The Myth of the Common School

D0881810

The Myth
of the
Common
School

Charles Leslie Glenn, Jr.

ICSPRESS

Institute for Contemporary Studies
Oakland California

This book is a publication of the Institute for Contemporary Studies, a nonpartisan, nonprofit, public policy research organization. The analyses, conclusions, and opinions expressed in ICS Press Publications are those of the authors and not necessarily those of the institute or of its officers, its directors, or others associated with, or funding, its work.

Inquiries, book orders, and catalog requests should be addressed to ICS Press, 1611 Telegraph Avenue, Suite 406, Oakland, California, 94612. (510) 238-5010. Fax (510) 238-8440. To order, call toll-free in the United States (800) 326-0263.

Cover design by Rohani Design
Set in Linotron Galliard by G&S Typesetters, Inc.

Library of Congress Cataloging-in-Publication Data

Glenn, Charles Leslie, 1938-
    The myth of the common school / Charles Leslie Glenn, Jr.
        p. cm.
Originally published: Amherst : University of Massachusetts Press, 1988.

Includes bibliographical references and index.
    ISBN 1-55815-522-8 (pbk.)
    1. Public schools—United States—History. 2. Education and state—United States—History. I. Title.
    LC89 .G54 2002
    371.01'0973—dc21   2002012132

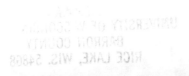

CONTENTS

PREFACE   ix

INTRODUCTION   3
The Common School Agenda   4
Who Promoted the Common School—and Why?   5
The Inevitable Conflict   10
Outline of the Study   12

1. GUIZOT: THE GOVERNMENT OF MINDS   15
Introduction   15
The Radical Agenda: The State and Its Children   16
    Emergence of the Program   16
    The Ideal School of Revolution   20
    Conflict over Implementation   23
    Education by Compulsion   25
    A Prescribed Curriculum   28
    Collapse of the "Republican School"   30
From Radical to Liberal Educational Agenda   31
    Education Reform under the Restoration   31
    The Doctrinaires   32
    The Threat of Social Disintegration   33
    "A Certain Government of Minds"   35

2. HOFSTEDE DE GROOT: THE DEFENSE
OF THE COMMON SCHOOL   38
Introduction   38
    Hofstede de Groot   39
    Origins of the Dutch Common School   40
    The Advocates of "Volksverlichting"   41
    Hopes and Fears   44
    The Nation-forming Institution   45
    The System Is Established   48
Conflict over the Common School   50
    De Groot and Popular Education   53
    Defending the Common School   55
    Conclusions   59

3. SOCIAL ANXIETY AND THE COMMON SCHOOL   63

A Time of Change and Fear   63
    Social Change in Antebellum Massachusetts   63
    The Irish Immigration   64
    Fear of the Immigrant   66
Education for Assimilation   73
    The Voluntary Impulse   73
    The State as Educator   75
    Horace Mann and the "Paternal" State   79
    The School in Place of Parents   82
Summary   84

4. SOURCES OF THE COMMON SCHOOL IDEA   86

The Social Mission of the Common School   86
Demand for National Education in the New Republic   88
    Samuel Harrison Smith   91
    Samuel Knox   94
    Robert Coram   96
    Lafitte du Courteil   96
    Significance of the Jeffersonian Essayists   96
The "Friends of Education" and Foreign Models   97
    Looking to Europe   100
    France   105
    Prussia   107
    The Netherlands   109
    Great Britain   112
    The Influence of Foreign Models   113

5. THE STATE ASSUMES EDUCATIONAL LEADERSHIP   115

The Debate over State Leadership   116
    Objections to State Collection of Education Data   123
    Objections to State Adoption of Books   124
    Objections to State Control of Teacher Preparation   132
The Unitarian Connection   140
Summary   144

6. THE COMMON SCHOOL AS A RELIGIOUS INSTITUTION   146

Background of the Religious Mission of the School   147
    Rejection of "Sectarian" Teaching   152
    The Concern about National Unity   155

The Problem of Horace Mann's Religion   158
    Mann's Official Statements   163
The Religious Program of the Common School   171
    Significance of the Debates over Common School Religion   177

7. THE OPPOSITION TO COMMON SCHOOL RELIGION   179

Overview   179
Protestant Opponents   180
    "The Spirit of the Pilgrims"   180
    The Orthodox Presbyterians   182
    Frederick Packard   183
    Matthew Hale Smith   187
    The "Witness" Controversy and Episcopalians   190
    The American Bible Society   195
Roman Catholic Opponents   196
    The Controversy in New York   198
    The Bishops State Their Position   200
    Conflict in Boston   202
Conclusions   204

8. ALTERNATIVES TO THE COMMON SCHOOL   207

The Effort to Create Alternatives   207
    New England before the Rise of Catholic Education   207
    Lutheran Schooling   211
    Orthodox Presbyterian Schools   213
    Roman Catholic Schools in Massachusetts   215
The Attack on Nonpublic Schools   219
    Horace Mann against Private Education   219
    Dutton Rallies Congregationalists   222
    Horace Bushnell and the Threat of Dismemberment   225
    The Gathering Protestant Consensus on Religious Schooling   230
Summary and Conclusions   234

9. THE TRIUMPH OF THE COMMON SCHOOL   236

France: *L'école laïque*   238
The Netherlands: *De gemengde school*   244
The United States: "The One Best System"   249
    Political Control of Schools   250
    Support for Confessional Schools   251
    The Issue of Language   256
Summary   261

10. THE COMMON SCHOOL CALLED INTO QUESTION   262
Recapitulation   262
France   264
The Netherlands   270
The United States   278
Conclusions   283

NOTES   289

BIBLIOGRAPHY   325

INDEX   367

PREFACE

IF I WERE a professional historian, this would be the place to acknowledge, with appropriate gratitude, the contribution of sabbaticals and travel grants, of fellowships and graduate seminars, perhaps of research assistants. It might even be the place to break a methodological lance or two with my colleagues.

But I am not a historian, nor does this claim to be a full-orbed account of the development of public schooling. I have researched and written in the spare moments of my life as a state official and the parent of five children. Think of this rather as an extended meditation on the history of an idea, indeed of a complex of ideas so powerfully enchanting in their continuing effect that they may fairly be called a "myth": the common school. The myth of the common school as crucible of a single national identity, as the hothouse in which young sprouts are trained to a single state-approved pattern, is my topic here.

I use the word "myth" not as a statement about truth and falsehood but as an acknowledgment of the unusual resonance of the idea of the common school. This resonance has been such that empirical research on the actual effect of schooling on beliefs and loyalties has been curiously meager. The common school has functioned above all as a statement of national intention and a symbol of national unity, and those who have laid a hand upon it have, correspondingly, been perceived as disturbers of the peace and of the national dream.

Jacques Barzun, in *Romanticism and the Modern Ego,* wrote that the "history of ideas cannot be written like an invoice of standardized goods. It is a subject requiring infinite tact. On the one hand, diversity must be reduced to clear patterns for the sake of intelligibility; and on the other, the meaning of each idea must be preserved from falsification by constant reference to its place and purport in history." It may be that my training, though not that of a historian, has its uses for working with the history of an idea. At Harvard College I studied comparative literature under the exacting direction of Harry Levin, followed by four years of theology and biblical studies in Berkeley, Tübingen, and Cambridge. More recently I have spent four years learning something about the sociology of knowledge with Peter

Berger at Boston University. These years of academic work have given me a nose for meanings and their context.

Of even more significance for this study, however, have been twenty-five years as an advocate of the racial integration of schools, seventeen of them directing the state effort to that end in Massachusetts. Countless times I have been called upon to articulate and defend the vision so important to Horace Mann, of the school as the place where social differences that threaten our national life and the achievement of justice are reconciled. Anthony Lucas in *Common Ground,* his account of Boston desegregation, refers to me as "implacable" in that cause, with a "passionate zeal on racial issues." Take it, then, that I have fundamental commitment to the common school.

I am also an Evangelical Christian, and a few years ago I began to be painfully aware that many of my fellow believers were deeply distrustful of public schools, and for reasons that had nothing to do (as I at first assumed) with race. Here only a brief narrative will do justice to how I stumbled into the research that lies behind this study.

A book by Rockne McCarthy and others associated with Calvin College, purchased almost at random in 1983, opened my eyes to reasoned and principled objections to our present system. This book also called my attention to an alternative model, in the Netherlands, of how to organize universal education. Several months later, on a bicycle trip with my oldest sons in that country, I bought a book with the promising title (when translated from the Dutch), "Theological and Philosophical Background to the Relationship of Church, State, and School in the Netherlands," and spelled out enough of it, with the help of a pocket dictionary, to realize that public education was anything but the almost natural phenomenon I had naively assumed it to be. The Dutch, I learned, had started out with common schools firmly in mind and then had turned and gone another way; these contrasting courses had a great deal to do with positions taken toward the Enlightenment and the French Revolution.

These clues were enough to send me searching through half a dozen libraries for what the education reformers and their critics and supporters—in France and the Netherlands as well as in Massachusetts—had said their intentions were. Much of this material had been mined by historians again and again, but the comparative perspective that I employed and my interest in the theological context within which the nineteenth-century debates developed have enabled me to add something to the ongoing discussion.

Where have I come out? Certainly not with abandoning the conviction that education is a matter of public concern and that the state should set

clear expectations for the education of every child—nor that these expectations, as Horace Mann insisted, must include qualities of character, of civic
virtue, as well as facts and intellectual skills. At the same time, however, I
have grown convinced that the state should not dictate the process by which
those goals are achieved or the context of meanings, the "symbolic universe," within which students are taught. A system of choice among public
schools, if centrally organized and monitored in the interest of equity (as in
Massachusetts) can permit diverse responses to the concerns and goals of
parents, different ways of achieving excellence, without losing its common
purpose.

Study of the controversies over public education in the three nations has
convinced me that the educational system of a democracy must learn to be
far more respectful of the convictions by which parents live and by which
they hope their children will also live. It is not enough to speak of "toleration"; as a Senate committee noted in 1829, "What other nations call religious toleration, we call religious rights. They are not exercised in virtue of
governmental indulgence, but as rights of which Government cannot deprive any portion of citizens, however small."

The mistake made by Horace Mann and his fellow reformers was not
their generous vision—universal education that would reach the heart as
well as the head of every future citizen—but their ungenerosity toward the
stubborn particularities of loyalty and conviction, the "mediating structures" and world views, by which people actually live.

This study of "the myth of the common school," then, has directed me
back to the challenge that faces public education in a pluralistic democracy,
to find ways not simply to tolerate deeply held convictions and particular
angles on the truth but to value them and to allow them scope to make
their contribution to our life together and to how we educate our children.

The Myth of the Common School

DESPITE the secularization of public life in the developed Western nations, the claims of religion and the state continue to clash painfully in the sensitive area of popular education. In France and in Spain, in Australia and Canada, in the Netherlands and in the United States, this conflict takes on new life every few years; whatever compromises are reached leave the potential for further clashes.

Although the immediate issues around which conflict arises vary, the underlying positions remain the same. On the one hand, there are those who assert the absolute right of parents to control the education of their . children, or to delegate that responsibility to the church or association in which they repose their confidence and by whose distinctive loyalties and beliefs they wish to see their children shaped. On the other, there are those who assert the absolute right of the state (or, in a softer form, of "society") to control the education of the next generation of citizens in a way that minimizes the differences distinguishing citizens one from another in the interest of national coherence.

From a close-up view, the rivalry is between the claims of the particulars of family or church and the universals of the nation-state. More broadly conceived, it may be between the universals of a worldwide religious faith and the particulars of national identity.

This study examines the first development of this distinctively modern tension in Massachusetts, with reference to parallel developments elsewhere in the United States and in France and the Netherlands, during the first half of the nineteenth century.

It is not another history of a period that, for each of the nations considered, has been the subject of repeated historical study, or of the institution of the common or public school. This is rather the history of an *idea*, a central component of the sustaining ideology of modern democracy.

We need to understand the resonance of the idea—even the "myth"—of the "common school" in order better to understand why we have so much difficulty accommodating the rich pluralism of American life in our system of public education.

The author is a state education official with responsibility for assuring that public schools both promote racial integration—the "common school"

3

goal—and also respond sensitively to ethnic and religious differences. In pursuing these divergent goals Massachusetts has developed the nation's largest program of promoting racial and social integration precisely through diversity and parent choice among public schools.

This study was undertaken with the practical intention of learning how to respond more wisely to the strains created by the attempt to bring these goals together. How much diversity and choice can we allow without undermining the social and national unity sought by Horace Mann? Did Mann and his successors go too far in attempting to promote a single form of American identity, at a cost that parents and children in a democracy should not be asked to pay? Why does the idea of "choice" arouse so much enthusiasm among parents but so much resistance among professional educators?

Other nations have responded rather differently to the same dilemma. Among democracies, France has sought most persistently to form a single national identity through a highly standardized educational system. The Netherlands, by contrast, has gone farther than any other nation to respond to the divergent goals of parents for the schooling of their children. Inclusion in my research of the development of popular education in both nations, and the very different balances they have struck between the goals of parents and those of the state, between private conviction and public orthodoxy, provides a valuable perspective on the American experience. There are many accounts of the development of popular education in each nation, some of them addressing the particular concerns of this study, but I have found none that look comparatively at the remarkably similar debates and the remarkably different choices that occurred in the three nations.

The Common School Agenda

We are familiar with the term "the common school" from its use by Horace Mann and other educational reformers before the Civil War. It refers, on the most obvious level, to the school that all the children of a community attend, in contrast to the schools that churches and religious foundations had long maintained for their own adherents or as missionary outreach.

The term refers also, however, to a program of educational reform, indeed of social reform through education. The heart of this program, which we will call "the common school agenda," is the deliberate effort to create in the entire youth of a nation common attitudes, loyalties, and values, and to do so under central direction by the state. In this agenda "moral education" and the shaping of a shared national identity were of considerably more ultimate importance than teaching basic academic skills. "Sectarian"

4

religious teaching was seen as a major threat to the accomplishment of this program of national unification through common socialization.

Horace Mann and his fellow reformers did not invent this agenda. It was an important element in the political theories of the French Enlightenment (often attributed to the virtuous Spartans as described by Plutarch) and of Rousseau and was expressly promoted by the Jacobin orators of the National Convention in the early 1790s. Around the same time, under this French influence, the idea of national schooling to mold citizens inspired a number of essays—though no practical measures—by allies of Thomas Jefferson. In the Netherlands a system of nationally supervised common schools, again under the influence of the French Revolution, was actually implemented in the first years of the nineteenth century, some thirty years before Mann began his twelve influential years as secretary of the Massachusetts Board of Education.

The common school agenda continues to shape discussions of education in the United States. We can see its enduring power in the extreme discomfort of "educationists" with the possibility of diversity and parent choice among schools and with any treatment of traditional Western religion in the curriculum.

This study asks how the idea of common schooling came to be so deeply rooted in our thinking about education, and why elements of the idea continue to have the power to shape our thinking about education.

Who Promoted the Common School—and Why?

Who were the promoters and organizers of the common school agenda implemented in most Western nations during the first half of the nineteenth century? Why were they so determined to establish universal and free popular education under state supervision, and how did they convince the broader public—and parents—to acquiesce to their designs? Were literacy and the communication of essential information at the heart of their concern, or were those concerns secondary to what has been characterized above as the common school agenda?

This question has attracted a great deal of scholarly interest over the past two decades. There is, for example, a "neo-Marxian" perspective that sees universal elementary schooling as a device of class domination, consciously intended "to inaugurate a new era of class relations."[1]

This study reaches a different conclusion. "Class interests" were served by the development of the common school agenda; these were not primarily the material interests of entrepreneurs and of property owners, however, but rather the ideal and material interests of an emerging class specializing

5

in law and government, in social and moral uplift. Far from acting as sur-
rogates for the large industrialists and other protocapitalists, this "new
class" often found itself deploring the industrial transformation of society.

If the interests of capitalists and of industry had driven the development
of the common school, we would expect it to have reached its first flowering
in Great Britain. In fact, Britain lagged well behind other nations in adopting the common school agenda, continuing to rely through most of the
nineteenth century upon a patchwork of private and semipublic institutions
to provide schooling for all social classes. The first successful implementation of common schools was in the Netherlands, which would not develop
significant industry until late in the century.

We can, therefore, accept only in part the basic premise of neo-Marxian
authors Bowles and Gintis, who argue that "the fact that changes in the
structure of production have preceded parallel changes in schooling establishes a strong prima facie case for the causal importance of economic
structure as a major determinant of educational structure."[2] Political and
not economic changes—above all changes in political thinking—are what
created the primary impetus behind the development of the common
school agenda.

It is true that the full implementation of the structure of public education
depended, in many cases, upon economic developments that created both
the resources and the demand for universal schooling. It does not follow,
however, that the idea or myth of the common school is the result of these
developments. In terms of Max Scheler's formulation of the sociology of
knowledge, "the 'real factors' [in this case, the factory system] regulate the
conditions under which certain 'ideal factors' [the common school agenda]
can appear in history, but cannot affect the content of the latter."[3]

In factory and mining communities in several nations, in fact, entrepreneurs resisted the development of popular education; literacy was not a
useful skill for workers and might indeed open them to radical influence.
Bowles and Gintis concede that "mass instruction was implemented considerably before the impact of capitalist expansion was felt" in Prussia and
Scotland, two of the pioneers in popular education.[4]

This is not to deny a connection between "technological production"
and bureaucratically organized universal education but to suggest that the
commonalities result from their common reliance upon and powerful tendency to create that form of consciousness that has been called "modernity."
The factory system itself is a powerful producer of the "symbolic universe
of modernity," quite apart from the support of formal schooling, as historical experience and Third World actuality demonstrate.[5] The Irish or Greek
peasant immigrants who came to Lowell, Massachusetts, fitted quickly into

6

the work discipline of the factory and developed the requisite supporting consciousness, without being subjected to the common school.

It is thus not historically accurate to assert that "labor and capital," in their continual struggle, operated "to construct an institution which would both enhance the labor power of working people and help to reproduce the conditions for its exploitation," with "the liberal professionals and enlightened school reformers" simply mediating compromises.[6] No, we must look elsewhere for the sources of the great crusade for state-led universal popular education that most Western nations experienced during the nineteenth century.

By and large, the promoters of this crusade were "new" men and women, members of social groups that emerged into prominence in the growing cities and provincial centers as commerce and industry developed, but were not themselves directly engaged in either. They were lawyers, clergymen, journalists, promoters of ideas and of causes. Though not profound thinkers, they were by and large members of an intellectual class that busied itself with "infusing into the laity attachments to more general symbols and providing for the laity a means of participation in the central value system." The "liberal and constitutional politics in great modern states," as Edward Shils notes (citing Guizot as one of his examples), "have to a large extent been 'intellectuals' politics.'"[7]

What motivated these supporters of universal popular education, if it was not the desire to create docile industrial workers, as the neo-Marxians argue? Some "revisionist" historians maintain that the common school was promoted by men and women concerned about an apparent breakdown in social discipline, that their underlying concern was less with pressing the pace of modernization than with containing its negative effects. The common school, in this version, was concerned not so much with industrial discipline as with social discipline.[8]

This was an important consideration for many of the school reformers. The Lowell industrialists were less concerned about the ability and willingness of their workers to adjust to the discipline of the factory than they were about the immigrants' native-born children on the streets and (eventually) in the voting booth. The "moral reform" movement, based largely in the evangelical churches, was a reaction to the apparent breakdown of social order in the growing cities.[9] Formal schooling was one aspect of the agenda of this movement, but the association is less close than is sometimes asserted. Horace Mann, for example, seldom mentioned urban disorder in his reports and speeches; his concern was not primarily with social control in a crude sense but with shaping the future of what was still primarily a rural society.

It is too simple to relate the concern of Mann and the other reformers exclusively to crime rates and ethnic conflict. The reformers were concerned about the diversity of society, especially as more and more groups entered political life, but their overriding preoccupation was with spiritual disunity, the growing gap between their own "enlightened" values and stubborn vestiges of what they regarded as superstition and fanaticism. It was this that led them to see rural Calvinists and immigrant Catholics as a profound threat to the emerging national society.

The relationship between material interests—capitalist factory-based production, social order, public and private morality, political stability—and the development of the idea of common schooling is more complex than many accounts allow. Horace Mann, Petrus Hofstede de Groot, and François Guizot saw their role as cultural and even spiritual; their evocation of religious imagery and purposes was in no sense cynical but reflected precisely their understanding of what the common school was all about.

Edward Shils observes that, in all times,

> the society without conflict, the highly integrated society, has not only been the reverently cultivated ideal. It has also been the object of government policies. . . . The Reformation settlement which declared that the religion of the ruler should also be the religion of his subjects was one sign of the desire of rulers not merely to gain the submission of their subjects but to integrate them into a single society through the uniformity of beliefs. When nationality became an object of passionate devotion . . . rulers found what was to them an almost ideal basis for the integration of the societies."

To inculcate and maintain the uniformity of beliefs upon which this integration was believed to rest requires that

> every society [acquire] alongside the central system of authority . . . a central cultural system. The central cultural system consists of those beliefs and expressive symbols which are concerned with the central institutional system and with "things" which transcend the central institutional system and which reflect on it. The central cultural system has its own institutional system. . . . The educational system is that part of the central power-institutional and cultural-institutional complex which inculcates considerable parts of the central cultural system into other sectors of the society. It contributes thereby to the formation, diffusion, and maintenance of the common culture.[10]

The education reformers were quite consciously seeking to create the unified cultural system that, they were convinced, was essential to the health and progress of nation-states in which the common people, for a variety of political, social, and economic reasons, were of increasing significance. It is no accident that in France, then in the Netherlands, then in France again, then in Massachusetts, the common school agenda was formulated and began to be implemented within three or four years of the disestablishment of the dominant church.

The "capital" of the new class that included the education reformers was counted not in property, in lines of credit or machinery, but in their own education, in their identification with national interests, their assurance of a place within a safely progressive society. The wrenching dislocations caused by industrialization, the migrations from country to city or from nation to nation that characterized the period in the United States and that brought the conservative religious views of rural New England or Ireland into a new prominence (just as such views seemed to have been routed in the established churches), were matched, in France and the Netherlands, by the growing political significance of the rural population. The new class found itself confronted by the continuing power of beliefs and loyalties that resisted integration. It was this confrontation that gave rise to deep concerns out of which the common school agenda developed.

The social strains, in another context, could easily have led to conservative reaction, to a determination to rely upon overt measures of social discipline. That it led to a "liberal" program of universal popular education may be attributed to the fact that the strains developed simultaneously with the emergence of a new class whose power was rooted in knowledge rather than property, for whom the social and economic developments created new opportunities for the employment of their skills. As a result, their reaction was not a conservative rejection of modernity but an optimistic determination to channel its effects through popular education. They would shape the children of the common people to share their own values, secure in the conviction that they were thus assuring social unity and progress.

Berger and Luckmann describe the process of "legitimation" by which the "meanings" already available in a society are integrated into a plausible and thus viable whole. "Legitimation justifies the institutional order by giving a normative dignity to its practical imperatives." [11] The common school was intended, by its proponents, above all as the instrumentality by which the particularities of localism and religious tradition and (in the United States) of national origin would be integrated into a single sustaining identity. It is central to the "myth" of the common school that, as Diane Ravitch observes, educators and policy makers have been convinced that it worked, that "the public schools had single-handedly transformed immigrant children into achieving citizens," a view that "took no account of the other factors that contributed to the assimilation of European immigrants or of the large number of immigrant children who were not successful in school."[12]

Unlike the advocates of popular schooling in contemporary Europe, the American reformers did not generally see it as a class-specific training. While they recognized that most students in the common school would not go on to secondary much less higher education, they never saw it as an exclusively "popular" form of schooling. Horace Mann urged "the professional men of Massachusetts" to put their own children in the common schools. The fact that, in an increasingly urbanized and class-ridden society, the education of most children has been anything but a "common" experience with classmates representing the full diversity of American life does not reduce in the slightest the power of the myth of "the long schoolbench" that would bring all classes and sects and ethnicities together.

It was the common school, the reformers in Europe as in America believed, that would "mold citizens" with the enlightened and tolerant attitudes held by the reformers themselves. To do so seemed to require that schools develop in their students the religious attitudes as well as the social habits of their betters.

The Inevitable Conflict

It is because the goals of the education reformers went far beyond teaching literacy or practical knowledge (indeed, did not even begin with those goals) that popular education has been the source of almost continuous political and social conflict. The "common school" about which Horace Mann and others grew so eloquent was surrounded with sacred associations. Rousseau had charged that Christianity, rather than attaching the hearts of citizens to the state, had the effect of detaching them from earthly concerns; government must establish a "civil religion" that would teach citizens to love their duties and their fellow citizens.[13] We will see how explicitly the education reformers in France, the Netherlands, and the United States sought to make the common school the established church of such a civil religion.

We must not look for this intention only in the specifically civic or moral teaching of the common school, though we will see that these elements of the curriculum were of decisive importance for the education reformers. The belief that "sectarian" values and convictions could be separated out from the rest of the educational experience led to attempts to remove whatever the advocates of traditional religious teaching found offensive. Such compromises could not succeed, for they failed to understand the claim of religion to explain all of reality. "Legitimation is not just a matter of 'values,'" Berger and Luckmann note. "It always implies 'knowledge' as well." [14] Formal education—like other forms of socialization—presents pictures or maps of reality that reflect, unavoidably, particular choices about what is certain and what in question, what is significant and what unworthy of notice. No aspect of schooling can be truly neutral.

The high ambitions that the reformers had for the common school brought them into inevitable conflict with social groups for whom traditional religion was of decisive importance. After all, as Shils observes,

> The increase in the integration of society occurs at the expense of parts of the society and some of the most important limits . . . are thrown up by the exertions of the communities, corporate bodies, and social strata to maintain an internal integrity which would be lost by a fuller integration into society. [15]

It was such exertion by groups that did not share the beliefs, values, and loyalties that the common school was intended to inculcate—or that attached central importance to elements excluded from the common school as "sectarian"—that made the history of popular education in the nineteenth century so frequently stormy.

If controversy continues to haunt public education, this is in large part the result of attempts by "cognitive minorities" to repel what they perceive as aggression by public educators seeking cultural homogenization at the expense of convictions stubbornly held. As Peter Berger has pointed out, "the fundamental coerciveness of society lies not in its machineries of social control, but in its power to constitute and to impose itself as reality." It is the reality-forming, the legitimating role of the common school, a role central to its mission from the start, that continues to be experienced as oppressive by many parents who have a different view of reality. They perceive instinctively that, as Guizot and others urged in making the case for state-sponsored universal education, it is the most powerful means available to the central cultural elite to impose its agenda on the "periphery" of society. To quote Berger again, "Society is the guardian of order and meaning not only objectively, in its institutional structures, but subjectively as well, in its structuring of individual consciousness." [16] It was precisely the beneficent intent of education reformers over the past two centuries—for nothing in this study suggests that they were less than sincere in wishing to benefit the common people of their respective nations—that made their "common school agenda" so profoundly threatening to cognitive minorities.

The sense of threat is reciprocal. Parents who hold beliefs and loyalties that diverge from or go beyond those sanctioned by the prevailing culture and are determined that these will shape the education of their children are

11

perceived, by the education establishment, as posing a threat far beyond their actual power. By raising their concerns they call into question the very "myth of the common school," that the values held and propagated by the cultural elite through public education are neutral, nonsectarian, and indeed obvious to any reasonable person. They challenge a dearly cherished self-image and way of understanding the purposes of education.

This continuing conflict, even as the common school has appeared to triumph, raises troubling questions in a democracy. How can the pluralism that we claim to value, the liberty that we prize, be reconciled with a "state pedagogy" designed to serve state purposes? Is there not wisdom in John Stuart Mill's remark that "all that has been said of the importance of individuality of character, and diversity in opinions and modes of conduct, involves, as of the same unspeakable importance, diversity of education. A general State education is a mere contrivance for molding people to be exactly like one another . . . in proportion as it is efficient and successful, it establishes a despotism over the mind." [17] Can government somehow assure that every child is educated in the essentials required by the social, political, and economic order without seeking to impose uniformity?

Outline of the Study

Our primary focus will be upon developments in Massachusetts. With Samuel Bowles and Herbert Gintis (though disagreeing in other respects) I stress that

> The emphasis on Massachusetts is no accident. The educational reform movement which marked the first turning point in U.S. educational history originated in the burgeoning industrial cities of this state and was dominated throughout its course by the example of Massachusetts and its educational leaders. [18]

In order to set the stage for an extended discussion of the motivations and strategies of education reformers in Massachusetts—and their opponents— the first and second chapters describe and discuss similar developments in France and in the Netherlands.

It was in France that the "hard" form of this agenda emerged, with Rousseau and later the Jacobins insisting that children belong primarily to the state, which must for its own protection mold them into loyal citizens with the "republican virtues." This program was implemented in the 1880s in an aggressively secularizing form that anticipated educational developments in the United States after World War II. More recently France, too, has had

12

to come to terms with resistance to the assumptions upon which the common school is based.

The focus of the first chapter is on the unsuccessful attempt at implementing state-controlled "Republican schools" during the revolutionary decade of the 1790s and on the far more successful efforts of statesman François Guizot in the early years of the "liberal" regime established in 1830.

It was in the Netherlands that the common school agenda developed in a relatively "soft" form, closely associated with liberal Protestantism. This would have a significant impact upon the American reformers. The focus of the second chapter is on the first emergence and implementation of the common school agenda in the Netherlands, and on its defense against growing criticism in the 1840s by theologian Petrus Hofstede de Groot.

The first two chapters, then, describe the conditions and the assumptions under which common schools were first launched in the 1800s in the Netherlands and the 1830s in France. Chapters 3 through 8 trace the development of this idea in the United States, its implementation, and its triumph over competing views of popular schooling, and Chapters 9 and 10 show "how the story turned out" in the three nations.

Chapter 3 describes the social changes perceived by Horace Mann and his contemporaries as requiring the remedy that only the common school could provide. The conviction that the state should assume the paternal role of discovering "by what appliance of means a . . . child can most surely be trained into a noble citizen" is traced in the writings of Noah Webster and Horace Mann, as is the assurance that "the Common School is the greatest discovery ever made by man." [19]

Chapter 4 presents the thoughts on "National Education" of a number of Jeffersonian Republican essayists in the 1790s, in evident parallel with the contemporary Jacobin educational program in France. The seed fell on stony and unresponsive ground in America. Four decades later, however, a generation of education reformers picked up much the same program in the more acceptable form that it had meanwhile acquired in the Protestant states of Germany and in the Netherlands. From Prussia, in particular, they took the example of the paternal state and, from the Netherlands, the teaching of a "common school religion."

Chapter 5 shows how James Carter, Horace Mann and other Whig reformers asserted educational leadership in Massachusetts, using three devices that had been crucial in the first systematic implementing of common schools in the Netherlands, thirty years before, and were being employed by Guizot, Cousin, and their other contemporaries in France. These indirect but powerful interventions in local school management—state collection of data, adoption of approved book lists, and training of teachers—were protested by some orthodox Protestants and by a powerful minority in the Massachusetts legislature, but Mann and his allies triumphed over their opponents.

The common school that Mann and others sought to create was profoundly and explicitly religious and saturated with moral purpose. Chapter 6 shows how this religious and moralizing function was understood and how it related to the actual religious beliefs then prevalent in Massachusetts. Chapter 7 describes the opposition to "common school religion," first among orthodox Protestants and then among the growing Roman Catholic population.

In Chapter 8 the attempts—of varying success—to create alternatives to the common school with a distinctively Protestant or Roman Catholic character are described briefly. The primary focus of this chapter, however, is upon the horrified reaction to immigrant demands for Catholic schooling. Influential Protestants closed ranks behind the common school. It is at this crisis point of national identity, with the massive immigrations starting in the late 1840s, that the common school passed from a proselytizing faith to something like an established religion, one of the dominating myths of American public life.

Chapter 9 describes the triumph of the common school agenda in the later nineteenth and early twentieth centuries in France and the United States and its failure in the Netherlands, where parent choice has become the basic organizing principle of education.

Chapter 10, finally, brings the story down to the contemporary policy debates and popular conflict in the three nations, and shows how deeply rooted they are in ways of thinking about the role of the school in molding citizens to a single pattern. The chapter concludes by suggesting that the consensus on the moral content of schooling that permitted development of the common school despite differences on religious doctrine no longer exists. Only through the expansion of parent choice and thus of diversity in schooling can broad support for public education be rebuilt.

1

Guizot: The Government of Minds

Introduction

UNIVERSAL popular education concerned primarily with shaping common attitudes and loyalties was high on the agenda of political theorists in France in the eighteenth century. For the leaders of the Revolution, particularly in its second, more radical phase, it was a matter of urgency to enact a scheme of state-controlled schooling. The town and village schools that, in an unsystematic way, had taught literacy and the essentials of Catholic doctrine to hundreds of thousands of students must be replaced by "republican schools" whose primary concern would be with the formation of citizens.[1]

In support of this objective, the Decree Concerning Public Instruction of 29 Frimaire, Year II (December 19, 1793)—during the Terror—placed schools under the surveillance of local watch committees and called for the denunciation of teachers whose teaching was "contrary to republican laws and morality." Successive governments devoted much of their attention, even when France was reeling from foreign invasion and civil war, to defining the objectives and requirements of popular education and commissioned textbooks that would present a new republican orthodoxy to young citizens.

These efforts were a complete failure. As we will see, parents launched a massive resistance to republican education, sending their children instead to alternative and illegal schools that provided religious instruction. The confiscation of religious endowments and the wealth of the Catholic church, and the proscription of religious orders, made schooling far less available than it had been under the *ancien régime*. During the chaotic decade of revolution popular education virtually collapsed, and began to be restored under Napoleon Bonaparte only by turning again to the church's teaching orders and to local initiatives; the revolutionary program was abandoned.

The radical or Jacobin program of popular education in the interest of the state and a new political order may have been a short-term failure, but it would make its way in modified form into the agenda of a dozen nation-states of Europe and the Americas by mid-nineteenth century. When Henry Barnard compiled his *Systems, Institutions, and Statistics of Public Instruction in Different Countries* and Emile de Laveleye his *L'instruction du peuple* (both published in 1872), it was with a sense that a common program of nation building through schooling was taking shape in every advanced society.

The Jacobin program became the liberal program of popular schooling, a systematic effort by the state to intervene in and shape society. This effort was promoted by political thinkers who in many other respects called for a limited state role.

It was historian and statesman François Guizot who, in the 1830s, provided leadership for the successful implementation of the Jacobin program of "government of minds" in its liberal form. His promotion of popular schooling was hailed by contemporaries among the American common school reformers as parallel to their own efforts, and the reports of his ally Victor Cousin on what French education could learn from Prussia and the Netherlands were translated and applied closely across the Atlantic as well.

Before describing the agenda pursued by Guizot and Cousin in the 1830s we show how this agenda emerged in the eighteenth century and describe the first, unsuccessful attempt to implement it during the 1790s.

The Radical Agenda: The State and Its Children

EMERGENCE OF THE PROGRAM IN THE EIGHTEENTH CENTURY. It is important to begin with a distinction between the actuality of widespread (though by no means universal) schooling under church and private auspices, and the proposals for schooling that were put forward—often with clerical or anticlerical intent—by political theorists and statesmen.

There is ample evidence that thousands of *petites écoles* offered at least the rudiments of instruction to all but the most impoverished families—at least in the more advanced regions of France—as well as free schooling for many urban orphans and paupers. By 1789, it has been calculated, there were sufficient school places in Paris and Lyon, the two largest cities in the kingdom, to accommodate every child. In the city of Nancy, with 30,000 inhabitants of whom about 4,000 were between the ages of five and thirteen, there were roughly 2,800 places available in schools, more than half of them in schools run by teaching congregations. In Grenoble there were fourteen fee-charging schools for boys and thirteen for girls, and teaching orders offered another 800 free places for indigent families.[2]

A distinction should be made between the hundreds of one-teacher schools operated as a form of private enterprise by teachers who offered to develop a mastery of specific skills at a price—so much for reading, so much more for writing, extra charges for the mathematical operations—and the schools founded by religious orders or wealthy patrons to serve essentially social and religious purposes.

Protestants took an early interest in schooling all of the children of their adherents; in Metz there were four Calvinist schools in 1562, ten in 1594, nineteen in 1662. The development of Catholic-sponsored schools tended to be strongest in areas where Protestants were active. When the new bishop of Montpellier undertook, in 1677, a crusade to bring Protestants back to the Catholic faith, his chosen instrument was village schools: In a decade, he increased their number from forty-seven to eighty-six.

It was this concern that drew the state into setting requirements for popular schooling. A royal decree of 1698 ordered that every parish in the kingdom maintain a school and that all parents be required to send their children unless they had made other appropriate (Catholic) arrangements; this was actually aimed exclusively at Protestants and recent converts from the Reformed faith. In many dioceses teaching orders were founded to reach the children of poor and middle-class families alike (though usually separately) with the principles of the Counter-Reformation. Some historians date the effective "Christianization" of France not to Clovis and Martin of Tours but to this seventeenth-century effort of popular instruction.[3]

The attitude of social and political theorists toward popular education was ambivalent. Some feared that half-educated peasants would fall prey to radical ideas or grow discontented with following the plow. Voltaire wrote that the common people should be guided, not instructed; they lacked the leisure to become enlightened and should be content to follow the example of their superiors.[4]

Others were convinced, however, that the hold of the Catholic church and of "superstition" could be broken only by education firmly under the control of the state. Thus the moralist Mably warned that good citizens could be formed only by public and universal schooling, and Breton parliamentarian La Chalotais claimed, in a widely noted essay written in 1763 as part of a concerted attack on the Jesuits,

> the right to demand for the Nation an education that will depend upon the State alone; because it belongs essentially to it, because every nation has an inalienable and imprescriptible right to instruct its members, and finally because the children of the State should be educated by members of the State. . . . It is then only by delivering us from this monkish spirit . . . which for more than two centuries has embarrassed civilized states by all kinds of obstacles, that it will be possible to succeed in establishing a basis for a general education.[5]

17

Perhaps the most distinguished statesman of eighteenth-century France, the economist Turgot, argued for a system of "national education" to train citizens, with prescribed textbooks to assure that "the study of the duties of a citizen and of a member of a family and of the State would be the foundation of all other studies, which would be arranged in the order of their utility to the country." Education in the hands of the state would create the sense of common citizenship that Turgot felt essential to a healthy social and political system and would weaken the influence of "different social orders which have no real unity."[6]

Some went further. Morelly urged, in his *Code of Nature* (1755), that "at the age of five children shall be taken from their parents and educated communally at government expense and on uniform lines." Du Pont de Nemours promised the king that the educational reforms he was proposing would totally transform the nation, make it "unrecognizable," in ten years. Baron Holbach, notorious for his outspoken atheism, saw education as the most effective way to free the people from the two powers most hostile to their progress, kings and priests.[7]

It was Rousseau, however, who applied this logic most consistently and influentially. Man must be *molded* to virtue, he argued, and this was the highest calling of the political leader: "He who dares to undertake the formation of a people must feel himself capable of changing human nature itself, and of transforming each individual."[8] Government should seek to shape not simply the behavior of citizens but their *will*, their loyalties, and their ways of understanding themselves and the world. In *Emile* Rousseau described how this could be accomplished by arranging a series of experiences through which virtue would be acquired without effort and indeed without conscious intent.

To the Poles Rousseau insisted that "it is education that must give to souls a national strength, and so direct their opinions and their tastes that they will be patriots by inclination, by passion, by necessity." To this end, youth must not be allowed even to play by themselves or following their own preferences but must always do so "together and in public, so that they will always have a common purpose to which all aspire [so as] to be accustomed early to rules, to equality, to fraternity, to competitions, to live under the gaze of their fellow citizens and to desire public approval."[9]

In his political writing, Rousseau stressed that purposeful national unity capable of imposing (or developing) universal virtue required not only state control of the education of children but also continual reinforcement through public ceremonies and through civil religion. Competing loyalties must not be tolerated; the General Will would be weakened by the existence of "partial associations" within the state.

Catholic leaders seeking to achieve spiritual hegemony and political thinkers seeking to limit—if not eliminate—the influence of the church were agreed that the formation of attitudes and loyalties was a more significant aspect of education than the acquisition of skills. For eighteenth-century *philosophes*, physiocrats, and parliamentarians alike it was above all essential to limit the educational role of the church by placing schools under the jurisdiction and guidance of the state, to "put schools into an immediate dependence upon the government" (Guyton de Morveau).[10]

The Revolution that began in 1789 and continuously unfolded over the following decade was not at first greatly concerned with education; the *cahiers* prepared in every part of France by the three estates give schooling (in the sense of the need for more literacy) only passing attention. It was only as it became clear that the old order—contrary to the expectations of almost all parties—had in fact been overthrown that legislators and polemicists turned to the more complex task of making that political change real in the soul of the nation. Just as Catholic leaders a century before had relied upon schooling to implement the Counter-Reformation, so the Jacobins saw it as essential to creating citizens with an equally fervent commitment to the Republic.

To a striking extent it is clear that the power of the Catholic church over the souls of the people—or what they imagined that power to be—was not only hated but also envied by the Jacobin and other radical leaders of the French Republic. They wanted not only to liberate the Sons of the Republic from the yoke of theocracy, as Marie-Joseph Chenier put it in a much admired discourse, but also to create an equally strong attachment to the Republic itself.

In November 1791, for example, a decree of the National Assembly required that all clergy take an oath of loyalty to the new constitution and threatened that any who failed to do so would be considered "suspect of revolt against the law and of sinister intent toward the *Patrie*." Even more affirmative measures to limit the independent influence of the church were called for:

> Since it is of utmost importance that the people be enlightened with regard to the snares which are constantly being set for them in the matter of so-called religious opinions, the National Assembly exhorts all worthy souls to renew their efforts and increase their teachings against fanaticism; it declares that it will regard as a public benefit the writings which are within the capacity of citizens of rural areas. . . . it shall have such writings printed at State expense, and shall compensate the authors thereof.[11]

In conscious imitation of the church, the National Convention ordered a new calendar (October 1793), "freed from all the errors which credulity and

19

superstitious routine have handed down to us from centuries of ignorance." Robespierre instituted the Cult of the Supreme Being and of Nature in May 1794, and countless ceremonies were held in all parts of France.[12] The Republic sought to draw to itself the prestige and authority, the ability to gain loyalty and to shape values, that it attributed to the church.

State-controlled schooling was an essential element of this program. As a colleague of Robespierre wrote in his *Elements of Republicanism* (Year I: 1793), consisting "largely of paraphrases of the *Contrat social* and elaborations of Rousseau's arguments,"

> You will lose the younger generation by abandoning it to parents with prejudices and ignorance who give it the defective tint which they have themselves. Therefore, let the Fatherland take hold of children who are born for it alone.

And Robespierre himself told the National Convention, the same year, that "I am convinced of the necessity of operating a total regeneration, and, if I may express myself in this way, of creating a new people."[13]

THE IDEAL SCHOOL OF THE REVOLUTION. A municipal report prepared in Paris under the Consulate of Napoleon Bonaparte and his colleages, at the end of the year 1800, complained that visits just made to several elementary schools by municipal authorities revealed that "public instruction is not yet at its dawn."

> The elementary schools are in a deplorable situation. It is nevertheless true that the earliest impressions are the most lasting. It would therefore be important that liberal ideas and republican morality be presented to youth with the earliest rays of their intelligence, as soon as they have a sense of good and evil. But what are they being taught today in elementary schools? They learn to read, to write, to calculate. Can this purely mechanical education suffice to prepare man for happiness? The citizen magistrate cannot think so.[14]

Several years earlier, in a more optimistic mood, the municipal authorities in Paris had proclaimed that "our children will be republicans. . . . they will be orators."[15] Later the same year (1798) they boasted:

> already the young students are no longer taken to mass or to other religious ceremonies; already (finally) elementary books have entirely chased away the books of superstition in most schools. . . . instruction is taking great strides toward its perfection. Emulation is reborn; the public examinations . . . on the *fêtes décadaires* contribute remarkably . . . to the conversion of their parents.[16]

The reference here is to the "republican" textbooks prepared at the orders of the national authorities as a substitute for the catechisms and devotional texts which had been employed in elementary schools under the ancien régime. These "elementary books" included an edition of the Rights of Man (adopted 1789), of the Constitution, and a specially prepared book called *The Heroic Traits of French Republicans* (intended to substitute for the lives of the saints). Others written in response to large prizes offered by the Convention included a *Republican Catechism* and *Republican Epistles and Gospels*.

The *fêtes décadaires*, by which the Republic attempted to provide a substitute for Sunday religious observances, are referred to in another municipal document a few months later. In many communities, the Paris authorities report, the schoolmasters and schoolmistresses have their students recite, each *décadi*, moral, scientific, and "always republican" discourses.[17]

The expectations for this republican education were high. "It is the role of teachers to complete and to confirm forever the French Revolution! . . . what glory awaits those who fulfil it worthily!" wrote one local school committee, while another proclaimed that "to enlighten the people is to destroy kings!"[18]

For another perspective on these expectations, as they were interpreted by teachers anxious to show their loyalty to the Republic, we can turn to petitions addressed to the authorities, asking that the successfully competing private schools be suppressed. A schoolmistress in Paris, *citoyenne* Roget, wrote:

> The law forbids fanaticizing the hearts of children. I have made my students take back home their catechisms, their gospels. I have banished from my classrooms all emblems of fanaticism, replacing them with the Constitution and the Rights of Man, with the liberty bonnet. Fathers and mothers seeing these changes have taken their children [out of her school]. . . . Regenerators of all Frenchmen, I demand of you a severe law against fanaticized schools. . . . I have made a joyful bonfire of the pictures of the king and queen, of the traitors Lafayette and Bailly. My students have shouted *Vive la République*. I make them sing republican hymns every day (after class) with the refrain *Vive la République!*[19]

In a similar vein, a schoolmaster in Eure-et-Loir describes his republican school to the authorities:

> In the morning school opens with a republican prayer; in the evening it concludes by the pious singing of hymns of Liberty. I have suppressed all the books of the old regime; reading consists only of the Rights of Man, the Constitution, the statutes, and issues of *Le Père Duchene* [a radical

publication]. I make my students celebrate the *décadis*. This direction doesn't please everybody. . . . Since we are using a suppressed church for our classes, we have made it a Hall of the Friends of the Constitution and of Liberty. . . . With the greatest joy I knocked down the symbols of the gods which were stuck up in niches . . . (many people hoped I would break my neck, but I knew that nothing could resist a true republican). . . . We have replaced these mummeries with the names of Marat, our friend, Le Pelletier [a Jacobin leader who had proposed that children be taken from their parents at the age of five and raised by the state] and other great men.[20]

To summarize the intention of the Revolution with respect to its schools, we cannot do better than to quote Danton's celebrated speech to the National Convention, in which he declared that

> It is time to reestablish the grand principle, which seems too much misunderstood, that children belong to the Republic more than they do to their parents. . . . We must say to parents: We are not snatching them away from you, your children, but you may not withhold them from the influence of the nation. And what can the interests of an individual matter to us beside national interests? . . . It is in national schools that children must suck republican milk. The Republic is one and indivisible; public instruction must also be related to this center of unity.[21]

The claim could not be stated more plainly; it would not again be stated quite so bluntly, even under the Third Republic. Other rhetoric was found, more acceptable arguments, but we will see that Danton's purpose has always been an element in the agenda of public education, whether in its radical or in its liberal form.

Albert Duruy (1844–87), son of the great education minister of Napoleon III, Victor Duruy, directed a telling critique against this program; it is worth quoting at length. Duruy did not write as a Catholic apologist, though he was strongly anti-Jacobin.

> Such was the pedagogy of the legislator of Year IV. Do not ask about its philosophy or its morality. It has none of its own; it has those which are furnished to it by the government. . . . In man it sees only one thing: the active citizen, the voter. Duty is made to consist solely in the love of the Republic and in obedience to republican commandments. Its gospel, its law, its ideal, its all, is the Constitution; it has nothing else.
>
> Now, take the child and ask yourself if the old state of affairs didn't correspond better to his spirit; if he didn't receive from it a more lasting and healthy imprint. Compare the two systems: on the one side, the narrow and limited cult of a form of government, that is, of an object essentially uncertain, contingent, an abstract cult, incapable of speaking to the

senses and thus to the imagination, dry and cold as a theorem in geometry; on the other side, an unchangeable doctrine, embracing in its breadth the entire human mind, preaching all forms of duty, at one moment opening to the imagination the dazzling perspective of eternal felicities, at another showing, in this life, the horrors of damnation; here, solemn declarations, pompous formulas, generalities and words empty of meaning for young minds: the Social Contract, the Sovereign People, the unity and indivisibility of the Republic; there, always images and forms which are concrete, tangible, always movement, color, and life, *le bon Dieu* in the clouds, the Virgin in glory, a sky peopled with pink angels and a hell full to the brim with little boys who were naughty.

What a contrast, how conclusive and compelling! How strongly the superiority of the old pedagogy leaps out! So much loftier and yet so much more accessible, broader and yet more understandable! . . . I can well imagine the small-time politician [*sectionnaire*], the party loyalist [*clubiste*], above all the blow-hard [*bavard*] this boy will become, nourished by revolutionary slogans and commonplaces; I search in vain for the upright and honest man that the church schools used to produce.[22]

It was in the same spirit that even the "constitutional" bishops, those reconciled with the Republic, resolved as early as 1795 that each parish should organize a school. In 1797 they warned parents, "Don't expect much from the arid and pompous teachings which they seek to substitute for the elements of religion." We can imagine how much more strongly the nonjuring priests to whom millions of Catholics looked for leadership condemned the schools of the Republic![23]

CONFLICT OVER IMPLEMENTATION. Those who sought to implement the radical program of popular education were continually frustrated both by teachers and by parents. Those teachers who were "patriots" were too often incompetent, whereas the more experienced teachers tended to be former priests or nuns and not to be trusted to teach pure republican morality. And parents seemed to prefer the bad old instruction of catechism and Bible stories, often refusing to send their children to the public schools. Since teachers were largely dependent upon the fees paid by parents, this put continual pressure on them to provide what the parents demanded, despite the surveillance of public authorities.

It appears that, by most measures, popular education actually worsened after the adoption of the educational program of the Revolution. In the Department of the Seine by the end of 1796 there were less than 1,200 students against a potential enrollment of 200,000. Of 599 communes in Meuse-et-Moselle, 566 had at least one school in 1789, at the start of the Revolution, but only about 200 had schools a decade later. Meanwhile, "private" schools, often taught by men or women who had previously worked in church-sponsored schools (or who were priests needing to support themselves) flourished. In the Seine (Paris region) in 1798 there were 2,000 private schools but only fifty-six public elementary schools.[24]

Whereas under the Convention administration in general was in deplorable condition, the Directory (1795–99) was a time of generally strong and stable government. An attempt was made to tighten up the implementation of a system of national schools. In a message to the legislative body (October 1798) the government observed that the education statute of 3 Brumaire remained valid, but little had been done to implement it; with the exception of a very few departments, elementary schools did not exist at all or had a very precarious existence. This would be corrected now by vigorous measures, including turning churches over to local authorities to use as schools, after pulling down their gothic belltowers. The Directory would issue fixed rules for instruction, would designate schoolbooks strictly, and would issue basal readers purified of superstitions.

Such central leadership was needed if the radical program was to be implemented. The reports filed with the Directory by authorities in each of the cantons of the Aube on the state of "the talents and morality of the teachers of youth, the principles which they profess, and the morality of youth" reveal how much remained to be done. In the instructions for this inquiry, they were reminded that the law of 3 Brumaire "severely prescribed the teaching of any religious cult" in the schools; it is clear from the replies that they were very aware of their impotence, despite government directives, to overcome the resistance of parents and of many teachers. Selections from some of these reports follow:

> education is still in its swaddling clothes. . . . teachers have not yet dared to confront the erroneous principles of certain parents. . . . all promise to support the views of the government. . . . I like to believe that they are in good faith, but I will watch scrupulously to assure myself of it.

> It's not that their morality is inferior; their principles are in fact superior, because they are republicans, but they will teach according to custom until the government takes measures which oblige the parents of students to conform themselves to the new mode of instruction.

> I believe it will be difficult to find good republicans to fill these positions because of the affronts which they experience; it will also be very difficult to introduce into their classes the [prescribed] elementary books unless the government takes measures to force teachers to use them.

> Whom do we have in our area to teach youth? Former schoolmasters, holding on to old prejudices, indoctrinated by refractory and fanatical

24

priests, making their students read in books filled with superstitious and lying rhetoric.

> all religious books are absolutely banned from the schools, at least in the public class, but I have a strong suspicion that everything is taught as in the past, such as the gospel, the catechism, "Christian thoughts," etc. What to do! shrug the shoulders and groan. . . . To revive republican spirit, it would be necessary that it have existed, but it has not yet been born.[25]

EDUCATION BY COMPULSION. "Citizen legislators," one complaining teacher wrote, "for how long will you permit true patriots to be oppressed?" He was facing competition from several priests and other persons who had organized schools and found that many parents preferred to entrust their children to them rather than to the "patriotic" school. Another petitioner asked that parents (he described them as "rebel and aristocrat," though he certainly did not mean by this that they were members of the *noblesse*) who failed to send their children to the public schools be subjected to a heavy fine. "National teachers will be useless," another insisted, "until parents are required to send their children" to their schools.[26]

This theme of compulsion toward parents was expressed again and again; nothing more clearly reveals the insecurity of a regime which, while claiming to represent the People, was in fact almost exclusively middle-class in its support and thus represented a very small part of the population. The People would have to be educated to be worthy of their new Liberty, and this whether they wished to be or not. As a leading orator argued in the Council of Five Hundred, the legislative body of the Directory, it was only logical for the Revolution to make attendance in its schools obligatory, in the name of Liberty itself. After all, if parents

> are friends of the present order of things, they will conform to the laws which it has established and will not recoil from confiding their children to republican teachers; if they are its enemies, I fail to see how you could claim for them a liberty which they would only abuse![27]

An emphasis upon the political consequences of permitting parents to choose schools that educated on the basis of the religious "prejudices" from which the parents themselves needed to be awakened is a common theme of government documents at this time, much more so than a concern about whether reading or writing is being taught adequately. For example, the administration of the Department of the Seine (Paris and vicinity) called for a rigorous inspection of schools. "Otherwise," it was feared, there will be two sorts of education in the Republic: In the public schools, our children will be raised on the principles of pure morality and republicanism; in private schools, they will suck the prejudices of superstition and of intolerance; thus the diversity of opinions, fanaticism, hatred will perpetuate themselves from generation to generation.[28]

The government of the Directory (1795–99), although it brought to an end the lawlessness and near anarchy of the Terror, was no less determined to carry out what could be called the "cultural" objectives of the Revolution, including its radical education program. The first phase of the Directory was a relatively liberal period of reaction against the excesses of the Terror and consolidation of middle-class control over against the Paris mob which had been such a powerful factor in revolutionary politics. During this period private schools seem to have been permitted to begin or resume operation in many areas. The coup of 18 Fructidor, Year V (September 4, 1797), opened a new phase in which "three categories of persons were the particular object of attack: brigands, émigrés, and priests." A law adopted in 1795 but not effectively enforced, forbidding public religious ceremonies and ordering the destruction of outward symbols of worship (like crosses on buildings), was revived; some 2,000 priests were imprisoned and ordered deported to Guiana; the observance of the revolutionary calendar and "Tenth Day worship" were promoted with "consuming zeal."[29]

Particular severity was shown toward teachers who failed to observe the new calendar. The minister of the interior wrote to departmental authorities about particular teachers who, it was reported, had failed to bring their students to the festivals of the Republic, and municipal authorities closed schools for the same offense. One local official wrote that ignorance itself was less dangerous than to allow the teaching of "lies, error, prejudices, and bad habits," and an envoy of the Directory urged that it would be better to have no schools at all in a community than to allow "pretended schools where [future] men . . . learn to prefer ridiculous illusions above their fatherland and their most sacred duties."[30]

The Directory was responsive to the complaints which it received from "true patriots" about the failure of the radical educational program; in 1798 it resolved to take vigorous measures to "arrest the progress of the fatal principles which a crowd of private teachers seeks to inspire in their pupils, and to cause republican education to blossom and prosper."[31]

In a decree adopted early that year the Directory ordered each municipal administration to visit all private schools within their jurisdictions at least once a month and on an unpredictable schedule. These visits were to determine:

1. whether the private schoolmasters take care to put in the hands of their students, as the basis for their earliest instruction, the Rights of Man, the Constitution and the elementary books adopted by the Convention;

2. whether they observe the *décadis*, celebrate the republican festivals, and honor one another with the title "Citizen";

3. finally, nutrition, hygiene, and discipline.[32]

The political and culture-shaping concerns are clearly to the fore; there is no mention at all of whether students are learning to read and write and calculate.

No effort was spared, by the Directory, to convey a sense of urgency about the enforcement of educational policy. As Letourneux wrote, in the fevered rhetoric characteristic of the period,

It will only be by such zeal and by constant surveillance that you will be able to snatch republican education from that sort of nullity into which the enemies of the laws and of the government have worked to plunge it to date, and give a final blow to those monstrous institutions in which royalism and superstition still agitate against the genius of liberty and of philosophy. It is against these lairs of royal and superstitious fanaticism, where greedy speculators smother in their vile and sordid bias the precious seeds of republican virtues and rob the Fatherland of its fondest hopes in the coming generation, that the Directory summons all your vigilance and your activity.[33]

The reports of municipal authorities in Paris reflect these new initiatives to implement the radical education program. It had been especially helpful, they wrote, that the Directory ordered all public officials and employees to send their children to public schools; nevertheless, additional measures were necessary. In the first place, all private teachers would be subject to screening by a committee before they were allowed to operate a school. At present, as fast as the authorities ordered the closing of a school, it opened again under the name of the teacher's cook or another subterfuge! In the second, all schools would now be considered "public places," and thus it would be illegal to have religious symbols displayed there.

The authorities explained that

Crucifixes found in several schools have provoked this measure, and it is particularly necessary to raise a wall of separation between education and the cults because many former nuns have become teachers and act as if they were still in their convents and in front of their boarding students.[34]

27

A PRESCRIBED CURRICULUM. The Committee on Public Education established by the Convention saw the development of a range of elementary texts as a principal means of overcoming the difficulties caused by an uncertain and uneven teaching body. In addition, until such texts were available schools would inevitably continue to use those provided under the ancien régime, the catechisms, lives of saints, and other material that was considered so much poison for young minds. The Convention therefore offered substantial cash prizes for new works that would serve this purpose.

One of those most widely referred to in the administrative reports is the *Republican Catechism*. This work answers in verse, intended to be memorized, such questions as "What are the rights of men and citizens?" and "What is God?" In answer to the latter question, students would learn,

I don't know what he is, but I see his work . . .
He escapes my senses, but speaks to my heart.[35]

This response strikes the master chord of "public school religion" as it was to emerge in the first half of the nineteenth century, in the Netherlands and the United States, as well as in France.

The Convention also endorsed a *Republican Epistles and Gospels*, *Catechism of Republican Morality*, a *Republican Thoughts for Each Day*, a *Republican ABC*, a *Universal Catechism*, a *Principles of Republican Morality*, *An Elementary Instruction on Republican Morality*, a *Manual for Young Republicans*, a *Republican Grammar*, and other works along the same line. In addition to these books in competition with the Catholic catechisms, lives of saints, and selections from Scripture, the Convention sponsored a variety of "service books" for use during republican worship on the *décadis*, such as *Hymns and Prayers for Use in Temples of Reason*.

The *Republican Epistles and Gospels* devoted its first epistle to Jean Jacques Rousseau, and its first Gospel began by describing the prediction of the "revolutionary of Judea" that priests would always be scoundrels. The author was "obsessed with his extreme hatred toward monarchy and religion" and attributed to them the intention of filling the earth with blood in order to increase their luxury. The National Convention awarded him a prize of 1,500 francs.[36]

The *Alphabet for Sans-Culottes; or, First Elements of Republican Education* asked, "What are the virtues of *sans-culottes?*" and answered, simply, "every virtue," while the *Historical and Revolutionary Catechism* provided, for the young reader, detailed descriptions of the decapitation of Louis XVI and Marie Antoinette, a somewhat risky proposition in view of contemporary attempts by the "underground" church to promote them as Catholic martyrs. Another book approved for elementary school use was "essentially a sex manual for patriotic mothers and fathers," advising them against intercourse during pregnancy, for the sake of the Fatherland! [37]

When the Directory turned, in 1798, to an attempt at strict enforcement of the radical education program, it determined to replace the "vicious" system of teaching spelling with new syllabaries freed from their superstitious elements. Local authorities were directed, as we have seen, to check on the texts being employed in private as well as public schools, to assure that all conformed with republican standards. The reports that came back were discouraging; parents persisted in sending their children off to school with the Christian books that had been used for so long, and most teachers did not dare to counter the wishes of those who paid their fees. Many teachers were themselves determined to continue to use their familiar books and to teach a faith that they shared. [38]

And despite the boast of some teachers, that they used the new "patriotic" hymns and prayers in their classes, the reports of school visits show how stubbornly the old practices continued. One inspector, for example, reports that he found eighteen students and their teacher at prayer in the old fashion and that, when he threatened to submit a complaint, the teacher was unmoved. Such responses were perhaps to be expected, given the high number of former nuns who were teachers (and who perhaps continued to live in little communities, by twos and threes). In Troyes, for example, of twenty-four schoolmistresses, thirteen had been nuns; all seemed attached to religion. The reports note "Catechism, prayers, Latin—everything is there!" or "Very religious, devout, bigoted, hypocritical," or "honeyed, sweet, reverential, but conniving." [39]

Teachers were not the only ones to resist the directly antireligious (or, at any event, anti-Catholic) character of the prescribed texts. In at least one community the mothers invaded the school and destroyed the republican books. The Republic found itself locked in a struggle with parents over the education of their children; "Citizen Minister," one local official warned, "don't expect anything without a regenerative violence, since the stubbornness of parents is such that it can only be overcome by conquering it." [40] In many others only those schools that did not use the prescribed books had fees-paying students, and so we hear again the complaint that the "culpable prosperity" of private schools "seems to grow as a result of the perversity of the principles which youth receive there." [41] Only under the Consulate did leaders like Fourcroy begin to recognize that, if private schools were prospering and public schools withering away, there must be something that public authorities could learn from that fact.

29

COLLAPSE OF THE "REPUBLICAN SCHOOL." Discouraging reports were received from all areas two years later when First Consul Napoleon Bonaparte sent out a number of top administrators to assess the success of the measures taken by the Directory to implement a system of popular education. It was their conclusion that the efforts of the previous regime had been doomed to failure because of their defiance of the convictions of parents. One of them observed that the failure to execute the law resulted from "the lack of moral education which conformed to the prejudices and habits of parents."[42]

These commissioners were no supporters of religion, but they saw religious education as an "inevitable evil." The preceding decade had been a disaster for education, with many children missing even the inadequate schooling available under the ancien régime. The chemist Fourcroy, who had earlier expressed his determination to continue Voltaire's work and "crush this infamous religion" and had served as president of the Jacobin Club, wrote to the first consul that his inspection trip had shattered his views on popular education.

> It is an error of some modern *philosophes*, into which I was drawn myself, to believe in the possibility of an education widespread enough to destroy religious prejudices. . . . The war in the Vendée has given modern governments a lesson which the pretensions of philosophy would seek in vain to nullify.[43]

The French Revolution was political far more than it was social or economic, and the primary agenda of its schools was correspondingly political. It was to create patriots, loyalists, fervent republicans; their literacy or more advanced skills were of comparatively slight importance. The quasi-religious observances, the prescribed texts, the anxiety about teachers with other loyalties show how seriously this effort was taken as the extension and guarantee of the work of the Revolution.

The motivation was essentially very little different from that of the Catholic church under the ancien régime: to bring up children in the True Faith, in the expectation that they would continue faithful adults. It was precisely this congruence of goals that set the stage for the *lutte scolaire* that has troubled France, intermittently, ever since. After all, if the sole concern of the state were to assure that its citizens possessed a variety of communication and computation skills, it would have no quarrel with the church's pursuing an entirely different agenda. But when the state is concerned to win the hearts of its citizens and sees divisions of belief and values as profoundly threatening, there can be nothing but war between the state and

30

any religious community that will not surrender the hearts of its children willingly. So it was to be in France.

From Radical to Liberal Educational Agenda

EDUCATION REFORM UNDER THE BOURBON RESTORATION. In the "false dawn" of Napoleon's first exile, in 1814, and in the early years of the restored Bourbon monarchy, popular education became a matter of intense interest among the intellectual and political elite. Popular ignorance, it seemed to them, had been the cause both of the excesses of the Terror and also of the acceptance of Napoleonic tyranny. Education of the common people would create the conditions upon which a stable political order depended.

Too much in France had changed for the restored monarchy to turn back the clock to 1788. One of the results of the Napoleonic era was the development of a new class of officials accustomed to broad responsibilities and of businessmen who had provisioned great armies and traded across occupied Europe. As the statesman Mole wrote, "only the new interests and the new men possess energy and skill in France. Have them on your side or perish!"[44] Another heritage was the Napoleonic organization of a wide range of institutions on a strongly centralized and rationalized basis. Despite the hostility of a revived Catholic church—an important ally of the Bourbons—to the University, with its authority over all secondary and higher education, the monarchy could not bring itself to abolish such a significant instrument of central control.

It was in this period that there emerged for the first time in France a well-informed middle-class "public" with a concern for reform and popular education. The Society for Elementary Instruction seemed, for a time at least, to have the potential of playing the same role for France that the Society for the General Welfare (Maatschappij tot Nut van 't Algemeen) had played for the Netherlands. Among its original members, indeed, was scientist Georges Cuvier, who had praised the work of the "Nut" in his influential study on Dutch education. At their first meeting, in June 1815, the members declared themselves

> convinced that education is the primary means to form virtuous men, friends of order, submissive to the laws, intelligent and hard-working, and that nothing else can serve as a useful and permanent foundation for the happiness and the true liberty of nations.[45]

31

Like the Nut, the new society founded schools for poor children in various parts of the country, encouraged new forms of instruction and teacher training, and sponsored the writing and publication of schoolbooks with a heavily moralistic emphasis. The society also appointed inspectors to visit its schools regularly and assure that their programs were of a uniform quality. One historian notes that "France was seized with a true fever for schooling"; it would be more accurate to say that middle-class reformers were seized with a fever to school the children of the poor. By 1820 there were 1,300 schools providing "mutual" or "monitorial" instruction to some 150,000 students.[46]

Mutual instruction was concerned primarily to teach basic skills in the most efficient manner possible, not to shape the values and beliefs of its students. This is a principal reason why it did not find favor in the Netherlands, where the moral purpose of schooling was always kept clearly to the forefront, and why Horace Mann would later disapprove of it. In France the new schools founded by the Society for Elementary Instruction came into conflict with those run by the Catholic teaching orders, even in the literal sense of students fighting in the streets. Soon the enthusiasm for reform through popular education began to wane, and by 1830 the society was supporting only a handful of schools, and its membership was reduced and apathetic.[47]

The failure of the mutual school movement refutes the contention of neo-Marxist historians that popular education took shape as a result of the determination of capitalists to develop a labor force broken to the discipline of the factory. No form of education ever conceived has been as factorylike as the mutual school, with its extreme stress upon efficiency and discipline, and indeed the Society for Elementary Instruction was first proposed at a meeting of the protocapitalist Society to Encourage National Industry.[48] Despite the support of many wealthy and powerful individuals—much more so than corresponding efforts in the Netherlands and in Massachusetts—the effort was ultimately a failure.

The comparative success of the efforts of Guizot, Cousin, and other middle-class reformers in the 1830s can be attributed to the fact that, like their contemporary Horace Mann, they stressed the moral and "generically" religious content of schooling. It was this, rather than efficient instruction in basic skills, that could attract broad support among the local notables, advocates, physicians, notaries, businessmen upon whose efforts the implementation of any program ultimately depended.

THE DOCTRINAIRES. In the flourishing of political thought under the Restoration, the group that came to be called "the Doctrinaires"—Royer-

Collard, Barante, Guizot, de Broglie, de Rémusat—have a particular significance for the development of the state agenda for popular education under the next regime. They occupied the Left Center of the political spectrum: opposed to attempts to restore vestiges of privilege from what they considered the "feudal" eighteenth century, hostile to the power of the Catholic church though not to religion as such, determined to protect individual liberties won by the Revolution of 1789, but equally determined to prevent a recurrence of the chaos of 1792, believers in progress and in property.

In economic thinking the Doctrinaires were liberals influenced by Adam Smith and the example of triumphant Britain. They believed that the unrestricted actions of individuals combine to serve the common good and that the privileges of guilds and associations were medieval relics and harmful to progress. Society should, in the same way, be unencumbered of the "artificial" restrictions of class, family, religious or regional loyalties, to permit unrestricted liberty. The individual should have no intermediaries between himself and the state, whose role should be reduced to a necessary minimum. All individuals should be equal before the law—this was the significance that they saw in the Revolution of 1789—with the enlightened middle class providing the leadership to which its qualities entitled it.[49]

Since the enlightened middle class was the active expression of society as a whole, a government based on a narrow means-tested suffrage that gave power to this class would, in Guizot's mind, be rooted in the living reality of needs and forces; it would be a government created by the action of society. Such a government could not in turn be passive, since it was the head of society, the instrument by which the middle class exerted its leadership. "Governments," Guizot wrote, "must be capable of supporting and guiding universal development."[50]

Guizot and his political allies counted upon the support of the new middle class that was emerging as the French economy entered the industrial age and that suffered in the slowdown of the late 1820s. Though Guizot himself made a brilliant career, serving eventually as prime minister for a decade, his background—provincial, Protestant, making a start in journalism on education and other social issues—was similar to that of the education reformers in the Netherlands a generation earlier and of his contemporaries James Carter and Horace Mann in Massachusetts.

THE THREAT OF SOCIAL DISINTEGRATION. While welcoming the disappearance of inherited privilege and institutions that restricted liberty, the Doctrinaires saw (before Tocqueville) that this created a new danger of unrestricted central authority. "The revolution has left nothing standing

33

except individuals," wrote Royer-Collard. "We have become *un peuple d'administrés.*"[51]

The political task that the Doctrinaires set for themselves was to build on the ruins left by the previous twenty-five years; not to rebuild the ancien régime but to create a rational form of government, a dispassionate politics founded upon science. Society could be transformed, they believed, and human nature perfected by a judicious application of new principles.

How could such a deliberate policy of political, social, even human reconstruction be reconciled with the limited role that the Doctrinaires, as liberals of their period, were willing to assign to government? Guizot wrote in 1821 that the effective "means of government" were not officials, prefects, mayors, tax collectors, soldiers. Having spread a network of such agents over the land, the monarchy was astonished to find that it had not achieved real power over the people.

> If those [agents] sufficed, why would the government be complaining today? It is equipped with such machines; there have never been so many or so capable. Nevertheless it replies that France is ungovernable, that everything is revolt and anarchy; it dies of weakness in the middle of its strengths, like Midas of hunger in the middle of his gold. But in fact the real means of government are not the direct and visible instruments of the exercise of power. They dwell in the heart of society itself and cannot be separated from it. . . . The internal means of government . . . are my concern.[52]

The art of government in modern society, Guizot argued, required using the inner workings of society itself. "Government and society are no longer two distinct beings. . . . They are one and the same." Thus the fundamental challenge was to "create a government by the action of society and society by the action of government." Government must interact with the interests, the passions, the opinions by which the masses are truly governed; it must be "anchored in the needs and forces which seem destined to determine the future fate of all."[53]

This was liberalism with a difference. While it asserted the natural right of the middle class, the "enterprising portion of society," to liberty unrestricted by government in pursuing its economic and other goals, it called for an active governmental role in extending middle-class influence throughout society. It was in fact essential to the security and continued progress of the new order that Guizot and other Doctrinaires hoped to establish, once government came under the control of the middle class, that it reach into the villages where the great majority of Frenchmen continued to live, to "introduce a moral influence amongst large communities over whom, in the present day, power seldom acts except by tax-gatherers, police officials, and gend'armes."[54]

"A CERTAIN GOVERNMENT OF MINDS." The "July days" that brought the enlightened middle class into political dominance also seemed to threaten an anarchy that would be worse than the mild repression of the Bourbons. Even as they planned a political takeover and the recognition of Louis Philippe as sovereign, Guizot and others were fearful that the popular movement offering that opportunity might soon pass beyond them. As he wrote later in his *Memoirs*, "the enemies of established order, the professional conspirators, the secret societies, the revolutionists at any price, the dreamers of an imaginary future, had rapidly thrown themselves into the movement, and became hourly more influential and exacting."[55]

The immediate crisis past, they were determined to avoid its recurrence by following their own prescription of penetrating the social masses with views that would assure stability and respect for the natural authority of a government based upon the middle class.

This concern led naturally to an emphasis upon popular education. As de Broglie would tell the Chamber of Peers in 1844, when the Doctrinaires were in power, "the state cannot be robbed of its double character of public teacher and executive power." In their thinking, in fact, the teaching role of the state was an essential aspect of its exercise of power; popular education was not so much a public *service* as a means of *control*. Guizot—now head of Louis Philippe's government—expressed this clearly in the same debate:

> The state obviously needs a great lay body, a great association deeply united to society, knowing it well, living at its heart, united also to the state, owing its power and direction to the state, such a corporation exercising on youth that moral influence which shapes it to order, to rules.[56]

Although, in common with other Liberals, Guizot believed that the various corporate bodies, including religious orders, that flourished under the ancien régime had prevented national and social unity and limited the individual liberty essential to progress, he recognized the positive role they had played in penetrating and organizing national life at those levels beyond the reach of Paris opinion. The "corporation" of public teachers offered the advantages without the drawbacks of the religious teaching orders and the network of parish clergy, since they could be made directly responsive to the state itself. As early as 1816 he had written that he and his allies wanted "a teaching corps belonging to the state, fed by the state, receiving its impulse and direction from the royal authority. . . . It is essential to establish and strengthen the ties of the teaching corps to the state."[57]

35

In 1832 Guizot was given the opportunity to begin to carry out this program, as minister of public instruction. Within days of his assumption of this office he began the effort to reach and reshape village teachers through the distribution of explicit instructional manuals and a periodical of approved educational practices. As he observed in his *Memoirs*, "I endeavoured to penetrate even to the very soul of popular teachers."[58]

Nationwide there was definite progress in the number of students attending elementary schools, and in the literacy rate. Between 1834 and 1848 the number of public elementary schools for boys increased from 22,641 to 32,964; those for girls increased much less rapidly and had only reached 7,658 by the latter date. The number of students in all schools, public and private, increased from 1,935,624 in 1831 to 3,240,436 in 1846, though more than 40 percent of all children did not attend school at all in 1848. The number of army recruits capable of simple reading increased from 420 in a thousand in 1827 to 634 in 1848. In brief, there was substantial progress in implementing the program of the Liberal Monarchy, to provide a simple and heavily moralizing education to the common people.[59]

Although this progress was uneven, it is significant that much of the information available for historians seeking to study the condition of the common people and of the communities of France in this period is that derived from the reports of school inspectors. After the immemorial functions of tax collection and raising recruits for the army, public education was the most consistent effort of the state to create a network reaching to every community.

Unlike the other forms of state action at the village level, the extension of popular education was an attempt not to take something from the people (their money and their sons) but to *affect* the people, to make them different, to carry out a program of social change. It was at once more benevolent and more deeply intrusive.

Guizot expressed this perfectly when he wrote that "the great problem of modern societies is the government of minds."

> It has frequently been said in the last century, and it is often repeated now, that minds ought not to be fettered, that they should be left to their free operation, and that society has neither the right nor the necessity of interference. Experience has protested against this haughty and precipitate solution. It has shown what it was to suffer minds to be unchecked. . . . for the advantage of progress, as well as for good order in society, a certain government of minds is always necessary.[60]

In support of this objective he sought to enlist schoolmasters as the agents of the state in every community, overseen by inspectors whose authority derived directly from the central government via its prefects. To assure that teachers would carry out the program of moral education that he believed so essential to social peace, Guizot pressed the organization of teacher training institutions modeled on those long operated by Catholic teaching orders; he published a journal for elementary teachers, to reach them continually with the ideas and techniques he supported.

Guizot's most celebrated effort was the letter that he sent to more than 39,000 teachers, requiring that each of them acknowledge receipt and "state the impression it had left on their minds." This letter was prepared by his fellow Doctrinaire, Charles de Rémusat, and struck many of the themes this group had been promoting. The teachers were told that

> liberty can neither be assured nor regular, except with a people sufficiently enlightened to listen, under all circumstances, to the voice of reason. Universal elementary education will become henceforward a guarantee for order and social stability. . . . Faith in Providence, the sanctity of duty, submission to parental authority, respect to the laws, to the sovereign, and to the common rights of all;—such are the sentiments which the teacher must labour to develop. . . . The peace and concord he will maintain in his school ought, if possible, to prepare the tranquillity and union of future generations.[61]

Victor Cousin, Guizot's collaborator and successor as minister of public instruction, gave special attention to shaping those who would in turn train teachers in the "normal schools" established in all parts of France. Himself a celebrated professor of philosophy, he sought to make his "eclectic" philosophy into "a sort of secular religion . . . claiming for the state the rights which the Ultramontanists demanded for the church."[62]

> Formerly [Guizot wrote], the church alone possessed the control of minds. . . . All this is over. Intelligence and science have become expanded and secularized. . . . But precisely because they are now more laical, more powerful, and more free than formerly, intelligence and science could never remain beyond the government of society. . . . the government should not remain careless or ignorant of the moral development of succeeding generations, and . . . as they appear upon the scene, it should study to establish intimate ties between them and the state.[63]

Although dressed out in the rhetoric of liberalism rather than in the radical terms used by the Jacobins in 1792, the program implemented by Guizot and his allies was equally concerned to use popular education to extend the influence and control of the central state over its people.

2

Hofstede de Groot:
The Defense of the
Common School

Introduction

ALTHOUGH the idea of a common school in the service of social and political unity was attended with more rhetoric than results in revolutionary
France, a system of nationally supervised common schools was actually implemented in the Netherlands in the first years of the nineteenth century,
some thirty years before Horace Mann became secretary of the Massachusetts Board of Education. French and American reformers made a point of
visiting the flourishing Dutch elementary schools in the 1830s, as interest in
this agenda revived, and singled out for praise the presence, side by side, of
Protestant and Catholic students receiving a common instruction saturated
with morality and nonsectarian religion.

Unitarian minister Charles Brooks, addressing "the schools and citizens
of the town of Quincy" on July 4, 1837, the year Mann was appointed first
secretary of the Massachusetts Board of Education, quoted Dutch education leader Adriaan van den Ende's insistence that

> The primary schools should be Christian, but neither Protestant nor
> Catholic. They should not lean to any particular form of worship nor teach
> any positive dogmas; but should be of that kind that Jews might attend
> them without inconvenience to their faith.

As in the Netherlands, Brooks declared, the schools of Massachusetts
should not confine themselves to teaching mechanical skills but should give
as much attention to the "moral" as to the "physical constitution." This
would, of course, require having "purposely-prepared teachers." [1]

It is one of the ironies of educational history that Mann and the other
reformers of the 1830s looked to the Netherlands for their example of how
a common school could serve a religiously diverse population, whereas critics of the common school today look to the Netherlands as the leading

example of educational diversity and choice. Another irony to set beside it is that Massachusetts, which took the lead in implementing the "common school agenda," is today giving national leadership in exploring how the common school can be made more responsive to the rich diversity of American life. Horace Mann's successors are asking how parents can be empowered to make choices for the education of their children, without sacrificing Horace Mann's goals of equity, social harmony, and national unity.

HOFSTEDE DE GROOT. Petrus Hofstede de Groot, a leading liberal Protestant theologian in the Netherlands through the middle decades of the nineteenth century, articulated and defended the agenda of state-controlled popular education, stressing its mission of shaping the values and attitudes of a diverse population.

Hofstede de Groot (1802–86) was a contemporary of Horace Mann (1796–1859) and of French education reformer François Guizot (1787–1874), but unlike them he did not help to launch a system of common schools; such a system was being established in the Netherlands at the time of his birth and had acquired an international reputation before he was out of elementary school himself.

The significance of Hofstede de Groot lies in his spirited defense of the "common school project," the effort to unify and enlighten the nation through a monopolistic system of popular elementary education concerned even more with attitudes and values than with skills of literacy and numeracy. De Groot articulated this defense in the 1840s as Dutch common schools were coming under a mounting attack from Roman Catholics and orthodox Protestants. Ironically, it was in this very period that education reformers in France and the United States were pointing to the Netherlands for evidence that schools could gain broad support for the teaching of a "common religion."

Unlike Guizot and Mann, Hofstede de Groot's career was exclusively academic; he was a professor of theology at the University of Groningen from 1829 to 1872. In 1833 he accepted appointment to the part-time position of school inspector, in which capacity he visited each school in his district annually and held "in-service training" sessions for teachers several times a year. For twenty-eight years he served in this capacity, resigning in 1861 in disagreement with a new policy that threatened the diffusely Christian character of government-sponsored schools, at a time when the very idea of the common school was coming under increasing attack from Catholics and orthodox Protestants alike.[2]

39

De Groot's principal defenses of the common school agenda were written in the 1840s. The institution and the program of popular "enlightenment" that he defended had taken shape decades before.

ORIGINS OF THE DUTCH COMMON SCHOOL. A true *system* of public elementary schooling emerged in the Netherlands in the first years of the century. A process that began officially with the education law of 1801, followed by those of 1803 and 1806, produced such notable results that by 1811 it could be presented to France—then occupying the Netherlands—as the model of what was possible. In that year scientist Georges Cuvier and a colleague visited Dutch schools on behalf of the French government, and their report on the well-organized instruction, and especially its uplifting moral character, created a sensation in France.[3]

A generation later philosopher Victor Cousin, soon to be minister of public instruction in France, prepared an equally enthusiastic report.[4] This later report contributed significantly to the revival of the common school agenda in France and was cited by American reformers as well.

Cuvier and Cousin were clear about the aspect of Dutch education that had greatest appeal to them as to other education reformers: its consistent concern, in all aspects of instruction and discipline, with inculcating morality and natural religion.[5] This overriding purpose was suitable because schools were under the control of the government, not of religious authorities, and thus served national rather than sectarian interests. The state, in the spirit of the Jacobin program of 1791, was seen as the incarnation of the national identity and interest, of Rousseau's "General Will." Thus Cousin wrote:

> Undoubtedly, government is made for society, but it is government alone which makes society function; if you want to organize a society, begin by organizing its government; if you are serious about the education of the people, be well aware that the essence of this education is in the government which you give it.

Whereas in France the control of schools was still (in 1837) in the hands of local "notables," the Dutch had placed it from the start of their reforms directly under inspectors selected and compensated for their part-time services by the state. There was thus assurance of a consistency of effort in the direction set by central authorities.[6]

Compared with France, the Netherlands had a tradition of very weak central authority and an extensive reliance upon voluntary and local efforts to meet social needs. Dutch education in the twentieth century continues this tradition, with less than 30 percent of students attending schools under direct control of public authorities. The situation that attracted such admiration in the early nineteenth century was in a sense an aberration, but one that helps to explain the form that educational reforms were to take in the United States.[7]

In the Netherlands, as in France, Prussia, or New England, widespread though uneven schooling preceded the development of a centralized system responsive to a single vision, under government sponsorship and regulation. Churches and charitable foundations had long provided opportunities for primary education, and far more than that for the brightest (and luckiest) of poor children. Private schoolmasters also provided instruction at various levels and of varying quality.[8]

What was new in the Netherlands around the year 1800 was not the idea of a systematic effort to provide schooling with a consciously modernizing and nation-building intent; the idea was not new, nor were attempts to implement it, but the program achieved a remarkable success in the Netherlands contrasted with its almost total failure in contemporary France of the Revolution and Directory.

The immediate occasion of the powerful effort to organize popular education on a national scale was the French invasion of 1795. The victorious armies of the Revolution brought with them thousands of Dutch "Patriots" who had been in exile since an attempt to overthrow the stadholder and his Patrician allies. Not coincidentally, one of the priorities for the Batavian Republic they established was to realize the program of education absorbing so much of the energy of their allies then in power in France.[9]

Of even more powerful influence than this Jacobin program, however, was a natively Dutch movement for enlightenment and improvement of the popular classes that had been gathering strength for several decades.

THE ADVOCATES OF "VOLKSVERLICHTING." The program for the "enlightenment" of the common people was able to draw upon a network of local leaders for whom it was already a major concern. Advocates of popular education were primarily rising merchants, small manufacturers, notaries, lawyers, dissenting clergymen, and teachers, a new class living on their brains rather than their capital and owing little to the Golden Age of the seventeenth century or its theological certainties. As characterized by one Dutch scholar,

> Their Christianity was very watered-down, what would later be called "modernism," and their faith was essentially a faith in the improvement of the world and the educability of mankind through rational interventions. . . . They wanted to centralize and modernize the state and at the

41

same time dismantle the power of the old oligarchy. . . . The "democrats" wanted a centralized state in which citizens would form a homogeneous "nation"; separation of church and state was a necessary precondition, given the religious diversity of the population.[10]

Unlike the regents, "who controlled not only the towns and provinces, but the States General, the Council of State, and the Dutch East India Company," or the larger rentier class with its investments more in foreign than in Dutch enterprises, the emerging class had everything to gain from a restoration of the energy and sense of common purpose which (in their imaginations, at least) had once characterized the Dutch Republic.[11]

The gradual growth in the literate middle class during the course of the eighteenth century supported a new periodical literature, on the model of Steele's and Addison's *Spectator*. These publications, the first of which appeared in 1731, addressed themselves to an emerging class that lacked a classical education but possessed a lively curiosity about new developments in science and social life. The Dutch "spectators"

> stressed middle class self-respect, praised friendship and marriage, criticized the loose morals and aristocratic aspirations of the patricians, and preached natural sociability: the conviction that mankind could lay a basis for knowledge, virtue, and happiness through voluntary association in circles of friends, organizations, and societies.[12]

These publications sought to inspire and advise, with a particular focus on the reasonable, virtuous life based upon a right understanding of human nature and of duty. While they upheld Christianity as the basis of virtue, they called for tolerance and criticized prejudices on the basis of doctrinal differences.[13]

This relatively small but inordinately active element in the Dutch population created many local and several national organizations intended to promote various forms of progress, rather parallel to the "benevolent societies" that flourished contemporaneously in Great Britain and would play such an important role in the United States in the 1820s and 1830s. Such groups met to read and discuss books, offered prizes for the best essays on current issues, and in other ways sought to apply the new energies stimulated by the Enlightenment to social improvement.

Most significant for the future of education in the Netherlands was the Maatschappij tot Nut van 't Algemeen (Society for the General Welfare), founded in 1784 and continuing in existence today. Significantly, this was launched not in Amsterdam among the urban elite but by provincial clergymen, teachers, local government officials, and others who had been holding weekly meetings in Edam to discuss natural religion and other interests. Mennonite pastor Jan Nieuwenhuijzen of Monnickendam, the founder, reported later that he had been greatly influenced by a publication of the Holland Society of Haarlem "On the Moral and Physical Education of Children."

> It's too bad, I thought, that as a result of its high price this can't be bought and read by the common man; after all, without a good education, children cannot become upstanding people, true patriots, virtuous Christians, nor can they come to know, to value, and to exercise wisdom with all her noble virtues.[14]

He and his friends resolved to form a society that could publish inexpensive works on religious, civic, and practical subjects. Soon the group turned to improving schools, seeing this as the most essential "foundation for the formation, improvement, and cultivation of citizens." By 1787 there were eleven branches of the Nut, and its publications—religious essays, schoolbooks, uplifting biographies, works of popular morality, folksongs—were appearing in large editions of five or six thousand copies.

These publications were influenced by Enlightenment themes, but as mediated through an essentially conservative liberal Protestantism. Contemporary German educational reformers—Basedow, Campe, Salzmann, von Rochow, von Zedlitz—were more directly influential than were Rousseau and Diderot. The ground had been prepared by pietism, with its emphasis upon teaching directly relevant to young minds,[15] but the authors favored by the Nut had taken this a step further, convinced that children could not appreciate the doctrines of sin and redemption and should be exposed only to a "natural religion" that avoided these difficult doctrines and stressed only the goodness of God as revealed in Nature and Jesus' teaching of virtue and duty.[16]

By 1800 several dozen Nut primary schools were in operation, and teacher training institutions had been established in Amsterdam, Haarlem, and Groningen; there were fifty-two local branches with 3,678 members.[17]

The first prospectus issued by the Nut, in 1784, was strongly critical of other societies for not concerning themselves with the advancement of the common people. In fact, however, the ground had been thoroughly prepared; "thanks to the activities of these societies the goals of the Nut had already become commonplace by 1784."[18] Lacking a monarchy, the Netherlands did not possess an institution parallel to the British Royal Society, the French Académie des Sciences, or the Berlin Academy, dominating debate and organizational life. It was through private initiative that societies were formed.[19]

It was the newly emerging literate middle class, the *brede middenstand*, and not the traditional, classically educated elites that formed the active membership of the Nut. W. W. Mijnhardt shows that of the sixty-two members of the Nut in Utrecht in 1786–87, about a third were from small-scale business and industry, with the next largest group coming from the free professions: doctors, lawyers, notaries, surgeons. Forty-three percent belonged to the (liberal) dissenting churches, compared with their 0.4 percent representation in the population as a whole; the four clergymen were all dissenters. Sharply underrepresented were Catholics, then almost exclusively of low status in Utrecht; and members of the established church, which included both the social and economic elite and many workers, were somewhat underrepresented.[20]

HOPES AND FEARS. In the implementation, as in the planning, of the program of popular education, a major role was played by members of this emerging middle class—almost all of the original group of school inspectors, for example, were clergymen. It was their hopes and anxieties for the future of their nation, rather than a calculation of labor-force needs, that inspired their efforts. They shared a concern for the gradual decline of the prosperity of the Netherlands over the previous century, and they tended to attribute this more to the corrupting influence of luxury and religious indifference upon national morale than upon the competition of the growing British and French imperial economies.

This concern was widely shared among the reform-oriented middle class. When the Hollandsche Maatschappij offered a prize for the best essay on moral education, nearly thirty years before, forty-three essays were received in response, a record for the eighteenth century.

"With what heavy darkness the majority of the Nation is still covered," wrote Y. van Hamelsveld in 1791, in an influential book entitled *The Moral Condition of the Dutch Nation at the End of the Eighteenth Century.*

Van Hamelsveld deplored not only what he believed was a serious decline in morality but also the "unbelief and superstition" (*Ongeloof en Bijgeloof*) which he held equally responsible. "How small is the number of true Christians!" he lamented.[21] The decline threatened to end in disaster, Van Hamelsveld warned. "Netherlands, Netherlands, you stand on the very brink of your own destruction. Your ruin is inevitable unless reforms . . . can avert the fatal blow." Virtue and duty could be restored to social life by reforms to increase the moral influence of schools, prisons, and almshouses.[22]

But virtue was not enough. In contrast with the provincial elites that controlled Dutch life—and had a stake in a weak central government—this emerging class desired national unity in the interest of national strength and prosperity. This became especially clear when, in the aftermath of the French invasion of 1795, the Patriots in power proclaimed that "the Netherlands Republic no longer exists . . . as a confederated state of independent territories, but as one single sovereign People."²³ As a leading Dutch historian describes the political reorganizations of the period of French influence or control,

> The endeavour to suppress federalism appeared in the division of the territory into eight departments . . . , their boundaries agreeing as little as possible with those of the old provinces and their names, after the French model those of the rivers, recalling in no respect the old division. . . . a state was to be founded one and indivisible, governed in accordance with the will of the people manifested through a representation elected by all the citizens . . . with a powerful central administration.²⁴

In the face of a "crisis . . . of national self-esteem," the program of national unification came to be of overriding importance for that emerging class for whom local and provincial privileges held no advantage. Thus the "Representatives of the People of Rotterdam" proclaimed in the year of the French invasion that

> without Unity our Republic can never succeed in being either important and valuable for her allies [that is, republican France] or redoubtable to her foes. Common interest dictates that the whole Batavian nation unite to form a single indivisible Republic.²⁵

THE NATION-FORMING INSTITUTION. The role of popular education in this program was of critical importance—popular education not simply, or even primarily, to teach literacy or other skills but to develop the common attitudes and values considered essential to a society in which broader and broader circles of the population were entering into public life. As a German theorist of public policy wrote at about the same time, "the needy people pays little attention to improving the hearts of its children, to instilling in them a love of fatherland, or leading them into virtue and righteousness."²⁶ Schools, it was believed, would make all the difference.

The educational program of the Batavian Republic was essentially based upon the initiatives and the publications of the Nut, and those appointed to implement it were selected for their sympathy with the goals of this unofficial organization. The presence of this organization in all parts of the country, coordinating activities through frequent correspondence and annual meetings, was profoundly significant as the semiautonomous provinces of the United Netherlands were forged into the Batavian Republic and then the Kingdom of the Netherlands. It goes far to explain why popular education developed so rapidly in the Netherlands as it did not in France.

In 1796 the Nut issued *General Reflections on National Education* in which it called upon the new Batavian National Assembly to undertake a comprehensive program of popular education:

> Every well-ordered society constitutes the unity of its citizens for the ordering of the general happiness. . . . Society has the right to demand from each of its citizens full and unstinting collaboration in the achievement of this goal. Society is especially obliged to its young citizens to provide them with the necessary knowledge for their future participation in the *national commonwealth*.[27]

What was the program of an "enlightened" minority before the French Revolution came to seem an urgent necessity to liberals and conservatives alike in the early nineteenth century. Education could no longer be left to private initiative or allowed to take as many different forms as there were sponsoring organizations; too much was at stake, especially for political liberals with their commitment to broadening the franchise. The Batavian Republic "transferred the enthusiasms of philanthropists, educationalists and amateur entrepreneurs from the voluntary into the public domain," and in no sphere more than that of popular education.[28]

> Through education and propagation of (Liberal) "culture" among all classes the circle of citizens could be broadened and the basis of the state as well. On this course a homogeneous Dutch nation would come into being, and would naturally take on a liberal coloration. This is the political core of the liberal school policies. The school as *nation-forming institution* must not be divided among competing "sectarian schools" or left in the hands of an exclusive political or church party. The Liberals considered themselves *algemeen* [that is, common, nonsectarian, nonpartisan].[29]

Thus, in Utrecht the new provincial authorities issued regulations for all schools, including charity schools operated by religious foundations. These included required book lists and teaching general Christianity "above" doctrinal differences to assure that the schools would be suitable for students from families of all religious views. Among the required books for religious instruction was one prepared by the Nut entitled "What proofs do nature and reason provide for the existence of God; to what extent can we know this Being; and what reasonable consequences can be drawn from this?"[30]

A key figure in the implementation of this common school agenda was Johannes Henricus van der Palm (1763–1840), a Protestant clergyman and university teacher who shaped the first school law of 1801. Van der Palm had been a leader in Patriot circles in the provincial city of Middelburg, and when Dutch Jacobins seized power in 1798 from an ineffectual interim government he was a natural choice to serve as the "Agent" for National Edu-

46

cation. This was a new function, indeed a new concept for the Netherlands, explicitly borrowed from contemporary developments in France. Van der Palm's policies and advice to the inspectors through whom he sought to give a single new direction to what had always been a local affair have a significance for the development of the Dutch common school comparable to that of Horace Mann's celebrated annual reports for American education. He was, it has been observed, the first true "minister of public instruction" in history.

For Van der Palm as for other Patriots the primary source of national weakness was political and religious factionalism, "old prejudices supported by new violence . . . to create a new lordship of ignorant priestcraft and oppression." National regulation of schools was essential to assure that local authorities would not appoint or retain "opinionated and fanatical idiots in the position of teacher, lest rural youth in particular remain submerged in the wallow of prejudices whose destructive results have become all too apparent in these days of civic dissension."[31] In place of such prejudices, youth should be taught a "Christianity above doctrinal differences."[32]

An important aspect of Van der Palm's assignment as Agent for national education was "the maintenance of public virtue, the formation of a national spirit of patriotism and civic duty." Disestablishment of the Reformed church in 1796 had made it seem all the more crucial that a correct understanding of religion be broadly propagated in schools as the basis for morality. The detailed instructions for the development of education adopted by the Representative Body (the Patriot-controlled National Assembly) in 1798 insisted in terms characteristic of the Enlightenment program that "the reverential knowledge of an all-governing Supreme Being strengthens the bonds of Society, and thus in all possible ways must be impressed upon the hearts of the Fatherland's Young People."[33]

Religious instruction was essential, but it must not be the traditional exposition of the doctrines codified at the Synod of Dordt in 1618–19 by which the Reformed church differed from Roman Catholics and from the Mennonite, Lutheran, and "Remonstrant" minorities. Loyalty to these "distinctives" was already seriously eroded among educated churchmen and, as we have noted, dissenters were particularly active in the Nut and its efforts for educational reform. As the representative assembly in Utrecht had declared in 1796,

> the establishment and maintenance of schools by a Nation that is made up of various religious communions cannot and should not be characterized by the propagation and favoring of any particular religious fellowship in itself, but by the spreading of general Christian and moral basic principles.[34]

47

Consistent with this charge, the proposal for a national system of education that Van der Palm put forward in 1800, and that was substantially enacted as the first school law in 1801, described the content of schooling as reading, writing, the first principles of arithmetic and the elements of religion and morality, designed

> through development of the reasoning capacity of children to form them into reasonable beings, and in addition to impress upon their hearts the knowledge and feeling of everything which they owe to the Supreme Being, to Society, to their parents, to themselves, and to their fellow men.[35]

In order to realize this program in the face of local authorities controlled, he complained, by "fanatical, ignorant and ungenerous creatures" with no desire "that their children learn any more than they had," Van der Palm reached the conclusion that the central authority would have to control curriculum and pedagogy, approved books, examinations, and school inspection, leaving to regional authorities the financial support of teachers. Decentralization was the great enemy of school reform.[36] Thus he redefined all schools as public (*openbaar*), including those operated by charitable foundations and churches, in order to bring all schools under government oversight.

THE SYSTEM IS ESTABLISHED. Considerable progress had been made by local chapters of the Maatschappij tot Nut van 't Algemeen in founding schools that reflected this new pedagogy of moral uplift. These schools taught "natural religion" and avoided mention of inborn human sinfulness and redemption through the death of Jesus Christ.[37] Presumably, the fact that enrollment was voluntary minimized conflict over the nature of this religious teaching. Resistance to school reform began as soon as efforts were made to implement it through the authority of the state, especially when this required changes in the curriculum of the many schools sponsored by pious foundations.

Within a year of Van der Palm's first measures to require teaching of "reasonable religion" as the basis for morality, sufficient resistance had developed that the School Law of 1803 weakened considerably the powers of central authority in education. Local authorities and parents reacted against the attempt to eliminate doctrinal teaching and demanded the return of the catechism. As provincial authorities wrote from heavily Catholic Brabant, "fanaticism against the particulars of the various religions is also fanaticism."[38]

Authorities accused some inhabitants of the province of Overijssel of "prejudice and stupidity based upon fanaticism and a desire for control," to be accused in turn of seeking "to subject us to your authority in order to teach our children entirely in accord with your own ideas; is not this a desire for control and can it not be described in a certain sense as enthusiasm and fanaticism pushed too far?"[39]

The pendulum swung back with the School Law of 1806—though Van der Palm had meanwhile left office—with a symbolic victory for religious orthodoxy, which was nevertheless essentially a confirmation of the Nut program. Enlightenment-tinged language was removed from the legislation, but schools were directed to provide "general Christian" teaching and to leave doctrines and catechism lessons to the churches. Van der Palm's assistant Adriaan van den Ende (also a clergyman) began his long career guiding Dutch education along the lines of a heavily moralized curriculum permeated with an uplifting "schoolhouse religion" making selective use of Christian vocabulary.

This compromise guided the development of the Dutch common school over the next thirty years, a period when it attracted international admiration for its broadly liberal yet religious and moral spirit. The Nut celebrated the triumph of its program of national revival through universal popular education in a characteristic way, with an essay contest. In a preface to the winning essay, printed in 1810, the Nut lamented that "in some places prejudice, attachment to old ideas, and a poorly understood self-interest continue to resist these so fatherly provisions" for elementary education. It was to help "root these out" and thus to further "the enlightened and enlightening designs of the Government" that the Nut had called for essays on "how wise and beneficial" the government's requirements were.[40]

The new direction in popular education was not abandoned when, at the end of the period of French hegemony three years later, the former stadholder returned as King William I. Van den Ende continued to oversee the system and its network of inspectors and gave a clear message that the highest goal of schooling would continue to be the forging of national unity. In an 1813 circular to school authorities, he wrote that

> Only through unity can our state become what it once was . . . through the uprooting of old enmities . . . and an unlimited trust and the most hearty support for the present government. Develop therefore among all of your students a mutual love, unity, and unselfishness so that, when they are fully grown, they may carry the same principles over into society and into all their relationships. To this end, inflame your hearts with love for the Fatherland, for the prince who rules it, and for Christian virtue.

To this end, Van den Ende provided lists of approved books, permeated with religious and moral themes. The youngest children read about Jesus, "the best child ever in the world"; older ones read a book prepared by the Nut, a "Description of the Religious and Reasonable Character of Jesus." Perhaps the best-known were two readers written a few years later by N. Anslijn, "Virtuous Hendrik" and "Virtuous Maria." As the titles suggest, the eponymous hero and heroine exemplify, to the highest degree, the qualities that the common school was intended to develop in children. These qualities include a simple piety directed to God as Creator and as providentially active in nature.[41]

The sentimentality and moralism of such books reflect the Romantic rediscovery of religion, religion purged of its more demanding characteristics and its more offensive doctrines, a "religion without crisis," tamed to serve social and national goals. Religious instruction along these lines, most notably as promoted by the Swiss education reformer J. H. Pestalozzi, was intended to produce a popular enlightenment free from the harsh glare of rationalism—virtually no one in this period continued to advocate the Jacobin program of overt hostility to religion—as it was also free from the uncompromising doctrines of Trent and of Dordt. The common school was intended to produce a popular enlightenment bathed in kindly mists of sentimentality.

Despite continuing resistance, the common school and its compromise religiosity proved workable for several decades. The "common school for the whole nation" (*algemene school voor heel de natie*) was an important part of the program of the restored Orange dynasty, and it was purged of the more objectionable echoes of the Jacobin program. Instruction was in fact permeated with religion, as Cousin and other foreign visitors noted. The goal of the school, as defined in law, was to raise children up "to all Social and Christian virtues."

The more "advanced" pastors of the Hervormde Kerk tended to be closely involved with local schools as well as with Nut-sponsored popular libraries and other vehicles of *volksverlichting* or popular enlightenment. Thus Petrus Hofstede de Groot, as a young pastor in the village of Ulrum, helped to organize a discussion group and gave the first lecture, in December 1828, on "the origin and value of the popular enlightenment of our days." He also bought himself a copy of Pestalozzi's didactic novel *Lienhard und Gertrud* and reported years later that he had learned from that book "what education is, how education must serve upbringing, how our life on earth must become an upbringing to a higher life."[42]

Conflict over the Common School

The compromise could not last forever. Trouble began in the 1830s, just as France and the United States began their own vigorous efforts to implement the common school agenda. Explicitly Christian content had grown thinner and thinner, reflecting the extreme religious liberalism of some educational leaders but even more their desire to respond to Roman Catholic complaints about the Protestant character of the schools. These complaints gained weight with the successful revolt of the larger part of the Kingdom of the Netherlands, which became Belgium. The revolt was successful because the Catholic majority of the population, aggrieved over the education policies of the Dutch government, joined in the demands of middle-class Liberals for political reform.

It became a matter of some urgency, in the wake of this setback to the Dutch government, to conciliate the remaining Catholic minority in the Netherlands. Dutch Roman Catholics had indeed taken some part in the agitation, in 1829, of their Belgian counterparts for "freedom of education" or the right to operate their own sectarian schools.[43] An attempt was made, as in the United States two decades later, to deflect these demands by removing elements from the religious instruction that were offensive to Catholics. As in the United States, such efforts were unavailing; the basic concern of Catholics was not so much with the presence of Protestant elements as with the lack of distinctively Catholic elements.

Although these changes did not satisfy Catholics, they had the unintended consequence of offending orthodox Protestants. The 1820s had seen a religious revival within the semiestablished Reformed church, with increased stress upon religious experience and the ethical consequences of faith. This revival (or Réveil) took several forms, one of which was a rediscovery of orthodox Calvinist teaching. The preaching of sin and redemption in some parishes found an eager response among the common people, many of whom had long nurtured the tradition of orthodox pietism in "conventicles" with lay leaders. This led to serious strains with the socially conservative but theologically liberal church leadership. In 1829 the ruling body of the Reformed church deplored criticism of (liberal) pastors by the laity and in 1833 condemned "unlawful gatherings" in which "ignorance and fanaticism go hand in hand."[44]

Such protests were unavailing. Orthodox Protestants directed increasing criticism at the watered-down theology of church and school, and a secession developed that took thousands of lay people and a handful of trained ministers into several new, theologically conservative denominations.[45] Significantly, the events that precipitated this secession took place in Ulrum, where Hofstede de Groot had been the pastor.

Hofstede de Groot's successor, Hendrik de Cock, was responsive to the deeply rooted faith of his parishioners in a way that De Groot—who saw them as mired in darkness and fanaticism—had not been. According to an unfriendly (and anonymously published) account by his predecessor and chief adversary, De Cock "wasn't up to the demands" of a congregation divided into

> the two elements that the Dutch Reformed church [De Groot was writing to a German audience] had long contained: the old limited Particularism founded on the Synod of Dordt, and the new, free Universalism developing out of enlightened study of the Bible and more extensive education.[46]

De Cock engaged in a polemic with his liberal colleagues, including Hofstede de Groot, accusing them of denial or evasion of the doctrines to which they had promised to be loyal. This brought down upon him the wrath of both church and state. After all, as the chairman of the national synod had remarked to De Groot the previous year, "Purity of teaching can no longer be maintained, but purity of life can be." By insisting upon the official doctrines of the Reformed church, De Cock created conflict and hindered the program of reinterpreting Christianity from a salvation faith to a system of morality.

Those who joined him in this opposition were mostly farmers, artisans, dayworkers. In the Schoolstrijd or "school struggle" that began in the 1830s and would mark Dutch political life for nearly a century, these class lines were clearly drawn, more so indeed than in relation to any economic issue of the times.

In scores of villages and towns a deep cleavage developed between the enlightened landowners and local notables, often members of the Nut, interested in "modern agricultural methods, science, medicine, and biblical studies," and their humbler neighbors—bakers, tailors, shoemakers, carpenters, small farmers—who held to traditional religious convictions.[47] The latter, whom their great political leader Abraham Kuyper would later refer to as the *kleine luyden* ("little people"), resisted the benevolent program of their "betters" in the Nut to "raise the children above the condition [and backward convictions] of their parents." They in turn were considered bigots, fanatics, hopelessly mired in superstition.

These backward views, this determination to cling to the ways and beliefs of the fathers, came to seem the principal threat to progress and prosperity. The early optimism of Nieuwenhuijzen and the other founders of the Nut that the poor would adopt their values and goals if only given the opportunity for enlightenment gave way by mid-nineteenth century to a testy determination to force enlightenment upon the children of the poor. In 1834, for example, local authorities in Smilde ordered the police to issue a warrant against orthodox Protestants who had started to educate their children in a barn to avoid the objectionable teaching of the common school. The school inspector offered an official opinion that "the founding of a new school is a disruptive movement against the standing order of things"—no light charge in that period of social unrest.[48]

A few years later a group of orthodox Protestants in another community addressed a petition to the king, "Sire, do not deny us any longer the tender interests of our children. We would rather see our goods consumed than our flesh and blood corrupted." They were willing, they wrote, to "provide for teachers and schools ourselves without making demands upon the national or local treasuries" if permission were granted; it was not.[49]

It was out of such refusals to allow parents to have their children educated in accordance with their own convictions that the Schoolstrijd began. It was to serve as the primary vehicle for the emergence of the "little people" into political and institutional life.[50]

The real issues were stated clearly at the very start of the Schoolstrijd by Guillaume Groen van Prinsterer, the historian and statesman who would provide political leadership to orthodox Protestants for the next four decades. Speaking up for the simple people then undergoing persecution, in his 1837 essay *De Maatregelen tegen de Afgescheidenen* [The measures against the Seceders], Groen observed that the Constitution made education "a continuing matter for the *concern* of the government" but that it had become a matter for the government's *control*, in the supposed interest of national unity. By providing an education directed against sectarianism, the government had directed it against all varieties of Christians. Because of a "longing for quiet and unity," the common schools were teaching "a general religion, a Deism with Christian vocabulary and coloration," which would always be unacceptable to Christians for whom there was "only one source of true godliness and virtue, for whom God could not be known apart from Christ, for whom there was only one way of salvation."[51]

On this, there could be no compromise.

DE GROOT AND POPULAR EDUCATION. Hofstede de Groot described, years later, his own experiences as a young pastor in Ulrum. There were two parties within the church and community, diametrically opposed to one another: on one side the "cultured," who placed their confidence in Nature and Reason; on the other seamen and farmers, who held to the "special Revelation" found in the Bible. One Sunday several members of the latter group visited their young pastor with volumes of seventeenth-century divinity under their arms to say that "Pastor preaches very well, but it would be more up-building if he would model his preaching on these books that they had brought him."[52] Such advice was highly unwelcome; De Groot was already convinced that Calvinism was a "foreign import,"

53

imposed upon what he saw as the liberal Dutch theological tradition at the Synod of Dordt, in 1619, and appropriately driven out in 1795.[53]

Hofstede de Groot's own theology had been profoundly shaped by Philip Willem van Heusde, professor of philosophy at Utrecht from 1804 to 1839. Van Heusde stressed, in lieu of the traditional doctrine of a good Creation and subsequent Fall and Redemption, that the story of mankind was one of harmonious development into wisdom and resemblance to God. The same idea had already made a powerful appearance in Lessing's 1780 book, *The Education of the Human Race*, and would be echoed in Hofstede de Groot's influential popular lectures in 1847 on "the history of the education of mankind through God up to the coming of Jesus Christ." God's revelation in nature and in history were essentially identical, reaching their highest but not unique point in the life—not the teaching as such—of Jesus.[54]

The education of children, then, should be modeled on the education of mankind by God (as understood by Van Heusde and Hofstede de Groot). The "Groningen direction" in theology—De Groot and such Groningen University colleagues as J. F. van Oordt and L. G. Pareau—and the common school

> were as if made for one another. The common school, which from the beginning of the century had a tendency to "general Christianity," and the Groningen direction, in whose way of thinking the concept of education, education of mankind by God, had such a major part, and which therefore considered all denominational differences as of subordinate importance.[55]

There was no place for hard-and-fast doctrines in this approach to teaching; teachers should develop the "intimations of the divine" that were already present in their students. This required that the teachers of the common people be themselves enlightened men and not "fanatics" who continued to hold to the doctrines of sin and salvation as defined at the Synod of Dordt.

Van Heusde, writing at the time of Van der Palm's reforms, saw education as restoring the Dutch people to their former unity and glory, much in the spirit of his Prussian contemporary Fichte. In his celebrated *Addresses to the German Nation*, delivered in Berlin during the French occupation, Fichte had called for a truly "national education" to fashion a "new self," a "new life," to "mould the Germans into a corporate body, which shall be stimulated and animated in all its individual members by the same interest."[56]

Sharing this goal, Van Heusde—and De Groot after him—sought to define a distinctively Dutch approach to education and to the role of religion in the formation of a national character. This led to an emphasis upon the instrumental, subjective side of religion, its role in the progressive development of the human personality, coupled with a disregard for the orthodox Protestant and Catholic teaching that such "sanctification" is a stage subsequent to and dependent upon an objective act of redemption by God in history.

Forty years later De Groot saw that effort, which he served as a part-time school inspector, threatened by new demands for sectarian teaching. He did not agree with Groen's characterization of the issues at stake. He and the other theologians who made up the Groningen school stressed the "enduring truth" that lay behind "changing opinion."[57] History, they believed, showed a progressive improvement in understanding religious truth. Education—even that of the children of the common people—should teach this enduring truth as the basis for moral and enlightened participation in society.

DEFENDING THE COMMON SCHOOL. In his 1837 defense of the common people who were seceding from the Reformed church, Groen van Prinsterer included the education system among the government-sponsored measures that he found contrary to the rights of parents.

> I don't want to take anything away from the high praise for the improvements in teaching methods . . . in recent times; my concern here is exclusively with the Christian upbringing of youth. In this regard I believe that I can say, without exaggeration, that where the present law [of 1806] is implemented in the spirit in which it was written, that upbringing is not Christian.[58]

This has been described as the first of what would be thousands of polemical writings on the school question over the next eighty years.[59]

Three years later Groen, appointed to Parliament, spoke of popular education as one of the most important national issues. He was concerned about the right of parents to found their own schools, but he was also concerned that the government's schools demonstrate a distinctively Christian character. Under the requirement to avoid offending any conscience, education had become not only "un-Christian" but "anti-Christian,"

> overlooking the unique Mediator, [schools teach] a Supreme Being; overlooking the chasm that sin has produced, [they teach] a general Father of Mankind. . . . Thus they preach to youthful hearts a God who is a fantasy of human wisdom, an idol set up through renunciation of the living God of Revelation.[60]

55

Groen was not alone in expressing this concern; the same year, Roman Catholic leaders submitted a petition to King William I complaining of the unreligious character of the common school. With the voluntary abdication of the latter in favor of his son, the moment seemed to have come to put education on a basis more satisfactory to Catholics and orthodox Protestants. William II appointed a commission in November 1840 made up of two Catholics, Groen, and three supporters of the common school.

The results of this commission were disappointing; as in the United States a few years later, an attempt was made to remove the offense by insisting upon the civic and social character of the moral development that schools would provide. Groen's proposal, that public schools abandon the attempt to be "common" and instead provide for voluntary choice of Catholic or Protestant instruction, was rejected. This is the direction that public education would take in most of the German states, but the commitment among Dutch liberals and conservatives alike to the common school prevented such a compromise until it was too late and public education itself was abandoned by a majority of parents.

Meanwhile, such discussions were alarming to those—particularly political conservatives—for whom the common school was an essential element of popular enlightenment and national unity. De Groot was convinced that the questioning of the common school represented a Jesuit plot, an attempt to stir up unrest as in Belgium a few years before. In 1841 he devoted ninety pages in the journal of the Groningen theologians to an examination of the views of four contemporary thinkers on the role of religion in education. The Catholic position, that the state should provide for the cost of Catholic education (as in other European nations) he characterized as a demand that the clergy be allowed to dominate education at the state's expense even if it meant that the state itself would be overthrown.[61]

In 1844 De Groot published a little book asking, in its title, "Are Separate Schools for the Various Church Fellowships Necessary or Desirable?" Attacks on the common or "people's" school by Catholic leaders and certain orthodox Protestants provoked this defense, in which he answered his question with a resounding no!

An invocation of "Divine Providence," the critics claimed, was not sufficient to assure that instruction was distinctively Christian; that was a belief that the heathens shared as well. The fact that stories out of the Bible were read in a school did not, by itself, assure that the essential Christian doctrines were taught. As one Protestant critic had written several years before, the ban on teaching offensive to the conscience of any students meant that

no Christian, no religious instruction may be given in the school; thus only the teaching that there is one God, but certainly not that Jesus is our

Redeemer, and even less may sin and forgiveness, repentance and rebirth be taught in the school. So that Jews will not be annoyed in our schools, everything that is Christian must be banned; our schools are purely *civic* and thus *anti-Christian, unreligious, morally corrupting*.[62]

De Groot reminded the critics that Van den Ende, Van der Palm's assistant and successor in national leadership, had stressed that no attempt should be made to divide the schools: The goal must be a single school, a "people's school for the entire people." Such schools were in fact authentically religious, teaching "common Christian principles" with which every parent could be comfortable.

> These common religious and moral principles consist of respect and love of God, love for all mankind, eagerness to be of service, modesty, humility, etc. These common Christian principles are taught the children on the basis of those matters on which *all* Christians agree (and surely these are the most important?), through biblical history.[63]

The demand of Groen van Prinsterer and other laymen for schools that would teach the distinctive beliefs of the various communions was thoroughly unjustified, theologian De Groot insisted, even on theological grounds. After all, God had created not only the Family and the Church, each with its rights and duties, but also the State, with its rights and duties. One of the basic rights and duties of the State was to control the education of its children, to prevent the spreading of the destructive doctrines, for example, of Jesuits or Communists. Imagine if a school could be established "where perhaps the children learn to write well, to do sums rapidly, to read accurately, but are also taught that the Dutch were wrong to rise against Philip II, that they should have obeyed the fatherly discipline of Alva."[64]

This would be a disaster for the Netherlands, where at present all children, "Romish and un-Romish," sit "next to each other on the same school-benches, offer a single prayer to the same God. . . . But if schools should come for the various communions—*Ach, mijn Vaderland!*" The Netherlands would in an instant return to the condition of the sixteenth century: "church quarrels would tear us apart again; fanaticism would be injected into the receptive hearts of children, and the gentle nation would become a prey to the most horrible of evils: *religious hatred*." For its own protection, and because of the impossibility of overseeing what was going on in every schoolroom, the State must insist upon common schools.

> The only way to keep fanaticism out of schools is to have common schools [literally, "mixed schools"] where the teachers, because of the different religious confessions of the children, *cannot* fall into such ruinous matters. Only in this way can youth receive at least somewhere a shaping that will arm them somewhat against the divisive and hate-evoking principles that

they will hear later. But let the government neglect this provision and it will abandon the moral life of the nation to wind and waves, to all the cabals and intrigues of known and secret enemies, and prepare (let us speak plainly) *the destruction of the people*.[65]

De Groot returned to this theme in 1848, the tense year when revolutions swept much of Europe. In response to unrest in the Netherlands, the Liberal statesman Thorbecke developed and guided to enactment a major revision of the Dutch Constitution, including provisions for "educational freedom"—the right to establish schools—intended to still the complaints of Catholics and orthodox Protestants alike. De Groot published a short book asking, in its title, "What do we have to look for in the proposal for constitutional changes with respect to religion and education?" If enacted, he predicted, these would "stave in" the "advance of *popular education* through a national school system" and would leave the Netherlands "a prey to all the political and churchly parties that would like to tear it apart."[66]

His opponents claimed that educational freedom was necessary to respect the rights of parents, but were these rights primary? After all, the Nation protected children against physical mistreatment, disinheritance, and forced marriage; must it leave them to the arbitrary will of parents in the most important matters of all? Would it really permit schools to be opened in which "all sorts of socially disruptive tenets could be imprinted in youth, tenets of riot, assassination, class hatred, deceit, plunder, of communism, religious warfare, atheism?"[67] Would the State really give up its control over education, "by which alone the population can make a *good use* of their rights and truly form one *Nation*. How would that make any sense?"

Few parents were capable of making judgments about the effectiveness of education; teachers would make their schools as pleasant as possible in order to attract students, and the long-term results would be the collapse of morality and increasing poverty. Because of the two sharply divided religious camps in the Netherlands, the common schools would in an instant become sectarian schools, and religious warfare would soon follow.[68]

Speaking to a gathering of the Groningen branch of the Maatschappij tot Nut van 't Algemeen later the same year, De Groot praised the society's contribution to maintaining the unity of the Dutch people. "How can we continue to feel that we are one Nation," he asked,

> despite all the differences in politics, religion and schools that already exist, and that could now increase vigorously? What can hold us together, with all these divisions in State and Church, as citizens, as men, as Christians, so that we will not come into daily conflict with one another as enemies?

The only answer was to continue to promote generalized Christian "principles" and to do so through the Nut's own schools and through the common schools modeled upon them. These principles must continue to be "deeply rooted in Dutch hearts."[69]

Petrus Hofstede de Groot's son and disciple, the theologian Cornelis Philippus Hofstede de Groot, published a study in 1858 of William Ellery Channing, the Boston Unitarian minister who (as we shall see) had helped to persuade Horace Mann to take on the challenge of the "intellectual and moral improvement" of future citizens. In his highly laudatory account, C. P. Hofstede de Groot argued that Channing had been "a member of no sect," because he taught that true Christianity was evolving into a purer phase beyond sectarian differences.[70] The claim that extreme liberal Protestantism was in fact nonsectarian and could be the basis for schools permeated with religion yet inoffensive to any parent was common to Dutch and American education reformers; each group justified the claim by pointing to what they understood of practices in the other country!

Although ill-informed about the actual situation in Massachusetts—he reported that Unitarians made up the great majority of the population!— C. P. Hofstede de Groot accurately captured the argument that Channing, Horace Mann, and other Unitarians had made a few years earlier in their crusade for a religiously saturated but "nonsectarian" common school. Criticizing the "unreasoning zeal" of the abolitionists (he was writing in 1858), De Groot described a religious ideal that placed more emphasis upon religious freedom than upon specific teachings, that was more concerned with tolerance and the search for "truth" than with conveying any particular truths. In this ideal, the highest goal of a teacher was to reveal to children the God in them, not to teach them what others had experienced or believed about God and his purposes.[71]

CONCLUSIONS. De Groot's extensive and laudatory treatment of Channing was in a long-standing tradition in European social or political controversies of calling upon the example (or what was imagined to be the example) of the New World in support of a prescription for the Old. Channing's Massachusetts, in De Groot's version, exemplifies the triumph of the nonsectarian, undoctrinal, but deeply religious consensus Christianity that De Groot and others sought to develop in the Netherlands through the common school. This consensus was coming under increasingly heavy attack from those who held to traditional versions of Christianity, and Channing served as an authority for the view that such versions were destined to pass away as Eternal Truth was progressively unveiled. The elder De Groot had of course held and taught the same view for thirty years.

Channing and his allies in Massachusetts themselves called upon European models to justify the development of state-directed common schools and the Netherlands in particular was frequently cited by them as evidence that schools could be permeated with nonsectarian religion.

Channing called, in the pages of the Unitarian *Christian Examiner*, for state action to establish a system of popular education on the Prussian model, pointing out that

> In Prussia . . . the Department of Instruction is organized as carefully as that of war or of the treasury, and is intended to act on every district and family in the kingdom. In New England, it is no man's business to watch over public education.

Thus "Monarchical Prussia does more for the intellectual and moral improvement of her subjects, than republican America has ever thought of doing for her citizens."[72] A few years later he helped to persuade his parishioner Horace Mann to accept the responsibility of carrying out moral reform through education on behalf of the state.

Mann and his fellow reformers drew encouragement from accounts by Cousin and others of the nonsectarian but deeply moral and religious character of instruction in Dutch common schools; Mann himself visited Prussian and Dutch schools in 1843 and devoted one of his celebrated reports to the lessons that American education should draw from these examples.

There are striking similarities between the concerns expressed by Hofstede de Groot and those of contemporary education reformers in the United States. The most notable difference, that Mann and his allies were on the way to victory in the effort to implement the common school agenda whereas De Groot and his allies were on the way to defeat in the effort to maintain it, only brings into sharper focus the themes they shared.

Most basically, they were concerned about social unity and nation building and believed that the common school provided the only means to achieve unity in an age of political and social emancipation, an age with neither an established church nor an absolute monarchy. As liberal Protestants they shared an essentially optimistic view of human nature emancipated from inherited dogmas and superstitions while exaggerating the menace that the latter continued to represent.

It would be a mistake to equate their position with the rationalism of the eighteenth-century Enlightenment. Those who implemented the common school owed more to Schleiermacher and German Idealism, to Benjamin Constant and Lamennais than they did to Voltaire. Although deeply religious, their faith was above all in the human spirit as a reflection and expression of the inborn divine. They believed that they were *more* religious than their orthodox opponents, in the sense that they saw all of reality permeated with a diffuse spirituality and sought, through education, to develop the hearts of their students more than their minds.

Given this goal, it is understandable that De Groot, like Horace Mann, saw religious particularism and "fanaticism" as the greatest threats. In their place he sought to promote tolerance, which he insisted was entirely different from religious indifference. Traditional Christianity, with its stress on the total depravity of the human spirit apart from God and the crisis of redemption, left no room for the gradual development of the seeds of goodness and godliness planted originally by God in each human breast.

De Cock complained that De Groot and other religious liberals misrepresented Calvinism, making it appear dark and cruel, a charge that Lyman Beecher similarly leveled against the Unitarians in Boston.[73] It is true that their famous tolerance did not extend to their orthodox opponents; De Groot, as a school inspector, arranged for the firing of a young teacher who criticized one of his anonymous pamphlets from an orthodox Protestant perspective. The same teacher was then employed by a group of parents in Smilde—unwilling to send their children to the common school— resulting, as we have seen above, in a legal prosecution. The school inspector for that area (like De Groot, a clergyman) accused the teacher of "mystical thinking."[74]

This intolerance of strongly held beliefs had been characteristic of the philosophes and scoffers at religion, of course, but what is notable in the early nineteenth century is its prevalence among those professedly (and professionally) religious. When Nicholas Schotsman published a book in honor of the two-hundredth anniversary of the Synod of Dordt the clerical reaction was strongly negative, and he noted that "experience throughout the ages has shown that those who esteem tolerance in matters of faith most highly are the most intolerant of any who speak up for the truth."[75]

"There is one tolerance that is from God, another that is from the Evil One," wrote Isaac da Costa in his 1823 polemic against "the spirit of the age" from the perspective of a convert to orthodox Protestantism. True tolerance was based upon a recognition of human sinfulness and helplessness before God, not upon a proud human spirit raising itself up in judgment upon God's ways.[76]

For De Groot and the other advocates of the common school, by contrast, such "fanaticism" was a "great evil which spreads contagiously from city to city and from village to village and, like an undermining sickness, drains away the noblest strength."[77] It was the highest mission of the common school to teach in its place mutual love based upon a form of Christianity purified of those elements that were a stumbling block to anyone.

At its heart, then, the common school agenda was—and to some extent continues to be—concerned above all with the muting of strongly held passions, the sentimentalizing of deeply felt convictions. Its "truth" had to do more with the process of social accommodation than with the drama of a living religion. The present-day assault on the common school by parents for whom traditional religious belief is a central reality is not unprovoked; to the contrary, such conflict is implicit in the very goals of the institution.

By the same token, many of the strongest defenders of the common school continue to share with Petrus Hofstede de Groot and Horace Mann religious convictions of a liberal Protestant, Reformed Jewish, or humanistic cast. For them as little as for their orthodox opponents is the primary function of schooling to teach basic skills and essential knowledge. With their opponents they hold that the heart of education is the formation of loyalties and convictions, though they would center these on universals rather than on particulars. The common school, then, is anything but "secular."

3

Social Anxiety
and the Common
School

A Time of Change and Fear

SOCIAL CHANGE IN ANTEBELLUM MASSACHUSETTS. Ralph Waldo
Emerson, attending a lecture by Horace Mann in September 1839, found it
"full of the modern gloomy view of our democratical institutions, and
hence the inference to the importance of schools."[1] Mann and his fellow
education reformers set out to convince the public to support universal
popular education in "common schools" by warning of a social and political
crisis that must inevitably ensue if any part of the next generation was not
reached and molded into the enlightened citizens that America required.

It is tempting to dismiss these warnings—as Emerson did—as essentially
self-serving and even insincere, but a fair assessment would echo the conclusion reached by Bernard Bailyn in his groundbreaking study of the pamphlet literature of the American Revolution.

> I began to suspect that they meant something very real to both the writers
> and their readers: that there were real fears, real anxieties, a sense of real
> danger behind these phrases, and not merely the desire to influence
> by rhetoric and propaganda the inert minds of an otherwise passive
> populace.[2]

The argument for the common school was based upon deep pessimism
about the economic and population changes that American society, including Massachusetts, was undergoing. As one historian describes these
changes,

> At the beginning of this period [1824–48], Massachusetts was approach-
> ing a great economic development. At the end, it had been practically
> transformed from an agricultural and seafaring community into a manu-
> facturing region. . . . as the wealth of Massachusetts concentrated under
> the direction of Bostonian financiers and urban interests grew more pre-
> dominant, sounds of rural discontent rose high.[3]

Historians Carl F. Kaestle and Maris A. Vinovskis observe that

> Massachusetts was more urbanized than the rest of the nation throughout the nineteenth century. The proportion of urban dwellers in Massachusetts rose from 32.0 percent in 1800 to 91.5 percent in 1900. . . . The rate of increase in the percentage of the population urbanized in Massachusetts is particularly significant in the two decades between 1830 and 1850. The surge of urban growth in the 1830s and 1840s coincided with a shift from commercial seaport dominance to the rise of numerous manufacturing cities in Massachusetts. . . . As we would expect, the proportion of the population engaged in manufacturing increased with urbanization, making its biggest gains in the 1840s.[4]

Poverty was an increasing problem, as urban conditions developed, and the poor were more and more perceived as to be feared as well as pitied. Henry Ware, Jr., a leading Unitarian and professor at Harvard Divinity School, wrote in the 1820s of

> dark and comfortless cells, where hunger and cold are perpetual afflictions, . . . where parents and children converse only in words of blasphemy and reviling. . . . it is difficult to say whether the wretchedness be more deplorable, or the depravity more hopeless.[5]

The population of Boston increased by 73 percent during the period 1800–20 and by 115 percent during the period 1820–40. The rate of growth was increasing; from 1830 to 1850, roughly the period when the common school took shape, Boston's population increased by 123 percent, and that of new industrial centers such as Lowell grew explosively.

A financial crisis in 1837 led to a change in the American mood, a loss of the self-confidence that had so impressed visitors previously.[6] This was the year that the Massachusetts Board of Education was established, as part of a general effort by the social, economic, and political elite to employ state action to contain and resolve the emerging social "crisis."

THE IRISH IMMIGRATION. Urbanization was not the only change that Massachusetts was experiencing. Slowly at first but with dramatic intensification starting in 1845, Irish immigrants poured into Boston, the nearest seaport in the United States. The problem of urban (and thus visible) poverty and social conflict took on a much more troubling character as it came to be associated with religious and cultural differences.

Although the earlier population growth in Boston, Lowell and other Massachusetts cities came largely from rural New England, there had been a steady flow of fairly prosperous Irish immigrants, many of them passing through on their way west. Evictions encouraged by the Irish Poor Law of

1838 and the potato rot that began in 1845 stimulated Irish immigration tremendously and changed its character in ways that would have profound consequences. Oscar Handlin observes of the immigrants who came from Ireland in the 1840s that "no other contemporaneous migration partook so fully of this poverty-stricken helplessness." These were not ambitious farmers and artisans seeking to improve their circumstances in a new land but involuntary refugees from economic catastrophe.

> Imperfect as they are, the statistics of immigration reflect this situation. Before 1830 the number landing there annually never exceeded 2,000; before 1840 it reached 4,000 only once (1837). Distributed among many nativities, most were transients, westward-bound. . . . Thereafter arrivals increased rapidly from 3,936 in 1840 to 28,917 in 1849. The newcomers were overwhelmingly Irish. . . . By 1850, about 35,000 Irish were domiciled in the city; five years later there were more than 50,000. . . . The other foreign groups in the city were exceedingly small.[7]

This rapid immigration developed *after* Horace Mann and the Board of Education began their work of defining the mission of the "common school" in 1837. There are scattered references to the presence of the Irish and their significance to this mission, however, such as a report from the Roxbury School Committee in 1841 (reprinted in Mann's *Common School Journal*) that

> there are numbers of boys, who seem to be growing up without any school education at all. The greater part of them belong, we suppose, to our foreign population. We learn their parents generally wish them to attend school, and indeed direct them to go; but they seem not to have sufficient authority, or do not exercise it with sufficient energy, to enforce obedience . . . They may generally be distinguished from our school children of the same class in society, by shabbiness and dirtiness of dress and person, by the obvious want of self-respect, by bad manners and bad language. . . . How much power have teachers and committees to enforce their attendance at school when their parents desire it?[8]

Mann makes passing reference to the immigrants in his later reports, though they were clearly not a major concern for him. For example, in his *Twelfth Report* (1849), devoted largely to defending his position on religious instruction in the common school, he refers to a recent study of the Boston primary schools that found that, of 10,162 students, 5,154 were of foreign parentage; his point is that only religiously neutral schools could hope to enroll such children.[9]

Others were more directly concerned about the immigration. The chairman of the school Visiting Committee of the Boston School Committee observed, in 1846, that "it is a matter of daily remark, that immigration is constantly countervailing the Puritan leaven of our people, and reducing the scale of public morality and public intelligence."[10] The following year Mann's close ally George B. Emerson lamented, on behalf of the Boston School Committee, that "there are great masses coming in upon us who are not educated, except to vice and crime; the creatures or the victims of the oppression, or the overpopulation of the old world."[11] The issue of foreign children was forcing itself upon education authorities: Over 37,000 Irish immigrants landed in 1847, when Boston's total population was around 114,000, and the foreign part of the population grew from 32.6 percent in 1845 to almost 46 percent in 1850.[12] By 1860 foreign-born parents for the first time produced more children in Massachusetts than the native-born, according to a report of the Board of State Charities.[13]

Foreign students (which included the children of foreign-born parents) became a major issue in the term of Mann's successor, Barnas Sears, who took office in 1849. Sears wrote, in his report on the year 1855, that

A people may, as is now the case with us, be subject to influence from the presence of a foreign race of men. . . . the gregarious life of childhood and youth in our numerous manufacturing towns and villages, furnish peculiar facilities for the diffusion of corrupt principles and morals.[14]

Governor Henry J. Gardner took office the same year as part of a landslide victory of antiimmigration "nativist" candidates. In his inaugural address in January, Gardner observed that

The most prominent subject before our State and Nation at the present moment . . . concerns our foreign population;—the duties of republicanism towards them, its dangers from them. . . . The remarkable spectacle presented to the eyes of our people, naturally and wisely jealous of their nationality, of a foreign immigration in the ten years from 1840 to 1850 outnumbering the whole previous influx since the organization of the republic, progressing too in an equally increased ratio since the latter date, and probable European convulsions threatening a steady augmentation of this flood . . .[15]

FEAR OF THE IMMIGRANT. The concerns expressed by Gardner were part of a venerable tradition in American life, the fear that the society would not be able to absorb a massive influx of immigrants with different traditions and beliefs. Thomas Jefferson had expressed this fear in 1781–82, in his "Notes on the State of Virginia," observing that

It is for the happiness of those united in society to harmonize as much as possible in matters which they must of necessity transact together. . . .

[Immigrants] will bring with them the principles of the governments they leave, imbibed in their early youth; or, if able to throw them off, it will be in exchange for an unbridled licentiousness. . . . These principles, with their language, they will transmit to their children. In proportion to their numbers, they will share with us the legislation. They will infuse into it their spirit, warp and bias its direction, and render it a heterogeneous, incoherent, distracted mass.[16]

Suspicion of foreigners was even stronger among Jefferson's Federalist opponents, whose stronghold was Boston. Federalist newspapers told native Americans around the turn of the century that the United Irishmen (primarily an organization opposing British rule in Ireland) were "so many vipers within your bosom" and "a force sufficient to form an imperium in imperio."

Controversies with France led in 1798 to the adoption of the Naturalization Act (requiring a waiting period of fourteen years), the Act Concerning Aliens, and the Act Respecting Alien Enemies. Harrison Gray Otis of Massachusetts insisted in Congress that America should not "invite hordes of wild Irishmen, nor the turbulent and disorderly of all parts of the world, to come here with a view to distract our tranquillity, after having succeeded in the overthrow of their own Governments." The same year the Massachusetts legislature proposed that the federal Constitution be amended to bar naturalized citizens from holding office, lest immigrants "contaminate the purity and simplicity of the American character."[17] As Otis wrote to his wife at the time, "If some means are not adopted to prevent the indiscriminate admission of wild Irishmen and others to the right of suffrage, there will soon be an end to liberty and property."[18]

Liberty and property were at risk, the Federalists believed, but so was that national unity so dear to Jefferson and the Republicans as well. Thus Hamilton wrote in 1802 that

the influx of foreigners must . . . tend to produce a heterogeneous compound; to change and corrupt the national spirit; to complicate and confound public opinion; to introduce foreign propensities. In the composition of society, the harmony of the ingredients is all-important, and whatever tends to a discordant intermixture must have an injurious tendency.[19]

Over the next thirty years a significant shift occurred in the nature of opposition to foreigners. The *religion* of the immigrants, specifically their Catholicism, became the primary sticking point, as it had not been for the generation of the founders. We may attribute this shift in part to changes in the immigration pattern itself; eighteenth-century immigrants, whether from Ireland or from Germany, were predominantly Protestant, but economic circumstances brought an increasing number of Catholics as the nineteenth century progressed. At the height of the antiforeigner agitation, nativist leaders made clear that they continued to welcome "respectable Protestant immigrants."

This was also a period of renewed aggressiveness on the part of the Catholic church in several European nations, after its partial collapse under the impact of Enlightenment and revolution. The nativist conspiracy mongers were not inaccurate in accusing the papacy of wanting to add the United States to the company of Catholic nations—after all, the Catholic hierarchy was reestablished during these years in Britain and the Netherlands, the two most staunchly Protestant nations in the world—even if nativists greatly exaggerated the real threat that this represented.

At the same time, resurgent evangelical Protestantism in the United States replaced the religious indifference or "reasonableness" of the previous generation. Under this impulse, some thirty religious newspapers were founded in the United States by 1827, all of which made anti-Catholicism one of their regular themes.[20]

Anti-Catholicism was a respectable sentiment across the Protestant spectrum. Thus the ultraorthodox *Biblical Repertory and Theological Review* pointed with concern, in 1830, to the "tide of infidelity and Romanism settling strongly into" the Mississippi Valley, and especially to the efforts of Catholic missionaries to establish "free schools, and female seminaries," in which "the most ruinous doctrines" would be taught.[21] The same year the Unitarian *Christian Examiner* noted an exposé of the evils of Catholicism in Italy and reviewed the book again in 1835 when it was reedited with the titillating title *Female Convents: Secrets of Nunneries Disclosed*.[22]

The theme of convent life received its classic exposition in the pages of the *Protestant Vindicator*, founded in New York City in 1834. Some of the "revelations" that appeared in this publication became the book *Awful Disclosures of the Hotel Dieu Nunnery of Montreal* (1836), by Maria Monk. Such attempts to exploit popular fears of "popery" were related to fears that there was an actual conspiracy on the part of European autocrats, especially the Austrian emperor, to bring down the American democracy.

In 1835 Samuel F. B. Morse published his *Foreign Conspiracy against the Liberties of the United States*, originally a series of newspaper articles devoted to this alleged conspiracy. Morse argued "the perfect fitness of the instrument, *Catholic missions*, to accomplish the political designs upon this country of Austria and her despotic allies." There was "a vigorous and unexampled effort . . . by the despotic governments of Europe to cause Popery to overspread this country." Austrian funding for mission and educational work among Catholic immigrants was, Morse argued, motivated by political rather than religious ends; he disclaimed any wish to address the *"purely religious* character of the tenets of the Roman Catholic sect." The most critical issue was educational.

> Popery is the natural enemy of *general* education. . . . It is conforming for the present from policy to the spirit of Protestantism around it, that it may forge its chains with less suspicion. If it is establishing schools, it is to make them *prisons* of the youthful intellect of the country.

In answer to this Catholic and despotic threat, Morse argued, "Protestant patriotism" must give generously to support education.

> Does Austria send her tens of thousands [of dollars] to subjugate us to the principles of darkness? We must send our hundreds of thousands, aye our millions, if necessary, to redeem our children from the double bondage of spiritual and temporal slavery, and preserve to them American light and liberty. The food of Popery is ignorance.[23]

Another collection of newspaper articles was published in 1835 under the title *Imminent Dangers to the Free Institutions of the United States through Foreign Immigration and the Present State of the Naturalization Laws.* The author, "An American," charged that

> emigrants are selected for a service to their tyrants; not for their affinity to liberty, but for their mental servitude, and their docility in obeying the orders of their priests. They are transported in thousands, nay, in *hundreds of thousands*, to our shores.

This threat was particularly acute because

> the notorious ignorance in which the great mass of these emigrants have been all their lives sunk, until their minds are dead, makes them but senseless machines; they obey orders mechanically, for it is the habit of their education, in the despotic countries of their birth.

Thus *education*—of the wrong sort—was an essential part of the problem. The newcomers had not been educated for participation in a republican form of government and would be fit tools for the conspiracy to overthrow American freedoms.

The author stressed that the danger could not be identified with the visible Catholic church alone, since its Jesuit agents were infiltrating themselves among the general mass of immigrants.

> They are not confined to one class in society; they are not merely priests, or priests of one religious creed, they are merchants, and lawyers, and editors, and men of any profession, and no profession, having no outward

badge (in this country) by which to be recognised; they are about in all your society. . . . They can be Democrat today, and Aristocrat tomorrow. They can out-American Americans in admiration of American institutions today, and "condemn them as unfit for any people" tomorrow. These are the men that Austria has sent here, that she supplies with money . . . and whose officers (the Bishops) are passing back and forth between Europe and America, doubtless to impart that information orally which would not be so safe committed to writing.

Thus *all* immigrants must be suspect and either excluded or kept in a second-class status by denial of citizenship and eligibility for office.[24]

Massachusetts was fertile ground for such fears. A Society for the Diffusion of Light on the Subject of Romanism was organized in the state in 1835, and a branch of the American Society to Promote the Principles of the Protestant Reformation a couple of years later.[25] Typical of the mood of the time is a "Memorial of 282 Citizens of Sutton and 325 Citizens of Milbury, in the State of Massachusetts, against Foreign Emigration" submitted to Congress in 1838.[26] These rural voters must have had very little direct experience with foreigners, but they asked Congress to ascertain

> 1st. Whether there are not designs against the liberties of our country by means of this great influx of foreign immigration?
>
> 2d. Whether the *character* of many of the emigrants does not auger a vast increase of pauperism and of crime in our land?
>
> 3d. Whether there are not those now amongst us, who, by their oaths of allegiance to a foreign despotic Prince or Power, are solemnly bound to support his interests and accelerate his designs?
>
> 4th. Whether there is not a foreign *conspiracy* existing against the government of this great republic?

The General Association of the Congregational Churches of Massachusetts adopted, in 1844, a *Report on Popery* which stated that the Catholic church was in fact more idolatrous and abominable than the pagans themselves,[27] and the Unitarian *Christian Examiner* of Boston stressed the "debasing and corrupting influences of the Roman Catholic religion" and lamented the necessity of allowing Catholics to found the College of the Holy Cross in Worcester.

> We should grieve for our beloved Commonwealth if we saw any reason to apprehend that the gross perversion of the Christian faith and life which Romanism involves would ever renew its blighting influences here. . . . our fathers sought this wild, dreary region, hard and inhospitable as it was, for the sake of an everlasting riddance of Popery, with all its forms

and substance. They hated it, they were absolutely and irreconcilably disgusted with it. They hoped never to see a rag or a remnant of it on this side of the great deep. . . . It is almost too much for the children of the Puritans to bear. Out from the heart of our beloved Commonwealth are now to graduate, from year to year, Jesuit priests,—the O'Briens, the O'Flahertys, and the McNamaras. Ireland and Rome together make a combination of a not very attractive character to the sons of New England sires.[28]

These developments in Massachusetts were part of a much broader nativist impulse during this period of uncertainty and social change. Delegates from around the country gathered in Philadelphia in 1845 for a Native American National Convention and issued a "Declaration of Principles" that lamented the peril to American civil institutions created by "the rapid and enormous increase of the body of residents of foreign birth, imbued with foreign feelings, and of an ignorant and immoral character."

The mass of foreign voters, formerly lost among the Natives of the soil, has increased from the ratio of 1 in 40 to that of 1 in 7! a like advance in fifteen years will leave the Native citizens a minority in their own land! Thirty years ago these strangers came by units and tens—now they swarm by thousands. . . . having been sent for the purpose of obtaining political ascendancy in the government of the nation; having been sent to exalt their allies to power; having been sent to work a revolution from republican freedom to the divine rights of monarchs. From these unhappy circumstances has arisen an *Imperium in Imperio*—a body uninformed and vicious—foreign in feeling, prejudice, and manner, yet armed with a vast and often controlling influence over the policy of a nation, whose benevolence it abuses.[29]

Public authorities in Massachusetts were equally concerned about the impact of immigration upon the increase of pauperism and disease. A joint committee of the legislature issued a report in 1848 that contrasted the current immigration with that in the past.

Those now pouring in upon us, in masses of thousands upon thousands, are wholly of another kind in morals and intellect, and, through ignorance and degradation from systematic oppression of bad rulers at home, neither add to the intelligence nor wealth of this comparatively new country. . . . their ignorance, and total inability, even when in perfect health, to adapt themselves to the requirements of society here, without a long and tedious training . . .[30]

The following year the Massachusetts Sanitary Commission submitted to the legislature an exhaustive report on the extent of foreign pauperism, drunkenness, criminality, and insanity in Boston and charged that foreign paupers and idiots were being shipped to America to empty the poorhouses of Europe.

> Massachusetts seems to have resolved itself into a vast charitable institution. . . . the managers of the pauper-houses of the old world, and the mercenary ship-owners who ply their craft across the Atlantic and pour their freight freely in, each smile at the open-handed, but lax system of generosity which governs us, and rejoice at an opportunity to get rid of a burden, or make a good voyage.[31]

Inevitably, these concerns about a growing pauper class (by no means unfounded) and xenophobic fears found political expression in Massachusetts, as elsewhere. In 1845 Thomas Davis was elected mayor of Boston on the ticket of the newly formed American Republican party; controversies in New York City over Catholic opposition to use of the King James version of the Bible played a role in this election. Several years before, Lyman Beecher, formerly an evangelist and pastor in Boston, had made a fund-raising visit for his theological seminary in Ohio. Echoing his 1835 book *A Plea for the West*, Beecher told Massachusetts Yankees that the Catholic church was seeking to subvert America and could be resisted only by "a competent evangelical ministry and revivals of religion"; Bible reading in schools was also essential. Davis's candidacy benefited from these concerns.[32]

It was in 1854 that nativist concerns came to a head in Massachusetts politics, resulting in an almost complete sweep of the elections of that year. The American Republican party outpolled the other four parties by 81,500 to 54,000 in what has been described as "an uprising against the prestige and power of a bourgeois aristocracy" as well as a reaction against foreign immigration. Of over 400 Massachusetts legislators, all but three were members of the American or Know-Nothing party. Only thirty-four of them had had previous legislative experience.[33]

This powerful political reaction against immigration is the context of Governor Gardner's remarks about the dangers created by the "foreign population." Gardner's inaugural address after the landslide election of 1854 called for a vigorous use, by the state, of education as the primary means of shaping the immigrant to the American pattern.

> It is a great problem of statesmanship wisely to control the mingling of races into one nationality. The dominant race must regulate the incoming class. . . . It is the only salvation of both. . . . Legislation must cooperate with time and circumstances in working out this decree of God, this axiom of political philosophy, this theory of nationality. . . . To dispel from popular use every foreign language, so great a preserver of unassimilat-

ing elements of character—to print all public documents in the English tongue alone—to ordain that all schools aided by the State shall use the same language . . . to cultivate a living and energetic nationality—to develop a high and vivid patriotism—to Americanize America—to retain the Bible in our common schools—to keep entire the separation of church and state—to nationalize before we naturalize, and to educate before either.[34]

The Know-Nothing program was essentially not to exclude but to assimilate, concerned to make immigrants "be as we are."[35] This intention had been expressed by Mayor Davis of Boston in his inaugural address in 1845, when he insisted that

It is not the object of the American party, by word or act, to engender unkind feelings between native-born and foreign-born citizens. Its object is, by the establishing of general and salutary naturalization and registry laws, by education and moral means, to place our free institutions upon such a basis that those who come after us, the descendants both of the foreign and of the American citizens may be free and independent.[36]

The assimilating intention evident in Governor Gardner's program of a decade later would become a primary theme in the development of the common school, and one of the leading factors in its "triumph" as the preeminent American institution.

Education for Assimilation

THE VOLUNTARY IMPULSE. It was not at first clear that the responsibility for assimilating immigrants and shaping them into upright Americans would be taken up by the state. The lead was indeed first taken by churches and church-related voluntary associations. Alexander Hamilton had called in 1802 for a "Christian Constitutional Society" to aid immigrants and win their loyalty, and a number of voluntary associations—such as the Massachusetts Society for Promoting Christian Knowledge (1807), the Boston Society for Religious and Moral Instruction of the Poor (1816), and the Society in Lynn for the Promotion of Industry, Frugality, and Temperance (1826)—included this among their objectives.[37]

When the prominent citizens who made up the Boston Society visited the homes of the destitute on a fact-finding mission, they discovered that many had no Bible and that a distressing number of children were both illiterate and ignorant of Christianity. The first response was to begin to organize Sunday schools that would teach literacy and moral principles through readings of a devotional character. In 1817 the society petitioned the selectmen for the use, on Sundays, of the grammar school bordering the Common, in an area with a high proportion of Negro and foreign-born families.

> Our objects in attending to Sunday schools are, to reclaim the vicious, to instruct the ignorant, to secure the observance of the Sabbath, to induce the children to attend public worship, and to raise the standards of morals among the lower classes of society.[38]

By 1837, the year when the Massachusetts legislature set up the Board of Education to give state direction to popular education, the Boston Sabbath School Union was enrolling 2,602 regular students, with 376 volunteer teachers.[39] It has been suggested that pan-Protestant cooperation in the Sunday school movement created the precedent for supporting the nonsectarian common school, with much the same motivation of popular uplift.[40]

Related to the establishment of Sunday schools was the effort to distribute copies of the Bible to every family. The American Bible Society adopted this as its mission in 1830, with a special concern to reach immigrants with the Bible. Thus the society reported, in 1835, on the work of one of its agents at Le Havre, a major port of embarkation for German immigrants. The agent wrote that he told them "that in America everyone has his Bible, and that American Christians wish everyone who comes to the country to have one also. It must produce a moral impression that will not easily be effaced from their minds."[41] A decade later a Massachusetts delegate reminded the society that

> we are trying to sweeten not a bitter fountain only [a reference to Exodus 15:22–25] but a mighty river which is continually flowing down upon us like the vast Mississippi, with all its waters and something I fear of its mud, carrying desolation in its track, and scarcely leaving a trace of cultivation behind. More than one half, at least, of these immigrants are Roman Catholics.[42]

Missionary efforts among poor urban immigrants were a major concern of the Protestant denominations in this period; by 1838 Boston had at least ten "ministers-at-large" supported by church funds to carry out such ministries. The pioneer of this group, Unitarian Joseph Tuckerman, had begun his work in 1826 with the conviction that he was engaged not only in relieving material needs but also in building character. As he wrote later,

> I do not believe there ever was or that there is a human being in whom there was or is no element of goodness; no element of moral recoverableness; no unextinguished spark of moral sensibility which, with God's blessing, may not be blown into a flame.[43]

Tuckerman was opposed to state interventions to improve the conditions under which the poor lived or to promote moral reformation. "Moral suasion was the only means of reform he could bring himself to endorse; he was convinced that all reforms based on legal coercion were bound to entail greater evils than they were supposed to remedy."[44]

It is no exaggeration to say that Protestant leaders of this generation believed that they were engaged in a mighty struggle with ignorance, moral degradation, and popery and that voluntary efforts could play a major part in this struggle. The nation was faced with a choice between "superstition and evangelical light,"[45] and the chosen role of Protestant churches went far beyond ministering to their members. They saw themselves as charged with shaping the culture, its institutions, and its future citizens.

THE STATE AS EDUCATOR. There were those, however, who looked to more than voluntary and church-associated measures, who believed that the state was in the last analysis the appropriate agency to take on the task of reshaping immigrants into Americans. One of these was James Carter, who more than anyone else prepared the way for the measures taken by Horace Mann to redefine the mission of the common school and led the legislative efforts that established the Board of Education in 1837.

Carter wrote in his highly influential *Essays on Popular Education* (1826) that

> Upon this topic of popular education, a *free* government must be *arbitrary*. For its existence depends upon it. The more ignorant and degraded people are, the less do they feel the want of instruction, and the less they will seek it. . . . if any one class of men, however small, be suffered as a body to remain in ignorance, and to allow their families to grow up without instruction, they will increase in a greater ratio compared with their numbers, than the more enlightened classes, til they have a preponderance of physical power.[46]

Thus popular education could not be left to chance, or to the zeal and efforts of voluntary associations; indeed, "every private establishment . . . detaches a portion of the community from the great mass, and weakens or destroys their interest in those means of education which are common to the whole people." Only a *universal* and *mandatory* system could achieve what was necessary:

> The ignorant must be allured to learn, by every motive which can be offered to them. And if they will not thus be allured, they must be taken by the strong arm of government and brought out, willing or unwilling, and made to learn, at least, enough to make them peaceable and good citizens.

Carter called for essentially a state monopoly of popular education, by which he meant the elementary schools, which alone were attended by the broad mass of the people. After all,

> free governments are the proprietors of all literary and scientific institutions so far as they have the tendency to diffuse knowledge generally among the people. The free schools of Massachusetts, as the most efficient means of accomplishing that object, should therefore be the property and peculiar care of government.

The objective of this state-controlled system of popular education had little to do with economic or egalitarian goals; it was to shape future citizens to a common pattern. Like the Jacobin orators on "republican education" during the French Revolution, Carter turned to the example of Sparta, as presented by Plutarch in his life of Lycurgus. Plutarch described an idealized Sparta in which boys were taken from their families to be raised by the state in a pattern of martial virtue. For Carter as for other education reformers of the time, this represented the potential of the common school. After all, "if the Spartan could mold and transform a nation to suit his taste, by means of an early education, why may not the same be done at the present day?"

The same intimate connection between a "free" or republican form of government and schooling was a primary consideration with Edward Everett, governor of Massachusetts in 1837, when the Board of Education was created by the legislature, and thus the appointer of the original board. Everett told a county common school convention the following year that

> on the system established in the United States, where the people are not only in theory the source of power, but in practice are actually called upon, constantly, to take an efficient part in constituting and administering the government, it is plain that education is universally and indispensably necessary. [47]

Carter and Everett were harking back to a theme that had been stated a generation earlier by Noah Webster, the author of the most widely used spellers in the early Republic. In an essay that first appeared in his *American Magazine* in 1787–88, Webster stressed that "our national character is not yet formed" and that therefore

> it is an object of vast magnitude that systems of education should be adopted and pursued which may not only diffuse a knowledge of the sciences but may implant in the minds of American youth the principles of virtue and of liberty and inspire them with just and liberal ideas of government and with an inviolable attachment to their own country.[48]

Popular education was not only the most effective but indeed the only effective means of creating future citizens.

> Laws can only check the public effects of vicious principles but can never reach the principles themselves, and preaching is not very intelligible to people till they arrive at an age when their principles are rooted or their habits firmly established. . . . The only practicable method to reform mankind is to begin with children.

Thus the churches could not effectively serve as the primary socializing agency of society, nor could such an essential element of social control be left to chance; it must become a primary object of government.

> Education, in a great measure, forms the moral characters of men, and morals are the basis of government. Education should therefore be the first care of a legislature. . . . A good system of education should be the first article in the code of political regulations. . . . no legislature can be justified in neglecting proper establishments for this purpose.

Webster was very clear about the socializing function of schooling: "The *virtues* of men are of more consequence to society than their *abilities*, and for this reason the *heart* should be cultivated with more assiduity than the *head*." Properly used as an instrument of republican government, popular education could shape children to the needs of a virtuous society. Of all possible reforms, this was clearly the most desirable, since "until legislators discover that the only way to make good citizens and subjects is to nourish them from infancy . . . mankind cannot know to what a degree of perfection society and government may be carried."

The concerns that Webster was expressing around the time when the Constitution was adopted had to do with the general challenge of forming citizens for a republic. Thirty years later the development of urban life and of new economic strains were turning his attention, and that of others, to the problem of poverty and of the incorporation of the poor into the social order. In 1819 Webster wrote to Massachusetts Governor John Brooks, urging him that

> To form plans for diffusing literary and moral improvement among the poorer classes of citizens, in connection with religious instruction, will be no less our pleasure than it is our duty. To draw from the obscure retreats of poverty the miserable victims of ignorance and vice, to enlighten their minds and correct their evil habits, to raise them to the rank of intelligent, industrious, and useful members of society will never cease to be the object of deep solicitude with a wise legislature.[49]

Immigration was still a minor part of the problem of social coherence in 1819; indeed, in the period 1821–26 less than 4,000 passengers would land at Boston, most of them transients going farther south or west (by contrast, in 1846–51, 112,664 passengers landed at Boston).[50] The assimilation of those immigrants who came seemed a matter of course; in 1818 Secretary of State John Quincy Adams wrote to a European inquirer that immigrants were welcome in America, but they must "cast off their European skin, never to resume it."[51]

Growing immigration does not account, initially at least, for the new concern for direct state intervention in the provision of popular education, though Governor Seward of New York identified this as a serious educational issue in 1840. Massachusetts, unlike New York, was not an attractive goal for immigrants until the economic crisis in Ireland sent over a wave of the truly impoverished who had no choice but to land at the nearest American port. It was *poor* students and not *foreign* students who, initially at least, were the primary concern of the Massachusetts education reformers.

This concern is reflected in the complaints in the 1820s and 1830s of the educational journals, which did so much to form the climate in which popular education became the preeminent social reform, that educators were doing too little about the "vicious" and "ignorant." Schools were needed to "purify the thick atmosphere of moral pollution which they have always breathed, and which still envelopes them." The editor of the *American Annals of Education* stressed that "the question for *every individual* is whether he shall aim at the highest degree of security for his property and life, by educating every individual around him."[52]

Historian Whitney Cross has suggested that the economic panic of 1837—initiating a period of retrenchment and confusion that lasted until 1844—led to "a more modest estimate of the country's immediate potentialities" and a turn, on the part of temperance and other moral reform forces, "from moral suasion to legal compulsion." Cross's contention is that the habits of thinking about the causes and remedies of social problems created by the "religious ultraism" of the preceding decade carried over into the reform movements of the subsequent period.

> Disillusion recommended less faith in the goodness and automatic accomplishments of the regenerate man and more faith in measures calculated to make men behave aright. . . . Reform was still to be accomplished rapidly, in great strides, not painstakingly and patiently by slow, small steps. The objective continued to be an absolute, not a relative, improvement. People must still be brought to an emotionalized state of intense conviction to accomplish anything.[53]

HORACE MANN AND THE "PATERNAL" STATE. Something of this fervor was very much a part of the character of Horace Mann, and of his success; French education reformer Gabriel Compayré likened Mann to "a Peter the Hermit who preached a crusade against ignorance."[54] His first crusade, however, was concerned with controlling adult behavior, with drunkenness and insanity, through state action. Elected to the Massachusetts legislature in 1827, Mann "found the environment of the General Court conducive for further development of his sense of stewardship and social responsibility." Taking stock of the laws that had been passed in the legislative session of 1830, Mann wrote that, "after such reflections, I feel my desire for human and benevolent effort invigorated." Biographer Jonathan Messerli notes that "Mann would cast himself in the role of a humanitarian reformer and be instrumental in defining the right of the state to intervene in curbing the appetites of the intemperate and treating the insane."[55]

This role proved a great success for Mann; thirteen years after his admission to the bar as an obscure lawyer with no social connections to the Boston elite, he was president of the Massachusetts Senate and a valued ally and agent of that elite. In this role he was instrumental in creating the Board of Education and was a natural choice (despite his lack of previous interest in popular education) to lead the most significant reform effort of all.

Two days after accepting the position of secretary of the board (at the end of June 1837), Mann wrote to a friend:

> I have abandoned jurisprudence, and betaken myself to the larger sphere of mind and morals. Having found the present generation composed of materials almost unmalleable, I am about transferring my efforts to the next. Men are cast-iron, but children are wax.[56]

Two weeks later he wrote in the same vein, to his sister, expressing his intense concern whether "I can discover by what appliance of means a non-thinking, non-reflecting, non-speaking child can most surely be trained into a noble citizen ready to contend for the right and to die for the right."[57]

Although he was discouraged by the resistance of adults to the efforts of state-led reform to mold them to a more virtuous pattern, he did not abandon his interest in such efforts. He retained a conviction that "If temperance prevails, then education can prevail; if temperance fails, then education must fail."[58]

In its *Third Report* (1840), Mann's Board of Education stressed that "the state, in its sovereign capacity, has the deepest interest in this matter" of popular enlightenment through common schools and the libraries which they urged that each should contain. In this way the state could "call into existence an order of men" who would lay the basis for future prosperity and social progress. "It is a corollary from the axioms of its constitution, that every child, born within its borders, shall be enlightened. In its paternal character, the government is bound, even to those who can make no requital."[59]

In the introductory remarks to the first issue of his *Common School Journal*, an immensely influential publication aimed at teachers and "friends of education" (November 1838), Mann reviewed the essentials of his educational creed.

> The germs of morality must be planted in the moral nature of children, at an early period of their life. . . . If we would have improved men, we must have improved means of educating children. . . . Of all the means in our possession, the common school has precedence, because of its universality.[60]

He stated the claim even more boldly in the introductory remarks to the third year of the *Common School Journal*, in January 1841:

> *the Common School is the greatest discovery ever made by man.* . . . Other social organizations are curative and remedial; this is a preventive and an antidote; they come to heal diseases and wounds; this to make the physical and moral frame invulnerable to them. Let the Common School be expanded to its capabilities, let it be worked with the efficiency of which it is susceptible, and nine tenths of the crimes in the penal code would become obsolete; the long catalogue of human ills would be abridged.[61]

His introductory remarks the following year (January 1842) summoned all true patriots to join in this effort, which he suggested was equivalent to that of the American Revolution (an early use of the "moral equivalent of war" argument!):

> what sphere of patriotic exertion is left open for the lover of his country, but the sphere of improving the rising generation through the instrumentality of a more perfect and efficient system for their education? . . . For this improvement of the race, a high, a generous, an expansive education is the true and efficient means.[62]

Mann's confidence in the almost infinite power of popular education was not confined to his public rhetoric; for example, he wrote to his ally Henry Barnard, then promoting school reform legislation in Rhode Island, in June 1844, that "If Rhode Island passes that bill . . . in one generation it will regenerate the mass of her people."[63] After all, he wrote the next year, "our schools foster the interests of morality, and act as a restraint upon those formidable vices which are everywhere starting up around us."[64]

In his *Tenth Report* (1847) Mann provided an extensive review of the legal and other provisions for education in Massachusetts; this summary was reprinted two years later in an expanded version by order of the legislature, with 10,000 copies distributed. Mann asserted that "Massachusetts is *parental* in its government" as evidenced by its provisions for popular education, and by its concern for the poor: "For the support of the poor, nine tenths of whose cost originate with foreigners or come from one prolific vice, whose last convulsive energies she is now struggling to subdue, she annually pays more than three hundred thousand dollars." This is one of his first references to the social problems created by immigration, and it is notable that he writes of "foreigners" in parallel with those impoverished by intemperance.[65]

In the last of his twelve reports, and after his decision to take the seat in Congress vacated by the death of John Quincy Adams, Mann employed his usual vehemence to portray the infinitely threatening nature of a society in which the young have not been shaped to honor the social virtues.

> As the relations of men became more complex, and the business of the world more extended, new opportunities and new temptations for wrongdoing have been created. With the endearing relations of parent and child, came also the possibility of infanticide and parricide; and the first domestic altar that brothers ever reared was stained with fratricidal blood.[66]

He continues in this vein for three pages, then notes the various efforts that have been made throughout history, including the exhortations of the clergy, to contain evil, all in vain. But, he concludes,

> there is one experiment which has never yet been tried. . . . Education has never yet been brought to bear with one hundredth part of its potential force, upon the natures of children, and, through them, upon the character of men, and of the race. . . . Here, then, is a new agency, whose powers are but just beginning to be understood, and whose mighty energies, hitherto, have been but feebly invoked. . . . Reformatory efforts, hitherto made, have been mainly expended upon the oaken-fibred hardihood and incorrigibleness of adult offenders; and not upon the flexibleness and ductility of youthful tendencies.

"Reformatory efforts," so directed, could banish from the world "the dark host of private vices and public crimes which now embitter domestic peace and stain the civilization of this age." This would, in fact, accomplish the long-deferred promise of the Founder of Christianity, since when Christ taught his disciples to pray, "Thy kingdom come, thy will be done, *on earth* as it is done in heaven," did he teach them to pray for what shall never come to pass? And if this consummation is ever to be realized, is it to be by some mighty, sudden, instantaneous revolution, effected by a miracle, or is it to be produced gradually by that Providence which uses human agents as its instruments?

For Mann, the question answered itself.

THE SCHOOL IN PLACE OF PARENTS. Historian Stanley K. Schultz has provided a masterful narrative of the growth of the conviction, among the Boston elite, that the common school and mandatory school attendance were essential to social stability and to the control and assimilation of an immigrant population. He relates this conviction to the "discovery of child-hood" that was such an important element in the international romantic movement of the early nineteenth century and that was abundantly re-flected in the new sentimental children's literature of the period. If "the child is father to the man," the education of the rising generation was ob-viously of overwhelming importance. "Although Americans had always re-garded their youth as the promise of the future, more than ever during the three antebellum decades they promoted the present generation as either the salvation or the destruction of the nation."[67]

It was no longer possible to rely upon the home to train this generation in those qualities of character that were essential to the survival of a free republic or Christian commonwealth. In 1843 a Baptist periodical in Boston charged that parents had abandoned their responsibility for moral educa-tion and that this laxity could destroy the nation.[68]

Horace Mann made the same charge in his *Eighth Report*. The context of his remarks is a concern to refute charges made by certain orthodox Protes-tants that the common school tended to undermine religious faith; actually, he wrote, he and the board had actively promoted the use of the Bible in schools and had required it in the state normal schools where future teach-ers were trained. Thus the common school, he wrote, was "the nursery of piety." After all,

> though undoubtedly it is the duty of parents and of religious teachers, to cooperate with the Common School teachers in their religious instruc-tions, yet it is only in the Common School that thousands of the children in our Commonwealth can be thus instructed. How many are there of those, who swarm in our cities, and who are scattered throughout our hundreds of towns who, save in the public schools, receive no religious instruction? They hear it not from the lips of an ignorant and a vicious parent. They receive it not at the sabbath-school, or from the pulpit. And

if in the Common School, the impulses of their souls are not awakened and directed by judicious religious instruction, they will grow up, active in error, and fertile in crime.[69]

The following year Mann expressed his concern over the neglect of moral training by many local school committees, as reflected in their annual reports to him.[70] He feared that many schools concentrated too exclusively on developing the intellect and even had a negative impact—through reliance upon competition among the students—upon the development of character.

Do they cultivate the higher faculties in the nature of childhood,—its conscience, its benevolence, a reverence for whatever is true and sacred; or are they only developing, upon a grander scale, the lower instincts and selfish tendencies of the race? . . . are we equally sure that our schools are forming the character of the rising generation upon the everlasting principles of duty and humanity?

In the strength of his conviction that the mission of the school was to make children better than their parents, and thus better than their parents could make them, Mann came as close as his Unitarian beliefs and his emphatic rejection of Calvinism would permit him to an assertion of something like "original sin." The human situation, for him, was as hopeless as a Calvinist would have painted it; the significant difference was that, for Mann, the agent of redemption was the common school.

How shall the rising generation be brought under purer moral influences [so that] when they become men, they will surpass their predecessors, both in the soundness of their speculations and in the rectitude of their practice? . . . The same nature by which the parents sunk into error and sin, preadapts the children to follow in the course of ancestral degeneracy. Still, are there not moral means for the renovation of mankind, which have never yet been applied?

Note that Mann hoped for an improvement in "the soundness of their speculations," by which he meant that progressive purification of Christianity from the superstitious inheritance of "priestcraft" (Protestant as well as Catholic) to which he often referred.

In approval of such efforts, the influential Congregationalist journal *New Englander* pointed out that "these schools draw in the children of alien parentage with others, and assimilate them to the native born. . . . So they grow up with the state, of the state and for the state."[71]

83

Summary

With the growing immigration of the late 1840s and early 1850s, the assimilating task of education seemed ever more essential. By 1852 over 6,600 of the 11,800 students in the Boston primary schools were of foreign parentage, and one of the city's educational leaders boasted of what the schools were doing to "Americanize" these children.[72] Two years earlier the School Committee had urged that

> We must open the doors of our school houses and invite and compel them to come in. There is no other hope for them or for us. . . . In our Schools they must receive moral and religious teaching, powerful enough if possible to keep them in the right path amid the moral darkness which is their daily and domestic walk. . . . unless we can reclaim this population in their childhood by moral means, we must control them by force, or support them as paupers, at a maturer period of life.[73]

It is the growing immigration—and the fears that it elicited—that explains why the common school came to have such a "mythical" significance in nineteenth-century America. The essential program had been laid out for the common school before immigration became a major preoccupation. Absent a national church, a monarchy, an external threat, there seemed little to hold the new nation together. Those concerned with public affairs found the burgeoning of Protestant denominations and even of new religions, the unbridled competitiveness of the marketplace, the rapid rise and fall of political parties deeply unsettling. The common school as imagined by Horace Mann (who never taught in one) would be above religious and political divisions and would teach students higher motivations than "emulation." It was the reform from which all other reforms would flow.

What in the 1830s was a cause appealing to a relatively limited elite, concerned to shape the American people in their own enlightened image, came in the next two decades to be perceived as an urgent necessity by virtually all Americans of social and political influence, including orthodox Protestants who otherwise might well have insisted upon more direct doctrinal content in the schools.

Anxieties about the assimilation of the immigrant prevented the development of a religiously differentiated educational system, as in most European nations in this period, and made the common school the supreme American institution.

The crisis in confidence in public schools so evident today draws much of its irrational quality from the exaggerated hopes that we have cherished over the past century and a half. We have expected that our schools would banish crime and social divisions, that they would make our children better than we have ever been. Horace Mann and others promised us that, and we believed them. It is no wonder that suggestions that the common school be diversified, that the "public education monopoly" be broken up, that our society's secular church be disestablished arouse the deepest anxiety and confusion today.

4

Sources of
the Common School
Idea

The Social Mission of the Common School

POPULAR—or elementary—schooling in Massachusetts in the years that followed the Revolution was provided by an assortment of local arrangements that do not fit into our present categories of "public" and "private" education. The schoolmaster might be hired by a town or district committee of citizens, or might set up school on his or her own initiative, especially in the larger communities. In either case, the school would be supported largely by the fees paid by parents, though various arrangements were made to pay the fees of the children of families for whom this would have been a burden. The clergy frequently took a leading role in sponsoring and overseeing schools; though few were explicitly church-controlled, most schools made religious instruction and devotions a normal part of their program.

The educational reformers of the 1830s and subsequent decades derided such arrangements for schooling as hopelessly inadequate, but recent research suggests that they were rather effective. Literacy and basic mathematical skills were nearly universal, and those students whose social status or natural ability made secondary education possible were prepared for such further study. It was effective, that is, in providing the instruction necessary for the farmer, craftsman, or small tradesman of the day and in laying a basis for further study for those who were in a position to go on.

It will be helpful to the discussion that follows to adopt a distinction current in the debates over education policy in France during the Revolution, between *instruction* and *education*. The former was used to refer to the teaching of skills and information necessary for economic life, whereas the latter referred to the shaping of the character, values, and loyalties of students as future participants in political and social life.

This distinction itself tells us much about the changing and expanding role attributed to formal education under the influence of the Enlightenment. For influential eighteenth-century thinkers, and for those school re-formers who sought to implement their program, popular *education* was essential as a counterweight to and eventually a replacement for that which had been provided by the churches through preaching and catechism. A certain amount of *instruction* in reading, writing, and computation was also seen as useful—literacy would banish "superstition," the philosophes be-lieved, not anticipating the new forms of superstition it would nourish!—but that was a secondary consideration in the creation of systems of popular education under state control.

The *instruction* provided in Massachusetts in the early nineteenth century was, in general, quite adequate to the needs of the day; the "common school revival" that began in the late 1820s and received definitive form under the leadership of Horace Mann was a struggle over *education*, over the role of schools in shaping the character of the American people. Mann and others set about creating a system of popular education in support of their convictions about the necessary direction of American life.

A concern for the improvement of instruction—in the narrower sense—was among the reform movements of this era of benevolent activity, pro-moted in much the same manner as other reforms and efforts to improve society that gained broad support about the same time, through voluntary associations, "networking," and local initiative by local elites.

Within a few years, however, the emphasis shifted from voluntary initia-tives to improve the techniques and resources available for instruction to state action in the interest of a uniform system of education. Voluntary efforts lost credit. Local diversity was defined as a problem, and schools not accountable to the political process were condemned as a threat to the best interests of society. The goal became the transformation of popular school-ing into a powerful instrument for social unity.

In Massachusetts the common school revival was essentially an effort by a Protestant/Whig minority to reshape popular beliefs and values after a single pattern. State action was necessary, in their view, primarily to over-come the undesirable diversity of teaching. This diversity was seen as harm-ful to progress, to social and national unity, and to the interests of an emerging elite whose position was based upon manipulation of the sym-bolism and management of the new institutions necessary to this unity.

Although the common school revival took place in the era of "Jacksonian democracy," efforts by some historians to relate it to the demands of the common people have been less than convincing. It would be more accurate to say that the liberal elite developed a program for a certain type of popular education as a reaction against the perceived threat of emerging class inter-

87

ests and of the "irrationality" of revivalistic religion. Through the *common* school, they believed, class antagonisms would be overcome and sectarian divisions reconciled.

This set of assumptions about the role of a unitary system of popular education acquired a new salience when the increase of Catholic immigration in the 1840s and 1850s seemed to pose a graver threat than any that the Republic had yet faced. From the crusade of an elite, the common school became the favorite public institution of the great Protestant majority.

Our concern here is not to trace the steps by which a congeries of workable though uneven and uncoordinated provisions for popular schooling was developed into the outline of a state-directed *educational system*. We will seek rather to identify some of the key influences and elements that served to define the program of Horace Mann and other educational reformers.

An extensive and selective use of foreign examples helped to shape the direction taken by the education reforms of the 1830s and 1840s. The strong role of the Prussian state in promoting popular education, and especially its use of state-controlled teacher training institutions or normal schools, was widely cited in support of a similar program in Ohio, New York, Pennsylvania, and Massachusetts. The attempt (which then appeared highly successful) in the Netherlands to teach religion and morality in common schools without concessions to the religious diversity of the students offered hope that the same approach would be a success under American conditions.

These continental examples provided the elements of an educational program that promised to shape the values of future generations of citizens in accord with those considered most appropriate by the liberal elite of the period.

Much the same program had already been proposed, some forty years before, by several gifted essayists under the direct influence of the French Enlightenment and the educational agenda of the radicals during the French Revolution. In this naked form, it found little support; mediated through the examples of the Protestant states of Europe and clothed in the rhetoric of liberal Protestantism, it was able to triumph in the decades before the Civil War.

Demand for National Education in the New Republic

In the years immediately after the American Revolution there was an extensive reciprocal influence between "republican" circles in the United States and in France. Most Americans hailed the French Revolution, as even arch-

88

Federalist Alexander Hamilton conceded in 1793, writing to a friend that "the popular tide in this country is strong in favor of the last revolution in France."[1] It was claimed, indeed, that more cannons were fired by Americans in 1795 to celebrate the fall of Amsterdam to the French than the French had fired in taking it.[2]

Thomas Jefferson and his political allies continued to support the French Revolution even after the excesses of the early 1790s. Jefferson wrote, in characteristically exaggerated terms, that "the liberty of the whole earth was depending on the issue of the contest, and . . . rather than it should have failed, I would have seen half the earth devastated."[3]

The exciting debates on education in the French National Assembly awoke echoes in Jeffersonian circles in the United States. Jefferson himself called schools the most important instrument of society for "ameliorating the condition, promoting the virtue, and advancing the happiness of man," and in 1786 he had written (from prerevolutionary Paris) that

> by far the most important bill in our whole code is that for the diffusion of knowledge among the people. No other sure foundation can be devised, for the preservation of freedom and happiness. . . . Preach, my dear Sir, a crusade against ignorance; establish & improve the law for educating the common people.[4]

This was not an unfamiliar theme to those who, like Jefferson, were soaked in Enlightenment discussions of the means of the progress of nations. Benjamin Rush wrote (in 1786) that "Our schools of learning, by producing one general and uniform system of education, will render the mass of the people more homogeneous and thereby fit them more easily for uniform and peaceable government."[5] Thus, by a sort of perpetual-motion process, Rush believed that popular education would produce the millennium in the new nation:

> From the combined and reciprocal influence of religion, liberty, and learning upon the morals, manners, and knowledge of individuals, of these upon government, and of government upon individuals, it is impossible to measure the degrees of happiness and perfection to which mankind may be raised. For my part, I can form no ideas of the golden age, so much celebrated by the poets, more delightful than the contemplation of that happiness which it is now in the power of the legislature of Pennsylvania to confer upon her citizens by establishing proper modes and places of education in every part of the state.

This is precisely the hope that inspired the Jacobin education reformers in the National Convention in France. Thus, for example, Napoleon's future chief of police, Fouché, told the Convention in 1793 that

If our schools are organized promptly and as we wish, the most glorious revolution will be achieved; every success depends upon *that* success; it bears all our hopes and all our fears; no other consideration may be set in the balance against such a powerful interest. . . . The French people no more want a half-schooling than they want a half-liberty; they want to be entirely remade, like a new creature coming freshly out of the hands of Nature.[6]

In their confidence that popular education could completely transform the French people, could create them anew as though they had no past and no attachment to beliefs, loyalties, and habits, Fouché and his fellow Jacobins reflected one of the dearest convictions of the Enlightenment. By putting such a transformation forward as a popular demand, they were articulating a desire of which we may be sure the French people to whom they attributed it were unaware. As the sequel—the dismal failure of attempts to implement the radical education program in France, despite all the threats and the formidable organizing energy of the Jacobins—shows, the common people were determined *not* to be reshaped according to the new "republican" model.

Like the Jacobins, Rush had absorbed the Enlightenment conviction that the state should seek to refashion its people by a popular education concerned more with civic virtue and national loyalty than with literacy and other skills. The impulse to seek to shape the future through molding the children of the common people was almost irresistible to this generation of liberal idealists.

The *present time* is peculiarly favorable to the establishment of these benevolent and necessary institutions in Pennsylvania. The minds of our people have not as yet lost the yielding texture they acquired by the heat of the late Revolution. They will *now* receive more readily than five or even three years hence new impressions and habits of all kinds.[7]

The essential ruthlessness of this ambition comes across in Rush's statement that

I consider it as possible to convert men into republican machines. This must be done if we expect them to perform their parts properly in the machine of the government of the state. That public is sophisticated with monarchy or aristocracy that does not revolve upon the wills of the people, and these must be fitted to each other by means of education before they can be made to produce regularity and unison in government.[8]

It was in this spirit that Rousseau had written, in his essay *Sur le gouvernement de Pologne* (1772) that

90

It is education which must give to souls a national compulsion, must so direct their opinions and tastes that they will be patriots by inclination, by passion, by necessity. The child must see the fatherland when he first opens his eyes, and must see nothing else until he closes them in death.[9]

Some of the essays on education in this period when the national purpose was defined are prophetic of later developments, though they produced slim results at the time. As in Europe, it was only when these "radical" ideas had been clothed in liberal Protestantism that they were able to make headway in a climate that did not favor direct attacks upon religious orthodoxy and its institutional expressions.

A characteristic form of policy debate during the eighteenth century was the prize essay, written in response to a question of current importance posed by one of those learned societies that were so prolific in that age; often a number of the responses were published and achieved significant impact. This was the means by which Rousseau first achieved a broad audience and the primary vehicle of the discussions out of which the great movement of educational reform in the Netherlands emerged.

In the same spirit, the American Philosophical Society (of Philadelphia) offered a prize in 1795 for the best essay on a national system of education. The prize was shared in 1797 by Samuel Knox (a Scots-Irish Presbyterian minister sympathetic to the religious views of Jefferson) and Samuel Harrison Smith (editor of the *National Intelligencer*, the official paper of the Jefferson administration). In their suggestions we can see boldly stated the views that Mann and his generation of reformers would restrain themselves from expressing openly but would translate effectively into new institutions and new assumptions. Of particular interest is the influence of recent and continuing debates in France, still admired by Jefferson and his political allies.

SAMUEL HARRISON SMITH. Smith does not mince his words: "it is the duty of a nation to superintend and even to coerce the education of children and . . . high considerations of expediency not only justify but dictate the establishment of a system which shall place under a control, independent of and superior to parental authority, the education of children." To this end, it should be "made punishable by law in a parent to neglect offering his child to the preceptor for instruction." "Society must establish the right to educate, and acknowledge the duty of having educated, all children. A circumstance so momentuously important must not be left to the negligence of individuals."[10]

This echoes the insistence of the Jacobins on the right of the state to educate all of the children of the nation in common schools, not only to

91

overcome possible neglect by indifferent parents but to counter the views of the parents themselves. Thus Citizen Le Clerc proposed as the first article of the education statutes with which the Convention proposed to transform the French people,

> No one will be excused from sending his children to the *écoles du citoyen*. . . . By means of common instruction, you will set the hearts of the children free from the aristocratic ideas of their parents, from their pride, from their fanaticism. . . . does that offend against the authority of parents? No. It simply exercises that of the Fatherland.[11]

With respect to the content of such instruction, Smith argued that it must give primacy to the development of that "virtue" essential to the civil order and of the "wisdom" necessary to the exercise of virtue. Since the purpose of education was essentially civic and secular, it should limit itself to

> the admission into the young mind of such ideas only as are either absolutely true or in the highest degree probable. . . . should it not be thought treason against truth and virtue to instill prejudice and error into the young mind? . . . what shall we say of those who inculcate principles which they know to be false and attempt in this way to establish systems that only exist in the midst of human carnage and destruction? . . . Let then those truths in which all men agree be firmly impressed, let those which are probable be inculcated with caution, and let doubt always hang over those respecting which the good and the wise disagree. Above all things let the infant mind be protected from conviction without proof.

Thus, "the most solemn attention must be paid to avoid instilling into the young mind any ideas or sentiments whose truth is not unequivocally established by the undissenting suffrage of the enlightened and virtuous part of mankind."[12]

Here is a full load of Enlightenment themes, familiar from Diderot, Condorcet, and others who discussed systems of national popular education. First, that much of orthodox religion is untrue and that those who teach its doctrines are self-serving hypocrites who know that it is untrue (by the 1830s the accusation had changed, both in Europe and the United States: they were "twisted fanatics"). Second, that religious systems have been productive only of "carnage and destruction." Third, that "the enlightened and virtuous" basically agree on both truth and morality, and thus there is a basis for a common teaching which can be entirely uplifting and which could not offend any right-thinking parent.

Since education would be compulsory, the resistance of those parents who might cling to beliefs on which the enlightened and virtuous do not agree could be dismissed. Note, however, that the need for compulsory education is a tacit admission that there would not be universal agreement on this program. Horace Mann himself did not initially call for compulsory education, trusting in his powers of persuasion and in the growing enlightenment of the age, but the resistance he experienced brought him finally to the conviction that it was necessary; Massachusetts adopted the first compulsory attendance law in the United States in 1852.

Smith adumbrated several other themes of the later program of public education, under the influence of the proposals then current in France. One was the need for the development of appropriate schoolbooks that would reflect the new objectives and premises of education from a national perspective. Such works "explaining and enforcing plain and undeniable truths and avoiding prejudices or falsehoods" were not available, Smith wrote, but by "offering large rewards for books of this nature" (as had become the practice of the French revolutionary government) it would be possible to develop a set of "approved books" that would render education independent of the inadequacies of particular teachers.

> The indispensable economy of arrangements which are to pervade a whole society will prohibit the employment of preceptors of either great or original talents. It will therefore be fit that the preceptor, instead of inculcating his own immature ideas, should be guided by prescribed works.

Presumably Smith had in mind the development of American equivalents of the *Principes de la morale républicaine*, the *Catechisme républicain*, the *Epîtres et évangiles du républicain*, and other works developed several years before at the invitation of the National Convention in France.[13]

It is clear that Smith's concern is not with improved methods of teaching reading or arithmetic (with "instruction") but with "education," with the ideological content of schoolbooks. This is for him a matter of transcendent importance, as it was then to the Jacobins in France.

> If any one circumstance be more connected with the virtue and happiness of the United States than another it is the substitution of works defining correctly political, moral, and religious duty in the place of those which are at present in use. . . . Every new work, then, which comes from the pen of a citizen may be deemed an important acquisition, a stay to our virtue and a shield to our happiness.

After all,

> it is true that some nations have been free without possessing a large portion of illumination, but their freedom has been precarious and accidental, and it has fallen as it rose. . . . Discord and strife have always proceeded

93

from, or risen upon, ignorance and passion. When the first has ceased to exist and the last shall be virtuously directed, we shall be deprived of every source of misunderstanding.

By establishing a national system of education in the United States, "the first result would be the giving perpetuity to those political principles so closely connected with our present happiness."[14]

SAMUEL KNOX. Samuel Knox, who shared the essay prize with Smith, shared with him also an approval of the recent efforts to create a national education system in the service of the French Revolution.

> What has lately been done in France excepted, I know of no plan devised by individuals or attempted by any commonwealth in modern times that effectually tends to the establishment of any uniform, regular system of national education. . . . The good effects of such a system are almost self-evident. . . . Diversity of modes of education also tend not only to confound and obstruct its operation and improvement but also give occasion to many other inconveniences and disagreeable consequences that commonly arise in the various departments of civil society. . . . But were an approved system of national education to be established, all these imperfections of its present state would, in a great measure, be remedied and at the same time accompanied with many peculiar advantages hitherto unexperienced in the instruction and improvement of the human mind.[15]

This rage for a "rational" uniformity, this conviction that national education is the key to the progress of humanity, echoes the debates in the French National Convention.

Another note that is more peculiarly American, and that would gain increasing importance in the future, was a concern to create a national unity out of the diverse population of the United States through an educational system deliberately geared to assimilation. Knox argued that this was essential for

> such a wide extent of territory inhabited by citizens blending together almost all the various manners and customs of every country of Europe. Nothing, then, surely, might be supposed to have a better effect toward harmonizing the whole in these important views than an *uniform system of national education*.

This required, as Smith had insisted, an exclusion of revealed religion, which was productive only of further divisions, from the educational process.[16] In characteristically Jeffersonian terms Knox noted that

It is a happy circumstance peculiarly favorable to an uniform plan of public education that this country hath excluded ecclesiastical from civil policy and emancipated the human mind from the tyranny of church authority and church establishments. It is a consequence of this principle of our happy civil constitution that theology, so far as the study of it is connected with particular forms of faith, ought to be excluded from a liberal system of national instruction, especially where there exist so many various denominations among the professors of the Christian religion.

Not that religion itself, in an extremely general sense, would be excluded. The school day should begin and end "with a short and suitable prayer and address to the great source of all knowledge and instruction."

It might, also, be highly advantageous to youth, and in no respect interfere with the different religious sentiments of the community, to make use of a well-digested, concise moral catechism. In the first part of this catechism should be inculcated natural theology or the proofs of the existence of the Deity from his works. . . . The second part might properly consist of the first principles of ethics, the nature and consequence of virtue and vice, and also a concise view of economics and the relative virtues. The third and last part should inculcate, concisely, the principles of jurisprudence; the nature of civil government.

He then goes on to recommend a daily reading aloud, by one of the students, of a selection from a book of meditations for each day of the year, translated from a German work, which sounds remarkably like one of the most "religious" works in the Common School Library that would be adopted by the Massachusetts Board of Education in the early 1840s. These *Reflections*, Knox says, "are calculated to present the most sublime ideas of the Deity and to excite to the love and study of science," and their use would "impress on the tender mind a reverence of the Deity, a sense of His government of the world, and a regard for morals."[17]

Like Smith, again, Knox called for a national board of education that, among other duties, would adopt a "uniform system of the most approved schoolbooks." In each state there would be a "president," who would also serve as a member of the national board and would make annual reports on the condition of all schools. To assist him in the "superintendence" of the schools, there would be a "rector" for each county to visit schools and supervise the examination of students. These arrangements are parallel to those discussed though not effectively implemented at the time in France and to those implemented effectively a little later in the Netherlands and then in Prussia.

ROBERT CORAM. Another contemporary essayist of the same political and educational views was Robert Coram of Wilmington, Delaware. Coram's *Political Inquiries: To Which Is Added, a Plan for the General Establishment of Schools throughout the United States* (1791) complained that

> In the savage state education is perfect. In the civilized state education is the most imperfect part of the whole scheme of government or civilization; or, rather, it is not immediately connected with either, for I know of no modern governments, except perhaps the New England states, in which education is incorporated with the government or regulated by it.[18]

Coram was writing before the education debates in the French National Convention (the Committee on Public Education was elected in October 1792), but he was a teacher of French and his essay is permeated with ideas of the French Enlightenment, including its optimism and urgency about popular education under state control:

> To make mankind better is a duty which every man owes to his posterity, to his country, and to his God; and remember, my friends, there is but one way to effect this important purpose—which is—by incorporating education with government.—This is the rock on which you must build your political salvation!

LAFITTE DU COURTEIL. A French immigrant and schoolmaster, Amable-Louis-Rose de Lafitte du Courteil, expressed similar views in an essay published in Philadelphia in 1797. Lafitte argued that

> there is not a true national character in the United States of America, nor any of those public establishments which announce a nation, and . . . the education of the youth of each sex is almost nothing and the houses of instruction very defective

compared with the specialized secondary schools of prerevolutionary France. Lafitte's concern, unlike that of those discussed above, was not with popular education but with the formation of a national elite, but he was led to the same conclusion, that "the creation of such institutions belongs only to the beneficent and paternal hand of government." Only in this way could a remedy be found for "the absense of a national character, an indifference for every public establishment."[19]

SIGNIFICANCE OF THE JEFFERSONIAN ESSAYISTS. The most significant aspect of the essays on the need for a "national education" for the development of a "national character" in the first decades of the Republic is that they had so little impact. Even though some of them, like editor

Smith or Dr. Rush—a signer of the Declaration of Independence—were otherwise influential, they wrote on education to an audience that was not ready to accept an essentially radical position about government intervention in matters that had been the concern primarily of parents and of churches.

The fact that the American Philosophical Society, the leading Enlightenment institution in the United States, offered a prize for the best essay on a national system of education and selected those by Knox and Smith makes it clear that the "radical" educational agenda of the French Revolution, derived in turn from the philosophes, was familiar to and even supported by some of the elite of the new nation. The complete rejection of these proposals and the lack of *any* contemporary action by Congress to create national uniformity and federal leadership in education reflect a very different view among Americans in general about how education should be controlled and by whom its objectives should be set.

For all their interest in the history of American education, we do not find Mann and other reformers of the 1830s and 1840s citing Knox or Smith or Rush in support of their very similar proposals: an active role for the state, a board of education, regular reports on the performance of local schools, adoption of standardized school texts, avoidance of religious instruction in distinctively Christian doctrines, and compulsory education as an assertion of society's prior claim to children, whatever the views and desires of their parents.

We may speculate that they recognized that the naked Enlightenment program of education by and for the state was too radical still for the American people, too closely associated with the atheism and social radicalism that continued to give France a fearsome reputation. They looked to other models, to those piously Protestant states of Europe that had managed to cast the Enlightenment program in acceptable terms and to direct it toward goals that were explicitly moral and only indirectly political.

The "Friends of Education" and Foreign Models

Colonial education, though required by provincial laws in some cases, was controlled locally with little coordination or communication other than that provided by the discussions of ministerial associations and by such benevolent associations as the Society for the Propagation of the Gospel in Foreign Parts. It was only in 1799, according to Henry Barnard, that the first education association was formed, in Middlesex County, Connecticut.

Samuel May, later a normal school principal in Massachusetts and a prominent abolitionist, was one of a group of Connecticut ministers who issued a call, in 1826, for a convention "to consider the defects of our Common Schools" and formed a society the next year in Hartford to improve them.[20] It was not until 1830, however, that a really influential association was organized.

The American Institute of Instruction grew out of a convention of nearly 300 "teachers and other friends of education" held in Boston in March 1830. Local conventions had been taking place over the previous four or five years, encouraged by the lyceum movement that brought together adults for lectures and discussions on various matters of common interest. This movement was a typical benevolent enterprise with strong local roots; by 1832 there were said to be 900 lyceums in the United States, some with as many as the 1,200 members in Salem, Massachusetts.[21]

The convention in 1830 was called "to receive reports on the progress of lyceums and the condition of common schools, and to acquire information as to the organization of infant schools, and the use of school and cheap scientific apparatus."[22] The participants visited "public schools and humane institutions of Boston" and discussed a wide variety of topics. A committee was formed to plan "a permanent association of persons engaged and interested in the business of instruction," and this group in turn called a further convention at the statehouse in Boston that August, drawing participants from fifteen states.

The "Introductory Discourse" was given by Brown University president Francis Wayland, who stated that

> We have assembled today, not to proclaim how well our fathers have done, but to inquire how we may enable their sons to do better. . . . we, at this day, are, in a manner, the pioneers of this work in this country. Education, as a science, has scarcely yet been naturalized among us. Radical improvement in the means of education is an idea that seems but just to have entered into men's minds. . . . God helping us, then, let us make our mark on the rising generation.[23]

Wayland was asserting, it should be noted, not that education itself was unavailable or in short supply—he knew perfectly well that almost universal literacy was the rule in New England—but that the *science* of education was undeveloped; this led to a limited capacity to make an impact upon the next generation. Wayland himself was author of a highly regarded text on moral education, and his concern to "make our mark" had to do more with what we would now call values and attitudes than with reading skills.

Another participant in these early meetings, George B. Emerson, recalled later that they had met

> to see what could be done to strengthen and advance the cause in which they were interested and engaged. . . . They have continued to meet for the purpose of elevating the character of instruction, of widening its sphere, of ascertaining more clearly what should be its objects, and of perfecting its methods; . . . for the purpose of making more apparent to our fellow-citizens the absolute importance of education to the existence and continuance of our free institutions, and to the advancement of our race. . . . In short, they meet to quicken to a warmer glow the fire in their own breast, and to kindle it as far as possible in the breast of others.[24]

For Emerson, who was a practicing educator, the first headmaster of Boston's English High School and then of a private school for girls, the original impulse was one of mutual support and the advancement of a profession by helping the teacher feel "how high and noble is the work in which he is engaged."

There is nothing in these early discussions, as they have come down to us, suggesting that the goal was a state-controlled system of education in which teachers would be employees carrying out centrally defined tasks. To the contrary, the thrust of the organization, so far as can be judged from the papers given at the annual conventions, was to increase the skills of teachers, seen as individual practitioners, and the scope of their concept of their mission.[25] In other words, the focus of these efforts was on improving *instruction*, though it is clear from Wayland's remarks (and from his widely influential *Elements of Political Economy* of 1837) that they enjoyed an elevated opinion of the significance of such efforts for the future of the nation.

Legislation to improve common schools had been enacted or revised in a number of states throughout the previous decade, but this legislation, like that during the colonial period, was designed chiefly to specify that local communities must provide schooling and did not create a state leadership role or specify educational objectives and procedures.

Historians David Tyack and Elisabeth Hansot observe that, although most of the participants in the institute were teachers, they were not from the "rank and file of district school instructors, who were young, female, and with only modest training." Almost all were male college graduates, and a majority taught in private academies[26]—those institutions that, a decade later, Horace Mann would be criticizing so harshly as competitors with common schools and state-operated normal schools.

In order to promote the exchange of ideas and practices among essentially isolated teachers, a number of education journals were founded in these years, some twenty before 1840. These included the original *American Journal of Education* (William Russell), the *American Annals of Education* (W. C. Woodbridge), the *Common School Assistant* (J. Orville Taylor), the *Connecticut Common School Journal* (Henry Barnard), and the *Common School Journal* (Horace Mann).[27] Barnard later revived the *American Journal of Education* and made of it a major organ of information about European practices and the history of the common school movement.

It was to Europe that the members of the American Institute of Instruction and other education reformers of the 1830s turned for their models of "scientific" education, and it was to a Europe which, in a revolutionary age of nation building, had developed the educational theories and institutions that gave popular schooling the primary mission in shaping political and social life.

LOOKING TO EUROPE. The influence of foreign models, epecially that of two Protestant states of the Continent, Prussia and the Netherlands, was of critical importance in shaping the goals and the arguments of the education reformers. It was through the nation-building role of popular schooling in those countries that key ideas of the Enlightenment and the French Revolution of 1789 became central elements of what was virtually a consensus program among elites in the United States throughout the century and a quarter beginning around 1830.

Ironically, the direct proposals for nation building through popular education that surfaced in the years following the American Revolution received little support, in part because they resembled the detested French models too closely. It was as mediated by the Protestant Enlightenment in the Netherlands and Prussia that such ideas became acceptable to the heavily Protestant elite in the United States.

That the alternative model offered by England, where education remained essentially in the hands of private, ecclesiastical, and charitable enterprise until the twentieth century, did not have more appeal suggests how strongly Enlightenment concerns for national unity and uniformity dominated the thinking of the leaders in the common school movement in the United States. These concerns were fueled by various strains and anxieties, including fears about divisive religious and social conflict and especially about the impact of immigration and Roman Catholicism upon the national identity.

Under these circumstances, the safely Protestant models of Prussia and the Netherlands seemed to offer justification for strong state leadership in popular education. This justification was used to good effect by Horace

Mann and others predisposed to seek to address many social ills through state action. The puzzle is that those who did *not* share this confidence in state action and this desire for uniformity did not put up a more effective opposition. By the Civil War, in fact, popular education was one of the few areas of social and economic life in which the states at least pretended to the primary role.

Visits to Europe and study of continental models are a constant theme in the 1830s. In Barnard's *American Educational Biography*, for example, we read of William Woodbridge's European trip in 1825–29, including long stays at Hofwyl in Switzerland to study Pestalozzi's methods and in Frankfurt, southern Germany, and Brussels. Similarly, Lowell Mason, the pioneer in music instruction, visited Germany and Switzerland in 1837 to perfect his methods. George Emerson was not able to make a similar tour until 1855, but he had studied eagerly the accounts of others.[28] Horace Mann's honeymoon trip to Europe in 1843 produced one of his most widely read annual reports.

Perhaps the most respected voice among orthodox Congregationalists, Amherst College president Heman Humphrey, published an account of his trip in 1835 to Great Britain, France, and Belgium. Humphrey, who served subsequently on the Massachusetts Board of Education and played the key role in disarming its orthodox critics, was critical of the vaunted parish schools of Scotland, while observing that New England schools also were "susceptible of great improvements."[29] Such improvements were particularly needed, he wrote, in the stress "laid upon the importance of *religious* instruction in our schools."

A few years earlier John Griscom, a professor of chemistry and natural philosophy in New York and a founder of the American Bible Society, had published an account of his European journey in 1818–19. Griscom had strong praise for education of poor children in the Netherlands and for the positive state role in bringing this about.[30]

Another influential American traveler was Alexander Dallas Bache, grandson of Benjamin Franklin and president of Girard College in Philadelphia, an institution for orphan boys. Bache was sent on the tour by his trustees as part of the planning for the institution. He had particular praise for the popular instruction provided in the Netherlands, singling out the system of school inspection, the provision for the education of poor children, and the method used in nonsectarian religious instruction:

> while the necessity of religious instruction has been strongly felt, it has been made to stop short of the point at which, becoming doctrinal, the

subjects taught could interfere with the views of any sect. Bible stories are made the means of moral and religious teaching in the school, and the doctrinal instruction is given by the pastors of the different churches on days appointed for the purpose, and usually not in the schoolroom.[31]

Presumably Bache felt a special interest in this aspect of Dutch education because the will of Stephen Girard, under which his institution was to be established, forbade religious instruction or the admission of any clergyman to what was to be a strictly cloistered boarding school, with the avowed intent of shielding students from religious controversy. This will was the subject of a celebrated lawsuit (instituted in October 1836) in which Daniel Webster was to argue before the Supreme Court, in 1844, that the teaching of Christianity was essential to any program of moral education and thus of the schooling that could be promoted in a Christian nation.

Bache's account of European schools was read eagerly; *The Princeton Review*, chief organ of orthodox Calvinism in the United States, cited Bache's report in 1840 in support of the acceptability of religious instruction in public schools.[32] Henry Barnard, then secretary of the Board of Education in Connecticut, wrote to his Massachusetts counterpart Horace Mann in March 1840 to ask whether he had read Bache. Barnard's comment is significant: "our school systems on this side of the water look very disjointed and imperfect when compared" with those of Europe.[33]

A description of Dutch and German schools by an English Quaker, W. E. Hickson, was also read with interest and excerpted in Mann's *Common School Journal* in March 1841. Hickson concurred with Bache in attributing great merit to the system of school inspection in the Netherlands as the keystone of an active government role in the promotion and standardization of popular education; he saw no difficulty about permitting "a spirit of honourable rivalry between the conductors of public schools and those of private establishments." Hickson also noted the importance of the neutral religious instruction provided in the Dutch schools as a key to the support they enjoyed.[34]

Mann was not alone in featuring reports on European education in his journal. Henry Barnard wrote to him in December 1838 about his intention of bringing out an issue of the Connecticut journal devoted to "teacher seminaries," including reports by Thomas Gallaudet, "Dr. Julius' account of the Teacher Seminaries of Prussia; Mr. Baird, of those of France; Cousin's, if I shall be able to lay hands on his volume, of those in Holland."[35]

Julius, a citizen of Hamburg, had already exerted a considerable influence on developments in Massachusetts by his friendship with Unitarian minister Charles Brooks of Hingham. Having met in London in August 1834, they shared a compartment on board ship for the forty-one-day trip from

Liverpool to New York; by the end of the voyage, Brooks was a convinced proponent of teacher education by the state through a system of normal schools, and he would be one of Mann's most vigorous allies.[36] He himself published, in 1846, an account of his observations of education in Europe, offering as a Prussian maxim that "whatever we would have in the State we must first introduce into the school-room." Credit for the first effective use of this strategy "to provide for the safety of the state by enlightening the public mind and fortifying public morals" Brooks gave to the Netherlands, with Prussia imitating in 1819 what the Netherlands had instituted in 1806.[37]

The most influential foreign commentator on education during the period when the American common school was shaped was undoubtedly the French philosopher Victor Cousin. His report on education in Prussia (Paris, 1832; translation in the *Edinburgh Review*, 1833; New York, 1835) had a profound impact in the United States as well as in France and was quoted constantly. His subsequent report on the Netherlands was only relatively less influential.

Francis Bowen, the Unitarian professor of moral philosophy at Harvard, in a contemporary review, called the publication of the American translation of Cousin's report on Prussia "a judicious and timely step, as the work contained the outlines, and even the minute details, of the most elaborate and complete system of common schools which had yet been devised in the civilized world."[38] Like many of his peers in the American elite, Bowen welcomed an account of a "complete system" that might be emulated, choosing to overlook the fact that it had been developed by an absolute monarchy concerned to control its subjects more efficiently.

Similarly, William Ellery Channing published a review, in the Unitarian *Christian Examiner* of November 1833, in which he drew particular attention to a summary of Cousin's account of Prussian education. "Monarchical Prussia," Channing concluded, "does more for the intellectual and moral improvement of her subjects, than republican America has ever thought of doing for her citizens." Channing does not seem to have reflected that it was *because* Prussia was ruled by a despotic government determined to transform its citizenry that it laid such stress on controlling and directing their "intellectual and moral improvement." "How much would be gained," he mused, "if every state should send one of its most distinguished citizens to examine the modes of teaching at home and in Europe, and should then place him at the head of a seminary for the formation of teachers."[39] Less than a decade later essentially this program would be carried out in Massachusetts.

Cousin gave prominence to the themes, sounded also by Bache and Hickson, that progress in education depended upon strong leadership and inspection by the state, a positive but neutral religious teaching in the ele-

103

mentary schools, and the preparation of teachers through special institutions under the control of the state, to assure that they would manifest the desired attitudes and commitments. He was to play a key role in implementing this program under the July Monarchy in France, first as adviser to Guizot and then as minister of public instruction in his own right.

Although he did not visit the schools of Massachusetts as he had those of Prussia and the Netherlands, Cousin showed a keen interest in the information he received from Charles Brooks and also from an account by a Cuban visitor, Ramón de la Sagra, who had praised the Massachusetts schools. A few years later Cousin questioned Senator Charles Sumner closely about education in Massachusetts and "asked particularly about Mr. Mann."[40]

The American traveler with the greatest influence was Calvin Stowe of Ohio, husband of Lyman Beecher's daughter Harriet. Stowe published his own account of *The Prussian System of Public Instruction and Its Applicability to the United States* in Cincinnati in 1836. Originally a lecture to an association of teachers, this book drew heavily upon Cousin. The same year Stowe was commissioned by the Ohio legislature to make a study of Prussian education in connection with a trip he was making to Europe. In 1837 he published a *Report on Elementary Public Instruction in Europe Made to the Thirty-sixth General Assembly of the State of Ohio*, a document that was republished the next year by order of the legislatures of Massachusetts, Pennsylvania, and other states and given wide circulation.

Like many other periodicals, the *Churchman* provided extensive coverage of Stowe's report for its Episcopalian readers. Stowe's insistence on the necessity of religion in education—for which he gave the Prussian schools as authority—may have influenced the agreement at the 1838 General Convention of the Episcopal Church that the church should keep a close watch on the education provided in common schools and also consider the development of its own schools.[41]

Henry Barnard, while superintendent of common schools in Connecticut, published an exhaustive compendium called *National Education in Europe: Being an Account of the Organization, Administration, Instruction, and Statistics of Public Schools of Different Grades in the Principal States* (1854) and followed it in 1872 with a two-volume study covering much the same territory, as well as studies of "English Pedagogy," "German Pedagogy," "Pestalozzi and Swiss Pedagogy," "German Teachers and Educational Reformers," and "French Teachers, Schools, and Pedagogy." Much of this material he had already published in the *American Journal of Education*. Barnard's influence on the development of thinking about public education was massive; it is significant that he returned again and again to European examples, with a particular emphasis (despite his use of the word "pedagogy") on organizational and governmental characteristics of the various national systems.

Barnard's objective was, indeed, a "national education" for the United States, and it was to this end that he agitated for a national bureau of education during and after the Civil War. The war had realized the favorite nightmare of the educational reformers, the breakdown of national unity, and their prescription of education as the great unifier was given a new urgency. In this campaign Barnard was supported by Brooks and others of the New England reformers who had been articulating this agenda for thirty years and more.

The example of the national systems of education in Europe, then, was constantly in the minds of the reformers of popular education in the 1830s and subsequent decades, to an extent that contrasts markedly with the general ignorance of European education that prevails in the United States today. Immediately after he accepted leadership of the common school movement in Massachusetts, for example, Mann took a few days to read two British works: Maria Edgeworth's *Practical Education* and Frederic Hill's *National Education: Its Present State and Prospects*; the latter may have helped to shape his convictions about the role of nonsectarian religious teaching in common schools.

It remains to ask *why* the continental example was so powerfully attractive, whereas that of England was appealing only to the advocates of elite private education. In an era when Congregationalists and Episcopalians in England were founding thousands of schools for the common people, and Calvinists in the Netherlands were beginning their great effort of developing schools reflecting their beliefs, it is notable that Protestants in the United States showed only the most limited interest in following their example.

What explains the attraction, among American Protestant elites, to the statist and ultimately secularizing educational systems of continental Europe? Which elements of European popular education attracted them?

FRANCE. France was neither admired nor emulated by this generation of reformers. The brief revolutionary episode of the early 1790s, when the National Convention sought to transform society through a program of heavily political education, caused horror among American friends of orderly progress and of property. It was in the years after 1830 and very much in parallel with efforts in the United States that Guizot, Cousin, and others worked to build a system of popular education at least semi-independent of the church. In these efforts they had the sympathetic support of Americans, who dreaded above all the domination of Rome and noted "the weight of clerical displeasure" at educational progress in France and to the use of the Bible in schools.[42]

France was, however, frequently cited as a horrible example of the necessity of a moral and religious basis for social progress. Thus the Massachusetts election sermon in 1843 noted that

> Human passion is the great leveller of states. This is not subdued, but often rendered more intense and ungovernable by external advantages. No modern nation has been more conspicuous as an example of such reliances, to the exclusion of moral means, than France. . . . overlooking in a great degree moral and religious influences, almost her entire wisdom and policy have been exerted to secure physical results. . . . Her subsequent revolutions and changes of dynasty, her conspiracies and attempted regicides, her unquiet and revolutionary tendencies, to say nothing of the abject condition of the millions of her peasantry, are a practical comment upon the impolicy of trusting to outward improvements for national happiness.[43]

This is very far from accurate. The French experience over the previous fifty years had in fact been characterized by a continual concern, on the part of "republicans" and "clericals" alike, to stress the moral basis of education and to use it as a means of building a social order in which spiritual motives were seen as paramount. It is significant, however, that France was seen as at once benighted in religious superstition and hopelessly wasted by infidelity and skepticism. Educational ideas from such a source could have little appeal in Massachusetts. It was through the liberal Protestant educational program of the Netherlands and Prussia that key elements of the radical educational agenda of the French Revolution became a part of the assumptions of American educational leaders.

This program was not the "materialism" of which the French were accused but an alternative system of belief in which the nation, personified by the state, became the focus of hope and of dedication, and popular education was seen as the primary means of forming the convictions, attitudes, and loyalties of future citizens. Common schools thus became a priority concern of the state, not so much in the interest of the progress and welfare of individuals as in that of social and national coherence.

Alternative means of achieving what could be called the social welfare goals of education, such as literacy and numeracy, which were not under the direct control of the state but were instead sponsored by the Catholic church, could be tolerated barely, if at all, since they tended to cultivate competing beliefs and values. The century-long conflict of public and nonpublic popular schooling in France was thus a conflict over what ultimate loyalties should be taught to future citizens.

PRUSSIA. What seems to have fascinated foreign observers about Prussian education was its organizational elaboration. Though France had given the intellectual lead by asserting a state interest in controlling the education of its future citizens, and the Netherlands had developed the first effective nationwide system of popular education, Prussia had implemented this program with a bureaucratic thoroughness that reform-minded observers found irresistible. Attendance was compulsory, parents were punished for withholding their children from school, teachers were trained in a network of normal schools controlled by the state, and efforts were made to make curriculum and instruction uniform. To Americans seeking effective ways to shape a nation, Prussia seemed to offer a convincing model.

In Channing's discussion, for the *Christian Examiner*, of a summary of Cousin's report on Prussia, he noted that

> In Prussia every child is taught, and must be taught, for a penalty is inflicted on parents who neglect to send their children to school ... In Prussia, the Minister of Instruction is one of the most important ministers of the state. The Department of Instruction is organized as carefully as that of war or of the treasury, and is intended to act on every district and family in the kingdom. In New England, it is no man's business to watch over public education.[44]

A few years later Channing and other members of the Unitarian elite in Massachusetts would persuade senate president, lawyer, and noneducator Horace Mann to become the man whose business it was, on behalf of the state, to watch over public education. There can be little doubt that it was the authoritarian model of Prussia they had in mind, suitably adapted to the political circumstances of Massachusetts.

When the American Institute of Instruction directed a *Memorial* (February 1836) to the Massachusetts legislature in support of the appointment of a "Superintendent of the Common Schools of the Commonwealth" (the initiative that led the following year to establishment of the Board of Education and appointment of Horace Mann as its secretary), they pointed out that this individual "could collect and present to the legislature the experience of other states and foreign countries on subjects interesting to the common schools." After all, "several of the states of Germany have, with wise policy, put into operation systems for the complete education of all their inhabitants."[45] It was this state assumption of authority and direction in the interest of a comprehensive and compulsory system that was so appealing.

As a Protestant state, strongly influenced still by pietism, Prussia seemed a safer model than papist/infidel France in the sphere of religious instruction that was so important to the American reformers. They were reassured by Cousin's observation that "the fundamental character of that law" of 1819, regulating popular education in Prussia, "is the moral and religious spirit which pervades all its provisions."

> The first vocation of every school [says the law of 1819] is to train up the young in such a manner as to implant in their minds a knowledge of the relation of man to God, and at the same time to excite and foster both the will and the strength to govern their lives after the spirit and the precepts of Christianity. . . . Every complete elementary school necessarily comprehends the following objects:—1. Religious instruction, as a means of forming the moral character of children according to the positive truths of Christianity.[46]

The religious character of Prussian education was highly commended by Calvin Stowe in his popularization of Cousin. "The *religious* spirit which pervades the whole of the Prussian system, is greatly needed among ourselves. . . . The [contrasting] experience of Germany and France has shown that, in Christian communities, school government cannot be maintained without religious influence."[47] After his 1837 visit to Prussia, Stowe gave a detailed report on the actual content of religious instruction there at each grade level and concluded that "its morality is pure and elevated, its religion entirely removed from the narrowness of sectarian bigotry. . . . If it can be done in Prussia, I know it can be done in Ohio."[48]

What Stowe did not make clear, however, was that Prussian schools were designedly "sectarian" in the sense that almost all were either Protestant or Catholic in the religious instruction offered. *Simultanenschule*, in which Protestant and Catholic children were educated together but with separate religious instruction, received only very limited acceptance. The Prussian approach to providing universal education without religious controversy did not commend itself to Americans. It may be that, for Stowe and other Americans for whom the sectarian divisions among Protestants were the primary concern, the fact that the Prussian government had forced together its Lutheran and Reformed churches and offered a single form of Protestant religious instruction was more significant than the Protestant/Catholic distinction, not yet a major concern among elites in the United States of the mid-1830s.

The failure to recognize that the admirable organization and support for popular education in Prussia rested upon a frank accommodation to the religious diversity of the Prussian territories and to the desire of parents to see their children educated in their own beliefs was unfortunate. In particular, it made it impossible for educational policy makers whose ideas had been shaped by Stowe, Mann, and others to respond adequately to the growing Catholic population of the United States.

THE NETHERLANDS. Although it was Victor Cousin's book on Prussian education that caused a sensation in the United States and inspired the further reports by Stowe and others, Cousin himself believed, as he wrote to Charles Brooks, that his account of Dutch education would be more useful, "inasmuch as Holland is an ancient commercial and industrial republic, whose manners and institutions bear a strong analogy of those of the United States." [49]

Many contemporary observers, starting with Cuvier in 1811 (Dutch primary schools, he wrote, were "above all praise") and including Bache in 1839, gave the palm of excellence for primary education and for the education of poor children to the Dutch schools. [50] As late as 1861 the experienced English school inspector Matthew Arnold would write, "I have seen no primary schools worthy to be matched, even now, with those of Holland. [51] The Dutch solution to the problem of religious instruction was commonly preferred to the Prussian, which generally provided for separate Protestant and Catholic schools.

Since these were ostensibly matters of primary concern for the American education reformers, it is curious that they returned again and again to the Prussian example. Horace Mann, for instance, wrote about Prussian schools at length, while making only a perfunctory trip to the Netherlands; [52] he informed the readers of the *Common School Journal* (1844) that

the most interesting portions of the world with regard to education are the Protestant states of Germany. . . . we hesitate not to say that Prussia and some of her sister states, where the work of education, after the Prussian model, is going on, are rising more rapidly in the scale of civilization than any other of the nations in Christendom. [53]

How can we explain the relative lack of interest in Dutch popular education, as contrasted with that of Prussia? It may have been the absence of strong state control and prescription, by comparison with Prussia, that made Dutch education less appealing to American reformers whose chief interest was in the levers of power by which a uniform and nation-building system could be put in place.

Alexander Bache saw clearly how well the largely decentralized system of education in the Netherlands would have fitted American circumstances, but when he commended the Dutch approach, he was identifying the very element that made it less appealing than the Prussian to Horace Mann, Calvin Stowe, Henry Barnard, and other advocates of a strong state role:

The system of primary instruction in Holland is particularly interesting to an American, from its organization in an ascending series; beginning with the local school authorities, and terminating, after progressive degrees of representation, as it were, in the highest authority; instead of emanating, as in the centralized systems, from that authority. A fair trial has been given to a system of inspection which is almost entirely applicable to our country, and which has succeeded with them.[54]

The Dutch school legislation adopted in 1806, under the Batavian Republic, remained in force for a half-century; it provided for local school inspectors, generally pastors or other local notables working part-time, who came together as provincial boards of inspectors to set policies and sent representatives annually to meet on a national basis. Over this period little was done from the center to tinker with a system that was working well. Nongovernmental organizations took an active and significant role.

As Bache observed, this approach to school improvement would have been highly consistent with American institutions and modes of cooperation, as described by Tocqueville and other observers. That no attempt was made to put it to work in Massachusetts may be attributable to a lack of confidence in local leadership or to impatience with the demands of gradual improvements in education. It seems more likely, however, that this choice of the alternative model of Prussia reflected a sympathy with the nation-building drive of the Prussian leadership, a drive that had flourished briefly in the Netherlands after the French occupation of 1795–1814 but was long since quiescent. Prussian nationalism, by contrast, was a striking success, both "conservative" and "progressive," and exercised a tremendous attraction for would-be nation builders in the United States.

Central state-level leadership under American political conditions, in the last analysis, *did* depend upon local initiatives, and contemporary observers pointed out that many of the towns of Massachusetts were totally unaffected by Horace Mann's highly visible term as secretary of the board. Under American political and social conditions, the Prussian model of top-down educational leadership was a chimera; nonetheless, it made a powerful appeal to those who saw themselves as the leaders.

The one aspect of Dutch education that was discussed favorably by every observer, including Mann, was its approach to religious instruction. It was in the Netherlands that liberal Protestantism had the most profound effect upon schooling. The spirit of toleration and the concern for religious teaching that would engage the emotions and elevate the ideals of children without introducing issues of religious controversy were profoundly appealing to the Unitarians and liberal Protestants who took the lead in defining the agenda for the common school in America.

110

Barnard quoted an English observer who summed up the Dutch approach to religious instruction:

The law of 1801 proclaims, as the great end of all instruction, the exercise of the social and Christian virtues. In this respect it agrees with the law of Prussia and France; but it differs from the law of these countries in the way by which it attempts to attain this end. In France, and all the German countries, the schools are the auxiliaries, so to speak, of the churches; for, whilst the schools are open to all sects, yet the teacher is a man trained up in the particular doctrines of the majority of his pupils, and required to teach these doctrines during certain hours, the children who differ from him in belief being permitted to absent themselves from the religious lessons, on condition that their parents provided elsewhere for their religious instruction. But, in Holland, the teachers are required to give religious instruction to all the children, and to avoid most carefully touching on any of the grounds of controversy between the different sects.

He goes on to quote Cuvier and Noël, the observers sent by Napoleon's Imperial University in 1810, in commendation of the Dutch system under which "those truths which are common to all religions, pervade, are connected with, and are intimately mixed up with every branch of instruction, and everything else may be said to be subordinate to them."[55]

This approach, under which religion was to be present in the schoolroom in such a generalized and idealized form that no one (in theory) could take offense, was the very formula that Horace Mann and others were looking for. Thus Charles Brooks told the citizens of Quincy, Massachusetts, in an 1837 Fourth of July oration, that the leading figure in Dutch education (it was presumably Van den Ende) had recently urged that

the primary schools should be Christian, but neither Protestant nor Catholic. They should not lean to any particular form of worship nor teach any positive dogmas; but should be of that kind that Jews might attend without inconvenience to their faith.

"Do not think me extravagant," Brooks said,

if I ask for every one of our town schools the recognition of God, of Christ and of goodness. . . . Can we, fellow citizens, doubt that the moral element is emphatically *the* element which nature and society call for in all future school instruction? We shall not have *whole* men—true representatives of humanity—until the *whole* nature of man is recognized in our systems of public education."[56]

Thus the Unitarian Brooks was able to use the example of the (ostensibly) Calvinist Netherlands to "take the high ground" of calling for more reli-

111

gious and moral instruction in schools and so disarm in advance the orthodox Congregationalists of Massachusetts.

In the Netherlands, meanwhile, the consensus over "common school religion" was already falling apart, though it was only as Roman Catholics
and orthodox Calvinists became politically significant through extension of
the franchise to moderate-income groups that primary education began to
be a matter of public controversy. Under these new conditions the accommodations that had evolved after 1806 no longer worked. As early as 1840
Groen van Prinsterer, serving on a royal commission to respond to growing
complaints about the religious character (or lack of character) of the public
schools, called for "voluntary division" (*facultatieve splitsing*) of the schools,
with a local option to maintain separate Protestant, Catholic, and Jewish
schools, on the Prussian model.

These controversies did not, in general, become significant enough to
reach the notice of foreign observers until after 1848, though the Episcopalian *Journal of Christian Education* carried an intelligent discussion of the
issues in 1841, concluding that Groen's proposals for separate public schools
for Protestants and Catholics were the only feasible solution.[57]

When Mann and others launched their "crusade" for the common school,
the Netherlands offered a model of effective nationwide popular education
without forceful state intervention. It is significant that the reformers gave
this model little attention in their preference for the example of autocratic
Prussia. The one aspect of Dutch education that they most frequently singled
out for praise was the neutral religious instruction, failing to recognize that
this was by no means the result of national consensus. Such instruction was
in fact a favored program of an elite very similar to that formed by Mann
and his allies, seeking like them to undermine the power of traditional religious loyalties.

GREAT BRITAIN. English education was not much admired by the American reformers, and Scottish education was regarded as sadly decayed from
its former glory. British reformers would have agreed, because the headlong
urbanization of the population had left hundreds of thousands of children
unserved or poorly served by existing educational resources. A major reform effort was under way to respond to this need. It is curious that the
close sympathies that bound abolitionists, temperance advocates, and other
reformers in England and New England did not much extend to education.
The primary differences among educational reformers seem to have been in
the two areas to which we have been devoting attention: the role of the
state and the content of religious instruction.

English and Scottish popular education continued, throughout this period, to be provided largely by cooperation between denominational bodies and public authorities. The central government made little attempt to exert control and was untroubled by the diversity of religious teaching in the various schools. "Nation building" was less a concern in Great Britain than in any of the other nations discussed, and a practical toleration of various religious bodies had long since been worked out.

British tolerance of diversity was undoubtedly encouraged by a high degree of racial and linguistic homogeneity and a high rate of emigration, which carried away many restless spirits. There were deep economic and political cleavages, of course, and the debate over education policy had much to do with these social strains, but the problems were not those of cultural assimilation and national unity that were faced at the same time in Prussia, the Netherlands, and the United States.

The reliance upon semipublic and denominational initiatives in Britain had little appeal to Horace Mann and others; after all, this corresponded to the practices of their own New England past, which they were busy rejecting.

In brief, Britain did not offer models of vigorous state action, of unified religious teaching, or of nation building through popular education. It is no wonder that it attracted little positive attention from the American reformers.

THE INFLUENCE OF FOREIGN MODELS. The American education reformers found in Prussia the model they were looking for: centralized state action to assure that all children received a centrally prescribed education in the interest of national unity and economic progress. They managed to overlook the less appealing aspects of the Prussian state and its schools, dazzled as they were by the logic and apparent efficiency of the organizational approach employed. Such elements as compulsory attendance (adopted in Massachusetts in the 1850s but in the Netherlands not until fifty years later), state-controlled training and appointment of teachers, and state prescription of curriculum seemed the very components of an effective program for educational progress.

In the Netherlands American reformers found a model of religious instruction that was "Christian" but would not offend a Jew, sentimental and devout but hostile to strong convictions, moralizing but not ascetic or countercultural. Ironically, they took this as a model just as it began to come under attack in the Netherlands; the *Afscheiding*, or secession, of thousands of orthodox Calvinists who could not accept the liberalized teaching of the semiestablished Hervormde Kerk took place in 1834 and

113

quickly led to efforts to provide schooling that would be distinctively Calvinistic. Meanwhile, demands for Catholic schooling were growing increasingly insistent. It was only in his 1872 survey that Henry Barnard acknowledged that all was not well with the "religion above differences of opinion" taught in Dutch schools.

These continental models were of profound importance in the development of the goals pursued by Horace Mann and others, and they provided effective arguments against the opponents of the "common school" as the reformers sought to shape it. Prussia and the Netherlands seemed to demonstrate that an essentially "Enlightenment" program of reshaping human nature in the interest of political stability and social progress could be set in motion by the state and justified within the terms of liberal Protestant pietism. The struggle between "progress" and "superstition," between the Republic and the church, which had brought the effort of popular education during the French Revolution to a halt, could be avoided. The common school could indeed be seen as carrying forward in a purified form the enlightening and character-forming mission of the Protestant churches.

To a striking extent, the program outlined by the Jeffersonian essayists in the early years of the Republic, under the influence of the Enlightenment and of its expression in political measures by the Jacobins during the French Revolution, would be realized by Mann and his allies. Only the superstructure of national organization would yield to the realities of state dominance during the nineteenth century, when public education took its definitive structural form. In other respects, what we have called the "Enlightenment program," as mediated through the Prussian and Dutch examples, defined the role of education in society and put down deep roots in American thinking and institutional structures.

5

The State
Assumes Educational
Leadership

DURING the three decades before the Civil War two significant developments occurred in popular education in the United States: The foundations
were laid for effective state control, and the historic role of schools in transmitting religious traditions was attenuated into perfunctory observances
and moralizing. Those who played the primary role in these developments
made it their constant practice to deny any intention of promoting either.

Horace Mann responded vigorously to those of his critics who accused
him of seeking to establish state control and a schooling void of religion.
Was his role not simply to collect information about the condition of education in Massachusetts and to give publicity to promising practices? What
authority did he possess, or seek? Was it not one of his proudest accomplishments that the Bible was more commonly read in school than before
his efforts began? Did he not insist that religion and morality were an essential part of education in common schools?

Far more attention has been given, by contemporaries and by historians, to the religious controversies associated with the development of the
"common school" than to the context of governmental activism that made
those controversies inevitable. There was ample precedent, among the early
nineteenth-century proprietary schools in Boston and its vicinity, for the
liberal religiosity that Mann would seek to promote, and it had aroused no
conflicts. Only when this became the central program of a state-mandated
common school, with an explicitly moral and religious mission, did orthodox
Protestants object.

The educational reforms of the 1830s and 1840s, in Massachusetts, represented an attempt by an elite to respond to the tensions of an increasingly diverse and complex society by assigning a new function to a long-
established institution, the elementary school. Their primary instrument
was an extension of the state role in defining what would be taught and in
preparing those who would teach. This state role was exercised not so much

through regulations and enforcement as through exhortation and the advantages of a central position in a highly decentralized "system." Horace Mann, during his twelve years of leadership, made brilliant use of both.

The Massachusetts Board of Education was established by act of the legislature in 1837, and Senate president Horace Mann was appointed as its first secretary. Over the next decade, until he resigned to fill a seat in Congress left vacant by the death of John Quincy Adams in 1848, Mann served as the most effective "evangelist" and propagandist that the common public school has ever had. A leading figure in the French radical educational program of the Third Republic, Gabriel Compayré, described Mann with unlimited enthusiasm and sympathy:

> Mann was well aware that his real mission was first of all to conquer souls, to stir up good will, to create a movement of opinion. . . . A Minister [of public instruction] would have issued rulings, signed decrees. Mann could only hold conferences and issue reports. One could define his role precisely by saying that he was above all neither a philosopher of education, nor a practitioner, but a militant, a tribune, a missionary who went from city to city, from village to village, peddling his ideas and his faith, a Peter the Hermit preaching a crusade against ignorance.[1]

With the reservation that Mann's "crusade" (an image he used himself) was not against ignorance so much as it was against unenlightened attitudes and beliefs, this is a fair description. Mann and his allies did *not* seek direct authority over local schools, no doubt aware that this was out of their reach given the contemporary climate of opinion, but they did seek, through influencing local schools, to have a powerful impact upon the convictions and the loyalties of the developing nation.

The models for these efforts were the public school systems of the Netherlands and Prussia. These national systems were dominated by a Protestant and vaguely pietistic ethos in the service of an agenda set by elites whose primary concern was to create national unity by reducing the power of the particularisms of creed or region. The remoter influences of the French Enlightenment and Revolution, with their insistence on state-controlled and secularized popular schooling in the name of national unity and political progress, were hidden behind the reassuring form given them as they were adopted and transmitted by liberal Protestantism.

The Debate over State Leadership

In the period of the "common school revival," the conviction that the state should take the leadership in popular education was expressed only obliquely by Mann and others. Although they were only moderately respectful of local leadership and commitment, they were well aware of the power of local jealousies. These were expressed very clearly in the only real crisis that Mann experienced (though he was capable of seeing a mortal threat in every critical article or pamphlet), the move in the Massachusetts legislature to abolish the Board of Education in 1840.

Although Mann himself characteristically interpreted this legislative move as an outbreak of religious bigotry, the evidence suggests that it was based upon opposition to the attempt, by a liberal elite, to use the state to define a single educational experience for all students, whatever the views of their parents or of local citizens. The charges brought against Mann and his board are a reasonable statement of an alternative view of how popular education should be provided and by whose values it should be informed.

The Scottish phrenologist and education reformer, George Combe, sometimes served as a "cat's paw" for the American reformers by saying what they dared not. Combe was a highly influential author and lecturer in the period when Mann and the others were launching their "crusade." His study *The Constitution of Man Considered in Relation to External Objects* was published in Boston in 1829 and by 1838 had reached its sixth American edition, with the significant addition of "an additional chapter on the harmony between phrenology and revelation" by Joseph Warne. The same year he began an extended lecturing tour in the United States, where he became a close friend of Horace Mann and other members of the liberal elite. His *Notes on the United States of North America during a Phrenological Visit in 1838–9–40* (1841) entered with enthusiasm into the current debates over the extension of state leadership in popular education.

Mann reprinted, in the *Common School Journal* (May 15, 1841) a passage in which Combe discussed the recent move to abolish the Board of Education and observed that

> There are countries which have outstripped Massachusetts in some branches of education . . . her teachers stand in need of nothing more than the active agency of an enlightened central board, to collect and diffuse information on these subjects,—to urge them to adopt improvements,—to give advice to local committees, and to submit to their consideration rules which would benefit the pupils. . . . It is not to be expected that voluntary associations of teachers, the members of which are scattered through the State, and engrossed with local objects, interests, and duties, should acquire, digest, and diffuse information with the same success as a public board; and, besides, they would want that moral weight to induce the acceptance of improvements, which gives the Board its chief value.[2]

117

Combe put his recommendation in a broader context, arguing that "what above all things is wanted in every State in the Union" is

a *moral power* which shall address itself to the highest faculties of the people, and assist in forming and giving consistency and permanence to opinion, and which, without conflicting with the political, religious, or money powers, at present exclusively prevailing, may serve, through the influence of reason, to elevate, temper, and guide them all.

It was precisely this concern to establish, in the Board of Education, a "moral power" dedicated to the elevation and transformation of opinion and to the creation of a higher unity that troubled the Education Committee of the Massachusetts legislature. The committee report, though condemned by Mann and his allies as the ravings of backwoodsmen, was in fact a sophisticated statement of the problem of an enhanced state role in education.

The Board of Education was established, and Mann appointed, in 1837, midway in the governorship of Edward Everett, the epitome of Whig and Unitarian elitist reform. Everett had defeated his Democratic opponent, Marcus Morton, by nearly five to three that year, and the Whig elite seemed poised to carry out its program of internal improvements (profitable to merchants, industrialists, and financiers) and the moral reform of the common people. The common school was intended to be a primary instrument in this program of guided social improvement.

In 1838 the reformers overreached themselves, however, by the adoption of a law limiting the sale of liquor to quantities of at least fifteen gallons: Like so much of their program, this was reform directed exclusively at the lower orders, who could not afford to lay in such large stocks of spirits and did their drinking in dramshops. Marcus Morton, a representative of the rural and popular interests, was elected governor, though his fellow Democrats did not carry the legislature.

Morton took office with an address in which, among other elements of the program of his party, he stressed his commitment to public education, though with a different emphasis than that of Everett and Mann:

Its importance in a democratic government, which must be sustained by the intelligence and virtue of the people, cannot be too highly appreciated. The system of free schools, which has been transmitted from generation to generation, has improved in its progress, and is now in a high degree of perfection. But it is capable of still further improvement.[3]

Mann would have disagreed only with the impression given, that the progress of education had been continuous; he and the other reformers had a stake in presenting the common schools as having fallen into complete decay by the 1820s, when they began its rescue.

It was Morton's next statement, however, that indirectly challenged the efforts of Mann and others to bring local district schools under centralized town authority and to achieve some degree of uniformity among the town through the efforts of a state agency:

> To arouse that strong and universal interest in [the schools], which is so necessary to their utility and success, an interest that should pervade both parents and children, the responsibility of their management should rest upon the inhabitants of the towns. And the more immediately they are brought under the control of those for whose benefit they are established, and at whose expense they are supported, the more deep and active will be the feelings engendered in their favor, and the more certain and universal will be their beneficial agency. In the town and district meetings, those little pure democracies, where our citizens first learn the rudiments and the practical operation of free institutions, may safely and rightfully be placed the direction and the governance of these invaluable seminaries.

Mann carried a long extract from this speech in the *Common School Journal* and preceded it with an editorial comment expressing his pleasure at "the coincidence of views, in this particular, between the present and the former Chief Magistrate of the Commonwealth." He conceded that there had "not been wanting an apprehension amongst some of the friends of the cause" that Morton would change course with respect to support for common schools, while stressing that this was a sentiment "in which we never, for a moment, participated." [4]

Despite this politic assurance, however, we know from Mann's diary that he felt considerable anxiety about the defeat of his political ally Everett: "I enter upon another year not without some gloom and apprehension, for *political madmen* are raising voice and arm against the Board." [5]

Although Morton was defeated in 1841, he was elected governor again in 1842, and this time in his inaugural address he expressed his concern that the present system of common schools was promoting inequality among the citizens rather than, as intended, increasing equality. State assistance on a matching basis for school libraries (one of Mann's favorite measures, as we will see) had the effect of providing a benefit to wealthier districts that the poorer ones could not take advantage of. [6] Mann responded angrily in his private diary:

> This week, Governor Morton has come into power, and commenced his course by a most insidious and Jesuitical speech. He speaks of education, but not one word is said of the Board, or of the Normal Schools. There is

119

no recognition of the existence of improvements effected by them. Six years of as severe labor as any mortal ever performed—labor too, which has certainly been rewarded by great success—cannot procure a word of good will.[7]

More than a personal difference existed here. Morton represented the predominantly rural and western Massachusetts Democrats, who resented the efforts of Mann and others to impose their version of progress and the goals of education. The same year, indeed, the Connecticut Democrats, winning both governorship and control of legislature, abolished that state's Board of Education and deposed Henry Barnard as its secretary.

It was largely—though not exclusively—the Democrats in the legislature and not the religiously orthodox as such, as Kaestle and Vinovskis have shown in their careful study, who moved to abolish the Board of Education soon after Morton's 1840 address. This corrects the view put forward by Mann himself and repeated by most historians that the school reforms were opposed on grounds of religious obscurantism if not bigotry. Thus Mann wrote in his diary, a few months later, that "the bigots and vandals had been signally defeated in their wicked attempts to destroy the Board of Education."[8] In fact, as Kaestle and Vinovskis show,

> representatives from towns whose schools used Bibles or whose school committees included members of the clergy were less hostile to the board of education than legislators from communities whose schools did not use Bibles or did not have ministers on their school boards.[9]

The finding is significant because, as they observe, "Horace Mann and the Whigs never fully appreciated the depth of the fears of the Democrats that the creation of a state agency to do good might eventually result in a serious danger to freedom within the Republic."[10] The conflicts that were to follow cannot be understood apart from the inability on the part of Mann and his allies to recognize that their opponents were neither insincere nor unenlightened; they simply had a different view of the best interests of the emerging American democracy.

To return to the events of 1840, a special legislative committee had been appointed to consider how to reduce state expenditures, and it reported that the board was an unnecessary expense and a threat to political and religious freedom.

> District schools, in a republican government, need no police regulations, no system of state censorship, no checks of moral, religious, or political conservatism, to preserve either the morals, the religion, or the politics of the state. . . . Instead of consolidating the education interest of the Com-

monwealth in one grand central head, and that head the government, let us rather hold on to the good old principles of our ancestors, and diffuse and scatter this interest far and wide, divided and subdivided, not only into towns and districts but even into families and individuals. The moment this interest is surrendered to the government, and all responsibility is thrown upon civil power, farewell to the usefulness of common schools, the just pride, honor, and ornament of New England; farewell to religious liberty, for there would be but one church; farewell to political freedom, for nothing but the name of a republic would survive such a catastrophe.[11]

The vote to abolish Mann's position as secretary of the board failed narrowly, on a vote along strongly partisan lines.

Meanwhile, the usefulness of the Board of Education was studied by the Committee on Education; two Whigs and two Democrats produced a majority report calling for its abolition, while two Whigs and one Democrat supported the board. Some months later, after this resolution—despite substantial support—had been defeated in the legislature, Mann reprinted the committee reports for and against the board, together with the leading speech given on each side, in the *Common School Journal*. The report of the committee majority, recommending that the board be abolished, argued that

> since our system of public schools did not owe its origin to the Board of Education, but was in existence for two centuries before that Board was established, a proposal to dispense with its further services cannot be reasonably considered as indicating any feelings of hostility or of indifference towards our system of Common Schools. . . . the operations of that Board are incompatible with those principles upon which our Common Schools have been founded and maintained.[12]

The primary concern of the majority was with the potential for an inappropriate concentration, in the hands of the state, of responsibility and initiative for defining the objectives of education and thus of the character and convictions of the rising generation. The influence of the Prussian model and the more remote French example (which was not acknowledged by the education reformers themselves) was accurately recognized:

> After all that has been said about the French and Prussian systems, they appear to your Committee to be much more admirable, as a means of political influence, and of strengthening the hands of the government, than as a mere means for the diffusion of knowledge. For the latter purpose, the system of public Common Schools, under the control of persons most interested in their flourishing condition, who pay taxes to support them, appears to your Committee much superior. The establishment of

the Board of Education seems to be the commencement of a system of centralization and of monopoly of power in a few hands, contrary, in every respect, to the true spirit of our democratical institutions; and which, unless speedily checked, may lead to unlooked-for and dangerous results.

This concern led, in turn, to the further problem of religious and moral teaching in a society that was already pluralistic.

Your Committee has already stated, that the French and Prussian system of public schools appears to have been devised, more for the purpose of modifying the sentiments and opinions of the rising generation, according to a certain government standard, than as a mere means of diffusing elementary knowledge. Undoubtedly, Common Schools may be used as a potent means of engrafting into the minds of children, political, religious, and moral opinions;—but, in a country like this, where such diversity of sentiments exists, especially upon theological subjects, and where morality is considered a part of religion and is, to some extent, modified by sectarian views, the difficulty and danger of attempting to introduce these subjects into our schools, according to one fixed and settled plan, to be devised by a central Board, must be obvious. The right to mould the political, moral, and religious opinions of his children is a right exclusively and jealously reserved by our laws to every parent; and for the government to attempt, directly or indirectly, as to these matters, to stand in the parent's place, is an under-taking of very questionable policy. Such an attempt cannot fail to excite a feeling of jealousy, with respect to our public schools, the results of which could not but be disastrous.

The majority could have made a better case by using the example of Dutch schools, in which at that time there was a determined effort to teach a single form of religion and morality—explicitly distinct from denominational teaching—in the interest of social unity. French and Prussian schools were Catholic or Protestant according to the majority of the students attending them, and the state made no attempt to define a religious or moral teaching independent of that provided under the supervision of the local clergy.

Apart from this quibble, the argument of the majority is prescient of issues that would become and have remained sensitive and at times highly controversial in American education. They were so far-seeing, in fact, that they stressed problems that had not yet taken concrete form, and the committee minority had little difficulty in discrediting their arguments on the basis of the still undeveloped role of the board.

The majority of our Committee do not specify a single instance, so far as we can recollect, in which the Board of Education have attempted to control, or in any way to interfere with, the rights of towns or school districts. They seem to be in great fear of *imaginary* evils; but are not able to produce a single fact to justify their apprehensions. It is the alleged tendencies of the Board, to which they object. There is a possibility, they think, of its doing wrong; of its usurping powers which would endanger freedom of thought.[13]

The minority was right, of course; the board and its secretary (who is believed to have written the minority report) had little direct authority over local school districts. But the majority had seen correctly the potential, and even the contemporary impact, of what Combe would call the *moral power* of the board; in their report they even identified its essential elements, while they were still in embryonic form.

OBJECTIONS TO STATE COLLECTION OF EDUCATION DATA. The majority cited at least three instances of what it believed to be inappropriate interference on the part of the board. One had to do with

> some of the rules and regulations already devised by the Board of Education, and doubtless considered by it of a very useful tendency, [which] have proved, when carried into execution in the schools, very embarrassing, and have engrossed much of the time and attention of the teachers, which might better have been bestowed upon the instruction of their pupils, than in making out minute and complicated registers of statistics.

Virtually the only power that Mann and the board possessed was that of requiring annual school returns of statistics and other information, and Mann had used this aggressively to collect the information that he then used with great effect in his celebrated annual reports. (Complaints about such data-collection activities have not abated over the years!)

Mann's requests for information, and use of the information he received, were in some respects the key elements of his influence over the development of the common school. Some of the information was fairly obvious, such as the enrollment of schools and the number of days they were in operation; he used these reports to show how much needed to be done to improve the schools and, as the years went by, how much he had accomplished, exactly as any government official might do. (Kaestle and Vinovskis have reexamined the data and greatly qualified Mann's accomplishments with respect to attendance, though without denying his impact upon the development of the perceived mission of the common school.)

Mann also was in the habit of sending out questions that sought information of a more subjective nature, generally in anticipation of basing policy recommendations on responses whose tenor he anticipated; there are no instances in which such responses appear to have caused him to change his mind about an issue! Presumably he was more likely to receive responses from those school committees dominated by the "Friends of Education" who were his allies than from those that were resisting or attempting to ignore his efforts. We will see one instance, below, of his use of such responses.

Though the Committee on Education stressed only the inconvenience to teachers of filling out Mann's requests for data, it seems likely that they were also sensitive to the use that he was making of the data and the responses he received to point education in new directions.

Although Mann was not the last state education official to collect the data that he needed to support policies to which he was already inclined, he did so with unusual effectiveness. The resonance of his reports was immense, not only in the United States but in Europe as well. Their special force was based not only on his brilliant ability to articulate a sense of the mission of popular education but also on the impression he was able to give of objectivity and of being in touch with the course of developing modernity.

OBJECTIONS TO STATE ADOPTION OF BOOKS. A second instance taken by the majority as a warning of the potential for tyranny by the board had to do with the adoption of an approved "School Library," which all district schools were encouraged, though not required, to purchase. Such approved texts were the primary device which the National Convention had attempted to use to shape education in France and which the Dutch educational reformers had used with significant impact early in the century. Several of the Jeffersonian essayists discussed above also made this a part of their program. It was perhaps inevitable that the school library developed under Mann's patronage would become one of the most controversial aspects of his program. Certainly it was so for the majority of the Committee on Education:

> It is professed, indeed, that the matter selected for this library will be free both from sectarian and political objections. Unquestionably, the Board will endeavour to render it so. Since, however, religion and politics, in this free country, are so intimately connected with every other subject, the accomplishment of that object is utterly impossible, nor would it be desirable, if possible. That must, indeed, be an uninteresting course of reading which would leave untouched either of these subjects; and he must be a heartless writer, who can treat religious or political subjects, without affording any indication of his political or religious opinions.[14]

And then the majority states what has continued to be a major complaint about the treatment of religion in public school instruction. The context is

Mann's repeated assertion that the School Library was demonstrably neutral on religious matters, because each title had been reviewed and approved by the entire board, which included orthodox as well as Unitarian members.

> It is not sufficient, and it ought not to be, that a book contains nothing which we believe to be false. If it omit to state what we believe to be true; if it founds itself upon vague generalities, which will equally serve the purpose of all reasoners, alike; this very omission to state what we believe to be the truth becomes, in our eyes, a fault of the most serious character. A book, upon politics, morals, or religion, containing no party or sectarian views, will be apt to contain no distinct views of any kind, and will be likely to leave the mind in a state of doubt and skepticism, much more to be deplored than any party or sectarian bias.

In the April 1, 1840, announcement of the School Library in the *Common School Journal* (about three weeks after the majority report was released), Mann stressed that

> Being intended for the *whole* community, no work of a sectarian or denominational character in religion, or of a partisan character in politics, will be admitted. . . . The project is one of great extent, and vast importance; and, if properly carried out, must become of inestimable value to the young. Whether the anticipations of the Publishers, with regard to it, will be verified, time must determine; but, from the intellectual and moral, theoretical and practical, character of those who have engaged to aid in the undertaking, they have good grounds for presuming that much will be accomplished, and that, by their united efforts, many obstacles, now existing in the mental, moral, and physical improvement of youth, will be removed, or, at least, made more easily surmountable. . . . No work will be admitted into the Library, unless it be approved by every member of the Board of Education.[15]

Among the members of the board offered as evidence of the neutrality of the library was the Reverend Thomas Robbins, an orthodox Congregationalist in his midsixties and a noted antiquarian, who had been active some years earlier in temperance and the "revival" of education in Connecticut. His diary for the period when he was on the board makes no mention of reviewing books for the library or of any sense of the potential of controversy over the content, perhaps because the selections brought to the board by Mann were marked by the absence of positive doctrinal statements. That is, they represented a lowest common denominator of the beliefs then current among "enlightened" members of the various denominations. Robbins, though orthodox, was much absorbed (as his diary shows) by his book collecting and his ministerial duties and appeared not to have the slightest taste for controversy over doctrinal points.[16]

The other clergyman listed as a board member was the Reverend George Putnam, Unitarian minister in Roxbury (where Horace Mann's critic Mark De Wolfe Howe was his Episcopalian rival). A few years later, in a sermon on "True Religion," Putnam said that "the chief desire" of Unitarians had "not been so much to break down any existing theology as to do away with the idea that any one particular theological belief is necessary to make a man religious."[17] It might be said, not unjustly, that this is an excellent description of a primary function of religious instruction in common schools, as conceived by Mann and the other reformers in Massachusetts.

Though it is easy to see why this seemed an excellent objective in a religiously plural society, it is equally apparent that those within that society who were convinced, for example, that only through faith in the atoning death of Jesus Christ was salvation possible might object to their children being taught that this belief was not essential to "true religion." Few actually did so, among what were then the "mainline" denominations, because of the successful effort to identify the common school with Protestant interests.

One of the exceptions, and the only one among the members of the original board, appointed in 1837, was an Episcopalian layman from Pittsfield, Edward Newton. Newton resigned in disagreement with the policy of creating a School Library with all doctrinal teaching excluded and became the only member of the board to engage in public controversy with Mann.

The School Library over which so much controversy was to be generated contained very little of an explicitly religious character; this was the primary argument used *for* it by those who proclaimed its true neutrality among religious opinions, and the primary argument used *against* it by those who, like the majority of the Committee on Education, believed that it failed to present religious beliefs considered essential by most parents.

One of the first titles was Paley's *Natural Theology*, which had been a standard text of liberal Christianity for many years. A review of the School Library in the Unitarian *Christian Examiner* in 1840 expressed

> admiration of Paley's great work. . . . Well do we remember the glow and passion with which we first read it, and the hearty outbreak of enthusiasm which we could not and would not suppress, when we came to that simple, earnest declaration—for which all before it had so well prepared us—"This *is* a happy world, after all!"

The reviewer thanked "the Board of Education for giving this so prominent a place . . . where it must be seen and known by a class of readers of both sexes, to whom it has been for the most part, we fear, but a stranger."[18]

Another title in the library was *The Sacred Philosophy of the Seasons*, a collection of daily meditations on natural phenomena as revealing the providence of God, rather parallel to the work by Sturm recommended by Samuel Knox forty years earlier. The *Christian Examiner* expressed reservations, as a general matter, about such "artificial divisions" of material to fit a daily schedule of readings but approved it in light of the anticipated audience.

> We suppose, however, indeed all know, that there is a large class of readers to whom such divisions are a decided convenience, if not a solid advantage. And they are precisely the readers for whom these books as now published are designed. To be read by families as such, or by teachers to their schools in the way of moral and religious exercises, a chapter or marked portion each day of the week, and thus a volume in a season, and the entire work in the year,—the arrangement is admirable. Every one who knows the habits of those families who read but little, and wish that little to be of a moral and instructive character, will see what a temptation is offered, and what a security gained, by such a plan as this.[19]

The work was especially to be commended, the reviewer noted, because it had been revised for the School Library by "the substitution of a few unexceptionable religious papers in place of those that might offend some particular faith or feelings."

Local authors were represented by Royal Robbins's *Christianity and Knowledge* ("to show what Christianity has done for the human intellect, and what that has done for Christianity") and board member Robert Rantoul, Jr.'s *Moral Effects of Internal Improvements*, among others.[20] Other titles were historical, biographical, quasi-scientific, and moralistic in nature.

Rantoul's book could not be called nonpartisan, in view of the intense controversies in the Jacksonian era over the appropriateness of government support for "internal improvements."[21] Although Rantoul was a leading Democrat, he agreed with the Whigs in supporting "the granting of corporation charters, the use of mixed (state and private) enterprise, the aid given to railroad and canal companies." As an attorney, Rantoul played a leading role in setting up the Illinois Central Railroad. He differed in his position from that of the rural constituency of his party, resentful of the large profits earned by capitalists (and lawyers) as a result of these arrangements and of the competition from midwestern agriculture that "internal improvements" encouraged.

The inclusion of a book by a leading politician arguing, on high "moral" grounds, for internal improvements was "nonpartisan" only in the most technical sense. Its dissemination at public expense and in the name of the unassailable common school was an instance of that "moral power" which Combe had urged that the Board of Education exercise, to "assist in forming and giving consistency and permanence to opinion," and to which the majority of the Committee on Education objected.

A curious feature of the selections for the School Library is that they are aimed more at adults than at children in the elementary grades then offered by the common school, and indeed the announcement makes clear that there would be a "Juvenile Series" of fifty volumes and another series, also of fifty volumes, "for advanced scholars and their parents." It seems clear that Mann and his fellow reformers, many of whom prepared volumes for the advanced series, saw this as a powerful way of introducing their ideas into every community in the commonwealth, at the expense of local taxpayers. Perhaps Mann remembered how he had educated himself in the Franklin town library to make up for the deficiency of the instruction available in school.

> This library [he wrote in some autobiographical notes] consisted of old histories and theologies. . . . Oh! when will men learn to redeem that childhood in their offspring which was lost to themselves? . . . I have endeavored to do something to remedy this criminal defect. Had I the power, I would scatter libraries over the whole land, as the sower sows his wheat-field. More than by toil, or by the privation of any natural taste, was the inward joy of my youth blighted by theological inculcations.[22]

We can readily understand why he wanted to place the ideas of his circle within reach of other bright and ambitious small-town boys.

The enthusiasm of the *Christian Examiner*, principal organ of Boston and North Shore Unitarianism, seems to reflect an expectation that the views of liberal Protestantism would penetrate the backcountry through the library available in the district school. Some gifted village boy would feel a "glow and passion" in reading Paley and would, in a "hearty outbreak of youthful enthusiasm," accept the essential goodness of the world in defiance of the gloomy preaching of the local orthodox minister—so perhaps Mann hoped, remembering his own rebellion, at the age of twelve, against the teaching of the orthodox controversialist Nathanael Emmons in Franklin. The father or mother, gathering family around of an evening, would read from *The Sacred Philosophy of the Seasons* rather than from the Bible or *Pilgrim's Progress* or some old Puritan devotional work, and thus the light of "reasonable religion" would spread across the commonwealth.

Mann often cited the Massachusetts statute of 1827, which had given to school committees the authority to select the books to be used in the schools under their jurisdictions (a measure intended to address the problem of classes in which each child seemed to be using a different text, as selected by their parents), providing only that "said committee shall never direct any school books to be purchased or used, in any of the schools under their superintendence, which are calculated to favour any particular religious sect or tenet."[23] Despite this requirement, Mann reported that, on his first tour of schools in Massachusetts in 1837, he had "found books in the schools as strictly and exclusively *doctrinal* as any on the shelves of a theological library."[24] His standard was such, indeed, that he would conclude in his *First Report* (1838) that "among the vast libraries of books, expository of the doctrines of revealed religion, none have been found free from that advocacy of particular 'tenets' or 'sects,' which includes them within the scope of the legal prohibition."

His conclusion was not that the teaching of religion should be banished from the common school but that new books were required, selected or written on principles in keeping with the enlightened spirit of the age. After all,

> entirely to discard the inculcation of the great doctrines of morality and of natural theology has a vehement tendency to drive mankind into opposite extremes; to make them devotees on the one side, or profligates on the other; each about equally regardless of the true constituents of human welfare. Against a tendency to these fatal extremes, the beautiful and sublime truths of ethics and of natural religion have a poising power.[25]

It was a subsequent statute, of 1837, giving local school committees authority to expend public funds also to establish libraries in district schools, that provided the occasion for the development of a School Library free from the weaknesses of the books currently in use. Neither statute gave any role or authority to the state board, but their combination provided what must have been an irresistible opportunity to put the "moral power" of the board (and the economic leverage possible from broad distribution) behind books that promoted the political and religious view of the reformers. This was the easier to compass because their political views were high-minded and "nonpartisan" and their religious views were equally high-minded and "nonsectarian." That we can recognize them as the highly partisan and sectarian views of economic and religious liberalism does not mean that the reformers were insincere in believing that they constituted a "party above party divisions." It is entirely understandable, on the other hand, that their opponents accused them of hypocrisy and of concealing their true aims and their true convictions behind a manipulation of vocabulary borrowed from the common tradition but understood in a special way.

In his *First Report* Mann deplored, as had Knox and Smith forty years before, the current diversity in books used in schools and the diverse beliefs and values that they reflected. "There is," he wrote,

> a public evil of great magnitude in the multiplicity and diversity of elementary books. They crowd the market and infest the schools. . . . Truth

and philosophy, in regard to teaching, assume so many shapes, that common minds begin to doubt whether there be truth or philosophy under any. . . . When the (local school) committee fail in directing what books shall be used, a way is opened for the introduction of books which are expressly prohibited by law, as "calculated to favor the tenets of particular sects of christians." Under such omission, also, the school house may cease to be neutral ground between those different portions of society, now so vehemently contending against each other on a variety of questions of social and national duty. . . . Would the disciples of hostile doctrines look forward, and foresee to what results a breach of the truce in regard to the school-room must infallibly lead, it seems scarcely credible, that each should not agree, in good faith, to refrain from every attempt to preoccupy the minds of school children with his side of vexed and complicated questions, whether of state or theology.[26]

The following year Mann reported that, in his annual request for information from local school committees, he had asked, "Would it be generally acceptable to the friends of Education in your town, to have the Board of Education recommend books for the use of the schools?" Twenty towns containing 18,000 inhabitants were opposed, ten towns wished the board to recommend books so long as it did not prescribe them, two wished the board to recommend and prescribe, and one wished the legislature to give the board the authority to prescribe schoolbooks. It is not clear whether the remaining towns did not answer this question or indeed failed to file returns at all. Somehow Mann reached the conclusion that "the friends of education in towns containing more than seven-eighths of the population of the State, are in favor of having the Board of Education *recommend* books for the use of the Schools."[27]

Within the next few months he gained enough support for the idea on the board to begin to issue the School Library. Characteristically, he had the most exalted opinion of what such a collection of books could accomplish for human progress:

> Could a library, containing popular, intelligible elucidations of the great subjects of art, of science, of duty be carried home to all the children of the Commonwealth, it would be a magnet to reveal the varied elements of excellence, now hidden in their souls.

The goal was more than popular enlightenment: It was the creation, by the state, of its own future citizens on a new model:

> The State, in its sovereign capacity, has the deepest interest in this matter. If it would spread the means of intelligence and self-culture over its entire surface . . . it would call into existence an order of men who would establish a broader basis for its prosperity, and give a brighter lustre to its name. . . . By our institutions, the political rights of the father descend to

his sons, in course of law. But the intellectual and moral qualifications, necessary for the discreet use of those rights, are intransmissable, by virtue of any statute. These are personal, not hereditary; and are, therefore, to be taught anew and learned anew, by each successive generation.[28]

An arrangement was made with a private publishing house, with the condition that no work was to be included without the unanimous approval of the board. This was frequently cited as the best assurance against any "sectarian" elements.

> The character of these gentlemen is a sufficient guaranty, that the trust reposed in them will be executed with fidelity. There is not a man, belonging to either of the great political or religious portions, into which our community is unhappily divided, but will find, in the above list of names, a watchful sentinel, to guard his social and spiritual rights against aggression. Suppose I am a member of the Calvinistic or orthodox Congregational denomination, and I deem it a paramount duty to avert from the eyes and ears of my children, the peculiar views of the Baptists, Unitarians, or Universalists. I see in the list, the name of the Rev. Emerson Davis, of Westfield,—an orthodox Congregational clergyman, known to his brethren throughout the State. . . . Further down in the list I see the name of the Rev. Dr. Robbins. . . . can I ask for any higher assurance, that the books examined and sanctioned by these gentlemen will be found to contain nothing at which any orthodox man can justly take offence? Suppose I am a Baptist . . .[29]

and so forth.

The proposition seems reasonable enough; why did it arouse the hostility of the majority of the Committee on Education, as well as such polemicists as Matthew Hale Smith and Frederick Packard? Not because materials were included that were offensive to one or another of the religious groups then prominent in the commonwealth. Against that, the review process as well as the law of 1827 so frequently cited by Mann were sufficient protection, had such a protection been needed. From what we know of Mann's own religious views, it was not.

As a Unitarian of his time, Mann considered himself a Christian who would preserve all that was pure, noble, and true of the teaching of Jesus Christ, without the accretions of legend and speculative doctrine that, in his view, had been added by superstition and the calculation of a priestly caste. He was quite sincere in considering his views "nonsectarian." Teaching that sought to form a sincere piety directed toward the Creator, a morality based upon the example and ideals of Jesus Christ and conducing to civic peace and social righteousness—how could that "favor the tenets of particular sects?"

131

By and large his contemporaries agreed, including many who were themselves fully "orthodox." Those who—more clear-thinking, perhaps—did not agree insisted that what was presented was in fact a false religion, worse than no mention of religion at all, since it took no account of sin as a corruption of human nature cutting man off from God and from his own happiness, or of God's plan of salvation through Jesus Christ. By retaining only those aspects of Christianity with which Unitarians agreed, the proposed religious teaching was in fact identical with Unitarian teaching. Thus it *was* sectarian in the fullest sense. On the other hand, to teach about human sinfulness and God's redeeming grace could not be considered "sectarian," since these were simply facts accepted by virtually everyone and attested by the almost unchallenged authority of the Bible. Those who argued this position agreed that truly "sectarian" teaching should be excluded from the common school but would limit this characterization to such matters as the time and mode of baptism and the most scriptural form of church governance.[30]

That this orthodox position did not prevail must be attributed largely to the theological confusion and "softness" of the orthodox party at that time, when so much of its energies were being devoted to evangelization of the cities, the West, and the world, with an inevitable popularization of doctrine in the interest of the broadest possible acceptance. The common school seemed part of the triumph of Christian benevolence, particularly when Mann urged that the Bible be read and morality taught in every school. Only the especially insightful, like Charles Hodge at Princeton, were able to foresee the rapid abandonment by public education of all connection with the essential beliefs of Christianity.

Despite his success in disarming and outmaneuvering his orthodox potential opponents, the School Library continued to be a point at which Mann was subject to attack, and we hear less about it in the later years of his incumbency. Perhaps as a result of these controversies, Massachusetts has never been one of the states in which the state board has prescribed textbooks or curriculum.

OBJECTIONS TO STATE CONTROL OF TEACHER PREPARATION. The third specific complaint of the majority of the Committee on Education, in March 1840, was about "Another project, imitated from France and Prussia, and set on foot under the superintendence of the Board of Education, . . . the establishment of Normal Schools."[31]

Traditionally, many of the teachers in district schools had been graduates of the private academies or college students taking a year or two to earn the money to continue their studies; others were ministers who had not found or had lost a position. The majority report argued that the present system worked quite satisfactorily and that, if there were problems in some towns with finding adequately qualified teachers, that could be resolved by paying better salaries.

> Academies and high schools cost the Commonwealth nothing; and they are fully adequate, in the opinion of your Committee, to furnish a competent supply of teachers. In years past, they have not only supplied our own schools with competent teachers, but have annually furnished hundreds to the West and the South. There is a high degree of competition existing among these academies, which is the best guaranty for excellence.

The majority saw no advantage, to the commonwealth, of creating state institutions in competition with the academies and town high schools that provided what seemed to them an adequate training for teaching basic literacy and numeracy skills. After all, "every person who has himself undergone a process of instruction must acquire, by that very process, the art of instructing others." "An intelligent mechanic, who has learned his trade, is competent, by that very fact, to instruct others in it; and needs no Normal School to teach him the art of teaching his apprentices."

The underlying issue, though, was not a practical one of the best investment of the available resources. The majority summed up its opposition to the board and its initiatives in terms that had to do with a concept of society, with a commitment to a pluralism of goals of education and of the means of attaining these goals. From this perspective, they pointed out,

> the idea of the State controlling Education, whether by establishing a central Board, by allowing that Board to sanction a particular Library, or by organizing Normal Schools, seems to your Committee a great departure from the uniform spirit of our institutions,—a dangerous precedent, and an interference with a matter more properly belonging to those hands, to which our ancestors wisely intrusted it. It is greatly to be feared, that any attempt to form all our schools and all our teachers upon one model, would destroy all competition, all emulation, and even the spirit of improvement itself. When a large number of teachers and school committees are all aiming at improvement, as is doubtless the case, to a great extent, in this Commonwealth, improvements seem much more likely to be found out and carried into practice, than when the chief right of experimenting is vested in a central Board. With these views, your Committee have come to the conclusion, that the interests of our Common Schools would rest upon a safer and more solid foundation if the Board of Education and the Normal Schools were abolished.[32]

The development of normal schools, or teacher training institutions, in France, Germany, and the Netherlands as in Massachusetts, was directly related to a new concept of the role of popular education. As long as elementary schools were simply to teach literacy skills, some basic arithmetic, and the catechism, Bible verses, or liturgical responses as religious instruction, they could be entrusted to anyone who was literate and of unexceptional moral character. The church sexton, a disabled veteran, even a literate tradesman might be the teacher; even better, it could be an aspirant to the ministry. Teaching was a matter of passing on some skills that one possessed as a result of one's own education and of presiding over the memorization of some essential elements of the common religious heritage.

This was certainly a limited educational program, though it resulted in a high degree of literacy in New England and a respectable level in some parts of France, the German states, and the Netherlands. What it did not do, however, was to meet the new aspiration, growing out of Enlightenment views of society and of human nature, to use universal popular education as a primary instrument of a number of social objectives that had nothing to do with literacy. These objectives included a spirit of national unity, a commitment to the existing political order, and those "social and Christian virtues" that were necessary to progress and the security of property.

If elementary schools—the very term "common school" expressed a political and social program—were to produce such profound transformations in the popular mentality, they must be taught by a new kind of teacher, one for whom the moral content of instruction was at least as significant as academic skills.

The first models for such teachers were the members of Roman Catholic teaching orders, the earliest of which were organized as an instrument of the Counter-Reformation for the express purpose of educating and thereby converting Protestant children. These teaching brothers and sister received a "formation" designed to enable them to rule their schools by moral authority rather than by the rod and to have a profound impact upon the children entrusted to them. When teacher training institutions under government auspices were established in the German states, it was with the significant title of "seminaries," and one of the first (and characteristically abortive) efforts of the French Revolution to create a "republican education" was the establishment of a national Ecole Normale Supérieure in Paris to train the teachers of teachers who would mold the loyalties of future citizens.

Contemporary descriptions of normal schools during the nineteenth century, whether in Prussia, France, the Netherlands, or Massachusetts, almost never fail to stress the *moral* content of the formation of future teachers.

Thus a letter by Dr. Samuel Gridley Howe, one of Mann's chief allies and director of the Institution for the Blind in South Boston, was included as part of the minority report of the Committee on Education, supporting the board's initiatives; Howe wrote that he, like others, "entertained some theoretical objections to Normal Schools, as carried on by European governments," but that he was satisfied that the board's normal school at Lexington was free of such objections, since "the moral nature is as much cultivated as the intellectual."[33]

The next year we find a report in the *Common School Journal* from Cyrus Peirce, principal of the normal school in Lexington, stressing that "there are no subjects in which scholars manifest more interest than in questions of morals."[34] A biographical notice of Peirce stressed "the especial attention he has paid to the *moral* culture of his pupils" and his opinion that "the common education of our schools has in it too little of the moral element."[35]

The stress on moral education in the normal school at Lexington—as in the celebrated institution at Fontenay-aux-Roses in France under the Third Republic—was a means of shaping young women into common school teachers whose convictions would be as clear and as winning as those of a teaching sister in a Catholic school.

James Carter, a predecessor of Mann as an education reformer in Massachusetts, had early identified the potential of teacher training as a means of having a profound impact upon popular education. In a series of articles published in 1824–25 in the *Boston Patriot*, he urged a comprehensive scheme of education reform through state leadership. The key to the entire program was the training of teachers. "The character of the schools, and of course their political, moral and religious influence depend, almost solely, upon the character of the teachers." As a result,

> An institution for the education of teachers . . . would form a part, and a very important part, of the free-school system. It would be, moreover, precisely that portion of the system which should be under the direction of the State, whether the others are or not. . . . An institution for this purpose would become, by its influence on society, and particularly on the young, an engine to sway the public sentiment, the public morals, and the public religion, more powerful than any other in the possession of government. It should, therefore, be responsible immediately to them. . . . It should be emphatically the State's institution.

And then he warns, "If it be not undertaken by the public and for public purposes, it will be undertaken by individuals for private purposes."[36]

But what invidious private purposes can Carter have been thinking of? After all, the "private" academies had been training teachers in a quite satisfactory manner, and an "individual"—the Reverend Samuel R. Hall—had been operating a little school for training teachers in Concord, Vermont, for several years and would later be praised by the education reformers as a pioneer. Carter himself would attempt to operate a private teacher training institution a few years later. Apparently such efforts were not what he had in mind.

It seems likely that his concern was with the potentially sectarian character of any teacher training not under state control. His own efforts would not be sectarian, of course, to his own way of thinking; but having once announced the tremendous power of teacher training to "sway the public sentiment, the public morals, and the public religion," he could not have failed to recognize that it would be in the interest of the churches to exert their influence over the "engine" that promised to take over so much of their traditional role. It is common to find such oblique references, among the education reformers, to the ambitions and claims of organized religion, presumably because they recognized their own intention of moving the state into areas of public influence where religion had previously been almost unchallenged. As one commentator puts it succinctly, "the church was viewed with suspicion, but not the State."[37]

Carter's fellow Unitarian, the influential Professor George Ticknor of Harvard, supported Carter's program in the pages of the *North American Review* in 1827, insisting that "the *schools* are the pillars of the republic. To these, let the strong arm of government be stretched out. Over these, let the wisdom of our legislatures watch."[38] The same year Carter came within one vote in the Massachusetts legislature of obtaining an appropriation for such a teacher training institution.

In 1830 Phillips Academy at Andover opened a teacher training branch under the direction of the Reverend Samuel R. Hall.[39] Phillips Academy was one of those semipublic institutions that we would now consider "private." It provided group instruction as college preparation, by contrast with the private tutoring by which Horace Mann, for example, had prepared for Brown. The academy was chartered by the Massachusetts legislature in 1780, proclaiming that "the first and principal object of this Institution is the promotion of true Piety and Virtue." Governance was by an incorporated Board of Trustees, a common means at that time of small government of accomplishing a public goal through a semipublic means.[40] The development of a department to train teachers for the common schools was thus entirely consistent with the history and role of Phillips Academy.

Although the Andover program was an initial success, it did not satisfy the goal of placing teacher preparation under state leadership; indeed, it threatened to reinforce the predominant role of the private academies. In the meeting of the American Institute of Instruction held in Boston in 1836, a resolution was adopted to petition the legislature once again to "establish a Seminary for the education of teachers." In the 1837 session of the legislature at which the Board of Education was established, an attempt to obtain an appropriation for "some literary institution for the purpose of qualifying teachers" failed, but the new board urged action in its *First Report*. Significantly, the example of other countries was cited in support of the proposal.

Charles Brooks, the Unitarian minister from Hingham, had made normal schools his special cause since 1834, urging the example of Prussia which, as we have seen, he knew from his acquaintance with Dr. Julius and from Cousin's book. Brooks insisted that

> the nineteenth century demands a higher type of teachers; teachers who are more than a match for the intense mental activity of the age, and who can more that master its tyrannous selfishness. . . . school instructors should be as fully prepared for their duties as is the clergyman for his. Teachers, teachers, yes I say teachers, have an inconceivable and paramount agency in shaping the destinies of the world. . . . Competent teachers, whose learning is sanctified by piety, and whose characters are all radiant with love, will assuredly impart their nobility of soul to their pupils. Their spiritual magnetism will go out from them whenever innocent childhood presents itself as a conductor. Such teachers will unconsciously throw into the daily lessons some moral suggestion, moral hint, moral maxim, or moral query; thus giving moral polarity to everything.[41]

In 1836 he called a convention of teachers in Plymouth County, on behalf of which he petitioned and twice addressed the legislature to urge the founding of normal schools.[42]

Brooks is especially significant as the one who made the connection with European models explicit. Thus he wrote, in a second petition in January 1837,

> Over and over again the Prussians proved that elementary education cannot be fully attained without purposely-prepared teachers. They deem these seminaries of priceless value; and declare them, in all their reports and laws, to be the fountains of all their success. . . . we are confident that teachers thoroughly prepared, as they are in Prussia, would put a new face on elementary education, and produce through our State an era of light and of love.[43]

In 1838 Edmund Dwight, a wealthy financier who was one of the Whig/Unitarian circle that had selected Mann to head the efforts of the Board of Education, offered $10,000 for a state normal school if that sum were matched by the legislature. Like the others, Dwight had read Cousin on Prussia and had been informed (as the *Common School Journal* would report in 1839) that the reform of education in Prussia dated from and was based upon the establishment of "teacher seminaries."[44] Through his initiative the Lexington Normal School was opened by the board in July 1839 (with three students), that at Barre in western Massachusetts in September 1839, and that at Bridgewater in southeastern Massachusetts in August 1840. The Lexington Normal School moved, in 1844, to West Newton where Horace Mann was a neighbor of the institution that was his special pride and joy.

Much was expected of the early normal schools in Massachusetts. Through their agency a new type of teacher would be created and sent around the commonwealth, to shape the moral as well as the intellectual character of the next generation of citizens. As Governor Everett asked at the dedication of the normal school in Barre in 1839, "to how much of the intellectual and moral frame are not the first impress and shaping to be given at school?"[45] And Mann used characteristic exaggeration at the dedication of a building for the normal school in Bridgewater:

> I believe Normal Schools to be a new instrumentality in the advancement of the race. I believe that, without them, Free Schools themselves would be shorn of their strength and their healing power, and would at length become mere charity schools, and thus die out in fact and in form. Neither the art of printing, nor the trial by jury, nor a free press, nor free suffrage, can long exist, to any beneficial and salutary purpose, without schools for the training of teachers. . . . nay, the universal diffusion and ultimate triumph of all-glorious Christianity itself must await the time when knowledge shall be diffused among men through the instrumentality of good schools. Coiled up in this institution, as in a spring, there is a vigor whose uncoiling may wheel the spheres.[46]

All allowances made for the occasion on which these remarks were made, they reflect an expectation widely shared among the education reformers in France, Prussia, and the Netherlands as well as in New England. We have seen that Henry Barnard dedicated one of the first issues of the *Connecticut Common School Journal* to reports on normal schools in Europe, and the theme of teacher education—frequently in a vein as exalted as that of Mann's Bridgewater speech—appears constantly in the journals and books of the period.

Support for teacher education was not limited to liberal Protestants; in 1835 we find a writer in the leading journal of orthodox Calvinism, the *Biblical Respository and Princeton Review*, urging the use of state funds to support teacher training.[47] The significant difference, however, is that his proposal was to support such programs in the colleges, then almost exclusively under private and denominational auspices. For Brooks, Mann, and the others, however, what was needed was teacher "seminaries," which would be devoted exclusively to forming teachers and would be accountable directly to state education officials.

In order to accomplish this purpose, the new normal schools were to offer the intensive experience suggested by their alternative title "teacher seminary." Thus Cyrus Peirce led regular devotions for his students and required them to read George Combe's phrenological *Constitution of Man* in order to acquire a new perspective on human nature and capabilities; Samuel Blumenfeld refers to this as "public education's first venture into educational quackery."[48] Mann himself saw Combe's theories as possessing deep religious significance. We find him writing to Combe in March 1839:

> There have been some striking conversions, since you were here, to the religious truths contained in your "Constitution of Man." Some of these have happened under my own ministry. [One young man, a prospective teacher, to whom he had recommended the book] came again, not a little disturbed: he had read it again, comparing it with his former notions (for he was highly orthodox), and found that the glorious world of laws which you describe was inconsistent with the miserable world of expedients in which he had been accustomed to dwell. I spent an entire evening with him, and endeavored to explain to him that your system contained all there is of truth in orthodoxy. . . . He adopted my views on the subject, and is now, I believe, a convert beyond the danger of apostasy.[49]

Making all allowances for Mann's jocular intention, it seems clear that he saw Combe's system as a full-scale alternative to orthodoxy and did not hesitate to recommend it as such to a future teacher. We can safely assume that the prescription and discussion of Combe's book at the normal school had a similar effect, and presumably a similar intention.

The concern with the moral impact of normal schools marked a significant difference from what had been James Carter's emphasis on "the *science of teaching*."[50] Mary Peabody Mann made this clear in her biography of her husband, when she wrote that he was free to go on their honeymoon trip to Europe in 1843 because

> now it only remained to improve methods of instruction, and to bring the subject of moral education more fully before the public. To this end he had set in operation the most adequate means—the Normal schools—and placed them in the hands of men who, as far as he could judge, saw the importance of that element in human culture.[51]

The moral "element in human culture" was indeed the underlying focus of the efforts of Horace Mann and his allies and reflected their deeply religious motivations in what they frequently called their "sacred cause." To understand what this meant to them it is necessary to look more closely at the role of "liberal Christianity" in defining the terms of the "common school revival."

The Unitarian Connection

It is impossible to appreciate the heat aroused by the establishment of the first normal schools in Massachusetts, and other measures taken by Horace Mann and the Board of Education, without an awareness that they were considered by some of the orthodox as an instrument of Unitarian aggression and proselytism. The complaint was that the normal schools were permeated with a Unitarian spirit, that, in fact, they served as the seminaries in which Unitarian missionaries were prepared to penetrate those parts of the commonwealth in which orthodox beliefs remained predominant.

Though Mann denied such charges angrily, the semiofficial history of *Unitarianism in America* (1902) does not hesitate to claim for that denomination the leading role in the development of the common school revival in general and of normal schools in particular.

> Horace Mann was an earnest and devoted Unitarian, the intimate friend of Channing and Parker, to both of whom he was largely indebted for his intellectual and spiritual ideals. . . . In full sympathy with him in this work were such (Unitarians) as Dr. Channing, Edward Everett, Theodore Parker, Josiah Quincy, Samuel J. May, and the younger Robert Rantoul . . . Some of the staunchest and most liberal friends of Mann were of other denominations; but the work for common schools was thoroughly in harmony with Unitarian principles.

Thus Charles Brooks, the advocate of state action to create normal schools, was a Unitarian minister, as were Cyrus Peirce, the principal of the first such school, and his successor Samuel J. May.[52]

The influence of this denomination, then at the height of its prosperity when all things seemed possible, was in fact even greater than claimed later by its historian. The principal of the normal school at Bridgewater was a Unitarian layman, and the "special visitors" assigned by the board to oversee these institutions in 1839 were Jared Sparks, Rantoul, Putnam, and Mann himself,[53] two Unitarian clergymen and two Unitarian laymen. The original board was even more heavily Unitarian than suggested above. Of the eleven original members, eight were Unitarians, including the governor and the other moving spirits in the creation and selection of the board: Carter, Dwight, and Mann himself.[54]

One of the non-Unitarians on the original board, Edward Newton, pointed this out in an article in the Episcopalian *Christian Witness* of May 17, 1844:

> I am next to consider another ingenious resort of the Secretary (Mann), or his friends, which is to make me appear in the public mind as "hostile to the glorious system of our common school education." . . . My contest is not with that excellent system, *but against the construction given to it, the powers claimed under it, and the perversion of its ancient design and usage* by the Board of Education.[55]

Newton noted that orthodox Congregationalists, Episcopalians, and Baptists had cooperated together in support of the common schools for nearly two centuries, with Methodists joining them more recently.

> These four denominations, making together at all times, then and now, nine tenths of the population of the Commonwealth, have had no jealousies of each other on this head. In agreement, *essentially*, in matters of faith, the *great doctrines* of the gospel, as understood by them in common, were *allowed to be taught*, and *were taught*, in all our Common Schools.

All this had changed, he charged, with the arrival of the Unitarians upon the scene: "In the early part of the present century, a new sect sprang up amongst us, small in numbers but highly respectable in regard to individual character," and the Board of Education appointed in 1837 included eight members of "the new sect referred to." To the influence of these members Newton attributed the exclusion "of all matters deemed by them *sectarian* in religion, or, as we affirm, *vital* and *distinctive* in the Christian scheme, as held by Orthodox denominations."

For Newton, the very premise on which Mann based his insistence that he was furthering the teaching of true religion was false.

> The idea of a religion to be *permitted* to be taught in our schools, in which all are at present agreed, is a mockery. There is really no such thing unless it be what is called natural religion. There is not a point in the *Christian* scheme, deemed important, and of a *doctrinal* character, that is not disputed or disallowed by some. As to the "*precepts*" [of Jesus], perhaps, there may be pretty general agreement, and that this is one great branch of the Christian scheme we allow. But is this all—all that the sons of the Puritans are willing to have taught in their public schools?[56]

Mann counterattacked angrily in the *Boston Courier*, contesting Newton's estimate of the proportion of the population that was orthodox and insisting that the Board of Education had been selected with great care to represent the different religious groups in the Commonwealth. "All the great parties into which the State was divided were to be regarded. Religious views were among the most important. Political considerations could not be overlooked."

Governor Everett selected the original board, Mann explained from his inside involvement in the process, taking three members from the legislature who only happened to be Unitarians. Two businessmen were then added—Dwight and Newton himself—of whom one was Unitarian and one Episcopalian, and then two orthodox and one Unitarian clergyman were added (Davis, Robbins, and Sparks). What could be fairer? [57]

The reply was disingenuous. The cabal of education reformers who selected themselves and others for the original board took care to assure that they and their allies would be in a clear majority. They were Unitarians, but this religious affiliation was more a result than a cause of their basic orientation to popular enlightenment, reform, and elite leadership.

Unitarianism was not a militantly proselytizing faith, as its supporters admitted half-ruefully, and we may believe Mann when he asserts that it was not their intention to convert the entire coming generation to that denomination—which many Unitarians were unwilling to admit *was* a denomination or "sect" rather than simply purified Christianity. On the other hand, there is ample evidence that these education reformers saw strict orthodoxy as a threat out of the benighted past and were disturbed by every evidence of its resurgence in those years of revivalism and orthodox counteroffensive.

Mann took care to keep his own views on orthodoxy out of his speeches and reports, but he wrote to his ally George Combe,

> There are two classes,—the one who are orthodox only by association, education, or personal condition. These may be good people, though they always suffer under that limitation of the faculties which orthodoxy imposes. The second class are those who are born orthodox, who are naturally or indigenously so; who, if they had had wit enough, would have invented orthodoxy, if Calvin had not. I never saw one of this class of men whom I could trust so long as a man can hold his breath. These are the men who are assailing me. [58]

In his private journal, about the time that he took up his responsibilities as secretary of the Board of Education, Mann wrote:

> In my early life I was accustomed to hear all doctrines, tenets, creeds which did not exactly conform to the standard set up, denounced as heresies, the believers cast out from fellowship in this life and coolly consigned to eter-

nal perdition in the next. I think it would have made an immense difference, both in my happiness and character, had the genial, encouraging,
ennobling spirit of liberality been infused into my mind when its sentiments were first capable of being excited on that subject.[59]

Reflecting again on his life, years later, he wrote bitterly in another letter,
"what an unspeakable calamity a Calvinistic education is."[60]

Thus, although Mann and the other education reformers may not have
intended to promote Unitarianism as a denomination, they were deeply
concerned to assure that "liberal religion" would, through the common
schools, replace "fanaticism." The board could not be exclusively Unitarian,
of course, but they made sure that most of its members were either religious
liberals or, like Thomas Robbins, genial members of the first group of orthodox described by Mann—Newton was a miscalculation, but it is more
difficult to judge the religious position of a layman than that of a clergyman.
A Democrat was needed to balance the Whig majority, but Rantoul was an
enlightened member of his party, a Unitarian, and not a representative of
the rural and orthodox population. The three orthodox members selected
for the board lived far enough from Boston—Pittsfield, Westfield (near
Springfield), and Rochester (near New Bedford)—to assure that their participation in making policy or in reviewing the activities of their energetic
secretary would be intermittent and confined to the periodic meetings of
the board.

Were the normal schools some sort of Unitarian conspiracy, then? Only
in the sense that they represented the most effective means for the education
reformers (themselves mostly but not exclusively "liberal Christians") to
develop a supply of teachers who would share their own views about the
"pure religion" appropriate to offer as religious instruction in common
schools. Presumably most of the student-teachers were themselves from orthodox families, and we may doubt that any overt attempt was made to
shake their beliefs, any more than they were expected to shake those of the
children who would be entrusted to them. Orthodox beliefs were not confronted directly, but they were relativized, marginalized. It was by a selective emphasis upon certain elements of Christianity, in a vocabulary familiar
from childhood, that the idea was conveyed that these were the *real* essentials of the faith.

An anonymous article entitled "What Shall Be My Sabbath Reading?"
which appeared in Mann's *Common School Journal* of August 15, 1843, provides an interesting example of this approach.[61] Presumably it was by Mann
or at least so closely represented his views that he saw no need to attribute
it to anyone else; judging by style, it is intended for schoolteachers or students in the normal schools. The author expresses a resolution to

143

avoid what has a tendency to make me self-satisfied, or proud of my thoughts or opinions. . . . Is there not a danger of my becoming proud even of my religious opinions? . . . I must, therefore, not read anything that diminishes my charity for my fellow-creatures,—for their character, their purposes, or their opinions. Whatever is written in an uncharitable spirit, no matter what name it has, I will endeavour to avoid . . . [no less if it is] under the cloak of a sermon or a religious tract, than if it came under the name of scoffing or unbelief. . . . in the latter case, I should be on my guard; in the former, I should not. Whatever renders me uncharitable must be wanting in that Christian spirit.

Having thus warned against the publications of the tract societies, which frequently sought to put the orthodox on their guard against "infidelity" in the form of liberal religion, the author then condemns—in the name of tolerance—those books that assert human sinfulness and divine judgment, especially when associated with predestination. "Whatever book . . . makes me doubt of His goodness, His justice or His mercy, must be injurious, and ought to be avoided. . . . Those books must be bad or doubtful which make me selfish, or distrustful of my fellow-man, or despairing of his advancement."

Without ever mentioning his target, the author effectively cast doubt on the orthodox position and on the tracts and books that argued it. In the name of "charity" he made a concern about the truth of religious teachings appear un-Christian.

The indirect strategy was difficult to grasp and difficult to counter, but it was a singularly effective means of relativizing the claims of traditional Christianity—far more effective than the direct assaults of "infidelity," which then and throughout American history have elicited little favorable response. It offered little for the orthodox to object to, especially since Mann and the other reformers insisted upon their devotion to the use of the Bible in the schools. After all, Protestants believed in the individual right of conscience, informed by reading the Bible, as the final authority for understanding Christianity.

Lacking a tradition of doctrinal teaching by an authoritative church, it was difficult for such Congregationalists as Emerson Davis, Thomas Robbins, and Heman Humphrey to articulate an objection to the practices promoted by Mann. It was significantly an Episcopalian layman, Newton, who was the only member of the board to resign for religious reasons.

Summary

Public education in the United States has never been under centralized state control in the sense that this has evolved in France, and indeed Horace

Mann's Massachusetts has a particularly strong tradition of "local control" of schools. Formal structural considerations should not blind us, however, to the skilled and resolute efforts of Mann and other reformers to redefine the mission and content of public schooling and to do so in the name of a benevolent and unifying state. In so doing, they set up "sectarian religion" as the implacable foe of progress and social unity and presented themselves as its much persecuted opponents.

In fact, as the majority of the Committee on Education perceived clearly, the basic issue had to do not with particular religious views but with *who* should have the power to determine the values that would be the basis of instruction in each school. They were prevoyant enough to see, in the very small-scale activities of Horace Mann, a claim and a potential to set the agenda for local schools through shaping the very terms in which education would be discussed.

The collection and interpretation of educational statistics, ostensibly a perfectly neutral activity, had and continues to have the power to define perceptions of the salient strengths and weaknesses of the schools. The recommendation of reading material—and the banning of other material—had and continues to have the power to shape the range of topics that may be taught or discussed, and the framework in which they will be understood. The training—and eventually the certification—of teachers had and continues to have the power to determine what will occur in the classroom, far more than could any system of regulation or prescription.

The normal school, in particular, played an important part in the efforts of Mann and other "liberal Christians" to promote a form of "common school religion" that allegedly had no sectarian character but was in fact consistent with their own beliefs and profoundly subversive of that of their orthodox opponents. It was in the normal school, with its strong emphasis on the teaching of morality and on an atmosphere of liberal piety, that the teachers were formed upon whom the hopes of the education reformers rested.

Training teachers was thus an effective way of avoiding the problems that a direct assault upon local control of schools would have caused; it made it possible to argue, in all sincerity, that the common schools were under the direct oversight of local school committees elected by the parents and frequently chaired by an orthodox clergyman.[62] The real content of public education would be determined by the emerging profession of teachers, shaped by normal schools under control of the education reformers, and not by parents through their local representatives.

6

The Common School
as a Religious
Institution

FOR HORACE MANN and his fellow reformers of the common school, both religious and moral instruction were essential elements of sound education. It was beyond questioning that schools should seek to educate the heart and the will as well as to fill the mind with facts and skills. Their quarrel with orthodox Protestant and (a little later) with Roman Catholic opponents had to do with the nature and basis of such education rather than with whether it was necessary in common schools.

The connection between state leadership in popular education and an explicitly religious instructional content was by no means fortuitous. The primary goal of the common school crusade was to form the hearts of the next generation, to assure that they would, in the words of a leading Congregationalist journal, grow up "with the state, of the state and for the state." This goal was implicitly religious, and it was pursued with a proselytizing zeal by a generation of reformers for whom popular education was the supreme cause of the age—if not the culmination of the idealism of all ages.

Those critics who charged that Mann and others were somehow irreligious could not have been farther from the mark. It is true that the common school ideology was hostile to teaching the most distinctive doctrines of revealed religion, but to its expounders this was the only way to penetrate to the real intentions of "the Founder of Christianity," to offer a purified teaching of moral duty and spiritual exaltation.

As the religious *content* of schooling declined, in the first half of the nineteenth century, the religious *mission* of schooling actually became more important in the minds of the education reformers. These developments were directly related. It was as the school came to be seen as the primary bearer of a new civic faith, closely related to liberal Protestantism, that much of the traditional religious content of instruction was increasingly excluded as divisive and also as representing a lower form of religion than the "pure religion of heaven" taught in the school.

Background of the Religious Mission
of the School

Two streams merged in the expectation that common schools would stress religion and morality. One was the Puritan tradition of parish schooling, brought from England and reinforced by the specific prescriptions of the leaders of international Calvinism at the Synod of Dordt in the Netherlands (1618–19). Thus President Heman Humphrey of Amherst—later Mann's most valuable ally among the orthodox—stressed, in a bicentennial address about the Pilgrims in 1820, that

> To the religious education of their children . . . the early settlers of New England paid great and constant attention . . . and, in a word, made it their grand object, not to lay up riches for their offspring, but to "bring them up in the nurture and admonition of the Lord." . . . Whoever may think it worth his trouble, to look into the colonial laws of New England, will find the broad basis of our whole system of education, carefully laid by our wise and provident ancestors.[1]

Every contemporary discussion of the origins of the common school, including several by Mann, explicitly gives credit to the founders of the New England colonies.

Although colonial schools were under town rather than church control, the distinction is largely meaningless because ministers played the leading roles on local school committees, and instruction was permeated with the themes and content of Puritan theology.

These colonial schools had a religious function, then, but they did not thereby become *religious institutions*. The church was a religious institution, of course, and so was the family; both were based upon covenants to which God himself was a party and thus were of supreme importance in Puritan thinking about the divine economy. The civil society as a whole, the commonwealth, was in some sense a religious institution as well. The school, by contrast, was a necessary handmaid to church and family, one, indeed, that played an essential role in a well-ordered commonwealth, but it was not part of the great drama of salvation nor did it mediate the covenant mercies of God.

The second stream that contributed to the development of the nineteenth-century common school was the European liberal program developed in the course of the eighteenth-century Enlightenment. The American reformers were deeply interested in contemporary developments in Prussia and the Netherlands; thus Charles Brooks reported that as the result of discussions in 1834, "I fell in love with the Prussian system, and it seemed to possess me like a missionary angel. I gave myself to it, and . . . I resolved to *do* something about *State* normal schools."[2]

The educational reforms in Prussia during the period of intense national revival in reaction to defeat by Napoleon were inspired above all by Pestalozzi, celebrated by Fichte as the prophet of a new era in the development of humanity. As Henry Barnard's *American Journal of Education* told the American reformers, the aged Pestalozzi declared in 1818 that

> The artificial spirit of our times has also annihilated the influence which the religious feeling of our fathers exercised upon this centre of human happiness. This religious spirit . . . has sunk down amongst us into an insolent spirit of reasoning upon all that is sacred and divine; still we must also acknowledge that . . . the blessed spirit of the true christian doctrine appears to strike deeper root again in the midst of the corruption of our race . . . and, indeed, with regard to popular education, it is from this quarter alone that we can derive the expectation that we shall ever attain to measures really calculated to reach with sufficient efficiency the views, dispositions, appetites, and habits of our present mode of life, which we must look upon as the original source of our popular depravity and the misfortunes of our times.[3]

When Pestalozzi referred to "the true christian doctrine," however, he meant something very different from the Westminster Catechism; he had in mind a "religion of love" for which Jesus Christ was the great exemplar, not a religion of judgment and redemption for which he was the Savior.

A theology centered upon growth rather than conversion, upon the continuities between nature and grace, upon the human potential for growing into the likeness of God, was characteristic of the most influential school reformers of the early nineteenth century. Most of them, like Pestalozzi, were profoundly religious, even mystical. Some, like Friedrich Schleiermacher in Prussia and Petrus Hofstede de Groot in the Netherlands, were professional theologians. For them, the process of educating and enlightening the young heart gradually to piety and morality *necessitated* the rejection of traditional dogmatic teaching in the interest of a higher truth. It did not permit them to cooperate with others who sought to reach the heart through an emphasis upon the necessity for conversion and acceptance of atonement through the cross.

The expected role of religious teaching in Prussian schools is expressed in the education statutes of 1819, which state that

> The first vocation of every school is to train up the young in such a manner as to implant in their minds a knowledge of the relation of man to God, and at the same time to excite and foster both the will and the strength to

148

govern their lives after the spirit and the precepts of Christianity. Schools must early train children to piety.

This quotation is drawn, significantly, from Victor Cousin's *Report on the State of Public Instruction in Prussia* (Paris, 1833) in the translation by Sarah Austin, published in New York in 1835.[4] No other book, it is safe to say, had a more profound impact upon the developing program of educational reform in the United States, except perhaps Calvin Stowe's popularizations of Cousin's observations. Stowe observed, in a widely distributed little book on Prussian schools in 1836, that

> The *religious* spirit which pervades the whole of the Prussian system is greatly needed among ourselves.—Without religion—and, indeed, without the religion of the bible—there can be no efficient school discipline. . . . Religion is an essential element of human nature; and it must be cultivated, or there will be distortion of the intellect and affections. . . . there is enough of common ground here to unite all the different sects in this great object. . . . If our republic is to be prosperous and happy, all our children must be instructed in the elements of science and religion.[5]

Similarly, Massachusetts education reformer Charles Brooks wrote in 1837 that

> Our schools may help to develop the whole nature of man by cultivating the *moral* faculties. The affection of Love contains the great central principle of spiritual life and religious culture. . . . Man has a moral as evidently as a physical constitution. It is the implantation of divinity. . . . Let nothing go into their heads which has not been first filtered through their hearts. But, you ask, How can religion be introduced into our schools? I answer, as it was into every town school in Holland, Germany, Prussia. . . . The technicalities of Christian sects are not taught. By special statute they are prohibited. But those great and eternal principles of moral truth, which all sects allow to be indispensable in the grown-up Christian, are the principles which they carefully imbed in every youthful heart. . . . I wish that every school committee could feel that they have a divine command to bring up every child in the nurture and admonition of the Lord. Words cannot tell the loss our community has sustained in expelling the spiritual nature from our school houses. It is my firm conviction that the omission of christian instruction in our schools accounts for half the crime and more than half the unhappiness in society.[6]

That pillar of New England orthodoxy, Heman Humphrey, and the Unitarian minister Charles Brooks used the same biblical phrase about bringing up children in the "nurture and admonition of the Lord," even though they understood very differently the content of the Christian message. Orthodox

Protestants, although greatly in the majority among the population, found it impossible to form anything like a united front to insist upon religious teaching corresponding to their own convictions. They shared many of the anxieties of their liberal opponents about nation building, social tensions, and the assimilation of immigrants, but in addition they were reassured by the heavy use of a religious vocabulary and frame of reference in discussions of the mission of the common school. The education reformers, disproportionately Unitarians and other religious liberals, in fact adopted as their own the demand to increase the amount of "religious" teaching in the schools, and so the issue became thoroughly confused.

The proceedings of the American Institute of Instruction reveal how seriously this moral and religious mission was taken by the leading reformers who presented papers during the formative period of the common school. In 1831 we find Jacob Abbott lecturing on moral education, in 1835 R. Park on religious education, in 1836 J. H. Belcher on "Incitements to Moral and Intellectual Well-doing," in 1837 Joshua Bates on moral education, in 1839 Henry A. Miles on "Natural Theology as a Study in Schools," in 1842 George B. Emerson on moral education, in 1843 Heman Humphrey on "The Bible in Common Schools," and in 1844 Calvin Stowe on "The Religious Element in Education."[7]

Contemporaries found nothing incongruous in such language from a public official. The outstanding figure in Massachusetts public life, Horace Mann's patron Edward Everett, governor, senator, later ambassador to Great Britain and principal speaker at Gettysburg, insisted in a speech in 1837 that there was

> one living fountain, which must water every part of the social garden, or its beauty withers and fades away. Of course I mean . . . moral and religious, as well as mental education. . . . It is the elemental fire, which must lighten, warm, and cheer us, as men and citizens.[8]

It is fair to say that the origins and justification of the common school, as it developed in the 1840s and as it became a reigning symbol and expression of the developing American democracy through the nineteenth century, cannot be understood without coming to terms with this "moral and religious" emphasis. The very power of the idea of the common school had much to do with its perceived role as the "one living fountain" of meaning and inspiration, as a sort of universal church.

This is not to accept the usual historical judgment that the common school was a Protestant institution; indeed, contemporary critics like Charles Hodge of Princeton were correct when they saw the common school as profoundly subversive of the beliefs of most Protestants. Nor is it necessarily true, as David Tyack too readily assumes, that Mann's generation of educational reformers were "almost all . . . deeply religious men."[9] Whatever the individual convictions of any of this group, they clearly did not feel that they were promoting their own beliefs; the recurrence of the theme of the necessity of a religious element in education can best be understood as an expression of their understanding of social necessity.

To understand why religion figures so prominently in the early discussions of the common school it is essential to ask what meaning was assigned to "religion" by the education reformers and why that was so important to them. The reformers and their opponents tended to talk past each other, while they each insisted on the importance of religion, because they drew upon very different sources in reaching this conclusion. They are in fact an illustration of Karl Mannheim's remark that "the same word, or the same concept in most cases, means very different things when used by differently-situated persons."[10]

We can best approach the question of the meaning assigned to the concept "religion" by describing briefly the role that Mann and others proposed that religion would play in the common school and thereby in American society. Contrary to the accusations of some of their opponents, the reformers were not primarily concerned to promote Protestantism or even Unitarianism. That would have been contrary to the elitist and increasingly complacent character of Unitarianism after about 1825; indeed, William Ellery Channing, the decisive figure in the development of Unitarianism and Mann's pastor and friend, boasted that "there is not on earth a body of men who possess less of the spirit of proselytism than the [Unitarian] ministers of this town and vicinity,"[11] and their principal organ, the *Christian Examiner*, carried long discussions of the mission of Unitarianism to serve as a vanguard of the "pure and spiritual religion" that would eventually triumph in every denomination.

The primary objective of "common school religion," in the minds of Mann and other reformers, was social integration through the inculcation of certain common beliefs selected for their presumably uplifting character. The passionate conviction with which the reformers advanced this program was a case of "false consciousness" in the sense described by Mannheim: "knowledge is distorted and ideological when it fails to take account of the new realities applying to a situation, and when it attempts to conceal them by thinking of them in categories which are inappropriate."[12]

Briefly stated, the reformers attempted to deal with the real (though exaggerated) threat of social disunity, to which they themselves were contributing through their abandonment of the religious convictions of previous generations, by acting as though a newly defined "religion" rooted in no community of faith could serve to reintegrate the society. They attempted to apply to a period of intense religious competition a program appropriate to periods of unity. As a result, the common school was never truly common in the sense of enjoying the support of all parents and—despite the tremendous achievements of the next hundred years—public education in the United States has continued to promise more social integration than it has been able to deliver. The present crisis of confidence in public education reflects a flaw in the foundation that Mann and others laid.

THE REJECTION OF "SECTARIAN" TEACHING. It is possible to gain a clue to the concerns and intentions of the reformers by noting how consistently their discussion of the importance of religious teaching is accompanied by repudiation of any sectarian elements.

A controversy arose during Mann's years as secretary of the Board of Education over whether books reflecting the doctrines considered essential by many of the orthodox could be used in common schools. Mann and the board based their rejection of such books on an 1827 statute which had attracted little attention previously. This statute authorized school committees to purchase books for classroom use, but provided that "said committee shall never direct any school books to be purchased or used, in any of the schools under their superintendence, which are calculated to favour any particular religious sect or tenet."[13] When opponents argued, in 1844, that this statute was not intended to ban Christian texts such as had been used since colonial days but only to restrict those of a controversial and divisive nature, Mann received support from a prominent citizen of Worcester, Samuel Burnside, who had drafted the bill adopted in 1827. It had been the understanding of its supporters, Burnside wrote, that

> upon the ground presented by the section it was believed all sects of christians might walk harmoniously together—and that children and youth would be well fitted, by such instruction, to judge for themselves, in after life, what system of disputed doctrines was best entitled to belief.[14]

This position by no means reflected an opposition to religious teaching, properly understood. In a lecture to the American Institute of Instruction in 1832 Burnside described his purpose further; it was "to contend earnestly that the moral or religious nature of man (and in whatever I say, I make no distinction between them, for I know of none) is a proper subject of school education." This association of religious and moral elements in education is characteristic of the reformers; it is marked in the passage from Charles Brooks quoted above. On the one hand, they wished to give primary emphasis, in religion, to the prescriptive elements on which, they believed, there were no differences among Christians of various denominations; on the other, they preferred to clothe morality in a sentimental religiosity, presenting it as a matter of the heart rather than of the head.

Burnside then went on to reject, implicitly, the contemporary orthodox Protestant emphasis upon conversion, in terms that anticipate the influential discussion of "Christian nurture" by Horace Bushnell:

> If it be true . . . that piety is the natural fruit of religious instruction, and is seldom, perhaps never produced by extraordinary, supernatural influences, then this education assumes an interest, as vast as the eternal destinies of our race. . . . our desire is only to train children to the practice of Christian virtues from Christian motives; that is, from reverence of God, an habitual sense of his perfections, his presence, and of personal accountability, and from a love also of country, and the whole human family. . . . This is all I mean by a religious education, or a religious character, and whatever more is attached to these terms by others, it will not be denied, that such a character is wanted for the concerns of this life, and I would humbly trust, that it is some preparation for a better.[15]

Another of the lectures to the American Institute of Instruction, perhaps on the same occasion, called upon teachers to teach children

> that in the performance of their daily labors, the discharge of their social relations, the government of their hearts and lives—in all this, if done in the right spirit, they are proving themselves Christians, inasmuch as they follow the example of the Saviour. . . . all this you may accomplish without proscribing the tenets, or offending the prejudices, of any sect of professed Christians. . . . Their doctrinal views will ripen with time, and may undergo changes; their practical principles should be fixed at once, and remain ever after immutable as the laws of nature.

Once again, morality is considered the common ground upon which all Christians can unite—and religious truth is presented as evolving and unfixed, which is consistent with a primary emphasis of Unitarian teaching at the time.[16]

The Unitarian *Christian Examiner* returned repeatedly to the theme of the common school and its religious and moral mission. In 1831 an article urged that

> the course and the fate of this country depend, under Providence, on the character of the mass of its inhabitants. . . . the moral education of all classes, and all ages, but most particularly of the poor and the young, is the one thing needful.[17]

It was this journal, in 1833, that published William Ellery Channing's significant review of the *American Annals of Education and Instruction*.

Channing called for state leadership and for emulation of Prussian efforts "for the intellectual and moral improvement of her subjects."[18] As Horace Mann set to work as Secretary of the Board of Education, the *Christian Examiner* cheered him on: "Let the work go on, and some of the worst fears entertained for our country will be relieved; especially as there is an increasing disposition to make this popular education—moral—as well as intellectual."[19]

As the name of the publication suggests, Unitarians at this time continued to consider themselves Christians despite the refusal of the orthodox to recognize that claim. Unitarians believed that they were preserving the essence of Christianity, purged of "sectarian" and divisive doctrines which—they argued—were no part of the message of Jesus. This essential Christianity could and should be taught in the common schools, since it represented a "religion of heaven" to which no right-minded parent could object, whatever additional doctrines he might hold privately and teach to his children at home. After all, did not Jesus himself sum up the Law and the Prophets in the two Great Commandments to love God and love one's neighbor?

This argument was advanced by others besides Unitarians. In 1839 the *Christian Examiner* published an enthusiastic review of a book by an Episcopalian minister, Benjamin Peers, urging the creation of a system of national compulsory education for the United States. Peers argued that "a system of national education suited to the United States must aim, above all things, to impress a virtuous character upon the rising generation, and by means of the Bible as the instrument."[20] The reviewer comments that

> Mr. Peers has much to say upon the need of religious culture in common schools, and in all that he says shows great good sense, and what seems to us a singular liberality in a clergyman of the Episcopal Church. He is entirely opposed to the introduction of any of the dogmas of controversial theology into schools.[21]

After all, the reviewer observes,

> So long as Christians regard Christianity as based on controverted dogmas,—so long as the people regard the Church as a selfish party, or band of parties, so long the Bible will be, if not absolutely kept out of common schools, used with much timidity and jealousy, and with little good effect. . . . We do actually believe, that the good yeomanry of our country would be more likely to agree upon a system of moral and religious instruction for schools than our clergy would. They would discern, that the love of God and man, justice, truth, temperance, and even the eternal life, were principles acknowledged by the great mass of the church and people;

and insisting upon these, they would leave controversialists to dispute at will about their -*isms* and -*ologies*.

This line of argument, endlessly repeated by Horace Mann among others, was to prove brilliantly successful. It is one of the ironies of the situation that it was put forward by an intellectual elite, perhaps the most distinguished and coherent our nation has ever known, venturing to speak for the "common man" who, so the argument implied, had been deluded into his persistent orthodoxy by the fanaticism and self-interest of the orthodox clergy.

THE CONCERN ABOUT NATIONAL UNITY. The argument proved successful because many of the orthodox were also seeking a basis for retaining positive religious and moral teaching in common schools, convinced that this was essential to the process of building a single nation and people. Even before heavy Irish and continental immigration began in the 1840s there was a widespread feeling that national unity was threatened. This was a period of countless sects and enthusiasms, a period also when Jacksonian democracy—and such notorious radicals as Robert Owen and Fanny Wright—seemed to threaten church as well as property. A report to the Massachusetts Senate in 1838 pointed out the threat of an atheism that was hostile

> to all decency and regularity, to the peace of all communities, and the safety of all governments. . . . Atheism is a levelling system. In religion and in politics, it labors to overthrow all ancient customs—all established institutions.[22]

It is significant that these remarks were made by a Whig-dominated committee, since the Whig leadership was largely Unitarian; Horace Mann had just resigned as Senate president. Although opposed to orthodoxy, this Whig elite had an equal horror of anything that might undermine what they regarded as the essential religious underpinnings of popular democracy. It was all very well for free inquiry to flourish at Harvard, but social order and harmony required a religious sanction. Through the teaching of religion and morality in the common school, they believed, the popular mind could be secured for a sort of progressive conservatism; by excluding all "sectarian" elements, everything that tied religion to the traditional and mutually exclusive communities of faith, a primary cause of social conflict could be gradually eliminated and a new unity of heart could be developed among the American people, guaranteeing liberty and property alike. Arthur Schlesinger, Jr.'s comment that "the Whigs, in scuttling Federalism, re-

155

placed it by a social philosophy founded, not on ideas, but on subterfuges and sentimentalities"[23] is borne out by their educational program.

Though atheism was regarded as a social and political threat by the orthodox as well as by their liberal opponents—as witness Lyman Beecher's celebrated lecture on "political atheism"—the liberals had an equal concern about what they feared would be the divisive social effects of religious enthusiasm. Nathan Hatch has described how,

> At the dawn of the nineteenth century, the Federalist citadel of Essex County, Massachusetts, witnessed a major assault on its well-bred and high-toned culture. Religious enthusiasm had taken hold among the common people and its rude challenge to authority dismayed even the tolerant Jeffersonian diarist William Bentley of Salem. As late as 1803, Bentley had confided smugly that Essex County remained virtually free of sects. During the next five years, he watched with dismay the lower orders of his community championing "religious convulsions," "domestic fanaticism," and "Meeting-Mania." . . . What Bentley found most appalling was that "the rabble" not only noised abroad strange doctrine but actually went beyond what they were told, attempting "to explain, condemn and reveal" religious matters. The people, he groaned, were doing theology for themselves.[24]

This was a period of religious revivals, starting soon after the turn of the century and continuing until the eve of the Civil War, with some Congregationalist churches becoming more orthodox as others moved toward Unitarianism, and the rapid spread of Baptist, Freewill Baptist, Methodist, and Universalist churches. The Baptists alone organized over a hundred new churches in Massachusetts between 1800 and 1813.[25]

That this concern over religious sectarianism is not altogether groundless may be seen from the growth of denominationalism in Massachusetts during this period. To the traditional Congregational dominance, with a significant Baptist minority stemming primarily from the Great Awakening, an array of additional forms of Protestantism was added, with the first signs of what eventually would be a Roman Catholic dominance:

Churches	1785	1858
Congregationalist	330	490
Baptist	68	287
Episcopalian	11	65
Roman Catholic	1	64
Unitarian	0	170
Universalist	0	135
Methodist	0	310
Other	0	130

Note that this does not reflect *membership*, since church size varied widely between a large urban Roman Catholic parish, for example, and a little country Methodist or Universalist congregation. In terms of organized churches it is nevertheless significant that the share of the largest denomination dropped in this period from more than 80 percent to less than 30 percent.[26]

Political developments enhanced this anxiety about potential division in the new nation. The Hartford Convention of 1814 had raised the specter of New England secession from the Union, while the agitation of Calhoun and other southerners over the tariff in the late 1820s foreshadowed the secession of 1861. The response of Massachusetts Senator Daniel Webster in a celebrated speech in 1830 expressed his fear of seeing the sun shine "on the broken and dishonored fragments of a once glorious Union; on States dissevered, discordant, belligerent; on a land rent with civil feuds, or drenched, it may be, in fraternal blood!"[27]

Sectional discord was not the only problem; the political controversies of this period centered, as Lee Benson has shown in his study of New York State, on differing views of the role of government in promoting public virtue and harmony. Democrats charged that the Whig reform program— given classic expression by Horace Mann and the Board of Education— was elitist and interfered with the social order anchored in local realities and mores. The detailed analysis by Kaestle and Vinovskis of the votes to abolish the board demonstrates that the opposition to Mann in the Massachusetts legislature was along political and social lines rather than being based upon "religious bigotry" (as Mann himself claimed). It reflected a traditional resistance by the predominantly agricultural sections of the commonwealth to the hegemony of the merchants and lawyers of the Boston area. This was in no sense a resistance to education as such; rather, it was resistance to the attempt to use the common school as the instrument for developing a new unifying faith.

Thus there was a real threat to vested interests, one of which the reformers were deeply aware. "Demagogues, appealing to the worst motives in men, always lurked in the fears of Unitarian moralists, ready to pounce upon the land and destroy its carefully nurtured equilibrium." No wonder that these strains were of deep concern to the reformers who sought to make the common school an instrument to create social harmony far more than to teach literacy and other skills.[28]

In addition, Boston experienced anti-Catholic mob violence by workingmen in 1834 and antiabolitionist violence by a middle-class mob in 1835. "A climate of disorder obtained . . . which seemed to be moving the nation to the edge of disaster."[29]

Historian Russel Blaine Nye comments, of this period in the development of the United States, that

> The creation of solidarity out of variety was a vital task for the new society, as its shapers clearly realized; their adoption of the Roman *fasces* as a national symbol had real pertinence to their problems. The men of the period were acutely aware of the need for creating a stable, cohesive society. . . . the United States was by 1830 a tangled skein of loyalties to sentiments, symbols, sections, localities, groups, political divisions and subdivisions, and to economic, ethnic, ideological, and other interests, all of which held the individual in a sort of loose social orbit. *E pluribus unum* was not an idly chosen motto for the society of the new Republic.[30]

The Problem of Horace Mann's Religion

Whether Mann was "deeply religious" we perhaps will never be able to say, but there can be no question that he was both repelled and attracted by religion. To say that his advocacy of religious teaching served an ideological purpose is by no means to assert that it was arrived at as a matter of cool political calculation. The energy with which he entered into controversies over religion in the common school shows how deeply and painfully the subject touched him.

Mann's position on religion in the common school and the controversies that occurred during his years as secretary of the Board of Education have been the subject of many studies. These include, in addition to the general histories of American education, which invariably cover this as a key issue, Sherman M. Smith's *Relation of the State to Religious Education in Massachusetts* (1926), Raymond Culver's *Horace Mann and Religion in the Massachusetts Public Schools* (1929), Neil G. McCluskey's *Public Schools and Moral Education* (1958), William Kailer Dunn's *What Happened to Religious Education? The Decline of Religious Teaching in the Public Elementary School, 1776–1861* (1958), Charles Bidwell's "Moral Significance of the Common School" (1966), Jonathan Messerli's *Horace Mann: A Biography* (1972), and Kaestle and Vinovskis's *Education and Social Change in Nineteenth Century Massachusetts* (1980). Recently, Samuel Blumenfeld's *Is Public Education Necessary?* (1981) has gone over much the same ground from a perspective far more critical of Mann than any of the earlier studies.

No useful purpose would be served by covering this material again. Our concern here is not so much with Mann's own role, or the social and political circumstances that permitted his position to triumph, as with the significance of the positions that he and others took, what religion in the public school meant to them, and what lasting imprint their efforts had upon American education—and the strains it is experiencing today.

The primary source for Mann's personal religious convictions is the biography prepared by his second wife, the former Mary Peabody, after his death. The book includes a long extract from a letter Mann wrote to a friend, recounting his formative experiences growing up in Franklin, Massachusetts. The strongly orthodox teaching of Nathanael Emmons (1745–1840) produced a reaction, first of anxiety and then of rejection, according to this account. Mann writes,

> More than by toil, or by the privation of any natural taste, was the inward joy of my youth blighted by theological inculcations. . . . He was an extra or hyper-Calvinist,—a man of pure intellect, whose logic was never softened in its severity by the infusion of any kindliness of sentiment. He expounded all the doctrines of total depravity, election, and reprobation, and not only the eternity, but the extremity, of hell-torments, unflinchingly and in their most terrible significance; while he rarely if ever descanted upon the joys of heaven, and never, to my recollection, upon the essential and necessary happiness of a virtuous life. . . . The consequences upon my mind and happiness were disastrous in the extreme. . . . I remained in this condition of mind until I was twelve years of age. I remember the day, the hour, the place, the circumstances . . . when, in an agony of despair, I broke the spell that had bound me. From that day, I began to construct the theory of Christian ethics and doctrine . . . which, with such modifications as advancing age and a wider vision must impart, I still retain, and out of which my life has flowed.[31]

Mann's characterization of Emmons, though not inaccurate, fails to do justice to one of the most distinguished of the "New Divinity men" who carried forward the theological work of Jonathan Edwards and prepared the ground for the Second Great Awakening of the early nineteenth century. Historian Sydney Ahlstrom refers to Emmons as "a highly distinctive, almost eccentric theological genius" who "contributed creatively to the single most brilliant and most continuous indigenous theological tradition that America has produced."[32] At a time when the Calvinist theological tradition had run very shallow in Switzerland, the Netherlands, France and Germany and was able to put up little resistance there to either liberalism or revivalistic enthusiasm, the New Divinity men in New England continued to insist upon and to develop a doctrine centered on the sovereignty of God and the need for salvation not dependent on human righteousness.

In such sermons as "Moral Inability of Sinners" Emmons preached not an iron determinism but rather the necessity for a radical change of heart, worked by the Spirit of God, after an honest recognition of the depravity of the unconverted nature. Sinners, he insisted, "do not know that the plague of their own hearts lies in their total selfishness, and entire regard to their own personal safety and happiness. . . . whatever attempt they make to serve God, their ultimate design in it all is, not to serve God, but to serve themselves."[33] Only by caring for the glory of God above one's own salvation could one honor him properly. The criticism often expressed by Mann and other religious liberals, that the orthodox selfishly sought only their own eternal welfare rather than the happiness of others, finds no support in Emmons's sermons.

We can imagine Emmons's sermons providing solid nourishment to such congregations as Horace Bushnell described from his youth in rural Connecticut:

> They think of nothing, in fact, save what meets their intelligence and enters into them by that method. They appear like men who have digestion for strong meat, and have no conception that trifles more delicate can be of any account to feed the system. Nothing is dull that has the matter in it, nothing long that has not exhausted the matter. . . . Under their hard and . . . stolid faces, great thoughts are brewing, and these keep them warm. . . . give them anything high enough, and the tough muscle of their inward man will be climbing sturdily into it; and if they go away having something to think of, they have had a good day.[34]

On the other hand, it is easy to appreciate that such demanding and rather bleak preaching could provide little nourishment and the possibility of confusion for a child, and that growing up in the congregation of a hyperintellectual minister more concerned with theological controversy than with the concerns of daily life (Emmons "once refused to replace a fallen bar on his fence, lest it start him down the road to worldly preoccupations"!)[35] could provoke a rejection of the whole orthodox system.

Emmons would certainly not have preached "the essential and necessary happiness of a virtuous life," as Mann complained, and the complaint says a great deal about the facile optimism of the emerging liberal religion. It was unfair, on the other hand, to suggest that his preaching was not concerned with what Emmons called "Christian duties"; the essential difference was that Emmons took care to deny that good deeds possessed any merit for justifying a sinner, whereas for Mann they were the essence of Christianity and the drama of salvation had no real significance.

Hostility to Calvinism, as represented by Emmons's teaching, was a consistent theme throughout Mann's subsequent life. In response to an early attack on the Board of Education, questioning the exclusion of teaching about sin and salvation in the schools, he wrote in his diary:

Probably they will have no difficulty in making out that the Board is irreligious; for with them religion is synonymous with Calvin's five points. As
for St. James's definition of it, "Pure religion and undefiled is to visit the
fatherless and widows in their affliction," etc.; and that other definition,
"Do justice, love mercy, and walk humbly with thy God,"—the Orthodox
have quite outgrown these obsolete nations, and have got a religion which
can at once gratify their self-esteem and destructiveness. They shall not
unclench me from my labors for mankind.[36]

The charge is unfair, as Mann must have known. Not only were some of
his strongest supporters and allies—like Heman Humphrey and Thomas
Robbins—squarely among the orthodox, but this was the era when the
"evangelical united front" supported a bewildering range of good works
and reform efforts. It is significant that he found it necessary to condemn
his opponents on these grounds, however; he is not setting orthodoxy
against a secular rationalism but pitting two expressions of religion against
one another. Even in his private diary, Mann was concerned to present
himself as "religious" and indeed as religiously superior to his opponents.

Historians have tended to accept Mann's version of how he came to be
in opposition to the prevailing religious views, as a result of youthful emancipation from the oppression of a narrow fanaticism. He wrote in one letter,

I feel constantly, and more and more deeply, what an unspeakable calamity
a Calvinistic education is. What a dreadful thing it was to me! If it did not
succeed in making that horrible thing, a Calvinist, it did succeed in de-
priving me of that filial love for God, that tenderness, that sweetness, that
intimacy, that desiring, nestling love, which I say it is natural the child
should feel toward a Father who combines all excellence.[37]

Although this testimony to a deeply held aversion based upon personal
experience should not be discounted—and indeed calls into question
Mann's public protestations of benevolent neutrality toward all religious
beliefs—it is not necessary to have recourse to a psychological explanation
for the conflict that developed between Mann and his opponents.

The conflict between religious liberalism and orthodoxy was the leading
drama in Massachusetts for more than a generation, until abolition and
immigration came to replace it in the public consciousness in the late 1840s.
Given Mann's career pattern, as a small-town boy of modest circumstances
but outstanding gifts who made a career in law and politics in alliance with
the Whig elite, it would have been anomalous if he had *not* been a religious
liberal. As we saw in the last chapter, most of the members of the original
Board of Education (all of those from the vicinity of Boston) were Unitarians; they shared with Mann an optimistic, moralizing tendency. If Mann's

161

personal experiences were significant—and there is no reason to believe they were not—they were the experiences of an entire emerging social class.

What is entirely missing from Mann's various allusions to the contemporary religious scene is reference to the dynamics within orthodoxy. Orthodoxy was by no means on the defensive, as it had been during the era of the Revolution. The old religious consensus had indeed broken down, but liberalism was not permitted to enjoy its victory unchallenged. Mann preferred to see orthodoxy as a relic of a past age in human development, but in fact evangelicalism was evolving and expanding rapidly. The founding of Andover Theological Seminary in 1808 and of Park Street Church in Boston in 1809 was a direct response to Unitarian advances. A powerful revival that began in 1823 and the foundation of the orthodox journal *The Spirit of the Pilgrims* in 1828 gave the orthodox a sense that the initiative had passed to them. As Lyman Beecher wrote to one of his sons in 1823,

> There is unquestionably a great and auspicious change going on in Boston in respect to evangelical doctrine and piety. The orthodox have for years been delving in their Sabbath-schools and other evangelical efforts, and their zeal, and strength, and momentum, as to preparing the way for a revival are noble, and they are reaping their reward.

Not that these orthodox advances passed unchallenged; Beecher was to recall that

> There was an intense malignant enragement for a time. Showers of lies were rained about us every day. The Unitarians with all their principles of toleration, were as really a persecuting power while they had the ascendancy as ever existed. Wives and daughters were forbidden to attend our meetings; the whole weight of political, literary, and social influence was turned against us, and the lash of ridicule laid without stint.[38]

As we shall see, Mann shared with Beecher an inclination to describe the liberal/orthodox rivalry in dramatic terms.

The conflicts over the religious mission of the common school were not, as Mann presented them, a struggle between an outmoded and moribund (but still malignant) orthodoxy on the one hand and the forces of progress and love of humanity on the other but rather a conflict between two dynamic movements, both very different from their eighteenth-century predecessors, each determined to shape the mind of the growing nation.

We have noted that Mann saw himself as more truly religious than his opponents, rather than as a proponent of secularity. What was the content of his religious program for and through the common school?

MANN'S OFFICIAL STATEMENTS. In his *First Report* of February 1838 Mann referred to the necessity of an "entire exclusion of religious teaching" in the common schools, lest "the school house may cease to be neutral ground between those different portions of society, now so vigorously contending against each other on a variety of questions of social and national duty." This exclusion of "vexed and complicated questions"

> enhances and magnifies, a thousand fold, the indispensableness of moral instruction and training. Entirely to discard the inculcation of the great doctrines of morality and of natural theology has a vehement tendency to drive mankind into opposite extremes; to make them devotees on one side or profligates on the other; each about equally regardless of the true constituents of human welfare. Against a tendency to these fatal extremes, the beautiful and sublime truths of ethics and of natural religion have a poising power.[39]

Mann thus saw the function of the common school as prevention not only of the breakdown of morality but also of the excesses of religious enthusiasm. Through teaching natural religion, the disturbing power of revealed religion would be reduced in the rising generation; they would not, like their parents, be "devotees."

In order to provide "moral instruction and training" in common schools, Mann urged the need for

> a book pourtraying, with attractive illustration and with a simplicity adapted to the simplicity of childhood, the obligations arising from social relationships . . . supplying children, at an early age, with simple and elementary notions of right and wrong in feeling and in conduct.

Later that year Mann gave a lecture on "The Necessity of Education in a Republican Government," in which he defined education as "such a culture of our moral affections and religious sensibilities, as in the course of nature and Providence shall lead to a subjection or conformity of all our appetites, propensities, and sentiments to the will of Heaven."[40] It seems evident that in this instance, at least, he was clothing a program of moral education and character formation in the religious vocabulary of the day, without proposing any distinct program of religious instruction. There is no mention of the use of the Bible, which would become a favorite theme later as his program came under increasing attack.

He made a similar use of religious vocabulary in a lecture delivered in 1840, entitled "What God Does and What He Leaves for Man to Do in the Work of Education." "If, then, God is Truth,—if God is Love,—teach the child above all things to seek for Truth, and to abound in Love." He became more specific about the positive content of instruction, calling upon teachers in common schools to keep children

> unspotted from the world, that is, uncontaminated by its vices; to train them up to the love of God and the love of man; to make the perfect example of Jesus Christ lovely in their eyes; and to give to all so much of religious instruction as is compatible with the rights of others and with the genius of our government.

He added that "when the children arrive at years of maturity" they should be commended "to that inviolable prerogative of private judgment and of self-direction which, in a Protestant and a Republican country, is the acknowledged birthright of every human being."[41]

In his *Third Report* (1840), Mann observed that

> any attempt to make the public schools (supported as they are by the common expense for the common benefit) an instrument for advancing or depressing the opinions of any sect of christians would meet what it would merit, the prompt rebuke of every considerate citizen.

This did not mean that the teaching of religion could safely be neglected; to the contrary, Mann expressed confidence that religion could and indeed must be taught.

> Although it may not be easy theoretically, to draw the line between those views of religious truth and of christian faith which are common to all, and may, therefore, with propriety be inculcated in school, and those which, being peculiar to individual sects, are therefore by law excluded; still it is believed that no practical difficulty occurs in the conduct of our schools in this respect.[42]

The following year Mann boasted of the universal support that this nonsectarian religious teaching enjoyed, arguing from the silence of those who might have held contrary views. In the reports submitted by local school committees,

> a majority of which, probably, were prepared by clergymen, belonging to all the various denominations in the State, there was not one which advocated the introduction of sectarian instruction or sectarian books into our public schools; while, with accordant views,—as a single voice coming from a single heart,—they urge, they insist, they demand that the great axioms of a Christian morality shall be seculously taught.[43]

His description of this unanimity, he reported in 1842, had drawn

> the applause of friends of education far and wide and had been quoted with warm commendation, in leading newspapers and periodicals of ad-

verse parties, both in our sister States and in foreign countries. The Commonwealth of Massachusetts has been congratulated on having reached that point in civilisation where men of all parties can cooperate for the promotion of a common object of acknowledged value, notwithstanding a want of uniformity on other subjects.[44]

In his *Seventh Report* (1844) Mann drew largely upon his extended visit, the previous year, to schools on the Continent and in Britain. He echoed Calvin Stowe's enthusiasm for Prussia and for the "absence of sectarian instruction, or endeavours at proselytism" in mandatory Bible lessons in some schools, while correcting Stowe by pointing out the denominational character of most Prussian schools.[45] In arguing that religious instruction, at its best, required no "formulas of a creed," Mann revealed much about his own concept of how it should be provided:

> It is when a teacher has no knowledge of the wonderful works of God, and of the benevolence of the design in which they were created; when he has no power of explaining and applying the beautiful incidents in the lives of prophets and apostles, and especially the perfect example which is given to men in the life of Jesus Christ; it is then that, in attempting to give religious instruction he is, as it were, constrained to recur again and again to the few words of sentences of his form of faith, whatever that faith may be.

The schools of England and Scotland, in which "religious creeds, and forms of faith, and modes of worship were directly taught," were, in his judgment, far inferior to Massachusetts schools in teaching "the common doctrines and injunctions of morality, and the meaning of the preceptive parts of the Gospel."[46]

Two years later he returned to this theme, asking rhetorically, "are there not moral means for the renovation of mankind, which have never yet been applied?" It was the fault of the clergy, through the centuries, that they had neglected the early moral training of youth. In the new era in the history of the world, which "opened with the war of the American Revolution and with the adoption of the constitution of the United States," he wrote, "we must expect a new series of developments in human character and conduct."[47] These were being promoted, above all, by the common school and the education reformers who were shaping its moral mission.

> Directly and indirectly, the influences of the Board of Education have been the means of increasing, to a great extent, the amount of religious instruction given in our schools. Moral training, or the application of religious principles to the duties of life, should be its inseparable accompaniment. No community can long subsist, unless it has religious principle as the

foundation of moral action; nor unless it has moral action as the super-structure of religious principle.[48]

Similarly, in a compendium of Massachusetts education law and policy, in his *Tenth Report*, Mann observed that "the policy of the State promotes not only secular but religious instruction."[49] As an indication of the support that Mann enjoyed, the Massachusetts legislature directed, just after his resignation in 1849, that 10,000 copies of this *Tenth Report* be printed and distributed to "exhibit a just and correct view of the Common School system of Massachusetts."

Under continuing attack for neglect of the distinctive teachings of ortho-dox Christians, those shared by most Protestants and Roman Catholics, Mann made even stronger claims in his *Eleventh Report* (1848), in which the major section was headed: "The Power of Common Schools to Redeem the State from Social Vices and Crimes."

> It is not known that there is, or ever has been, a member of the Board of Education who would not be disposed to recommend the daily reading of the Bible, devotional exercises, and the constant inculcation of the pre-cepts of Christian morality in all the Public schools. . . . as a matter of fact, I suppose there is not, at the present time, a single town in the Common-wealth in whose schools it is not read. . . . By introducing the Bible, they introduce what all its believers hold to be the rule of faith and practice; and although, by excluding theological systems of human origin, they may exclude a peculiarity which one denomination believes to be true, they do but exclude what other denominations hold to be erroneous. . . . If it be the tendency of all parties and sects, to fasten the mind upon what is peculiar to each, and to withdraw it from what is common to all, these provisions of the law counter-work that tendency. They turn the mind towards that which produces harmony, while they withdraw it from sources of discord.[50]

These "peculiarities," of course, included the belief that the death and resurrection of Jesus Christ were of decisive and irreplaceable importance for each person, a doctrine which, according to Mann, could not be taught in the schools. He appears sincerely not to have recognized the extent to which his own belief in human goodness and the centrality of morality to religion constituted an alternative faith—essentially that preached Sunday by Sunday in Unitarian churches—which could not fail to conflict with orthodox beliefs, whether of Protestants or of Roman Catholics.

In support for his contention that the common school was capable of achieving a moral revolution in society, Mann cited letters that he had received from a number of prominent educators to whom he had written.

One assured him that, "with teachers properly trained in Normal Schools and with such a popular disposition towards schools as wise legislation might effect," 95 percent of "the immoralities which afflict society" could be eradicated. Another was not willing to concede the possibility of failure in even one case in a hundred; yet another could not recall a single former pupil "who had been with me long enough to receive a decided impression, whose life is not honorable and useful." Several stressed the importance of reaching *all* the children and thus "training up the whole community to intelligence and virtue." Miss Catherine Beecher (Lyman's daughter and Calvin Stowe's sister-in-law) went so far as to promise that if

> *all* the children at the age of four shall be placed, six hours a day, for twelve years, under the care of teachers having the same views that I have . . . I have no hesitation in saying,—I do not believe that *none*, no, *not a single one*, would fail of proving a respectable and prosperous member of society; nay, more, I believe that every one would, at the close of life, find admission into the world of endless peace and joy.[51]

Fortified by these assurances, Mann went on to call, for the first time, for universal, compulsory popular education in the interest of social progress and virtue. After all, any children left out of the benefits of the common school would have "a poisonous influence . . . upon all the rest"; therefore, "universality in the end to be accomplished demands universality in the means to be employed." He expressed confidence that such a system— which he urged the next session of the legislature to enact—would enjoy the support of the great majority "and would thus leave but few of those unnatural cases,—of those parents who are *not* parents,—to be dealt with compulsively." This was, for Mann, the culmination of the whole reform impulse of the age, since

> in universal education, every "follower of God and friend of human kind" will find the only sure means of carrying forward that particular reform to which he is devoted. In whatever department of philanthropy he may be engaged, he will find that department to be only a segment of the great circle of beneficence, of which *Universal Education* is centre and circumference; and that it is only when these segments are fitly joined together, that the wheel of Progress can move harmoniously and resistlessly onward.[52]

With this continuing concern for the role of the common school in promoting social reform through inculcation of high religious and moral ideals, it was appropriate that the last of his celebrated manifestoes, the *Twelfth Report* (1849), was devoted primarily to defining why and how these should be taught.

"Moral education," he wrote, "is a primal necessity of social existence," yet

> Education has never yet been brought to bear with one hundredth part of its potential force, upon the natures of children and, through them, upon the character of men, and of the race. . . . Here, then, is a new agency whose powers are but just beginning to be understood, and whose mighty energies, hitherto, have been but feebly invoked.

Returning to the theme of the *Eleventh Report*, Mann claimed that

> if all the children in the community, from the age of four years to that of sixteen, could be brought within the reformatory and elevating influences of good schools, the dark host of private vices and public crimes which now embitter domestic peace and stain the civilization of the age might, in ninety-nine cases in every hundred, be banished from the world.[53]

Having recapitulated his views on social control and progress through moral education in less than ten pages, Mann devoted the remaining forty pages of his final report to a discussion of religious education. He began by stating his conviction

> that this grand result, in Practical Morality, is a consummation of blessedness that can never be attained without Religion; and that no community will ever be religious, without a Religious Education. Both these propositions, I regard as eternal and immutable truths. Devoid of religious principles and religious affections, the race can never fall so low but that it may sink still lower; animated and sanctified by them, it can never rise so high but that it may ascend still higher.[54]

Far from desiring to exclude religious instruction from the common school, as his accusers had it, Mann insisted, "I could not avoid regarding the man who should oppose the religious education of the young, as an insane man." His own position, he wrote, had been consistent over the twelve years of his term as secretary of the Board of Education:

> I believed then, as now, that religious instruction in our schools, to the extent which the constitution and laws of the State allowed and prescribed, was indispensable to their highest welfare, and essential to the vitality of moral education. Then as now, also, I believed that sectarian books and sectarian instruction, if their encroachments were not resisted, would prove the overthrow of the schools.

His advocacy of this position had continued despite years of suffering, "under misconstructions of conduct, and the imputation of motives, whose edge is sharper than a knife."[55] He had been strengthened by the conviction that "a true education would be among the most efficient means to prevent the reappearance in another generation of such an aggressive and unscrupulous opposition as the Board and myself were suffering under in this."

Mann then turned to an argument for a religiously neutral common school, which has—ironically enough—become familiar in recent years in support of public support for nonpublic schools, the argument of "double taxation":

if a man is taxed to support a school, where religious doctrines are inculcated which he believes to be false, and which he believes that God condemns; then he is excluded from the school by the Divine Law, at the same time that he is compelled to support it by the human law. This is a double wrong. It is politically wrong, because, if such a man educates his children at all, he must educate them elsewhere, and thus pay two taxes . . . ; and it is religiously wrong, because he is constrained, by human power, to promote what he believes the Divine Power forbids.

Apparently Mann could not see that, for some of his opponents, the confidence in human goodness and improvability that he wished the common school to teach represented a false doctrine, corrosive of the basis of their faith. In his mind—or at least in his argument—the Massachusetts common school was "more strictly religious than any other which has ever yet been adopted."[56] There could be no valid objection from any denominational perspective, he believed, to the positive religious teaching he advocated.

In what he clearly considered his unassailable argument, Mann pointed out that he and the board had continually promoted the use of the Bible in the common school, and "if this Bible is in the schools, how can it be said that Christianity is excluded from the schools?" The Bible was allowed to "speak for itself," and what could be more fair or reverent? Thus,

so far from its being an irreligious, an anti-Christian, or an un-Christian system, it is a system which recognizes religious obligations to their fullest extent; . . . a system which invokes a religious spirit, and can never be fitly administered without such a spirit.[57]

But this admirable and "Christian" system was under attack, and now not only from Protestant orthodoxy but from the claim of the Catholic clergy to provide education for the children of Irish immigrants. Nothing could be more unfortunate. It was, after all, "the first duty of every government in Christendom to bring foward those unfortunate classes of the people who, in the march of civilization, have been left in the rear."

169

The urgency of this concern was underlined by the fact, recently reported by a committee overseeing the Boston primary schools, "that of ten thousand one hundred and sixty-two children belonging to said schools, five thousand one hundred and fifty-four were of foreign parentage." Sectarian teaching in the common schools would inevitably drive these students away, and this would in turn strengthen the hand of those (presumably the Catholic clergy) who "propose to supersede the necessity of subduing free thought, *in the mind of the adult*, by forestalling the development of any capacity of free thought, *in the mind of the child*."

Mann believed that the common school ideal, "Free Schools for all, and the right of every parent to determine the (out-of-school) religious education of his children," was threatened by religious zealots on two sides: by orthodox Protestants and Roman Catholics.

> Some are attempting to withhold all means, even of secular education, from the poor, and thus punish them with ignorance unless, with the secular knowledge which they desire, they will accept theological knowledge which they condemn. Others, still, are striving to break down all free Public School systems, where they exist, and to prevent their establishment, where they do not exist, in the hope that on the downfall of these, their system will succeed.[58]

Mann's charges were unfair to both groups of his opponents; they are notable as an illustration of his unusual power, as a controversialist, to place the worst possible construction on the motivations and actions of his opponents and to do so in a manner many found convincing. If Mann's annual reports attracted and continue to attract more attention than those of any of his contemporaries or successors as "chief state school officer," it was not least because he managed to present the situation of education as simultaneously triumphant and imperiled. He created a genre of reports on education that, down to *A Nation at Risk*, has always reached for the dramatic image.

The charges are also an example of a theme—the fear of immigrants—that would be sounded with increasing vigor by supporters of the common school over the next decades and would contribute heavily to forming a "united front" among Protestants who otherwise might have been at each other's throats.

That Mann was not insincere in portraying himself as engaged in a mighty struggle is evident from his next, self-pitying remark that he was now bidding farewell "to a system with which I have so long been connected, to which I have devoted my means, my strength, my health, twelve years of time and, doubtless, twice that number of years from what might otherwise have been my term of life." After all, as he had noted earlier in the report,

> The preoccupancy of the public mind with error, on so important a subject, is an unspeakable calamity; and errors that derive their support from religious views are among the most invincible. . . . I was made to see, and deeply to feel, their disastrous and alienating influence, as I travelled about the State; sometimes withdrawing the hand of needed assistance, and sometimes, when conduct extorted approval, impeaching the motives that prompted it. By no cause, not dearer to me than life itself, could I ever have persevered, amid the trials and anxieties, and against the obstacles, that beset my path. But I felt that there is a profound gratification in standing by a good cause, in the hour of its adversity. I believed that there must be a deeper pleasure in following truth to the scaffold, than in shouting in the retinue where error triumphs.[59]

The reader of these lines would have little clue that the opposition to Mann's efforts was ineffectual and scattered, and his support not only broad but including virtually all of the political and financial elite. Kaestle and Vinovskis have demonstrated by careful analysis that the opposition to Mann and the Board of Education in the legislature in 1840 was correlated not with religious orthodoxy but rather with political resistance to what a later age would have called the "meddling do-goodism" of the Whig elite. In fact,

> representatives from towns whose schools used Bibles or whose school committees included members of the clergy were less hostile to the board of education than legislators from communities whose schools did not use Bibles or did not have ministers on their school boards.[60]

Mann did not espouse an unpopular cause or follow truth to any scaffold, but the fact that he saw himself in those terms reflects his vivid sensitivity to what he considered the threat of religious orthodoxy. Recent reactions, from the "education establishment," to controversies over the content of textbooks reveal how powerfully this sense of threat persists. A handful of "fundamentalist" parents, in Hawkins County, Tennessee, win the right of excusal for their children from certain aspects of instruction in the local school, and we are told that the "end of public education" is at hand!

The Religious Program of the Common School

"All those who are worthily laboring to promote the cause of education," Mann wrote in the *Common School Journal* in 1846, "are laboring to elevate mankind into the upper and purer regions of civilization, Christianity, and the worship of the true God; all those who are obstructing the progress of this cause are impelling the race backwards into barbarism and idolatry."[61]

As stated with particular clarity here, Mann saw the common school itself as having an essentially religious mission, a mission of "elevating" and "purifying" "the race." To carry out its mission, though, the school had to work against much that was considered religious by the orthodox, so that he wrote in the same essay, "He who is ignorant is almost necessarily superstitious. But a Christian education lifts off the whole, black, iron firmament of superstition from the soul, and brings life and immortality to light." Thus the school, though not, strictly speaking, salvific, was at least the revealer of essential human goodness and the pure morality that guaranteed happiness in this world and beyond. As one historian puts it, "the core of his religious philosophy was his firm belief in the infinite perfectibility of mankind through the process of education."[62]

Mann would probably have agreed with his Dutch contemporary, Petrus Hofstede de Groot, that God's primary purpose and form of activity in the world was *educational* and that therefore the school, because it worked in a systematic way with children when they were most impressionable, had a special part in the divine plan. Hofstede de Groot, a liberal Protestant theologian, school inspector, and author of an admiring book about Mann's mentor William Ellery Channing, saw in the nonsectarian religious teaching of the common school not an unsatisfactory compromise but an adumbration of the next, purified stage of Christianity.

Holding similar views, Mann was able to argue that he was actively engaged in promoting religion and that his opponents could only be motivated by fanaticism and hostility to the true interests of humanity.

In his private journal Mann wrote, just before taking up the post of secretary of the Board of Education (May 1837),

> For myself Natural Religion stands as preeminent over Revealed Religion as the deepest experience over the lightest hearsay. The power of Natural Religion is scarcely begun to be understood or appreciated. . . . And however much the light of Revealed Religion may have guided the generations of men amid the darkness of mortality, yet I believe the time is coming when the light of Natural Religion will be (to) that of Revealed as the rising sun is to the day-star that preceded it.[63]

This suggests that his public posture, that "the Religion of Heaven should be taught to children, while the creeds of men should be postponed until their minds were sufficiently matured to weigh evidence, and arguments,"[64] rested upon the assumption that, if the evidence and arguments were weighed by adults who had passed through the common school, the "creeds of men" or revealed religion would stand little chance of acceptance.

Mann also persuaded himself—and others—that "the Religion of Heaven" was in fact something different from, higher than, and in conflict with "the creeds of men." He expressed this view in one of his controversies with the orthodox, asserting that in their educational system

> The whole moral nature is left almost a waste, & the sublime pleasures, which attend its activity are not known & instead of cultivating the religious nature, all effort is expended upon the inculcation of doctrines and creeds, & the modes of adroitly defending them.[65]

In brief, then, Mann saw the common school as cultivating the moral nature and, at the same time and necessarily, developing the highest form of religious sentiment and piety of which children were capable. It was in the service of this mission, and not simply to avoid controversy, that the school must exclude the doctrinal tenets of orthodoxy. It was not that the exclusion of these traditional teachings from the school was an unfortunate consequence of the religious divisions in the community but rather that their inclusion would be fatal to the teaching of true religion and morality.

Mann was by no means alone in his views. We have seen that his immediate predecessors stressed the importance of nonsectarian religious instruction in order to have a deep impact upon the students. His immediate successor as secretary of the Board of Education, Barnas Sears, though a less flamboyant figure than Mann and theologically orthodox (he was a Baptist clergyman and president of the theological school at Newton), shared his conviction that religious training should be provided and that it should be nonsectarian. In the *Fifteenth Report* (1852) Sears wrote that

> The most perfect development of the mind, no less than the order of the school and the stability of society, demands a religious education. Massachusetts may be regarded as having settled, at least for herself, this great question of the connection of religion with the Public Schools. She holds that religion is the highest and noblest possession of the mind, and is conducive to all the true interests of man and of society, and therefore she cannot do otherwise than seek to place her schools under its beneficent influence. . . . What it needs for its own safety and well-being is the spirit of the decalogue as expounded by the Great Teacher of mankind, while varying creeds, which are so much in controversy, are not indispensable as a means of public education. . . . In the exclusion of distinctive creeds from the schools, religious persons, of almost every name, are singularly agreed. . . . The formation of a virtuous character is the natural result of a right religious training.[66]

173

The *Seventeenth Report* (1854) incorporates an address by George Emerson, Mann's ally and fellow Unitarian, at the dedication of a normal school building. Emerson's main theme, on this as on other occasions, was the importance of moral education, and he stressed that

> this moral instruction must be based on the Gospel, on those great principles of Christianity which are common to all Christians, the great principles of the immortality and accountability of man, of the holiness and omnipresence of God, of the authority of the teachings of Christ.[67]

Sears returned to this theme the following year, alluding to the fact that certain persons, years before, had pressed for the establishment of schools "having a distinctive religious character," whereas at the opposite extreme some school committees had gone to excessive lengths in forbidding all forms of religion in the common schools, even prohibiting prayer.

> Time, by giving opportunity for sober reflection and more careful observation, has done much towards correcting both these extreme views. The one class has become satisfied that . . . the children of emigrants, now swarming in our cities and manufacturing districts, will, unless brought into our public schools, soon form a dangerous part of our population . . . the very foundations of society will be rendered insecure, by the fearful amount of brute force that will be accumulating around us, breathing the spirit of riot and misrule.
>
> The other class have come to see that a government cannot long perpetuate itself by means of mere secular education; . . . that a reverence for divine things and for the Supreme Being, breathed by the conscientious teacher into the hearts of the young, especially of those who receive no such lessons at home, is indispensable for the preservation of social order among men.
>
> Considerations of this nature have done much to unite the great bulk of the community on the common ground of a Christian but unsectarian education for all the children of the Commonwealth. . . . Those who would deprive the teacher of so powerful a means of moral discipline as the Bible find little sympathy among the descendants of the Pilgrims.[68]

Two of the speakers before the American Institute of Instruction, in 1849, took a similar position. Benjamin Labarce argued that

> the most important interests of individual and of society, the stability and the permanency of our institutions, *imperiously demand* that our children and youth be thoroughly instructed in the principles of moral and religious obligations,

and Charles Brooks stressed that "Christianity, enthroned in the heart of any people, is the cheapest police that any government can maintain." The "animal ferocity" of the ignorant—especially immigrants—could be disarmed "by the implantation of moral principle."[69]

A decade later the mayor of Lynn, Massachusetts, a manufacturing city experiencing heavy immigration, declared that

> sound education of the heart and mind is the only sure basis of character. . . . The importance . . . of the public schools, in a community like ours, where they furnish to a large proportion of the youth the only means of acquiring such an education, cannot be over-estimated. What interest in any community can compare with the moral and religious education of the young?[70]

This conviction was not limited to Massachusetts. In 1856, as Detroit hosted the annual conference of the American Association for the Advancement of Education, the participants heard a paper by a local reformer, D. Bethune Duffield, entitled "Education, a State Duty; or, May the State Insist on the Education of Her Youth? And to What Extent Can She Go in This Direction?" Like Mann, the speaker had no doubt that the benefits of universal education would outweigh the element of compulsion involved and that this education should be essentially religious in its character.

> If the State is injured by the rearing of immoral and lawless citizens, she has a right to protect herself against the evil; not alone by prison bars and the hangman's cord, but by striking at the root of the evil, and adopting preventive measures. The only effective way to stop the streams of pollution is to close and seal up the fountains whence they flow. The only way to protect children from barbarism and vice is to furnish them the blessing of religious instruction and the elements of knowledge.[71]

Those who challenged such religious instruction as violating the Constitution misread its intention and would themselves create

> just what the constitution forbids; viz., a sectarian establishment, consisting of schools, in which the tenets and dogmas of sect are taught; for Infidels and Deists are as much a *sect* as Presbyterians, Catholics, or Quakers. You would then, by urging your objection, practically insist on having the mighty machinery of this government—which recognizes and has ever recognized Christianity—employed, not for the enforcement indirectly of its simple doctrines, but in building up an establishment directly at war with all its heavenly precepts. You would trample under foot the constitutional rights of the great majority of the people, and establish over their heads a small minority sect of infidels and deists. . . . We desire neither the barrenness of infidelity, nor the dwarfing of sectarianism. . . . all who are Christians profess to adopt these great cardinal principles and precepts as the rule of their lives, no matter by what name they are known.[72]

As a final example of the intense interest this question aroused among education reformers in this period, we note the debate that occurred before the same American Association for the Advancement of Education the previous year (1855), in New York. A resolution was offered to the effect that "moral and religious instruction should form a prominent element in all our systems of public education," and the seconder "thought it to be necessary in order that the public should know that the Association were not, as it had been sometimes feared, in favor of excluding the religious element from our systems of education." [73] Support was expressed by delegates from a number of states. One reported that he had found religious instruction in the schools at all levels in New York City; another noted that "the State of Indiana had placed the Bible at the head of their text-books." Massachusetts had just passed a law requiring the daily reading of the Bible in all schools, and the sole delegate from the South Atlantic states reported that "they were beginning to feel that intellectual character is a curse, unless moral and religious education go with it."

This chorus of support was interrupted by Episcopal Bishop Potter of Pennsylvania, who expressed concern over potential controversy. The essential was to "place in every primary school a devout conscientious enlightened Christian heart"; it was not dogmatic instruction but the daily example of such teachers that would do the job. "But you must recollect that they can only teach the ten commandments, the Lord's prayer, the Sermon on the Mount, and a few other similar passages, before they get over into the stoney region of polemics; God save the schools from that. (*Applause*)" He was afraid, he said later in the two-day debate, that

> affairs might take such a course that in ten years we should find the Protestants, the Catholics, and the unbelievers, all standing side by side, shoulder to shoulder, toppling that magnificent system (common schools) to its base; and if that time shall ever come I verily believe it will have been invoked by the excessive zeal and impatience of those wishing to introduce religious instruction in these schools.

And on that note the resolution, though supported by most of those who spoke, was tabled. [74]

Beneath the discussion was a continual undercurrent of concern growing out of Catholic opposition to the reading of the King James version of the Bible, in New Orleans as well as in New York and elsewhere. The new Massachusetts statute alluded to was in fact adopted as one of a series of antiimmigrant measures that helped to provoke the development of the parochial school system, as had similar developments earlier in New York City.

This key debate brought into sharp focus, at the heart of the educational reform establishment, the difficulty of operating common schools with a deeply religious mission and character while at the same time avoiding all controversy over religion. The solution urged by Bishop Potter, that the teacher provide a deeply Christian example while avoiding the specifics of religious teaching, would increasingly be the rationalization adopted by education authorities anxious to gain the broadest possible support for the common school, particularly in the face of growing immigration. His confidence that more and more teachers would find it possible to read from the Bible because of the "growing spirit of piety throughout this land" was shared by many other Protestant leaders, and they were content to pursue a flexible policy of pressing at the local level for what seemed unwise to pursue as a uniform program.

SIGNIFICANCE OF THE DEBATES OVER COMMON SCHOOL RELI-GION. Despite the continually announced concern of Mann and other education reformers to strengthen the religious mission of the common school, the evidence suggests that the actual *practices* of religious instruction, Bible reading, and prayer at the opening or closing of the school day were in decline throughout the nineteenth century. Perhaps the most comprehensive study is that of William Kailer Dunn (1958). Dunn cites a study of the textbooks in use, which found that religious themes were increasingly replaced by moral ones:

> the readers used in the colonies prior to 1775 devoted 85% of the space to religion and 8% to morals; those between 1775 and 1825, 22% to religion and 28% to morals; those between 1825 and 1875, 7.5% to religion and 23% to morals; and those between 1875 and 1915, only 1.5% to religion and 7% to morals.

Dunn's exhaustive survey concludes that "there was little in the textbook content by the time of the Civil War to give the public school child an understanding of natural theology, and even less of Christianity itself."[75]

The inadequate presentation of the role of religion in American life in textbooks, as noted in several recent studies, does not, then, reflect postwar aggression by "secular humanists" alone but indicates a long-term avoidance of such controversial material.[76]

It was not, according to Dunn, either concerns about the First Amendment or pressure by secularists that led to this purging of religious instruction from the schools. "The struggle over sectarianism . . . and not hostility or indifference to religion as such mainly caused the decline of religious teaching."[77]

My own review of the controversies supports this conclusion; the remarks by Duffield, cited above, are the only mention of the United States Constitution that I found, and there seems to have been an almost universal conviction that schooling should have some form of religious character. It was not hostility to or avoidance of religion, understood in the most general terms, that fueled the debates of these decades. After all, it was an Episcopal bishop who, at the debate in 1855, urged against taking a position on the specifics of religious teaching lest it cause controversy and a loss of support for the common school and its civilizing mission.

Dunn seems to believe, however, that the problem was simply shortsighted bickering among religious leaders. This leads to his conclusion that the time had come (1958) to reopen the issue and to restore the tradition that "religion belongs" as part of the "American way of life" (his quotation marks),[78] taking care this time to protect liberty of conscience more adequately.

This interpretation fails to take into account the historical evidence that Dunn marshals so thoroughly. After all, there was a continual chorus, by those in the leadership positions of American education, that religion was an essential part of the mission of the school. Is it credible to believe either that they were engaged in a vast conspiracy of insincerity, or that they were powerless to prevent the swift leeching away of something to which they attached so much importance?

I suggest a simpler explanation: that although explicit religious instruction was increasingly removed from the common school, largely in an attempt to enroll and thus to assimilate the children of Catholic immigrants, *the mission of the school itself became more rather than less truly "religious" over this period.*

The common school and the vision of American life that it embodied came to be vested with a religious seriousness and exaltation. It became the core institution of American society, the definer of meanings, and the only way to higher life—spiritually as well as materially—for generations of immigrant and native-born children alike. In close alliance with but never subordinate to the Protestant churches, the common school occupied a "sacred space" where its mission was beyond debate and where to question it was a kind of blasphemy.

7

The Opposition to
Common School
Religion

Overview

THE INITIAL objections to the character of "common school religion" were made by orthodox Protestants rather than by Catholics. They expressed concerns with the lack of instruction in the tenets of orthodox Christianity and also with the religious teachings that were offered in their place by Mann and others whose conception of the mission of the common school was profoundly "religious."

The objections raised were parallel to those of orthodox Christians in other countries where, during this period, an elite of educational reformers were creating "common schools" intended to shape the hearts as well as the minds of the rising generation. Although the reformers in the United States, Prussia and other German states, the Netherlands, France, and Great Britain were keenly aware of each other's efforts and kept in touch through visits as well as through correspondence, there is little evidence of similar linkages among their Protestant opponents or an awareness that they were not alone in their concerns. This was not the case with Catholics, given the strong European orientation of the emergent Catholic elite in the United States and the resonance of the battles for "Catholic freedom" and against the liberal state in one nation after another.

Voices from within the "mainline" Protestantism of the nineteenth century opposing the "religious" mission of the common school as Horace Mann and his allies defined it were isolated, even prophetic; they saw implications and consequences that most of their fellow Protestants, concerned over the "Catholic threat," chose to deny. These voices seemed, indeed, to threaten the institution upon which Protestant hegemony most depended. Catholic opponents, on the other hand, were in the position of defending a group solidarity that the common school was explicitly intended to undermine. They were not isolated critics but voices for an immigrant people that first found its voice, first became aware of its desire for

179

solidarity in addressing this issue. The German and Irish Catholic immigration created—as we shall see in the next chapter—the most extensive alternative to the common school; before that could occur, however, it was controversies over the common school and its religious mission that made Catholics a self-conscious community and began their political mobilization.

Protestant Opponents

"THE SPIRIT OF THE PILGRIMS." The Second Great Awakening of the early years of the century reached Boston most visibly in the ministry of Lyman Beecher, who led a revival there in 1823 and was called to form a new orthodox congregation, the Hanover Street Church, in 1826. Beecher soon founded a monthly journal to serve "that portion of the community, usually denominated orthodox," the *Spirit of the Pilgrims*. In the initial issue (January 1828), Beecher made no apology for a frankly aggressive position toward the Unitarianism prevalent in elite Boston circles. After all, he argued, "all the controversies with Unitarians, since the name was known in this country, have accelerated the progress of correct sentiments; have given strength, union and consistency to the orthodox," with the result that there had been "great accessions of numbers and strength to the body of orthodox Christians in Boston and the vicinity."

The orthodox, Beecher wrote, "feel themselves to be *the proper and legitimate representatives of their pilgrim fathers*" who, among other good qualities, had "*a true knowledge of human nature*" (emphasis in the original). As a result, "they tried no Utopian experiments." Nor did they shrink from controversy: "There is not a single principle of civil liberty or of religious toleration, there is nothing virtuous or honorable among men, for which . . . the Puritans were not obliged to contend against dangerous error." The *Spirit of the Pilgrims* would continue that tradition, Beecher promised, and would include "*Remarks on public measures* which have a bearing on the interests of religion and morality, and thus on the prosperity of the Redeemer's kingdom."[1]

Later the same year the journal turned to the topic of "christian education," in the promised spirit of honest controversy. "The natural state of children has commonly been mistaken by those who have written on this subject. It has been represented as a state of innocence and virtue," with the consequent misunderstanding that education was concerned primarily with preserving that innocence. The Christian parent, by contrast, had a realistic view of the ravages of sin in his children.

He is concerned for their respectability, usefulness, and happiness in the world; but much more for their eternal well being. He knows what they are by nature, and what they must be by grace; and although he cannot himself bestow converting grace, still he believes there is much which he can do for the promotion of their spiritual interests.

After all, "if means are used for the conversion of adults, why not for the conversion of children?" This required "direct religious *instruction*." Children

> should be made, if possible, to see and feel that they are sinners, involved in guilt and ruin. . . . The truths to be urged upon the minds of children are, not the abstrusities of religion, but the plainest and most important doctrines of the Gospel. These should be urged with the utmost simplicity, so that they may be understood; and with a degree of tenderness and affection, which can hardly fail to convince those to whom they are addressed that they are intended for their benefit. They should be urged also in a way to engage the *attention* of children, and to interest their feelings. They should be made as little repulsive and wearisome as possible.

In short, orthodox Christian doctrine should be taught in a way consistent with the new "romantic" concern for the capacities and feelings of children.[2] There are clear parallels to the pedagogy pioneered by German pietists at Halle in the previous century, to which ironically the Unitarian educational reformers could also have traced much of their inspiration.

One of the latter, Harvard divinity professor Henry Ware, Jr., was the target of a critical review several years later. His book *On the Formation of the Christian Character* was accused of leading to "that sentimentality which is a popular substitute for true religion" and of misleading the unsophisticated "by interweaving Orthodox terms into his composition" and thus giving it "a savour of evangelical piety."

> How affecting it is to find that the book provides no Saviour from this wrath to come but moral culture. . . . The sinner is directed to be a philosopher, and by retiring into himself and forming good resolutions, to fix the religious principle deeply, and attain to a spiritual mind. . . . The sublime contemplation of God is not religion; nor the philosophical admiration of the character of Jesus; nor the sentimental love of virtue, more properly called pride of character. . . . we are directed to ask for blessing because Christ was the founder of our religion. This is like feeding on dew. . . . This religion is too scholastic and subtile to reclaim a lost world to God.[3]

181

Here we see anticipated the objections that orthodox Protestants would make to the religious mission of the common school as it was described a few years later by Horace Mann and his allies. A religion without salvation, a religion of moral exhortation and sentimental images, was appealing to an educated elite confident of its own mastery and of the nation's inevitable progress, but it bore little relation to the powerful revival impulses that were shaping American Protestantism.

It should be clear that this was a *theological* objection, not a concern to prevent popular enlightennment or social change; indeed, Beecher's introductory statement of mission in 1828 stressed that one of the "grandest objects" of the Pilgrims had been to make "provision for universal education." What he objected to in Ware and other religious liberals was the removal of sin and redemption from the very center of the religious view of life; schooling that made this error could only be a "moral culture" in some ways worse—because misleading—than nothing.

THE ORTHODOX PRESBYTERIANS. Lyman Beecher considered himself fully orthodox and even Calvinist, but the logic of the "revival system"— with its emphasis upon human decision and thus free will—led him into theological compromises with the optimistic spirit of his age. He was in fact to be the object of a celebrated heresy trial within the Presbyterian church, gleefully reported by the Unitarian *Christian Examiner*, and his children drifted even further into such compromises (although a Congregationalist in background, Beecher came under Presbyterian discipline when he relocated to Ohio, under an interchurch agreement dividing up spheres of influence). As we shall see when considering the scattered Protestant voices calling for sectarian schools in which orthodox Christianity could be taught, Beecher shared many of the nation-building objectives for education of Mann and the other reformers and thus helped to prepare the way for the triumph of the common school.

This was not the case with his opponents within the Presbyterian church; the most orthodox wing had grave concerns about "common school religion." Princeton divinity professor Charles Hodge wrote, in 1828, that "unless some plan can be adopted of introducing religion into the common schools, we must consent to see a large portion of our population growing up in ignorance of the first principles of moral and religious truth."[4] Three years later he wrote that "it should be a constant object with the friends of religion, to try to secure a religious character to the instructions of the common school."[5] Addressing the American Sunday School Union in 1833, he charged that, when the Bible was excluded from schools, children were brought up under the influence of "heathen minds and models."

Such statements were common enough among the contemporary education reformers, but Hodge meant something very different than they did when he called for "religion" in the schools. He made this clear in an article in the *Princeton Review* in 1846, observing that the mingling of students in the common school required a "standard of doctrine" unobjectionable to the "lowest and loosest sects" to prevent an "outcry . . . about religious liberty and the union of Church and' State." The inevitable consequence was that "the whole system is in the hands of men of the world, in many of our states, and is avowedly secular"; such a system "cannot be neutral, and in fact is not neutral. . . . The people will never submit with their eyes open to a merely secular, which is another name for an irreligious, godless education."[6]

Hodge saw clearly that the issue of the *content* of religious instruction in schools was tied to a *structural* issue. As he observed in the same article, in a passage that would be quoted at length by Matthew Hale Smith in his controversy with Horace Mann later that year,

> What right has the State, a majority of the people, or a mere clique, which in fact commonly control such matters, to say what shall be taught in schools which the people sustain? What more right have they to say that no religion shall be taught, than they have to say that Popery shall be taught? Or what right have the people in one part, to control the wishes and convictions of those of another part of the State, as to the education of their own children? If the people of a particular district choose to have a school in which the Westminster or the Heidelberg catechism is taught, we cannot see on what principle of religious liberty the State has a right to interfere, and say it shall not be done; if you teach your religion, you shall not draw your own money from the public fund! This appears to us a strange doctrine in a free country . . . unjust and tyrannical, as well as infidel in its whole tendency.[7]

Hodge's view was shared by many of his fellow Presbyterians, and a brief effort was made to establish a system of Presbyterian elementary schools that would provide explicitly orthodox religious teaching; as we shall see in the next chapter, this effort collapsed under the perceived threat of the schools that immigrant Catholics actually *were* establishing.

FREDERICK PACKARD. Frederick A. Packard, although officially a Congregationalist, was associated with the orthodox Presbyterian position and wrote for Hodge's *Princeton Review*. Packard served as editor of publications for the American Sunday School Union, based in Philadelphia. This organization was one of the bright lights of the "evangelical united front" of the antebellum period and was "nonsectarian" in the sense that its board of review for publications included (in 1838) two Methodists, two Baptists, two Episcopalians, and two Presbyterians—though no Unitarians or Universalists! In an article reliably attributed to him, and written before the Board of Education was set up in 1837, Packard stressed his support for public schools in which teachers would bring to bear "the great truths of Christianity . . . on the minds and hearts" of the pupils,

> so that while, on the one hand, the school should be protected from the evils of bigotry, sectarianism, and fanaticism, it shall be secured, on the other, against the equally destructive influence of a heartless, intolerant infidelity. For it should never be forgotten that, in the present blindness and madness of the human heart, infidelity will always compromise with truth on the basis of mutual forbearance. She knows her position too well to refuse a treaty on those terms; and we ought to know ours too well to propose or accept it.[8]

Packard wrote to the recently appointed Mann in March 1838, inquiring whether one of the books in his series could be included in the "district school libraries" Mann was encouraging. Mann wrote in his journal that he would "rather no District Library should ever be formed, than to have them, if they must be composed of such books as that."[9] To Packard he wrote:

> The book would be in the highest degree offensive to the Universalists. . . . many if not most of them would rather see the whole system abolished than to have such a book introduced. . . . The whole scope and tenor of the book would ill accord with the views of Unitarians. . . . the book would shock the moral & religious feelings of a large portion of our community. . . . Many of our people believe that affection and love of God is a far higher and more desirable feeling to inspire than blind obedience, and that the book forgets the higher in urging the lower state of mind. . . . There is scarcely anything in the book which presents the character of God in an amiable or lovely aspect. . . . the whole book proceeds upon the ground, that children have a natural disinclination to love what is good & to hearken to what is wise in their maker.[10]

The book proposed by Packard, Abbott's *Child at Home*, placed a strong emphasis upon the final judgment as a sanction against misbehavior, with the possibility of ultimate condemnation for sins not repented of. Packard responded promptly, asking how "the principles of piety [can] be taught intelligibly without constant reference to the character of God and to the provisions and sanctions of His law as revealed in the Holy Scriptures."[11] Since the Massachusetts constitution *required* that schools inculcate the "principles of piety," it was essential that the law requiring the exclusion of sectarian teaching from the books provided by school committees not be interpreted to exclude the most basic doctrines of Christianity as to sin and salvation. After all, he must have thought, his organization was itself nonsectarian.

Mann's reply to this letter took the position that morality is to be promoted by pointing out the "sources of happiness" in following the course of duty; sin was a form of ignorance rather than of rebellion against God. Packard had argued that the awareness of the consequences of sin *in this life* was not sufficiently great or inevitable to enforce moral behavior. "And why?" Mann asked:

> Not as I believe from any mistake or oversight in the original constitution of man, nor from any love of error or wrong, into which they have since fallen, but because the earthly portion of their natures is highly cultivated, while their moral and religious sentiments are mainly neglected. The whole moral nature is left almost a waste, & the sublime pleasures which attend its activity are not known, & instead of cultivating the religious nature, all effort is expended upon the inculcation of doctrines and creeds.

Thus religion consists essentially of an educative process—the development of moral and religious sentiments—and education itself is essentially religious.[12] As for the *content* of religious instruction, it should be limited, as Mann wrote to Packard in July 1838, to "the Religion of Heaven," consisting of those doctrines upon which all could agree.[13]

What Mann did not appear to appreciate was that his original premise was itself unacceptable to those who believed that the sinfulness of human nature required conversion and redemption by God's intervention as a necessary prelude to the educative process of sanctification. Packard asked, in a further letter,

> who but men are to determine what is "the religion of heaven?" Does it include the holiness of God, the corruption of the human heart—the sacrifice of Christ for sin—the eternal punishment of the finally impenitent &c &c? No, you will say, these belong to the "creeds of men" & must be postponed until the pupil's mind is sufficiently matured to weigh evidence and argument.[14]

Packard continued his attack on Mann in a long article appearing in the *Princeton Review* in July 1841.[15] Noting that educational reform was attracting tremendous attention, he insisted that the essential question that must be answered first was "not after what order we shall build an inconceivably vast and expensive structure for the security and happiness of unborn myriads, but whether it shall be founded on a rock or on the sand."

185

He reviewed recent developments at the state level in Pennsylvania, New York and Massachusetts and charged that

the compromising system now prevalent in our country is the most un-christian thing that is to be found on the earth. In the mixed schools of other Christian countries, the essential doctrines of our common faith are honourably recognized—in ours they are contemptuously set aside.[16]

Discussing a recent New York State report, Packard suggested that

the doctrine is that the right of rejecting all religions must be respected as an element of religious liberty, and that the compulsory recognition of any [particular] religion is an invasion of that liberty. . . . A close comparison of these sentiments, with those we have drawn from the reports of the Massachusetts Boards, shows clearly that these two states, which are re-garded as taking the lead on educational subjects, have virtually discarded the Christian religion, and all inculcation of its doctrines, from the course of public instruction.[17]

The problem was in fact directly related to an increasing state role, based upon the concern, by a reforming elite, to use what until then had been a highly localized system of district schools as a means of forging a new social unity. Common schools would mold citizens who would share common loyalties and beliefs, free of the divisive sectarian convictions which, they believed, were accountable for the misery of human history. Packard spoke for those who did not accept this agenda:

we most earnestly protest against the doctrines which appear to find fa-vour in some of our oldest and most influential states, and those states in which the *machinery* of education seems to be most expressly and effi-ciently in motion. . . . We protest against the interference of the govern-ment with the matter and manner of instruction, and especially against annexing any condition to its grants, that shall affect in the slightest degree the independence of the whole district or of the teacher whom they em-ploy—and least of all on the subject of religious instruction.

In short, he was calling not for a state-imposed orthodoxy in public schools but for local freedom to provide orthodox religious instruction in those areas where that reflected the desires of parents.[18] In the context of Massa-chusetts, this would have meant essentially that schools in the central and western parts of the state—the more rural areas—would not have been controlled by the religious liberalism of the Boston area. On the other hand, Packard did not acknowledge the difficulty that Mann never wearied of stressing, that religious teaching could become a matter of local conflict

186

in those communities in which orthodox denominations coexisted with Unitarians or Universalists.

MATTHEW HALE SMITH. Another critic to whom Mann replied repeatedly and at length was Universalist-turned-Calvinist Matthew Hale Smith. Smith's objections were in fact more sophisticated and far-reaching than those raised by Packard. He entered the fray with a sermon preached before an orthodox congregation in Boston in October 1846 and promptly published, called "The Ark of God on a New Cart: Increase of Intemperance, Crime, and Juvenile Depravity—Its Cause and Cure." [19] Smith's text was taken from the episode in 2 Samuel 6, when the ark containing sacred relics was placed upon a cart rather than being carried, as had been prescribed by Moses; as a result, one of those involved was killed by fire from heaven. Smith pointed out that "his motive may have been good, but *a right thing must not be done in a wrong way*. So this history, so all experience, teach."

Juvenile delinquency and street crime were on the increase in Boston, Smith observed, and the reason was that the right thing—education—was being done in the wrong way.

> Modern reformers have taken the education of youth under their special care. Men, wise above that which is written [that is, the Bible], have made common schools the theatre of their experiments and labors. . . . We ask not that religion shall be sustained by the law; but we do ask that impiety and irreligion shall not be supported by the state. When religious and intellectual culture are divorced, is it strange that we have a harvest of crime?

The Massachusetts Board of Education had fostered this divorce in two ways:

> 1. By allowing an individual [Mann], under the sanction of its authority, to disseminate through the land crude and destructive principles, principles believed to be at war with the Bible and with the best interests of the young for time and eternity. 2. By a library which excludes books as sectarian that inculcate truths, which *nine-tenths of professed Christians of all names believe*, while it accepts others that inculcate the most deadly heresy—even universal salvation.

Smith was answered promptly by William B. Fowle, one of Mann's closest allies and the publisher of his *Common School Journal*. Referring to Smith's sermon as a "tissue of impudence and ignorance," Fowle sought to refute it by pointing out that the Bible was read regularly in most Massachusetts schools and that the majority of the members of the board were orthodox Protestants. The author of the sermon deserved, Fowle wrote in

187

a lapse of the "tolerance" that he ordinarily professed, to suffer capital pun-
ishment for "such wholesale calumny" and "falsehood."[20]

Smith is not an especially attractive figure and he has been treated by the
historians scarcely more sympathetically than he was by Fowle, but in fact
his objections were quite justified from his orthodox perspective, and Fowle
had not answered them. It was not the act of reading the Bible in school
(even Unitarians professed reverence for the "sublime truths" found in
Scripture) but teaching about sin and salvation that would have satisfied
Smith. This was made clear in an instructive exchange that followed between
Mann and Smith. In a complaining letter, Mann argued that "the whole
influence of the Board of Education, from the day of its organization to the
present time, has been to promote and encourage, and, whenever they have
had any power, as in the case of the Normal [teacher training] Schools, to
direct the daily use of the Bible in school."

Smith wrote back promptly, asking Mann to state clearly (*inter alia*)
whether he was in favor of the use of the *whole* Bible, "the Law, the Prophets, the Psalms, the New Testament. I suppose you to be willing that parts
shall be read. But are you in favor of the *whole* Bible as a school book?" In
addition, Smith wrote, he understood that with respect to religious instruction Mann would "rule out as far as you have power truths and sanctions
which nine tenths of professing Christians believe essential to sound morals
and an honest life, no less than to the salvation of the soul. If you are in
favor of religious instruction in schools, will you please state what you mean
by that term?"[21]

Mann's reply consisted primarily of an attack on Smith for not answering
his criticisms of the original sermon. As to the points at issue, he gave
characteristically evasive answers. His published writings showed conclu-
sively, he wrote, "that it is my belief that the Bible makes known to us the
rule of life, and the means of salvation, and that it is my wish (I have no
authority in the matter) that it should continue to be used in our schools."
We know from Mann's journals and private correspondence, in fact, that he
understood "the means of salvation" as being the pursuit of ever-higher
ideals, such as were exemplified in the life and teaching of Jesus, not faith
in the latter as Savior.

Mann did not answer whether he favored the use of those portions of
the Bible that were repellent to his fellow Unitarians, those that stressed
the condemnation of unrepentant sinners, for example. His position on this
was in fact very much parallel to that of his contemporary in liberal school
reform in the Netherlands, Petrus Hofstede de Groot, who argued that
candidates for ministry should be allowed to interpret their oath to uphold
the teaching of the Reformed church, "as it is revealed in Scripture," to

mean "to the extent that it is supported by Scripture," thus allowing each candidate to decide for himself what was truly biblical.

To the second question, Mann replied that he was "in favor of religious instruction in our schools, to the extremest verge to which it can be carried without invading those rights of conscience which are established by the laws of God, and guaranteed to us by the Constitution of the State." He did not, however, fall into Smith's trap of specifying what content this would include, nor did he explain why there was a right of conscience not to be exposed to orthodox teaching but no such right (apparently) to be protected from religious teaching directly contrary to the orthodox position.

Smith returned to the attack against his elusive opponent in a further published letter, charging that "no plan can so effectually get the Bible, ultimately, out of Common Schools, as that which rejects a part as not true, and another part as not fit to be read. . . . Those who believe and so teach, are displacing the Bible for human codes of ethics." As to religious instruction,

> You decline to define a term you are using frequently. You are willing, you say, religion should be taught in schools; but what you mean by religion, you will not define. . . . The [Massachusetts] Constitution commands that "*the Principles of Piety*" shall be taught in schools. . . . Certain views that you entertain, you call religion, or "piety." These you allow to be taught in schools. You enforce them in your lectures, reports, and Journal. Those which clash with your particular views, you reject as "dogmatic theology," or "sectarianism." By what authority do you settle those grave and important questions for every town and school district in Massachusetts? . . . You substitute, as far as you have influence, for the principles of piety allowed by the Constitution, nothing above, nothing more than Deism, bald and blank. This I am prepared to show from what you publish, from what you admit. . . . you teach the native purity of the heart. A little scum is on the surface, but it is all right, all sound at the bottom. What to us, then, is the Redemption of Christ, if men are not dead in sin? . . . those who are influenced by German Transcendentalism, which begins by denying the Scripture doctrine of human depravity, and ends by asserting the perfectability of man, without God—without grace—may also respond, of no necessity. But there is a religious pulsation in Massachusetts, yet. . . . The yoke our fathers would not bear—the yoke of Infidelity, allied to State dogmatic theology, in any form—the children will not wear.

Smith saw more clearly than did most of the other critics that Mann and his allies were promoting an educational program with a distinctively religious emphasis. He also saw, as did Packard, that this represented a new

189

form of religious establishment—"State dogmatic theology." He attempted to turn against Mann his own language about "dogmatism" by demanding that "the dogmatism of unbelief" be kept out of the schools.[22] The next year, in a further salvo, he made clear that

> I have not accused Mr. Mann of being opposed to what *he calls* religion in schools. On the contrary, I charge him with being a dogmatist—a sectarian, zealous and confident, as all sectarians are. I have accused him, and do accuse him, of deciding what those "principles of piety" are, which the Constitution demands to be taught in schools.[23]

THE "WITNESS" CONTROVERSY AND EPISCOPALIANS. Episcopalian leaders were generally supporters of the common school, but Horace Mann was to experience some of the sharpest attacks upon his interpretation of the religious mission of the school from this denomination. The issue had first surfaced at the national church level in 1838, when the journal *Churchman* printed extensive extracts from Calvin Stowe's reports on Prussian elementary schools. The next year a short-lived journal attempted to arouse interest within the denomination as to its responsibility for the education of its children, urging that "it is now generally conceded that the morals of children are not *improved* by their attendance at school. . . . we should be driven to the conclusion that education is favorable to vice."[24]

One of the original members of Horace Mann's Board of Education in Massachusetts was an Episcopalian banker from Pittsfield, Edward Newton. Newton was the only one of the board to resign in protest against Mann's policy on religious teaching in the common school, and he launched a controversy in the pages of the *Witness*, the diocesan periodical, edited by Roxbury minister Mark De Wolfe Howe. Mann counterattacked with characteristic vigor, and others joined in through a variety of periodicals.

The occasion for Newton's article was reports of the argument made by Daniel Webster before the Supreme Court in February 1844 in the celebrated Girard College case, an attempt by the heirs of Stephen Girard of Philadelphia to set aside his will, under which he left $2 million to endow a boarding school for white orphan boys. The trustees were to have complete parental authority over the students, who were not to leave the facilities until, at between fourteen and eighteen, they were apprenticed in some occupation. The free-thinking Girard provided that no ministers could set foot in the school and noted that,

> as there is such a diversity of opinion among [the "sects"], I desire to keep the tender minds of the orphans . . . free from the excitement which clash-

ing doctrines and sectarian controversy are so apt to produce; my desire is, that all the instuctors and teachers in the college shall take pains to instill into the minds of the scholars *the purest principles of morality*, so that on their entrance into active life they may *from inclination* and habit, evince *benevolence towards their fellow-creatures, and a love of truth, sobriety, and industry*, adopting at the same time such religious tenets as their *matured reason* may enable them to prefer.

In short, Girard intended to set up a "total institution" capable of molding rational, virtuous beings, uncontaminated by the superstitions and prejudices which he no doubt believed had always afflicted mankind, [25] a project very much in the spirit of the eighteenth century Enlightenment, which looked enviously at the convent education to which the Catholic church, supposedly, owed its continuing power.

In an argument that had nationwide resonance at the time, Webster asserted that the orphans "were to be left entirely to the tender mercies of those who will try upon them this experiment of moral philosophy or philosophical morality." This was itself a sectarian project, Webster argued, and derogatory because based upon the rejection of Christianity.

> It is all idle, it is a mockery, and an insult to common sense, to maintain that a school for the instruction of youth, from which Christian instruction by Christian teachers is sedulously and rigorously shut out, is not deistical and infidel both in its purpose and its tendency. . . . In what age, by what sect, where, when, by whom, has religious truth been excluded from the education of youth? Nowhere; never. Everywhere, and at all times, it has been, and is, regarded as essential. It is of the essence, the vitality, of useful instruction. . . . The earliest and the most urgent intellectual want of human nature is the knowledge of its origin, its duty, and its destiny. . . . *if a man die, shall he live again*? And that question nothing but God, and the religion of God, can solve. Religion does solve it, and teaches every man that he is to live again, and that the duties of this life have reference to the life which is to come. [26]

As for the argument that the multiplicity of Christian denominations, "persecuting when strong, tolerant when weak, hating each other in the name of the God of peace," was a scandal from which children should be protected—a favorite theme of Mann and his allies—Webster dismissed this as "the universal cant" of "all the lower and more vulgar schools of infidelity throughout the world";

> this objection to the multitude and differences of sects is but the old story, the old infidel argument. It is notorious that there are certain great religious truths which are admitted and believed by all Christians. . . . cannot

all these great truths be taught to children without their minds being per-
plexed with clashing doctrines and sectarian controversies? Most certainly
they can. . . . How have they done in the schools of New England? There
. . . the great elements of Christian truth are taught in every school. The
Scriptures are read, their authority taught and enforced, their evidences
explained, and prayers usually offered.

By contrast, Webster argued, the supposed "neutrality" that was to prevail
at Girard College would be nothing of the sort.

It has been said . . . that there was no teaching *against* religion or Christianity in the system. I deny it. . . . The children are . . . to learn to be
suspicious of Christianity and religion; to keep clear of it. . . . They are to
be told and taught that religion is not a matter of the heart or conscience,
but for the decision of the cool judgment of mature years; that at a period
when the whole Christian world deem it most desirable to instil the chas-
tening influences of Christianity into the tender and comparatively pure
mind and heart of the child.[27]

Webster was not himself an active participant—beyond this one case—in
the debates over the place and character of religion in education, but the
authority that he enjoyed, especially in New England, was such that a challenge in his name could not be taken lightly by Horace Mann, even if it had
been his nature to accept any criticism meekly. In addition, the Girard College case provided a particularly clear example of what some feared would
be the nature of every school under a system that rejected "sectarian" Christianity. Thus Episcopal Bishop White of Pennsylvania charged, in connection with the proposed Girard College, that

modern times have multiplied those pests of society who, under the profession of schoolmasters, lose no opportunities of infusing their poison of
infidelity into unsuspicious minds. . . . no one, acquainted with human
nature, will believe that such instructors, in teaching, will find reluctance
to the guarding of their pupils against the religious truths which will be
addressed to them on their entrance into social life, resolving what they
will hear into popular fable and superstition, which it is now high time to
lay aside.[28]

Edward Newton lost no time in applying Webster's arguments to the
situation in Massachusetts, publishing his charges on February 23, 1844.
This initial salvo consisted largely of reprinting four paragraphs of a newspaper account of Webster's speech, preceded by the question, "Can any one
tell wherein the system of Mr. Girard, and the present system of our 'Board
of Education,' or rather of its Secretary, differs; or where the *essential* line
of agreement varies?"[29]

Two weeks later the editor of the *Christian Witness*, Mark De Wolfe Howe, responded to criticism from Mann about the "suggestive query." It was true, Howe conceded, that the board had not discouraged the use of the Bible, or the involvement of the clergy on school committees, or the teaching of religion, provided it was nonsectarian. The author of the query had pointed out, however, that the effect was very similar to that intended by Girard:

> as all the teaching of what Orthodox men hold to be the doctrines of grace is excluded in the books furnished [to the student] to read, he may not, if the child of wicked, or indifferent, or ignorant parents, or guardians, ever truly know what is necessary to his salvation.[30]

Howe went on to quote from the report of the Committee on Education of the Massachusetts legislature, several years previously, opposing the effort of the board to create school libraries of approved texts, as a means of "moulding the sentiments of the rising generation."[31] Even though assurance had been given that the books selected would be free from sectarian material, the committee had pointed out that

> a book upon politics, morals, or religion, containing no party or sectarian views, will be apt to contain no distinct views of any kind, and will be likely to leave the mind in a state of doubt and *skepticism*, much more to be deplored than any party or sectarian bias.

A week later the *Witness* returned to the issue by reprinting with expressions of approval a paragraph from the *Christian Reflector*, a Baptist paper. The *Reflector* asked,

> is it not true that many of our teachers *dare not*, or do not venture to give any instruction whatever; that they never come nearer to it than the simplest principles of morality? But our fathers thought, and our statesmen affirm, that morality cannot be taught effectually without religion.[32]

At the end of March the *Witness* printed a long second letter from Mann, warning against sectarianism in the common school and arguing that in fact there had been a significant increase in the religious effectiveness of schools since he and the board had been at work.

> Allow our schools to become nurseries of proselytism,—battle-grounds where each contending sect shall fight for the propagation of its own faith,—and how long would it be, before we should have schools for the Come-outers, for the Millerites, and the Mormonites? How long, before one portion of the children would be sent to school in their "ascension robes," and before another portion, instead of the Bible, would carry a

Catechism, whose first doctrine would be that "God is the Lord, and Joseph Smith is his prophet"? . . . The Bible is more universally read in [the schools than before the board was established, in 1837]; thirty fold more of instruction in morality and in religious truth is given in them than was given seven years ago.[33]

The response is typical of Mann's controversial style as well as of what there is every reason to believe were his sincere convictions: imputing the worst motivations to his orthodox opponents, carrying to ridiculous lengths the dangers of sectarianism, and making the unprovable claim that his efforts had resulted in a far greater concern for the teaching of "religious truth" in schools. Mann stated again and again that he wished to increase the amount of such teaching; in his mind, of course, "religious truth" excluded the orthodox Christian doctrines.

Editor Howe printed, with Mann's long letter, an extended comment of his own. Mann had dragged in a variety of unreal issues, he wrote, but the *Witness* would not

be diverted from the great question, whether the exclusion of what is distinctive in Christianity, as a way of salvation, from our public schools, be not an unchristian measure which orthodox Christians ought to observe and think of. . . . You can learn what the Hon. gentleman regards as *un*-sectarian religion, by recurring to his own description of what he thinks suitable to be taught. . . . They are very well so far as they go; they are important to the social uprightness and welfare of man, but they leave untouched what we, and all Orthodox Christians esteem the essentials of Christianity,—the way of salvation by Jesus Christ. . . . of what particular sect does it favor the tenets, to teach that "God was in Christ reconciling the world unto himself," that "we are by nature children of wrath," that "the blood of Jesus Christ cleanseth from all sin," and that "by grace we are saved through faith"? Are these truths, which are the sum and substance of the gospel, distinctive of any "particular sect"? No, thank God, they are the common ground of the great body "who profess and call themselves Christians."[34]

In a response which the *Witness* declined to publish but which was carried in the *Boston Courier*, Mann made an unanswerable argument, given the assumption that the common school would provide a common instruction to all students: Who would select the teachers who would teach "the way of salvation?" And if some official screening process were established to assure the orthodoxy of those doing this sensitive teaching, "will you be so good as to tell me wherein your 'system' will 'differ' from an established religion!"[35] Given Mann's conviction that the schools must be centrally and uniformly guided and shaped, logic was on his side in arguing from the

194

difficulty of positive religious instruction. America had long since rejected the idea of a single state-prescribed religious orthodoxy in its churches, and there was no practical way to provide this in schools. Mann was on more solid ground here than when he attempted to demonstrate that the form of "religion" that *could* be taught in common schools was in fact the highest and best.

Mann's opponents differed with him not only about theology but also about how society should provide education for its children. This had been clear in the report of the Committee on Education four years earlier, and it was clear in Edward Newton's reply, again in the *Witness* (May 17), to Mann's letters. Newton wrote:

> we do not need this central, all-absorbing power; it is anti-republican in all its bearings, well adapted, perhaps, to Prussia and other European des-potisms, but not wanted here. All that we require is wise general laws, dependent for their execution on the virtue and interest of the people, leaving to the various sects the matter of watching against the improper encroachments of each other, experience having shown that they will be abundantly vigilant.[36]

Like Hodge, Packard, and Smith, Newton saw that the possibility of orthodox teaching was bound up with local control of the content of schooling and believed that a process of accommodation and mutual limi-tation would prevent the excesses that Mann predicted so vividly.

THE AMERICAN BIBLE SOCIETY. We have reviewed the forceful and of-ten very cogent arguments brought forward by Mann's orthodox Protestant opponents. As they frequently observed, they represented at least the nomi-nal beliefs of the majority of citizens. This was a period of rapid growth among the "evangelical" denominations, of frequent revival enthusiasm, and of self-confidence, by Protestant leaders, that they spoke for the nation. The question naturally arises: How were Mann and his allies able to impose their own vision of the common school and its religious mission upon the nation?

Part of the answer lies in Mann's own extraordinary skills as a controver-sialist. He was able to position himself as a stalwart advocate of the use of the Bible and the teaching of religion in common schools and to character-ize his opponents as narrow, bigoted sectaries. The position of the Ameri-can Bible Society, an unquestionably evangelical though nonsectarian or-ganization, during this period gives an indication of why Mann was able to isolate Smith and other critics.

At the twenty-third anniversary of the society, in 1839, Presbyterian minister Robert J. Breckinridge charged that

> It is to be feared that many who call themselves the friends of education are totally opposed to all religious influence either in the school or the community. . . . manifestly there can be no union of effort between those friends of education who exclude from their system all moral training, and those who make conscience of taking the Bible to school with them; and the sooner the question is made between them at the bar of the public, the better for the country; for the question between them is no less than this, Whether the education of a religious people shall be subject to an infidel or a christian control? . . . strifes and divisions are the price we pay for all that is precious in a sinful world.[37]

Mann managed to align himself among those supporting moral training and the use of the Bible in the common school. Thus he could have seconded the sentiments of John W. Yeomans, president of Lafayette College in Pennsylvania, at an American Bible Society convention two years later:

> We have a theory of education which contemplates the universal instruction of the people. . . . it awakens sad apprehensions to hear of high examples in which the Holy Scriptures are rejected as a book for daily use in schools. . . . Can we countenance a plan of education which excludes the Scriptures? Will a christian people tolerate a system which keeps God out of all the thoughts of the young; and which sets up a virtue opposed to Christian holiness, or beside it, as the aim and perfection of the moral man?[38]

Or the resolution of John Thompson of Poughkeepsie, seconded by John Tappan of Boston, adopted by the convention of 1842: "That the growing disposition manifested of late to use the Bible as a leading-book in common schools is an auspicious omen to our country."[39]

It was only when someone like Matthew Hale Smith or Charles Hodge pressed his position more closely that it became clear, to them at least, that Mann meant something very different by "religious instruction" than did most Americans and that the use of the Bible by itself would not assure orthodox religious teaching.

Roman Catholic Opponents

The objections of Roman Catholics to the public common schools shifted ground during the antebellum period. At first, the primary objection was to the allegedly Protestant character of the schools (however much orthodox Protestants might have objected to that description); subsequently, as

196

the first objection was met by removing religious practices, it was replaced by the criticism that the schools were "godless."

This shift naturally led to charges that Catholic leadership was hypocritically determined to destroy the common schools on any pretext, in order to preserve their own authority over the hapless immigrant. There was little inclination, among the elite groups who were the primary supporters of the common school, to listen sympathetically to the reasons given by Catholics for their position. Orthodox Protestants themselves did not appear to notice how close Catholic objections were to their own, so convinced were they that "popery" was distantly if at all related to Christianity. In this Charles Hodge of Princeton was an honorable exception.

This course of events was very different from that in the Netherlands, where orthodox Protestants and Catholics began to work together on school policy soon after the Constitution of 1848 gave both groups a measure of electoral power. Two factors may have been of particular significance in producing this difference: (1) Orthodox Protestants in the United States lacked the coherence developed in the Netherlands through struggle against a liberal established church backed by government authority and were further confused by revivalism, and (2) Catholicism in the United States was strongly identified with a foreign threat and with ignorance and lower status, whereas Catholics and orthodox Protestants in the Netherlands shared a modest status in the society. Though the alliances formed in the Netherlands required overcoming strong prejudices on both sides, they did not face such complications as in the United States.

The story of Catholic opposition to the common school is better known than that of Protestant opposition, and it is not necessary to cover it in such detail. Our concern here is particularly with the evolving reasons given by Catholic leaders for their demand, at first, that common schools be purged of "sectarian" Protestant teaching and, subsequently, that Catholic children be educated in explicitly Catholic schools, if possible with public financial support.

That Catholics attempted to develop schools at all levels in the early years of the Republic has no special significance; virtually every denomination made the same effort in those parts of the country where—unlike New England—there was inadequate coverage of town schools. Opposition to what was taught in those common schools was expressed in 1828, however, by two bishops in their suggestions for discussion at the First Provincial Council of Baltimore.[40] Bishop James Fenwick, S.J., of Boston wrote that "all the children educated in the common schools of the country are obliged to use books compiled by Protestants by which their minds are poisoned as it were from their infancy."

197

Despite this concern, the pastoral letter of 1829, adopted at this council, did not directly criticize the common school. It was content with stressing the importance of an education in the faith and the dangers of a "neglected or an improper education." Catholic parents, especially those of children ready for secondary education, should

> seek for those teachers who will cultivate the seed which you have sown [in the home]. . . . How well would it be, if your means and opportunities permitted, were you . . . to commit your children to the care of those whom we have for your special fitness placed over our seminaries and our female religious institutions.[41]

The undeveloped state of Catholic educational alternatives at this period may have contributed to the mildness of this statement compared with those of later decades, as may the fact that the common school had not yet acquired that sense of a homogenizing mission that was to develop under the leadership of Horace Mann and others.

THE CONTROVERSY IN NEW YORK. In the early 1830s there were five Catholic schools in New York City, to serve a population of some 35,000. Inevitably, many children were faced with attending the common schools operated by the Public School Society, a private organization with trustees drawn from the city's elite, serving a semipublic function with public funding support. Apparently an appreciable number of Catholic parents chose not to send their children to such schools. Bishop John Dubois petitioned the trustees in 1834 to make certain changes to "ensure the confidence of Catholic parents and remove the false excuses of those who cover their neglect under the false pretext of religion, which they do not practice."
According to historian Diane Ravitch, Dubois

> asked that the board permit him to recommend a Catholic teacher for P.S.S. 5, subject to examination and removal by the trustees; that he be allowed the use of the school after school hours, for religious instruction of apprentices and servants; that the trustees expunge any passages in schoolbooks which inculcated Protestant sectarian principles or defamed the Catholic religion; . . . that the bishop be permitted to visit the school occasionally and offer suggestions to the trustees for its improvement; that religious instruction be given to Catholic children between five and seven each evening by a clergyman designated by the bishop.[42]

The trustees rejected these requests, except for the removal of any objectionable passages that might be pointed out, an offer Dubois did not take advantage of. Ravitch suggests of a similar episode several years later, "the clergy did not cooperate in editing biased material out of the books, because they knew that to do so would remove one of the best complaints they had against the schools of the Society."[43]

As the controversy over public funds for elementary education developed in 1840, a Catholic spokesman rejected the argument that common schools could be religiously neutral. After all,

> The Catholic Church tells her children that they must be taught their religion by *authority*. The Sects say, read the bible, judge for yourselves. The bible is read in the public schools, the children are allowed to judge for themselves. The Protestant principle is therefore acted upon, slily inculcated, and the schools are Sectarian.[44]

And, again, "How can we think of sending our children to those schools in which every artifice is resorted to in order to reduce them from their religion?"[45]

One sees clearly why Catholic opposition to "common school religion" was more effective than that of orthodox Protestants. Mann could and did charge the orthodox with inconsistency in objecting to his policy of Bible reading without doctrinal interpretation, on the basis of their own commitment to the principle of individual interpretation. For Catholics, there was no such problem; they believed that those untrained in the doctrines of the church could not adequately interpret Scripture for themselves and that there were great dangers in the attempt.

A report prepared on behalf of Catholic citizens the same year took the opposite, but complementary, line, that the common schools were lacking in any religion and therefore hostile to it. As summarized by Ravitch, the report urged that

> only the cultivation of religious and moral understanding could mold virtuous and enlightened citizens. Nonsectarianism, it was argued, necessarily banished the Christian religion from the public schools; since the negation of Christianity is infidelity, therefore "the public school system in the city of New York is entirely favorable to the sectarianism of infidelity."

The address held that

> even the least perfect religion of Christian sectarianism would be better than no religion at all. . . . The transition will not be found difficult or unnatural from the idea of a common school to that of a common religion; from which, of course, in order to make it popular, all Christian sectarianism will be carefully excluded.[46]

Later in 1840 a petition to the alderman from "the Catholics of New York" rejected the claim of the Public School Society to provide an education to which no parent should object.

If they do, as they profess, exclude sectarianism, then your petitioners contend that they exclude Christianity and leave to the advantage of infidelity the tendencies which are given to the minds of youth by the influence of this feature and pretension of their system.[47]

Thus Ravitch concludes that

The Church did not want public schools which were truly common schools, where Irish children and other Catholic children might go without fear of prejudice. Because of the Church's view of the inseparability of religion and education, the kind of nonsectarian common school which had developed in New York City and in other parts of the country was wholly inimical.[48]

Although the charges that the common schools were "Protestant" and that the reading materials contained anti-Catholic biases were useful in controversy, it is clear that for the Catholic leaders the real issue was that education *should* be "sectarian," in the sense that it should include the explicit teaching of a particular religious tradition. Bishop Hughes believed that "if you exclude all sects, you exclude Christianity. Take away the distinctive dogmas of the Catholics, the Baptists, the Methodists, the Presbyterians, and so on, and you have nothing left but deism."

In this Hughes exaggerated the differences among the Protestant "sects," as Mann also was accustomed to do.[49] There *were* real differences among orthodox Protestants, of course, but their willingness to cooperate on revival campaigns in rural areas and on large-scale institutional ministries— the "Evangelical United Front"—is a constant theme of contemporary accounts. Methodists and Baptists might compete for members, but they worked together closely as well. There is no reason to believe that sectarian competition was as great a problem of local schools as Mann, Hughes, and others made it out to be. This was, indeed, what Webster called "the old story, the old infidel argument," a favorite theme in the Enlightenment critique of Christianity in the eighteenth century.

THE BISHOPS STATE THEIR POSITION. As the battles over support for Catholic schooling developed in New York City and State, the national Catholic hierarchy began to make its own position more explicit. The bishops observed in their pastoral letter of 1840 that "there are few subjects dearer to us than the proper education of your children" and warned of "the danger to which they are exposed, of having their faith undermined, the imperfect instruction which they receive, if they get any, upon the most important subject of religion." Despite, or because of, this concern the bishops opposed the use of the Bible as a class book in schools, lest it be "exposed to that irreverend familiarity which is calculated to produce more contempt than veneration." This danger "shows the necessity of your better exertions to establish and uphold seminaries and schools, fitted according to our own principles."

The bishops did not fail to repeat the accusation that the materials used in common schools were tainted with anti-Catholic prejudice.

> We can scarcely point out a book in general use in the ordinary schools . . . wherein covert and insidious efforts are not made to misrepresent our principles, to distort our tenets, to vilify our practices and to bring contempt upon our Church and its members.

Although they were not reluctant to "contribute whatever little we can to the prosperity of what are called the common institutions of the country," the bishops were "always better pleased to have a separate system of education for the children of our communion." [50]

Three years later the bishops returned to their criticism of the religious flavor of the common schools. This was the period when the American Bible Society was passing resolutions calling for the use of the Bible in the schools, and Mann and other reformers were disarming the orthodox majority by stressing the same theme. The pastoral of 1843 noted that

> We have seen with serious alarm, efforts made to poison the fountains of public education, by giving it a sectarian hue, and accustoming children to the use of a version of the Bible made under sectarian bias, and placing in their hands books of various kinds replete with offensive and dangerous matter. This is plainly opposed to the free genius of our civil institutions. . . . Let [parents] see that no interference with the faith of their children be used in the public schools, and no attempt made to induce conformity in any thing contrary to the laws of the Catholic Church. [51]

At this point the Catholic church was not in a position to provide schools of its own for the children of immigrants. A decade later, however, the bishops at the First Plenary Council (1852) rejected the idea that education could be purged of religious elements and warned lest youth be "involved in all the evils of an uncatholic education, evils too multiplied and too obvious to require that we should do more than raise our voices in solemn protest against the system from which they spring." [52]

The bishops were responding to the recent papal encyclical calling upon all bishops worldwide to provide for Catholic education. This initiative from Rome helped to set up what would become the bitter hostility between French radicals and the Catholic hierarchy over schooling. The encyclical also had an impact upon the course of events in the Netherlands, helping to break the alliance between Catholics and liberals and creating the conditions in which that between Catholics and orthodox Protestants was to evolve. No such alliance developed in the United States, and Catholics faced not only isolation but also condemnation from all sides for their efforts to establish their own schools.

CONFLICT IN BOSTON. Some of the sharpest conflicts over the religious character of common schools occurred in Boston. By 1850 one-half of the children in Boston aged five to fifteen were "foreign" (including the children of a foreign-born parent), with the proportion much higher in some sections of the city. Those overseeing the public schools were convinced that they were the primary instrumentality to "Americanize that class of our population" so that they would become "lovers of American soil and sustainers of American institutions."[53]

This program of assimilation rested upon a conviction that otherwise immigrant children represented a serious threat to society. Although there were generous impulses of extending an opportunity, there were also fearful ones of preventing social breakdown. Thus the Boston School Committee stressed in 1850,

> We must open the doors of our school houses and invite and compel them to come in. There is no other hope for them or for us. . . . In our Schools they receive moral and religious teaching, powerful enough if possible to keep them in the right path amid the moral darkness which is their daily and domestic walk. . . . unless we can redeem this population in their childhood by moral means, we must control them by force, or support them as paupers, at a maturer period of life.[54]

This explicit program of assimilation, since it rested upon a conviction of the superior moral value of Protestantism—an almost universal assumption among Protestants—met with resistance from Catholics. The periodical of the Boston diocese advised Catholic parents in 1853 that teachers had no right to enforce such sectarian practices as reading the King James version of the Bible or reciting Protestant prayers.[55] The year before the *Pilot* had told its readers that

> The general principle upon which these [education] laws are based is radically unsound, untrue, Atheistical. . . . It is, that the education of children is *not* the work of the Church, or of the Family, but that it is the work of the State. . . . Two consequences flow from this principle. . . . In the matter of education, the State is supreme over the Church and the Family. *Hence*, the State can and does exclude from the schools religious instruction. . . . The inevitable consequence is, that . . . the greater number of

scholars must turn out to be Atheists, and accordingly the majority of non-Catholics are people of no religion. . . . The other consequence . . . leads the State to *adopt* the child, to weaken the ties which bind it to the parent. So laws are made compelling children to attend the state schools, and forbidding the parents, if they be poor, to withdraw their little ones from the school.

The issue was becoming critical at a point when anti-immigrant feeling was at its height in Massachusetts, resulting in the election of an overwhelming majority of state legislators who were strongly opposed to Catholic claims to equal consideration. In 1852 the legislature passed the first compulsory school attendance law in the country, and vigorous enforcement followed; in 1853 the Boston truant officer reported 98 native and 559 foreign truants.[56]

In order to insure that immigrant children were exposed to the full program of Protestant moral teaching, the anti-Catholic "Know-Nothing" majority in the legislative session of 1855 adopted a law requiring the daily reading of the Scriptures in public schools. This had already become compulsory for the Boston schools in 1851, as was the use of the Lord's Prayer in 1857. That year the weekly recitation of the Ten Commandments was also required. The regulations made it clear that this was a devotional exercise.

The combination of vigorous efforts to bring Catholic children into common schools with explicit insistence upon religious practices led inevitably to conflict. The most celebrated instance occurred in 1859 at the Eliot School, where Thomas Wall, a Catholic boy, refused to recite the Commandments in their "Protestant" form. After a variety of developments that do not concern us here, Bishop Fitzpatrick wrote to the Boston School Committee that

> The Catholic cannot act in this manner. He cannot present himself before the Divine presence in what would be for him a merely simulated union of prayer and adoration. His Church expressly forbids him to do so. She considers indifference in matters of religion, indifference as to the distinction of positive doctrines of faith, as a great evil which promiscuous worship would tend to spread more widely and increase.

Compromises were made that reduced tension for a time, though the public schools would again become a battleground between Boston Catholics and Protestants several decades later.[57]

The logic of the Catholic position, as expressed by Bishop Fitzpatrick and others, did not really allow any alternative to Catholic-controlled schools. Sectarian Protestant teaching was utterly offensive, "neutral" religious practices reflected an objectionable "indifference," and the exclusion of religion altogether would teach "infidelity." Only the positive and authoritative teaching of Catholic doctrine could satisfy the sense, among the Catholic leadership, of what the defense of their faith required.

Conclusions

Roman Catholic opposition to the common public school has frequently been understood as reflecting an immigrant group's concern to preserve its traditions and coherence as it faced the acids of a new environment. The creation of a parochial system can be seen as perhaps the most massive and (for several generations) successful attempt in American history to prevent "cognitive contamination" by keeping the formal socialization of children within institutions in which the beliefs, values, and world views of parents would be presented consistently to their children. This may be seen as a less extreme form of the strategies employed by such groups as the Amish and Hasidic Jews.

Some support for this view may be derived from the fact that several smaller immigrant groups for whom a particular religious position was an important element of identity—German (mostly Saxon) Lutherans and Dutch Calvinists, for example—were also successful in creating and maintaining their own schools.

Though the sense of a threatened group identity is an important factor in the success of the efforts by Catholics and some other immigrants to create and maintain their own schools, this is not a sufficient explanation of why they believed that this struggle should occur primarily with respect to formal schooling. Other immigrant groups, including Jews and Scandinavian Lutherans, embraced the public school with enthusiasm and found other means of preserving group identity. Italian and Polish Catholics appear to have felt less strongly than did German and Irish Catholics about the importance of creating their own parochial schools.

A further difficulty with the "resistance to assimilation" thesis is that virtually every immigrant group was in fact eager to fit into American life and to assure that its children would not suffer under the stigma of being a foreign element. In some respects, in fact, parochial schools rivaled the public schools in their commitment to "Americanization." German and Irish Catholic immigrants were eager to embrace virtually everything about contemporary American life while providing an alternative educational system for their children. Group solidarity, though it explains how they were able to do so, does not explain why this seemed so important to them.

To understand this we must take seriously what their leaders said on the subject and the instructive parallels with what farsighted orthodox Protestants were saying at the same time. They were speaking against a background of the contemporary struggles in Great Britain (including Ireland), the German states, and the Netherlands between a triumphant liberalism concerned to use the common school aggressively and orthodox Christianity, Protestant and Catholic alike.

As we have noted, the orthodox Protestant opponents of the common school and of Horace Mann were not generally aware of the parallel struggles that were taking place in Europe, though the Dutch Calvinist and German Lutheran immigrants who were coming to the Midwest during this period were fresh from those struggles and acted accordingly in forming their own "sectarian" schools.

Catholic leaders, by contrast, were acutely aware of the controversies over schooling in Europe. Virtually all of them were French, Irish or German. Heated controversies were taking place in France, Ireland and Germany, and the papacy was taking the lead in rallying Catholics worldwide to resist what it not inaccurately saw as a liberal assault. This placed the creation of alternative schools—and, where that was not possible, the resistance to objectionable practices in public schools—at the top of the Catholic agenda in the United States. The Italian and Eastern European immigrants who came in their millions late in the century were much less concerned about the issue because schooling of any kind—and thus controversy about schooling—had been minimal in the areas from which they came, but church leadership continued to be almost exclusively in Irish and German hands, and thus the Catholic perception of a struggle with liberalism over education remained unchanged.

In this perspective it is possible to understand that the failure of native-born orthodox Protestants in the United States to resist "common school religion" was the result not only of their belief that common schools were necessary to protect their own stake in a culturally homogeneous society but also of their lack of a tradition of struggle with a secularizing liberalism over the content of schooling.

Liberalism in America took a "softer" form, often cloaking its antiorthodox purposes in the Christian vocabulary. This approach was not unique to the United States; indeed, it was in part learned from liberal Protestant education reformers in Prussia, the Netherlands, and even in France, but it was uniquely successful under American conditions. Horace Mann and his allies presented the mission of the common school in essentially religious, salvific terms to a Protestant majority that was quite prepared to identify the institutions of American society with the Kingdom of God.

Anxiety about the effects of immigration upon the homogeneity and moral coherence of American society provided the essential energy behind the triumph of common school religion over its opponents, but it was the theological confusion of nineteenth-century Protestantism that prevented an effective resistance. The orthodox Protestant majority that could have insisted upon religious teaching reflecting the views of parents and local communities, or public support for a choice of schools, was easily persuaded that a generalized civic religion was an acceptable and indeed necessary substitute.

Concerns about group solidarity under the assaults of an unfriendly social environment provided the essential energy behind the creation of alternative "sectarian" school systems by several immigrant groups, but it was the theological clarity developed in contemporary struggles in Europe that made this seem a necessity.

8

Alternatives to the
Common School

The Effort to Create Alternatives

NEW ENGLAND BEFORE THE RISE OF CATHOLIC EDUCATION. In the eighteenth and early nineteenth centuries, when most New England communities were religiously still fairly homogeneous, the colonial education provisions had become inadequate due to neglect and to population growth. "Nonpublic" schools (to use an anachronistic term), either for profit or operated by benevolent foundations, existed side by side with "public" schools without the perception of there being a significant difference. Such schools were not established as religious alternatives to public schooling, as were the later parochial schools, though religious motivations were commonly at work in their founding. The Great Awakening of the 1740s had indeed contributed significantly to the revival of education, with many joining Jonathan Edwards in calling for

> schools, in poor towns and villages, which might . . . not only . . . bring up children in common learning, but also might very much tend to their conviction and conversion, and being trained up in vital piety; and doubtless something might be done in this way in old towns and more populous places, that might have a great tendency to the flourishing of religion in the rising generation.[1]

One who responded was Samuel Phillips, Jr., of Andover, son of a wealthy merchant from orthodox stock. Phillips, who was to play a leading political role during the Revolution, complained of "the decay of virtue, public and private," owing to "the neglect of good instruction. Upon the sound education of children depends the comfort or grief of parents, the welfare or disorder of the community, the glory or ruin of the state."[2] The founding document (1778) of the academy that he endowed in Andover speaks in terms common to the Protestant Enlightenment, with its confidence in the improvement of the human condition through education, of the grand design of the great *Parent of the Universe* in the creation of man-kind, and the improvements of which the mind is capable, both in knowl-edge and virtue as well as upon the prevalence of ignorance and vice, dis-order and wickedness.

Horace Mann and his allies a half-century later could have echoed this view of the world and of the importance of education, as they would have applauded the insistence that the schoolmaster devote himself to the "*Minds* and *Morals* of the youth under his charge," but they could not have ap-proved the "sectarian" character of the religious instruction that would be provided to the students. The schoolmaster was charged

> not only to instruct and establish them in the truth of Christianity [which could mean virtually anything at that time]; but also early and diligently to inculcate upon them the great and important scripture doctrines of . . . the fall of man, the depravity of human nature; the necessity of an atone-ment and of our being renewed in the spirit of our minds; the doctrines of repentance toward God and of faith toward our Lord Jesus Christ . . . and of justification by the free grace of God through the redemption that is in Jesus Christ.[3]

This is uncompromisingly orthodox language, of course, and we should not disregard a polemical element in it at a time when the liberal tendencies that would become Unitarianism were emerging in Boston and on the North Shore. It was, after all, in Andover that the orthodox (with the help of the Phillips family) would three decades later locate the theological semi-nary, the "West Point of orthodoxy," established in opposition to the Uni-tarian takeover of Harvard Divinity School. The Phillips Academy was equally orthodox in intention, but it was established not in a spirit of op-position but to meet an educational and social need.

The new school was described as "a public free school or *Academy*" in its constitution, in the sense that it was intended to serve the public at large, though under control of independent trustees and enjoying a large endow-ment. At this point the terms "public" and "private" had not acquired the specific and heavily laden significance that would develop during the "com-mon school" movement.

Nonpublic schools were not limited to such relatively elite secondary institutions as Phillips Academy in Andover; they were a primary means of providing education at all levels in communities where population growth had outstripped the colonial arrangements.

In what Stanley Schultz refers to as "one of the earliest 'social surveys' of an urban population," the Boston School Committee carried out a ward-by-ward census in 1817. This survey, coordinated by architect Charles

Bulfinch, found that public school enrollment amounted to 2,365 students, with over 4,000 students attending free or tuition-charging private schools. Bulfinch suggested that the hundreds of students not attending any school could be accommodated within the existing structures, with the Overseers of the Poor continuing to pay tuition for those children whose parents could not afford to send them to private schools. He found important moral advantages to expecting those parents who were able to do so to take responsibility by paying tuition and thus devoting attention to the education of their children.[4]

Other citizens did not agree, insisting that the city should take responsibility for the education of all children in common schools in order to bring together in mutual harmony children of all the nationalities, races, and social and economic classes in Boston. It was this view that ultimately prevailed in the establishment of free primary schools under public control. These schools were managed by a Primary School Board made up of "the godly and well-to-do who could be depended upon to uphold the financial and moral interests of their class,"[5] appointed by the School Committee.

In effect, the first urban school *system* in the country was set up on behalf of the common people by an elite that itself undoubtedly patronized the better private schools for their children. The private charity schools and those that educated students from moderate-income families were quickly driven out of business, whereas private schools for the more affluent continued to serve their clientele.

As in Boston, it appears that much of the energy of the education reformers of the "common school revival" had less to do with the unavailability of elementary schooling than it did with opposition to such schooling under private auspices. Kaestle and Vinovskis, after a careful study of the data available, concluded that

> Americans' apparent indifference to the educational schemes of republican theorists in the early days of nationhood led to the myth of the "sleepy" period in our educational history. The illusion that there was little schooling prior to 1840 in the American Northeast can be traced to school reformers like Horace Mann and Henry Barnard, who were hostile to private schools, such as academies, as well as to the small district schools that prevailed in rural areas. They preferred the model of the mid-seventeenth-century New England town, where schools served the whole town and were required by colony-wide laws. As population dispersed, however, the district system developed in rural areas; and in the eighteenth century urban development fostered private educational alternatives.[6]

The data available on schooling in Salem—the second city in Massachusetts early in the nineteenth century—show that the shift from private to public, and the development of a state-assisted public school system, had little effect upon the proportion of children enrolled. . . . As this public sector grew in Salem schooling, the total enrollment remained remarkably stable. . . . Enrollment records for Boston tell the same story. In 1826, when 44.5 percent of all children aged birth to nineteen were in some school, 32.6 percent of all schoolchildren were in private schools. . . . by 1850, when the percentage in private schools had dropped to 12.2, the overall enrollment rate remained at 45.4 percent.[7]

Thus the growth of public school enrollment as a proportion of population, so lovingly documented by Mann in his reports, was largely at the expense of private schools rather than the result of enrolling out-of-school youth. Though private schools maintained their enrollment levels in terms of absolute numbers, it was by serving a more and more elite clientele, thus achieving the opposite result from Mann's stated goal of social integration through public education.

What occurred was not, then, a victory over separate elite schooling, as Mann would have liked, but a conversion of low-priced pay schools, local academies, and subscription schools (kept to prolong the common schools) into town-controlled, tax-supported schools.[8]

Efforts to organize schools on a "sectarian" religious basis in New England during the nineteenth century, then, were not so much threatening an existing unity of schooling—as Mann and his allies claimed—as retarding a program of suppressing established alternatives to the common school that had rendered good service. This program did not lack opponents, who continued to support nonpublic schooling, especially at the secondary level, but ironically enough these opponents were equally hostile to the new Catholic schools. Thus Edward Hitchcock, in an address at "Williston Seminary" (a secondary academy) in 1845, proclaimed that

in this country the government presumes that every parent is intelligent and judicious enough to judge what sort of an education it is best to give his children. . . . a free and intelligent people prefer to have the control of so important a business themselves; and it has come to be pretty well understood, that if we wish to have an institution fail, let the government start it and attempt to support it. . . . Were the government to deprive individuals, or parties, or sects, of the right to establish such seminaries, their own forced treadmill system would be a wretched substitute.[9]

Yet, just before saying this he had attacked "the system of the papist" as "utterly unadapted to this free Protestant country, as well as to this age." No alliance was in fact possible between a Protestant elite concerned to protect its institutions from the leveling and unifying claims of the liberal reformers and the clerical leadership of a Catholic underclass who were seeking to develop their own institutions in defense against the assimilating zeal of the reformers.

There was thus little tradition of nonpublic schools as religious alternatives in New England when Mann and others began to shape a program and develop a supporting ideology of the common school. Roman Catholic leaders found themselves without allies as they sought to develop their own school system. This may help to explain why Catholic education developed relatively slowly around Boston compared with other parts of the country where there was strong Catholic migration and also a stronger tradition of Protestant alternative schools.

LUTHERAN SCHOOLING. The German immigrants to Pennsylvania during the eighteenth century were in many cases refugees from Catholic religious oppression in the Palatinate, and some support for the schooling of their children was provided by the Pietist center of mission and educational energies at Halle. Their extreme poverty retarded these efforts, so that by the start of the Revolution only about forty German schools were in operation. Pennsylvania leader Benjamin Franklin was dubious about their attempts to perpetuate a distinct culture, writing in 1753, "All that seems to me necessary is to distribute them more equally, mix them with the English, establish English schools where they are now too thickly settled."[10]

A different approach was advocated in a report on education submitted to the Pennsylvania legislature by Dr. Benjamin Rush in 1786. Rush called for free schools in every township, with instruction in both German and English and provision that "children of the same religious sect and nation may be educated as much as possible together."[11] In effect, he was recognizing that the diversity of the population of Pennsylvania required that a system of public schooling be itself diversified.

German schools with explicitly Lutheran teaching developed further after the Revolution, with approximately 130 schools under the supervision of the Pennsylvania ministerium by the end of the century. Similar efforts were made in other centers of German immigration, such as New Jersey, North Carolina, and (a little later) Ohio. One historian calculates that there were 342 Lutheran schools in the United States by 1820.[12]

The role of ethnicity in this development is difficult to distinguish from that of religion; though virtually all such schools were initiated and controlled by local churches, "the major opposition to public schools came to be based on the question of language." As one correspondent wrote to the *Lutherische Kirchenzeitung* in 1841,

211

Whoever gives up his language, brings shame upon his parents and gives up his religion besides and becomes a Methodist. And is the English language then nobler and more beautiful than German? I think not. . . . But as soon as pride enters into the young people, they want to be English and are ashamed to talk German.[13]

That language was a major factor in the development of these Lutheran "parochial schools" is suggested by the fact that they gradually faded away in Pennsylvania as the German population adopted the use of English. Fear of Catholic immigration and of Catholic "sectarian" schools as the supposed consolidator of Catholic power was a major factor in the triumph of the common school among Protestants of all ethnic backgrounds. Thus the Lutheran East Pennsylvania Synod adopted "Resolutions on Common Schools" in 1853; they began,

> Whereas, The most industrious and insidious efforts are at present being made in this and other States by those in connection with the Roman Catholic Church to divert a portion of the Common School Fund . . . Resolved, That we regard the Common School System of Pennsylvania as *now* constituted as the pride and ornament of our State . . . and every effort to engraft upon it features of an obnoxious sectarian character we regard as a stab aimed at its vitality, whose only consummation can be its utter subversion and overthrow.[14]

While Lutheran schools were fading away in Pennsylvania and other eastern states, new ones were being established in the Midwest, where Saxon immigrants held to a strongly orthodox interpretation of Lutheranism. A background of controversies over the "Prussian Union" of Lutheran and Reformed churches in 1817 and over the nature of religious teaching in state schools made these immigrants particularly determined to preserve a religious tradition, more so than were the eastern Lutherans. Settling first in Saint Louis in 1839, this group established the Missouri Synod in 1847, with teachers among the original organizers. By 1871 the 419 congregations of this denomination supported 408 schools with 26,455 students. There can be no doubt that factors of language and ethnicity were also extremely important in the growth of this system of schools; indeed, the denominational publication for teachers was largely in German until 1885, when articles began to appear more frequently in English.[15]

A concern to maintain religious orthodoxy was of at least equal importance, however, to judge by the fact that other Lutheran groups who immigrated around the same time did not make as much effort to maintain their languages. The Scandinavian Lutherans, numbering nearly 2 million immigrants in the nineteenth century, did not have the same kind of background of religious controversy in their homelands and were much quicker to support the public common schools than were the Missouri Synod Lutherans.

> There was a general tendency among the Scandinavians for full-time schools to continue as such only for a limited period of years until the immigrant stocks . . . had become settled and adjusted and had acquired a knowledge of English. After a few years the need of the full-time elementary school was considered to have passed.[16]

The Norwegian-American press was calling upon parents to send their children to the common schools as early as 1850.[17]

Other groups of German immigrants, less orthodox theologically than those belonging to the Missouri Synod, were also much less interested in maintaining their own schools and satisfied themselves with pressing for the teaching of German in the public schools.

In short, the experience of Lutheran schooling in the United States suggests that the desire to preserve a minority language and culture was an essential precondition for the maintenance of sectarian schools but that such schools were in fact maintained only when a self-conscious religious orthodoxy made that seem of transcendent importance. This would suggest, reciprocally, that religiously orthodox groups would be more likely to maintain a distinctive language and culture as a concomitant to sectarian schooling.

ORTHODOX PRESBYTERIAN SCHOOLS. There is, at it happens, a test case of the hypothesis suggested above: The orthodox Presbyterians expressed a strong desire to develop their own system of schools to teach "pure religion, and undefiled" during the decades before the Civil War but were unable to carry out this program because of their lack of the essential precondition of a distinctive ethnic and linguistic heritage.

As early as 1799 the Presbyterian General Assembly noted that "a vain and pernicious philosophy has, in many instances, spread its infection from Europe to America" and urged elders to serve as school trustees to assure that neither teachers nor instruction were infected. In 1812 there was much discussion, in the Assembly, of a proposal for parochial schools. In 1838 Dr. Samuel Miller published an article in the *Biblical Repository*, observing that ministers should not be satisfied with the limited instruction possible in Sunday schools, and in 1840 he presented a committee report to the Assembly recommending that every congregation should establish one or more "Church Schools" for children from six to ten. This report was adopted by the Assembly in 1841.[18]

The context of this growing concern is the split in 1837 among Presbyterians into "Old School" and "New School" factions over the liberalizing theology of the latter. The orthodox Old School Assembly addressed a "pastoral letter" to the congregations in 1838 calling for teaching the doctrines of the church, especially through the use of the catechisms. As one Old School leader asserted, sound training of youth would protect against "that spirit of declension and fatal error which is abroad."[19]

In a series of reports and statements through the 1840s, the Assembly stressed the desirability of an instruction that would "direct the infant mind, not only to a meager natural religion, but to the whole round of gracious truth, as it is in Christ Jesus." After all, state schools could not teach the full doctrines of revelation, which put children "in a favorable position, by God's grace, for the salvation of the soul." Education was in fact the "peculiar and appropriate province" of the church, which, "by a strange perversion," had come to be attributed to the state.[20]

Despite strong support by J. W. Alexander, Charles Hodge, and other leading intellectuals among the Old School group, the project of organizing denominational schools produced meager results. Less than 1 percent of the congregations founded schools over the next twenty years, and the movement was already in decline by about 1854.[21] The orthodox rigor of this denomination gave it the will but not the means to maintain a system comparable to that developed by the Missouri Synod Lutherans in the same period, with 97 percent of the much poorer congregations supporting schools.

As further evidence that a combination of doctrinal rigor and minority cultural status was necessary to sustain a system of sectarian schools, we will mention briefly a system of schools in the Reformed theological tradition which were more successful than those of the orthodox Presbyterians, despite far smaller resources of talent and money.

The Dutch immigration to the Midwest after the *Afscheiding* ("secession") within the Hervormde Kerk that began in 1834 shared many characteristics with that of the Saxon Lutherans during the same decade. An early characteristic of the Afscheiding was the insistence of the "little people" upon controlling the education of their children in unauthorized schools rather than sending them to public schools in which a nonsectarian liberal Christianity was taught. After many prosecutions that destituted orthodox parents, several of their ministers organized an immigration to the United States where they could

enjoy the privilege of seeing their little ones educated in a Christian school—a privilege of which we are here entirely deprived, as the instruc-

214

tion in the state's schools may be called but a mere general moral one, offensive to neither Jew nor Roman Catholic.[22]

After a slow start, the system of Dutch Calvinist schools began to grow in the Midwest and elsewhere, including nearly 400 schools with more than 72,000 students at present. Maintenance of the Dutch language has not been an important consideration in recent decades, but it was the close-knit Dutch-American community that provided the soil in which the seed of theological conviction could grow. In addition—like the Saxon Lutherans and German and Irish Catholics—the Dutch immigrants brought a tradition of the school as the place to take a stand against liberal religious teaching. They were better prepared than were their orthodox Presbyterian co-religionists to see themselves as holding convictions that could not be satisfied by American common schools.

Efforts within the essentially "establishment" Presbyterian church to create sectarian schools were more difficult, precisely because many of its leaders were so heavily committed to the social mission of the common school. The Reverend R. J. Breckinridge, for example, served as superintendent of education for the state of Kentucky from 1847 to 1853 and urged that the state provide for the education of all of its people to insure "its own security." "Revealed religion" could be taught in the common school by the regular use of the Bible. In 1850 he urged the Presbyterian Assembly to avoid committing itself to providing a comprehensive education program.[23]

Breckinridge was one of those who in effect disarmed the orthodox by their insistence that the common school could meet their educational objectives and who refused to abandon the common school to "the spirit of popery which every where suppresses the word of God; the spirit of indifferentism, which treats it with total slight; and the spirit of infidelity, which openly rejects it," as he proclaimed to the American Bible Society in 1839. "No adequate moral instruction can be furnished generally in our public schools, unless the Bible itself be put into the hands of the pupils," he told the society, and he committed himself and it to working to insure that this occurred in the common schools "in all our States and Territories." This would, he admitted, meet with "infidel" opposition, but "strifes and divisions are the price we pay for all that is precious in a sinful world."[24] For many of the native-born orthodox, such calls to struggle for influence upon the entire nation through the common school must have seemed more appealing than a summons to withdraw into providing a Christian education to their own children alone.

ROMAN CATHOLIC SCHOOLS IN MASSACHUSETTS. Although Boston became an Episcopal see in 1808, the first Catholic school on record was not organized until 1820 under the impulse of Bishop Cheverus. Over the next decades several other schools were founded, some of them by the enterprise of schoolmasters from Ireland, but it was not until 1849 that an order of sisters began a systematic effort to provide education.[25] This order had originated in Belgium, where conflict over the control of education by the church or the government had been a major factor in the successful secession of 1830 from the Netherlands. Despite these efforts there were by 1855 only five free Catholic schools for girls, taught by sisters, and a few for boys taught by lay teachers.

To some extent the lack of full-time schools was compensated for by the organization of Sunday schools in emulation of the vigorous contemporary Protestant movement, which was seeking to enroll as many Catholic children as possible, with an eye to their conversion. Thus by 1845 (before the main Irish immigration began) there were 4,100 students enrolled in Catholic Sunday schools in Boston.[26]

The most interesting aspect of this development of an alternative Catholic education system was the arrangement made in the new industrial city of Lowell, where Catholic immigrants were beginning to replace the workers drawn from New England farms. In 1830 a committee was appointed to "consider the expediency of establishing a separate school for the benefit of the Irish population," and funds were appropriated the next year for such a school.[27] Despite this gesture, the Irish children continued to attend a school set up by their priest, and Bishop Fenwick wrote to local authorities stating the terms upon which Catholics would consent to send their children to the public school:

> I really do not understand how, in this liberal country, it can be made a condition to their receiving anything that they, the Catholics, shall be in that case debarred from having a Catholic teacher, learning out of Catholic books, and being taught the Catechism of the Catholic Church. We can never accept such terms. . . . it is all important that the person whom they select be one qualified to instruct children in the principles of their religion, for I would not give a straw for that species of education, which is not accompanied with and based upon religion.[28]

On the basis of this statement of principle the local pastor was able to negotiate an agreement with town authorities under which support for the two parochial schools would be taken over by the town. The public School Committee would examine and hire teachers, and the books used would be those prescribed for other schools, but the teachers would be Catholic and the books would contain no facts not accepted by the church and no remarks reflecting upon Catholicism. This arrangement was in effect from

1836 to 1852, though the schools gradually lost their distinctive Catholic character and non-Catholic teachers were appointed. A historian comments that "doubtless the school authorities had accomplished what they wished, they had coaxed the Irish into the public schools."[29]

Horace Mann, then in his last year as secretary of the Board of Education, expressed strong approval of the Lowell arrangement in the pages of the *Common School Journal* in 1848, reprinting a letter from John Green in Lowell. Green observed that

> By this mutual conciliation, we easily secured incalculable advantages; and from these small beginnings have grown up a class of large and highly respectable schools, drawn from our most degraded population. The Irish children may now be found in every school in the city in considerable numbers, even in our high school.[30]

With continuing growth of the Irish population and its dissatisfaction with the religious instruction now provided in the former parochial schools, new Catholic schools were founded starting in 1852. The breakdown of the Lowell arrangement was a reflection of an antiimmigrant campaign responding to the heavy immigration of the famine years (especially 1848 and 1849) and of an effort to require all of the Irish children to attend public schools where they could be assimilated to American habits and values. Barnas Sears, the secretary of the state Board of Education who followed Horace Mann, commented in his annual report of 1851 that

> The non-attendance of a part of those children for whose benefit the Public Schools are especially intended, particularly the children of foreigners in our large cities and manufacturing towns, is assuming a fearful importance; and it will not be safe long to delay such measures as may be necessary to avert the impending danger.[31]

Increased efforts were made by public authorities to compel school attendance by Irish children and to increase the explicitly socializing and assimilating impact of the common school by requiring daily Bible reading and other devotional practices that were clearly seen by both sides as a challenge to Catholic loyalty. These efforts led to growing tension and support within the Catholic community for the development of alternative schooling arrangements. Thus, while Barnas Sears's successor noted with satisfaction, in 1856, that the Catholic schools in the industrial city of Lawrence had been discontinued and 2,279 of their students had been received into the public schools, Bishop Fitzpatrick was devoting much of his energy to founding new institutions and obtaining teachers for them.

Conflicts over the refusal of Catholic students to join in recitation of Protestant versions of the Lord's Prayer and Ten Commandments, such as the celebrated Eliot School case in Boston in 1859, enhanced the solidarity of the Irish community in support of their own institutions and also in political involvement. As in the Netherlands, it was the insistence upon educating their children in their own convictions and loyalties that led to the initial political mobilization of a class that had previously been apathetic.

The support of Catholic schools was not easily accomplished by an immigrant population and was closely associated with a sense of alienation and helplessness with respect to the common school. As Bishop Fitzpatrick wrote in 1859,

> it is impossible to open catholic schools. . . . Already we find it almost impossible to provide churches for the hundreds of thousands of poor people whom the last ten years have sent to our shores. . . . No redress can be expected by petition to the authorities for the state is ruled by a vast majority of persecuting bigots who, a few years ago, were bound by oath, as members of the know-nothing party, to oppress Catholics. The very laws . . . were framed, no doubt, for the express purpose of corrupting the faith of Catholic children. The only alternative at present seems to be that the children, under open protest, submit to the tyranny exercised over them, but at the same time to loathe and detest its enactments. This very sense of unjust oppression may, with God's grace, strengthen them in their attachment to the faith.[32]

The same year, however, a Catholic priest was elected to the Boston School Committee, the more obnoxious features of the school devotional practices were removed, and at least four new Catholic schools opened in the diocese. Catholics were moving on two distinct tracks with respect to education, and not surprisingly they were accused of hypocrisy by some Protestant leaders: trying to make the common schools less religious, and thus less satisfactory to orthodox Protestants, while at the same time seeking to keep their own children out of those schools. The logic of the Catholic position was that their children should attend Catholic schools if possible, but to the extent that they could not they should attend schools with no religious character at all.

We have seen that there were financial obstacles to the organization of Catholic schools in the Boston diocese, but it may be questioned whether these were greater than those faced by the Saxon immigrants to the Midwest, or indeed by the German Catholics who created a substantial system of schools during the same period. A historian notes that there were "at least two hundred Catholic parish schools in the country in the year 1840. More than half of these were west of the Alleghenies. . . . the dioceses of Kentucky and St. Louis were better off for schools and teachers than the more populous dioceses of the East." [33] He attributes this to the "educational zeal or genius" of the western bishops, but they could not have been more concerned than Hughes in New York or Fenwick in Boston. It seems likely that the ethnic factor was at work here; indeed, several of the early Catholic schools in Boston served the city's small German population.

This appears to bear out our hypothesis that organization and support of a system of alternative religious schools required not only a sense of being in conflict with the religious character of the common schools but also a close-knit ethnic community concerned to preserve its language and culture. The Irish Catholics along the eastern seaboard were clear enough that the common schools did not support their own educational goals for their children, but it was not until after their much acclaimed participation in the Civil War that they began to acquire the self-confidence as a community that permitted them to build a system that, in Massachusetts, served 61,570 students by the year 1899.

The Attack on Nonpublic Schools

HORACE MANN AGAINST PRIVATE EDUCATION. Kaestle and Vinovskis observe that "Mann and other reformers presented the defeat of private schooling as a major objective." It is important to ask why. Perhaps the fullest presentation of Mann's views is found in a long series of articles that he wrote for the *Common School Journal* starting in May 1839, in which he asked "the professional men of Massachusetts,"

> Has not the course which some of you have pursued in relation to the education of your own children tended to reduce the reputation of our excellent free school system? . . . The consciousness that they are attending a school unworthy of the patronage of those whom they have been led to regard as the better part of the community, will degrade the children of the less-favored classes in their own estimation, and destroy that self-respect which is essential to improvement either in science or in morals. This feeling of degradation will hang like a millstone about the necks of the children of the poor. [34]

Equally seriously, the perpetuation of two classes of schools would lead to social and national disunity, "and so proves an injury to all classes."

> No one cause contributes so much to introduce the terms and the distinctions of other countries into our favored land. . . . in this way, the distinc-

tions of the dark ages, and of aristocratic governments, will be revived on these happy shores.[35]

Mann made a similar argument in his *First Report* (February 1838): The private school tended to draw away the "best scholars" and the children of those parents most influential and thus able to assure that common schools were of high quality. In so doing they depressed the education available to "more than *five-sixths* of the children in the state . . . dependant upon the common schools for instruction." Equally seriously, they reinforced social distinctions:

> It is on this common platform, that a general acquaintanceship should be formed between the children of the same neighborhood. It is here, that the affinities of a common nature should unite them together so as to give the advantages of pre-occupancy and a stable possession to fraternal feelings, against the alienating competitions of later life.[36]

So far the argument is the same as that advanced, at much greater length, in the articles in the *Common School Journal*. But Mann strikes two additional notes in his report. The first is a bold assertion, introduced in passing, of the idea that children belong ultimately to the state, which must watch over their early formation to assure that its own ends are met. Mann writes,

> After the state shall have secured to all its children, that basis of knowledge and morality, which is indispensable to its own security; after it shall have supplied them with the instruments of that individual prosperity, whose aggregate will constitute its own social prosperity; *then* they may be emancipated from its tutelage, each one to go withsoever his well-instructed mind shall determine. At this point, seminaries for higher learning, academies and universities, should stand ready to receive, at private cost, all whose path to any ultimate destination may lie through their halls. [Emphasis added.]

In other words, the state must control elementary education, in order to assure that all of its future citizens receive a common and uniform instruction, but need not control secondary and higher education. It was at those levels that preprofessional training occurred, and Mann was ready to concede that inequalities of fortune or of ability could lead students in different directions at that point. What he was *not* willing to concede, however, was that parents might demand for their children differing forms of preparation at the stage when the "basis of knowledge and morality" is being laid.

Mann's first concern about nonpublic elementary schools, then, was that they would tend to enhance social distinctions or, at least, frustrate the homogenizing role of the common school. A second objection to private schools introduced in the report had to do with the religious motivations that caused some parents to seek such schools. Here Mann allowed his strong feelings against "sectarian" religion to show:

> Amongst any people, sufficiently advanced in intelligence to perceive that hereditary opinions on religious subjects [that is, the beliefs of parents] are not always coincident with truth, it cannot be overlooked, that the tendency of the private school system is to assimilate our modes of education to those of England, where churchmen and dissenters,—each sect according to its own creed,—maintain separate schools, in which children are taught, from their tenderest years, to wield the sword of polemics with fatal dexterity; and where the gospel, instead of being a temple of peace, is converted into an armory of deadly weapons, for social, interminable warfare. Of such disastrous consequences, there is but one remedy and one preventive. It is the elevation of the common schools.

True religious conviction, then, could support only universal and compulsory public schooling; the spirit that would call for an education based on religious confession was that of sectarian fanaticism and not of real religion and thus could and should be disregarded.[37]

Mann returned to this theme in his *Fifth Report* of 1842, in connection with a school founded by the Shaker community in Shirley. The Shakers had refused to allow their teacher to be examined or their school inspected by town authorities, and it appears that Shakers in the town of Harvard were moving in the same direction. Mann described it as fortunate that, "if such a case must arise," it had "occurred amongst a sect, where the authority of numbers is not added to the weight of example," and "in a place, where all the residents upon the territory embrace one faith, and where, therefore, the children of parents who hold other views are not involved in the consequences of this violation of the law." That is, the danger to his reforms was not as great as if the orthodox Protestants or (a little later) the Roman Catholics had taken the same steps in communities in which they were preponderant. Nevertheless, Mann looked upon this as a very dangerous example:

> If a difference of opinion, on collateral subjects, were to lead to secession, and to exclusive educational establishments among us, it is obvious that all the multiplication of power which is now derived from union and concert of action would be lost. . . . if once the principle of secession be admitted, because of differences in religious opinion, all hope of sustaining the system itself must be abandoned. . . . our school system,—alike the glory of the past, and the hope of the future, would be broken into frag-

ments. . . . Civilization would counter-march, retracing its steps far more rapidly than it had ever advanced; and, amid the impulses of human self-ishness, and the rancor of spiritual pride, the heaven-descended precept, to "love one another," would practically pass into oblivion. . . . whoever would instigate desertion, or withdraw resources, from the common cause is laboring, either ignorantly or wilfully, to shroud the land in the darkness of the middle ages, and to reconstruct those oppressive institutions, of former times, from which our fathers achieved the deliverance of this country.[38]

If this seems rather extreme language to apply to the desire of the world-shunning Shakers to be left alone to raise their foster children, it is an indication of how much Mann believed was at stake in his efforts to insist upon a single system of elementary education under state direction. No doubt he was actually aiming his broadside at a more threatening challenge: the decision, the previous year, of the Presbyterian General Assembly to call upon every congregation to form a school. Mann was still under attack by Frederick Packard (for example, in the orthodox Presbyterian *Princeton Review* in 1841) for excluding Christian doctrine from the common school, and Packard had attempted to draw the Massachusetts Congregational General Association into the fray.

Mann's opposition to private schooling—or, in this case, to diversity within "public" schooling—had to do with theological as well as social and political views, all of them distrusting the capacity of the society to accommodate real diversity of beliefs and values without experiencing fatal divisions.

DUTTON RALLIES CONGREGATIONALIST OPPOSITION. There was in fact a certain amount of interest within the Congregationalist General Association of Massachusetts during the 1840s in the possibility of founding private schools "in which all the fundamental doctrines of Christianity could be taught," though this should be a last resort because of the importance of retaining an influence over the common schools.[39] A devastating counterattack was mounted by the Reverend W. S. Dutton in *New Englander*, a Congregationalist journal published in New Haven, in an article entitled "The Proposed Substitution of Sectarian for Public Schools." Dutton's article was serialized, with expressions of strong approval, in Mann's *Common School Journal* the same year.[40]

Dutton deplored the interest on the part of several denominations, including Roman Catholics and Episcopalians, in developing "schools which would be under their exclusive supervision," but his immediate concern was clearly with the recent developments in the orthodox wing of the Presbyterian and some elements of the Congregationalist denomination. "It is

with mortification and impatience," he wrote, "that we now see a movement virtually to subvert our common schools, so beneficent for purposes of unity and harmony, on the ground that they are not sufficiently
sectarian."

In addition to a variety of practical and financial difficulties with this
effort, it was highly threatening to the most critical mission of schooling in
a democratic society, the development of an enlightened and unified citizenry. The system of common schools served a high purpose:

> It is in accordance with the nature and necessities of our free institutions,
> with the comprehensive character of Christianity, and with the liberal
> spirit of the age.
>
> The influence of the church school system, on the other hand, will be
> sectarian, divisive, narrow, clannish, anti-republican.

For Dutton, as for Benjamin Franklin a century before, the common school had a particularly significant role in relation to an immigrant
population.

> It is unnecessary to dwell upon the importance of assimilating the people
> of this country,—of making them one in character and in spirit, and of the
> value of institutions and influences for this end. . . . The value of educa-
> tional institutions and influences, having this assimilating and uniting ten-
> dency, as have common schools eminently, can not be easily exaggerated
> in their relation to our native population, and especially in their relation
> to our immigrant population. As they come hither from all sections,
> nations and religions of Europe, it is important that their children should
> be neither uneducated, nor educated by themselves,—that they find here
> educational institutions for the *whole* people, which will command their
> confidence, and secure the attendance of their children.

This did not mean that instruction under denominational auspices was
not appropriate as a supplemental measure, but it should not represent the
core of education.

> The children of this country, of whatever parentage, should, not wholly,
> but to a certain extent, be *educated together*,—be educated, not as Baptists,
> or Methodists, or Episcopalians, or Presbyterians; not as Roman Catholics
> or Protestants, still less as foreigners in language or spirit, but as Ameri-
> cans, as made of one blood and citizens of the same free country,—
> educated to be one harmonious people. This, the common school system,
> if wisely and liberally conducted, is well fitted, in part at least, to accom-
> plish. While it does not profess to give a complete education, and allows
> ample opportunity for instruction and training in denominational pecu-
> liarities elsewhere, it yet brings the children of all sects together, gives
> them, to a limited extent, a common or like education, and, by such edu-

cation, and by the commingling, acquaintance and fellowship which it involves, in the early, unprejudiced and impressible periods of life, assimilates and unites them.

Proposals for denominational schools thus represented a profound threat to American society. It is clear that Dutton was not so much concerned by the prospect of Presbyterian schools as by the withdrawal of the patronage of one of the most respectable elements in the community from the common schools—this is similar to Horace Mann's concern about the "professional men"—and also the implicit support that would give to the desire of Roman Catholics for their own schools, in which their un-American characteristics would be reinforced.

And it is with serious regret that we see it recommended and zealously urged to substitute for this common school system, a system of dividing children into sectarian schools for the avowed purpose of teaching them sectarian peculiarities,—a system which is fitted to lay deep in the impressible mind of childhood the foundations of divisions and alienations,—a system well fitted to drive the children of foreigners, and especially of Roman Catholics, into clans by themselves, where ignorance and prejudice respecting the native population, and a spirit remote from the American, and hostile to the Protestant, will be fostered in them.

Not that there was, in Dutton's judgment, a real prospect of the creation of a Catholic system of schools, or even a serious intention of doing so. After all, he wrote, it was common knowledge that

the Roman Catholic church never has, in any country, secured, or favored, the education of *all* her people; and . . . in this country, she is not strongly disposed, and, if she were, would be unable, such is the poverty of a large proportion of her members, to sustain schools adequate for the purpose. Nothing is more certain than that, between the invincible repugnance of that church to send her children to schools of other churches avowedly sectarian, and her indisposition and inability to maintain adequate schools of her own, large masses of her children would be left to ignorance with all its dangers, crimes and miseries.

This was the first time, Mann wrote as editor, "so far as we know, in which the policy of abolishing the present system of *Common* schools, and establishing in their stead half a dozen or more kinds of sectarian schools, has received a full discussion in any periodical in this country."[41] With increasing Catholic immigration, it would not be the last; there would be repeated attempts to overwhelm with scorn the proposals to organize schools on a denominational basis. Another Connecticut Congregationalist minister returned to the topic five years later, with even more vehemence.

HORACE BUSHNELL AND THE THREAT OF DISMEMBERMENT. Horace Bushnell delivered a "public fast day sermon" in Hartford in 1853 on the role of the common school in relation to Catholic immigrants; his attack upon the desire of Catholic leaders for their own schools achieved special resonance because of his wide reputation as an advocate of undoctrinal religious teaching of children, not only as a political necessity in a pluralistic society but also as by far the best form of "Christian nurture."

Bushnell had achieved considerable fame—and notoriety—in 1847 for a little book, published then quickly withdrawn by the Massachusetts Sabbath School Society, called *Discourses on Christian Nurture*. The heart of his argument was that the churches and Christian parents should concentrate on bringing up children as Christians, rather than rely entirely upon a later conversion when the heart was already steeped in sin. At a time when many were wearying of the revival agitation "got up" by Lyman Beecher, Charles Finney and others in the preceding decades, Bushnell urged that, if possible, the child "is to open on the world as one that is spiritually renewed, not remembering the time when he went through a technical experience, but seeming rather to have loved what is good from his earliest years."[42] Parents should concentrate upon teaching their children a feeling of love for God, rather than upon any particular doctrines, and reinforcing the natural good and reverence that was already in the child's heart.

Bushnell struck a chord that found response across the theological spectrum. The principal Unitarian organ, the *Christian Examiner* of Boston, gave his book an enthusiastic review, asserting that "were its views generally adopted, they would revolutionize the life of the Christian world" and noting that there was a

> peculiar harmony between the views presented by Dr. Bushnell and those which we have been accustomed to cherish. . . . we do not know that we have any distinct objection to offer to any one of Dr. Bushnell's main positions. They state our own faith, expounded from another point of view.[43]

With endorsement from such a quarter, it is not surprising that many of the orthodox attacked Bushnell's book and that the Sabbath School Society came under the pressure that led to its temporary withdrawal from circulation. Curiously, though, it met with a certain amount of approval from the ultraorthodox Professor Charles Hodge in the pages of the *Princeton Review*. Hodge pointed out that Bushnell's stress on "organic, as distinguished from individual life"

> represents a great and obvious truth; a truth which, however novel it may appear to many of our New England brethren, is as familiar to Presbyter-

ians as household words. . . . it still has power to give his Discourses very much of an "Old-School" cast, and to render them in a high degree attractive and hopeful in our estimation.

Bushnell's stress on a child's participation and growth in the faith of his family was similar to that of Calvinists on the "covenant of grace." Thus Hodge found that he could commend two truths upon which Bushnell had stumbled (for he did not believe that Bushnell really understood why he was right!):

> First, the fact that there is such a divinely constituted relation between the piety of parents and that of their children, as to lay a scriptural foundation for a confident expectation, in the use of the appointed means, that the children of believers will become truly the children of God. . . . A second truth . . . is that parental nurture, or Christian training, is the great means for the salvation of the children of the church.[44]

This was by no means to say that Bushnell—though considered orthodox by New England Congregationalist standards—was anything but an awkward ally to true orthodoxy as understood in Princeton. Hodge picked up the consonance of Bushnell's optimistic anthropology with that of Schleiermacher, with his teaching that "Christ introduced a new life-principle into the world," on the basis of which godliness could now develop in the personality as a natural growth.

> The complaint against his book . . . is because he has not rested [his argument] upon the covenant and promise of God, but resolved the whole matter into organic laws, explaining away both depravity and grace, and presented the "whole subject in a naturalistic attitude." It is this that renders his book so attractive to Unitarians, and so alarming, with all its excellencies, to the orthodox.[45]

This background of Bushnell's thinking about "Christian nurture" helps to explain why he took so much more serious a view than did most contemporary evangelicals of the prospect of Catholic schools. Believing, as he did, that religious and other sentiments were shaped by a process of nurture rather than by divine intervention and conversion, he was deeply concerned that the nurture of the children of immigrants not be under the direction of the Catholic clergy, with their presumed determination to replicate Old World patterns of authority in the service of error in the New.

Ironically enough, it was because he shared with Catholic educators the conviction that early nurture was of extreme importance that Bushnell's opposition to their claims to educate the children of their denomination was particularly vehement. He showed none of the pragmatic tolerance that had led New York Governor Seward some years earlier to recognize that "the children of foreigners . . . are too often deprived of the advantages of our system of public education, in consequence of prejudice arising from differences of language or religion," and to "recommend the establishment of schools in which they may be instructed by teachers speaking the same language with themselves and professing the same faith."[46] For Bushnell, too much was at stake.

Americans had been extremely generous, he told his audience in Hartford, in admitting immigrants to all the privileges of a free society, but "they are not content, but are just now returning our generosity by insisting that we must excuse them and their children from being wholly and properly American." The ungrateful Catholic immigrants wanted "ecclesiastical schools, whether German, French, or Irish; any kind of schools but such as are American, and will make Americans of their children."

Bushnell saw a mighty struggle shaping up, provoked by the Catholic opponents of the common school, who had behaved with insincerity if not perfidy. In particular, he saw the menace of European-style clericalism in the request—pressed in several cities in the early 1850s—for tax support for Catholic schools.

It has been clear for some years past, from the demonstrations of our Catholic clergy and their people, and particularly of the clergy, that they were preparing for an assault upon the common school system, hitherto in so great favor with our countrymen; complaining, first, of the Bible as a sectarian book in the schools, and then, as their complaints have begun to be accommodated by modifications that amount to a discontinuance, more or less complete, of religious instruction itself, of our "godless scheme of education. . . . Evidently the time has now come, and the issue of life or death to common schools is joined for trial. The ground is taken, the flag raised, and there is to be no cessation, till the question is forever decided, whether we are to have common schools in our country or not."

Unlike Dutton, Bushnell did not admit that the challenge to the common school was coming from orthodox Protestants as well as Catholics; he presented the common school as the quintessential Protestant institution, an essential aspect of the national heritage. Speaking as though the society were still as homogeneous as in colonial New England, he insisted that

we have had the common school as a fundamental institution from the first—in our view a Protestant institution—associated with all our religious convictions, opinions, and the public sentiment of our Protestant society. We are still, as Americans, a Protestant people.

227

Bushnell articulated a "high" position of the role of the state in education, one that indeed had much in common with the views of the Jacobin party at the time of the French Revolution and with their sympathizers among the educational theorists of the early American Republic. He declared that

> the common school is, in fact, an integral part of the civil order. It is no eleemosynary institution, erected outside of the state, but is itself a part of the public law, as truly so as are the legislatures and judicial courts. . . . the teachers are as truly functionaries of the law as the constables, prison-keepers, inspectors and coroners. . . . an application against common schools, is so far an application for the dismemberment and reorganization of the civil order of the state. . . . the civil order may as well be disbanded, and the people given over to their ecclesiastics, to be ruled by them in as many clans of religion as they see fit to make.

Thus claims that the family and the church shared primary responsibility for education were rejected by this clergyman; those of the latter were a direct assault upon national unity and the civil order.

Bushnell saw the common school as a primary instrument of the state to create social cohesion and considered this instrumental role as by far the most important function of the school, above the teaching of skills or the enhancement of individual opportunities.

> This great institution, too, of common schools, is not only a part of the state, but is imperiously wanted as such, for the common training of so many classes and conditions of people. There needs to be some place where, in early childhood, they may be brought together and made acquainted with each other. . . . Without common schools . . . the disadvantage that accrues to the state, in the loss of so much character, and so many cross ties of mutual respect and generous appreciation, the embittering so fatally of all outward distinctions, and the propagation of so many misunderstandings . . . weakens immensely, the security of the state, and even of its liberties.

Given this high view of the school as an instrument of the state, Bushnell could not accept the existence of private schools as a harmless exercise of freedom. "Common schools are nurseries thus of a free republic, private schools of factions, cabals, agrarian laws, and contests of force." Such schools were a menace to society, and their religious justification was in fact no justification at all: "The arrangement is not only unchristian, but it is thoroughly un-American, hostile at every point to our institutions themselves."

228

Immigrants must cease abusing the hospitality and goodwill of their American hosts by rejecting the most essential institution of the society. They must not be allowed to re-create the divisions of the Old World in the New.

> We bid them welcome as they come, and open to their free possession all the rights of our American citizenship. They, in turn, forbid their children to be Americans, pen them as foreigners to keep them so, and train them up in the speech of Ashdod among us. . . . Our only answer to such demands is, "No! take your place with us in our common schools, and consent to be Americans, or else go back to Turkey, where Mohammedans, Greeks, Armenians, Jews are walled up by the laws themselves, forbidding them ever to pass over or change their superstitions. . . ." I said go back to Turkey—that is unnecessary. If we do not soon prepare a state of Turkish order and felicity here, by separating and folding our children thus, in the stringent limits of religious non-acquaintance and consequent animosity, it will be because the laws of human nature and society have failed.

Parochial schools would provide un-American education, and their students would not acquire those attitudes and loyalties essential to American society.

> They will be shut up in schools that do not teach them what, as Americans, they most of all need to know, the political geography and political history of the world, the rights of humanity, the struggles by which those rights are vindicated, and the glorious rewards of liberty and social advancement that follow. They will be instructed mainly into the foreign prejudices and superstitions of their fathers, and the state, which proposes to be clear of all sectarian affinities in religion, will pay the bills!

The context of these remarks is the common practice, at the time, of presenting the Protestant struggles of the Reformation as the precursors of nineteenth-century liberties and the Catholic Counter-Reformation as the very model of tyranny. Naturally, Catholic schools would not present history in those terms, and they were explicitly intended to teach children the "superstitions of their fathers."

Abandonment of the common school would also mean the failure of its religious mission, its all-important task of teaching a generic Christianity as the basis of social order. After all, if Catholics insisted on teaching their foreign prejudices and superstitions, why should not freethinkers organize schools around the equally un-American views of Tom Paine and other scoffers at religion? Indeed, "many children, now in our public schools, will be gathered into schools of an atheistical or half-pagan character, where they will be educated in a contempt of all order and decency."

The Catholic clergy were acting not only contrary to the interests of American society, Bushnell believed, but also contrary to the long-term interests of their own church, since future generations would reject those who had attempted to deprive them of American liberty in the form of its central institution, the common school. He insisted that

> they who exclude themselves are not Americans, and are not acting in their complaints or agitations, on any principle that meets the tenor of our American institutions. . . . their children of the coming time will at last find a way to be Americans; if not under the Pope and by the altars, then without them.

Bushnell found it "a dark and rather mysterious providence, that we have thrown upon us, to be our fellow-citizens, such multitudes of people, depressed, for the most part, in character, instigated by prejudices so intense against our religion." It was his hope, however, that through the common school "we may be gradually melted into one homogeneous people."[47]

THE GATHERING PROTESTANT CONSENSUS ON RELIGIOUS SCHOOLING. If Dutton and Bushnell achieved particular resonance with their attacks on sectarian schooling from the perspective of religious orthodoxy, they were not alone in their position. The initial interest, among some native-born Protestants, in an alternative to the nonsectarian character of "common school religion" was quickly derailed by what was perceived as the threat of Catholic determination to reproduce European religious divisions on American soil.

As early as 1844, the Congregationalist journal *New Englander* observed that the Catholic immigrants were "incomparably the most ignorant class of our population" and insisted on the importance of educating them in the common schools, even if that required the sacrifice of much of the distinctively religious character of those schools. "It is better that Roman Catholic children should be educated in public schools in which the Bible is not read, than that they should not be educated at all, or educated in schools under the absolute control of their priesthood."[48]

Also in 1844, the Methodist bishops warned in an address to the General Conference of the intention of "Papal Rome" to "wield the mighty engine of education to mould the minds of the rising generation in conformity to the doctrines of their creed," in order to

> assert and establish its monstrous pretensions in countries never subject to its . . . authority. With these weapons the Papal power has invaded Protestant communities with such success as should awaken and unite the energies of the evangelical Churches of Christ in every part of the world.[49]

The same year, Hiram Ketchum of New York addressed the American Bible Society's annual meeting on the recent controversies in that city caused by Catholic demands for support for their schools, in which he had been the primary spokesman for the Public School Society and thus an opponent of Catholic claims.

> Friends blamed us for having made too great sacrifices for the sake of quiet. We said we want to educate these children for the sake of society; we want to make Americans of them—to make them think and feel as Americans about American institutions and American people. But that was not what the Roman priests wanted . . . . They knew that in these schools the spirit of liberty would be growing up in their children's hearts; they would begin to exercise their right of private judgment, and this might diminish their respect for their spiritual fathers. They did not *want it so*.[50]

The expressions of concern and of anti-Catholic sentiment stimulated by these controversies in New York City in 1840 were mild compared with those a decade later, when the numbers of Catholics had grown and they had begun to behave in a more assertive fashion in calling for a share of tax support for their schools. The central figure of the earlier furor, Bishop (now Archbishop) John Hughes of New York, helped to stir feelings up again with a widely publicized sermon in 1850 on "The Decline of Protestantism and Its Causes."

> Protestantism pretends to have discovered a great secret. Protestantism startles our eastern borders occasionally on the intention of the Pope with regard to the Valley of the Mississippi, and dreams that it has made a wonderful discovery. Not at all. Everybody should know it. Everybody should know that we have for our mission to convert the world— including the inhabitants of the United States,—the people of the cities, and the people of the country, the officers of the navy and the marines, commanders of the army, the Legislatures, the Senate, the Cabinet, the President, and all![51]

This aggressive spirit was applied especially to the issue of education; in 1852 Hughes's organ, the *Freeman's Journal*, and other Catholic papers called on Catholics everywhere to demand tax support for their schools or, at the very least, the banning of Bible reading in public schools. Such efforts were mounted in a dozen states, evoking massive Protestant reaction.

This reaction had an abrupt effect on those Protestant denominations that were flirting with the idea of creating their own elementary schools. Creating sectarian schools, a Congregationalist journal argued in 1852, would have disastrous consequences. "The present system" of common schools, the *Independent* pointed out, "is an important check against Romanism; that [i.e., a system of denominational schools] would contribute to the strength and progress of the Roman system."[52]

Similar voices were raised within other denominations. An Episcopalian journal, the *Church Review*, pointed in 1855 to

> simultaneous and adroitly planned efforts put forth in all parts of the country, on the part of the Romish priesthood, either to banish the Bible from our Public Schools, so as to make them absolutely atheistic in character, or else to break down the whole Common School System altogether.

Interest, within the Episcopal church, in organizing a system of denominational elementary schools quickly faded away in response to the Catholic challenge.[53]

A similar process took place among the Dutch Reformed in the Middle Atlantic states. In 1851 their weekly *Christian Intelligencer* was asking whether the denomination should be forming its own schools, but in 1853 it warned about the Catholic threat and defended the common school.[54] As noted above, among the recent Dutch immigrants to the Midwest, fresh from the "school struggle" in the Netherlands, a very different attitude prevailed.

The same year the Baptist journal, the *Christian Review*, published an extended article on "The Catholics and the School Question," reviewing recent developments that seemed highly threatening. The author begins by noting that

> It is a somewhat remarkable coincidence that just as the Popular Educational Institutions of this country are beginning to attract the attention, and win the respect of enlightened men in the Old World, a systematic effort should be set on foot here to retard their efficiency, if not to effect their ruin, by destroying their catholic character, and making them the propagandists of a sect. That the measures which the Papists are now pursuing, in relation to our common schools, are the result of system and combination is manifest from the fact that, from New York to Cincinnati, from Baltimore to Detroit, they are enlisted in the same crusade.[55]

This was fair enough; as we have seen, there *was* a coordinated effort by Catholics to raise the school question at this point, though for the sake of their own children and not with a design to deny common schools for those who wanted them.

Compromises had been made, the author pointed out, because of the transcendent importance of maintaining the common school as the unifying institution of the society. "It was an evil to take the Bible from the schools, but it would have been a greater evil to have sanctioned a system

232

of sectarian schools to be supported by general taxation." It is striking that an evangelical publication was prepared to sacrifice the role of the Bible in education for the maintenance of a unitary system, though it should be noted that Baptists, always particularly strong supporters of the separation of church and state from their Anabaptist perspective, had never been strong advocates of sectarian schools or of explicit doctrinal instruction in public schools.

The Catholic leadership was demonstrating by its actions, the *Christian Review* believed, that it did not share the transcendent goal of national unity. "The only relation of the Papists in this country to our common school system, is that which is disclosed by their criticisms upon, and their complaints against it, and their efforts to modify or destroy it."

These Catholic leaders were not unrealistic in seeing the common school as a threat, the author believed, though it was not because their claims of Protestant indoctrination were justified. The very strengths of the common school were threatening to "popery":

> If they are Protestant it is because they cultivate a piety which is the growth of religious knowledge, and whose highest fruit on earth is a virtuous life, and encourage personal independence and freedom of thought. If they are unfriendly to the Roman Catholic church, they are so only because they give the Bible a place in their instructions, and promote the spread of intelligence among the people.

By contrast, sectarian schools were profoundly subversive of American society, productive of disunity, and promised future conflict.

> How can it be otherwise than that the children thus taught and reared, should regard themselves as separated from other classes, and look upon all their interests as distinct from, if not opposed to, those of the rest of the community? . . . They are not instructed in reference to the nature of our government, and the spirit of our institutions. But what is more, they are inspired with the most active jealousy, if not filled with the most bitter hatred, of all other denominations of Christians.

For the *Christian Review* as for Horace Bushnell, a great deal was at stake in the Catholic challenge to common schools. They saw two visions of society in confrontation. Their own found its highest expression in an idealized portrait of the common school, whereas they attributed to their Catholic opponents all the worst motivations of the Counter-Reformation as portrayed in a whole genre of conspiracy literature of the time.

> It is because this system realizes, in so adequate a manner, its true end— the promotion of intelligence and virtue—and fosters in its disciples so

233

high a degree of personal dignity and independence, that the leaders of the Roman Church hate, and seek to cripple or destroy it. But they must not be successful.

Summary and Conclusions

New England schools before the common school movement that began in the 1830s were usually explicitly religious, even doctrinal in their teaching, but they were un-self-consciously so. Schools created deliberately to provide a traditional *religious* alternative to publicly controlled schools were a reaction to the rise of the nineteenth-century common school with its unifying intent and its nonsectarian but religious content. It was the religious agenda of the common school, as elaborated by Mann and others, that elicited a demand for schools that served alternative religious agendas.

This urge was felt in a number of denominations but produced lasting results only in those cases where the seed fell in the receptive soil of a distinct and self-consciously minority ethnic community. Those immigrant groups that brought with them traditions of European conflicts over the religious mission of popular education, and were therefore clear about the significance of this issue, were especially likely to found and maintain such schools. For the denominations rooted in American traditions, however strongly they may have felt about their particular doctrinal views, there was always an uncertainty about the wisdom of breaking the solidarity of Protestant/American domination of the institutional means of the socialization of immigrants.

As might be expected, Mann and other education reformers reacted extremely negatively to the existence of schools not under public control. Mann objected to the social class distinctions that these were said to perpetuate (though the schools that the reform efforts drove out of existence were not elite institutions) and also to the threat they represented to the development of unified commitments and loyalties on the part of the rising generation. This reaction was predictable—nonpublic schools were a direct threat to the reform program of social progress and unity through a universal and uniform popular education.

Opposition came also from those orthodox Protestant quarters that might have been expected to seek to provide for the education of their own members in their distinctive beliefs. Despite many early expressions of interest in such denominational schools, the controversies that arose in the early 1840s and, much more strongly, a decade later as a result of Catholic efforts to obtain tax support for their schools drove orthodox Protestants (with the exception of some marginal immigrant groups) into alliance with

234

the education reformers in defense of the common school as the school for *all* Americans.

As we saw in the case of Horace Bushnell, the growing opposition to religious schools among traditionally religious Protestants was the effect not only of the heavy foreign immigration (mostly Irish and German) that began in the late 1840s but also of a changing appreciation of the role of *nurture* as contrasted with *conversion* in the transmission of faith.

Although revivals continued in this period, such key revivalists as Charles Finney and Lyman Beecher turned to leadership in higher education, and the denominations grew more self-consciously protective of their own membership and relative positions. Founding of hundreds of denominational colleges was one of the forms that this concern took; in this way the future elite would develop a loyalty to the denomination that presided over its higher education. Denominational energies were thus devoted to the training of leadership, whereas "Christian nurture" was entrusted to the common school.

The immigrant threat created near unanimity among Protestant leaders, by the early 1850s, in support of the common school. It is interesting to speculate whether systems of denominational elementary schools would have developed, at least in some parts of the country, had evangelicals discovered "nurture" a decade or two before the Catholic immigration reached disturbing proportions.

Liberal Protestants did believe strongly in nurture (and distrusted conversion) during the first decades of the nineteenth century, when evangelical energies were devoted to revivalism and to missionary enterprise. They shaped a form of common school religion that, for a time at least, gave a distinctively liberal Protestant flavor to common schools and to the normal schools in which common school teachers were trained.

As orthodox Protestants began to take nurture more seriously, they became concerned about the limitation of doctrinal religious instruction, but the perceived threat of sectarian Catholic schools (increased by aggressive Catholic moves in 1840 and 1852) quickly drove them into alliance with the liberal Protestant reformers. This led them, paradoxically, to support *further* limitation of the religious content of schooling.

The Triumph of the
Common School

THE PRECEDING chapters have described only the first stages of the process by which the common school came to be one of the dominant institutions of American life, legitimated by a myth of national integration through the inculcation of common beliefs and loyalties.

Let us define again what we mean by "the myth of the common school," as it emerged in the early nineteenth century in France, the Netherlands, and the United States.

"The common school," in the thinking of education reformers in all three nations, was to be a society-shaping institution, the most powerful possible means of forming the attitudes, loyalties, and beliefs of the next generation and thus of "molding citizens" to a common pattern. This ambitious program was promoted by an elite whose primary loyalty was to the dominant "common culture," rather than to any of the subcultures of creed, locality, or tradition to which many parents gave their loyalty. In Edward Shils's terms, they represented the societal "center" in its attempt to integrate the various peripheries of an expanding society. For these "common school reformers," the state was conceived as ultimate guardian and guarantor of a social order in which individuals would be liberated from intermediate traditions and loyalties, in the interest of progress, enlightenment, and national integration.

Robert Nisbet's observation that "the real conflict in modern political history has not been, as is so often stated, between State and individual, but between State and social group," is amply borne out by the process that we have traced of the use of state power, through common schools, to undermine competing sources of authority. The history of education in the nineteenth and twentieth centuries has been an essential episode in the "emancipation of the State from the restrictive network of religious, economic, and moral authorities that bound it at an earlier time."[1]

We have seen that the reformers shared a profound mistrust of diversity and of alternative sources of meaning, much in the spirit of Thomas Hobbes's description of social groups as "worms in the entrails of natural man." Through their efforts a great work of cultural homogenization has

236

been carried through, one directly dependent upon (and following from) the prior disestablishment of the locally dominant church. In this way, in Nisbet's phrase, "the State has risen as the dominant institutional force in our society and the most evocative symbol of cultural unity and purpose."[2]

The set of ideas and objectives that we have characterized as the "common school agenda" should not be confused with other elements of the case for public schooling. The myth of the common school is not just the belief that universal education is a good thing—that adults who have had some formal education are better citizens, better workers, better parents. Nor is it simply the policy resolution that the availability of education should be assured for all as a matter of public responsibility. Nor is it even the argument that *someone* should define a common content of education—including aspects of shared culture and political assumptions—that every child should master.

These convictions were closely associated with the program of educational reform successfully implemented by Horace Mann and others in the early nineteenth century, and they continue to enjoy broad assent today. It is unlikely that the reformers could have gained the support to implement the more global, society-forming, consciousness-structuring aspects of their program had they not so effectively built upon general assent to other essentially limited objectives.

This becomes clear when we stop to ask whether the objectives outlined above could not have been reached as effectively, and with far less continuing conflict, by a more modest approach than the common school agenda promoted by Mann and others.

The schooling of an entire people has never depended upon the state's serving as educator. New England was at least as literate—and as schooled—before Horace Mann as after him, as several studies have shown. The example of France is compelling: Some areas have been highly literate for three centuries, without government intervention, while others long resisted the reforms instituted by Guizot.[3]

Even granted that, under the conditions of modern life, government should appropriately serve as the ultimate guarantor of universal education, it is by no means clear that it need do so as "educator of first resort." The Netherlands, in which government schools today serve only about 30 percent of the school-age population, has a higher real literacy rate than the United States, where they serve 90 percent. Government in the United States chooses to assure the availability of other essential public services—such as health care services for elderly and low-income patients—through a "mixed" system of public, semipublic, and private providers.

Although the setting of common standards and goals for education in a democracy would seem an appropriate task for popularly elected government, the American experience demonstrates that there are viable alternatives. The waning impact of standards set by the private-sector College Board on the curriculum of a highly decentralized system of secondary education has been blamed for much of the confusion and "dumbing-down" of that curriculum. One of the most powerful instruments of maintaining at least a minimum of standards, on the other hand, has been the accrediting work of regional associations made up of public and private institutions. In both instances "semipublic" initiatives have addressed issues on which insufficient consensus existed for government action.

Is the argument for government as educator a matter of efficiency, then? By no means; a number of recent studies have found that government-operated schools may be more expensive and produce results inferior to those of schools under alternative auspices.

The most commonly used argument for the common school—since Horace Mann—has to do with the avoidance of conflict over beliefs and values; yet ironically it has been a prolific source of such conflicts in each of the nations discussed above. It has turned out to be extremely difficult to achieve the goal of instruction that, as Mann and Guizot urged, would offend no father truly concerned for the welfare of his children. Efforts to eliminate the causes of offense have had the effect, as we saw in the case of the accommodation of Catholic concerns in the 1850s, of producing a curriculum as offensive by its omissions as by its inclusions.

The contemporary controversies in Tennessee and in Alabama illustrate the futility of seeking a lowest-common-denominator curriculum. The parent-plaintiffs were as offended by what was left out of their children's readers as they were by what was put in; as the judge observed, ruling in their favor, "many of the objectionable passages . . . would be rendered inoffensive, or less offensive, in a more balanced context."[4]

No, the basic case for the common school agenda had to do with *control*, not with literacy, efficiency, or the avoidance of conflict. As Michael Katz has noted, "Only in the educational area, in the reform of human nature rather than in the reform of social systems, were reformers willing to apply coercion or conceive radically new solutions."[5] What has become evident as we reviewed the arguments used by its promoters would be amply confirmed as systems of popular education were actually implemented, later in the nineteenth century.

France: *L'école laïque*

We have noted the anomaly that the creation of a centrally controlled system of popular education in France was the work of a "liberal" regime attracted, in other respects, to the English pattern of a restrained use of state power and reliance upon individual initiatives to serve the common good. Guizot argued that the Revolution of 1792 had rooted out those local and traditional institutions that could otherwise have been relied upon to shape opinions and habits in ways conducive to social peace. It was thus necessary for the state to create and make deliberate use of a system of popular schooling as "a guarantee for order and social stability."

It may well be that this agenda gained the support of the local "notables" without whom little could be accomplished because it was introduced by a regime reflecting their concern for social stability and economic progress, with a mildly anticlerical flavor. The idea of a great army of lay teachers, "belonging to the State, fed by the State," and "owing its power and direction to the State," was appealing as long as the state itself had a very limited agenda to promote.

The Revolution of 1848 put an end to this period of harmony between local leadership and the state apparatus of popular education. The more radical wing of the Republicans who gained a short-lived power understood that education could serve their political goals as well as it could those of their opponents. Having extended the electorate from 250,000 to over 9 million men, the Republicans were keenly aware that the conservatism of the rural population could be their undoing, as indeed it would be. Thus Hippolyte Carnot, minister of public instruction, told his colleagues in the National Assembly that "the inauguration of universal suffrage imposed on me, as my first duty, the prompt development of primary instruction, in order that a large number of citizens might understand the interests of the country."

Carnot proposed to make primary education free and compulsory and to further centralize control over teachers. In a circular to teachers just before the elections he urged them to go among the people and explain to them what to look for in a "good representative," stressing that a "worthy peasant" would be preferable to a wealthy and well-educated candidate who was "blinded by interests different from those of the mass of peasants." In support of this effort, Carnot called upon regional education authorities to prepare "Republican catechisms" for teachers to use.[6]

This last-minute effort had little impact; the new legislature was distinctly moderate, and Carnot's attempt to use state control of popular education for political goals contributed to the reaction that elected Louis Napoleon Bonaparte as president later the same year. Fear of social revolution triumphed over the anticlericalism that had characterized the "friends of order"; thus Thiers proposed turning primary education entirely over to the Catholic clergy:

239

The primary school must above all serve [character-building] education, and give to children the eternal truths of religion and morality. Primary education must defend society against revolution. Society has been so deeply shaken [by the recent events] that it can recover its security only by seeing grow up around it new generations that will reassure it.

Thiers characterized the primary teachers whose support Carnot had sought as "thirty-seven thousand socialists and communists, true anti-priests." His charge was echoed by influential Catholic layman Charles Montalembert, who described "two armies face to face, each of about thirty to forty thousand men: the army of teachers and the army of priests. The demoralizing and anarchical army of teachers must be countered by the army of priests."[7]

The antagonism between teacher and parish priest, adumbrated rhetorically in the aftermath of the popular revolts of 1848, would become a reality later in the century. The conflict was prepared by twenty years of collaboration between the Catholic church and Louis Napoleon, who mastered the use of nationwide plebiscites in which the clergy helped to mobilize a series of overwhelming votes of support. In exchange, the church was given a substantially free hand in education, and many local authorities chose to invite teaching congregations to provide schooling at public expense. The membership of religious orders increased from 37,000 in 1851 to 190,000 two decades later. The Republican opposition was confirmed in its determination to ban clerical influence from popular education.

One of the most influential of the Republican thinkers, Edgar Quinet, stressed that the issue was not to keep separate a secular and a spiritual sphere; Catholicism was identical with *political* reaction, and the Republic with *spiritual* progress. In 1789 two irreconcilable religions had come into confrontation, Jules Michelet argued in his influential history, and the future depended upon the victory of the faith expressed in the Revolution. Alone among modern nations, Quinet wrote in 1846, France had tried to carry out a political and social revolution without having completed a religious revolution by destroying Catholicism entirely. "This liberal," one historian notes, "became a terrorist himself when it came to religion, and would have desired a half-century of iconoclastic terrorism."[8]

The opportunity of the Republicans to realize their own educational program did not come until 1877, when a commission chaired by rabid anti-clerical Paul Bert proposed a legislative package of more than 100 articles. Over the next few years this program—lay-controlled teacher training in each department; universal, free, and obligatory schooling; and state inspection of schools operated by the church—was enacted and implemented as a matter of highest priority for the Radical wing of the Republican majority.[9]

The concern of the Radicals was far more with assuring the secular and republican content of schooling than with using education to bring about social change. They did not touch, for example, the existing system of two classes of schools for the common people and the elite; the Radicals hated religious "fanaticism" more than they hated social inequalities. Their educational program was a "preemptive strike" against clericalism and political reaction based in an unenlightened electorate.

In support of this objective the education law of 1886 required a public elementary school in every commune, even if sufficient provision was already available in a Catholic school. Instruction in public schools could henceforth be given only by lay teachers, and these were forbidden to exercise liturgical functions (such as being a cantor or reader) in any church, even on a voluntary basis. Nonpublic schools could not use antirepublican books that had been forbidden by the government, and they would be monitored regularly by public officials.

Three years later elementary teachers became employees of the state rather than of municipalities, and in 1904 all teaching by religious orders was forbidden.

A republican regime committed to personal liberties found itself, in the crucial sphere of education, denying the right of parents to educate their children in schools that corresponded to their own beliefs. Thus Jules Ferry, as minister of public instruction, condemned Catholic schools as

> establishments which are maintained as schools of counterrevolution, where one learns to detest and curse all of the ideas which are the honor and the purpose of modern France. . . . the youth who come out [of Catholic schools are] raised in ignorance and in hatred of the ideas that are dear to us. . . . Let this go on for ten years more, this blindness, and you will see all this lovely system of liberty of instruction . . . crowned by a last liberty: the liberty of civil war.[10]

Ferry was anticlerical but not antireligious; he believed that the supreme mission of the Republic, through its schools, was to create a new social order based upon a new spiritual unity. He—and many of his Radical allies—looked for this unity in the positivism of Auguste Comte, who had taught that the "fixity of fundamental maxims" was the basis of a true social order and that the tensions and periodic conflicts in French society were the result of the resistance of outmoded philosophies to the progress of the scientific spirit. Only a consistently positivist education could assure that intellectual regeneration necessary to the renewal of society.

The schools of the Third Republic, then, placed a heavy stress upon moral and civic education, as a means of "endowing men with a moral tie superior to or at least equivalent to that which they once found in super-

241

natural beliefs," as one of his allies wrote to Ferry in 1879.[11] What was needed was not neutrality but a new form of spiritual authority capable (as Comte had written in 1824) "of replacing the clergy and organizing Europe through education." The common people could never be converted to the disinterested love of humanity through rational argument, but only through emotional appeals. Ferry and others sought to replace the love of God with the love of humanity and of France.

John Stuart Mill observed, in his essay "On Liberty" (1859),

> some of those modern reformers who have placed themselves in strongest opposition to the religions of the past, have been no way behind either churches or sects in their assertion of the right of spiritual domination: M. Comte, in particular, whose social system ... aims at establishing (though by moral more than by legal appliances) a despotism of society over the individual, surpassing anything contemplated in the political ideal of the most rigid disciplinarian among the ancient philosophers.

But only in this way, the Radicals believed, could the Revolution truly be completed. As Michelet had written in a history that served almost as a sacred text for the Radicals,

> In the first age, which was the correction of the age-old grievances of humankind, an *élan* of justice, the Revolution formulated into laws the philosophy of the eighteenth century. In the second age, which will come sooner or later, she [the Revolution] will transcend the formulas, will find her religious faith (on which all the laws of politics rest), and in that divine liberty which only excellence of heart provides she will bear an unknown fruit of goodness, of fraternity.[12]

Or, as his friend Quinet wrote from exile under Napoleon III, "the real education of a people is its religion; beside it all other teaching is as nothing." Only by opposing to the "Roman religion" an equal power could its hold over the people be broken and the nation be transformed.[13]

During the closing decades of the nineteenth and into the twentieth century a crusading *laïcité* or secularism sought—not without success—to promote an alternative to Catholicism. This could go to comical lengths, including the replacing of all street names in Lyon associated with religion with names expressing the secularizing program: Saint Elizabeth was replaced by Garibaldi, Saint Blandine by Diderot, Saint Dominique by Zola, Sacred Heart by Paul Bert, and Saint Helen by Jules Ferry. Secular ceremonies were invented as a replacement for the way the parish church had marked the stages of life: laicized baptisms, first communions, marriages, burials, processions, and feasts on Good Friday.[14]

Having identified the Catholic church as the primary enemy of the Republic, the Radicals paid it the compliment of seeking to emulate the church by creating a state-controlled system of education that was centralized, unified in its doctrines, and concerned above all to transmit values and to shape loyalties. In doing so, they relied above all upon the formation of teachers in normal schools that resembled nothing so much as seminaries of a secular religion; such leaders in this program as Ferdinand Buisson (whose speeches were collected in a volume called *La foi laïque*), Félix Pécaut, and Jules Steeg were also leaders in liberal Protestantism. They turned also to the power of the state to drive Catholic teaching congregations out of France and to force parents to send their children to *l'école laïque*.

It was, as Paul Bert insisted, "the supreme task of the school" to create "elevated sentiments, a single thought, a common faith" for the French people. "This is the religion of the Fatherland, it is with this cult and this love, at once ardent and reasonable, that we wish to penetrate the heart and mind of the child, to impregnate him to the marrow; it is that which will constitute civic education." [15]

France, then, more explicitly than any other democratically ruled nation, implemented the common school agenda of seeking to shape the hearts of the rising generation through popular schooling. It did so through the exercise of state power, not only promoting government-controlled schools with the utmost vigor and moral passion but taking increasingly drastic steps to foreclose an educational alternative. The education provided in the state's own schools made no pretense of neutrality; indeed, those who shaped it would have considered a value-neutral school an abomination. Their goal was to inculcate a "secular faith."

Emile Durkheim observed, in his lectures on moral education (1903), that

> The last twenty years in France have seen a great educational revolution, which was latent and half-realized before then. We decided to give our children in our state-supported schools a purely secular moral education. . . . if, in rationalizing morality in moral education, one confines himself to withdraw from moral discipline everything that is religious without replacing it, one almost inevitably runs the danger of . . . an impoverished and colorless morality. . . . we must discover the rational substitutes for those religious notions that for a long time have served as the vehicle for the most essential moral ideas.

Without providing a secular replacement for the transcendent foundations of morality, French schools would "risk having nothing more than a moral education without prestige and without life." The task of educational leaders, then, was to "discover those moral forces that men, down to the present time, have conceived of only under the form of religious allegories."[16]

In support of this program, several hours a week of lessons in morality were prescribed for French schools at all levels, and readers in secular moral education were prepared and sold by the million. These works were a continual irritation to Catholic parents and provoked a recurrent *guerre des manuels*.[17] There is an unbroken line from these controversies to the struggles in 1983 and 1984 over the Socialist program of public school monopoly.

The Netherlands: *De gemengde school*

The common school triumphed in France, in the closing decades of the nineteenth century, just as it was losing its early advantage in the Netherlands.

In both cases broadening participation in political life after the continentwide disturbances of 1848 provided an opportunity for the churches to promote the type of educational programs—with traditional religious content—desired by many parents. Having struggled to extend the franchise to the common people, the liberal and radical elite found that the new voters supported their opponents, especially on educational issues.

The Dutch Constitution of 1848 included a guarantee of the right to operate a school, subject to minimal regulation by public authorities. The government school monopoly was, in principle at least, brought to an end through the leadership of Liberal statesman J. R. Thorbecke; he had consistently defended a "free enterprise" right to establish schools, with schooling provided by public authorities only in those cases in which private provision was insufficient.[18] This position was both a cause and a result of the close alliance between Thorbecke's Liberals and the emerging Roman Catholic interests.

Thorbecke's Conservative opponents, closely allied with the semiestablished Reformed (Hervormde) church and the Groningen theology represented by Hofstede de Groot, were appalled at the prospect of surrendering the monopoly position of the public school as "protector and symbol of the unity of the nation." The governing Synod—in its only official statement on the school question during the nineteenth century—noted that the spirit that ruled in public schools was the very same spirit that the Synod sought to maintain in the churches and warned lest the fanaticism of hyperorthodox Protestants be spread through private schools. "The members of the . . . Synod, always so apathetic about the confession of their church, became suddenly very active in protection of their own belief in a generalized Christianity."[19]

Events would show that the Liberals were scarcely more receptive to the idea of confessional schooling than were the Conservatives: They shared an elitist disdain for "fanaticism" and a conviction that "the public school must remain a nation-forming institution for all religious communities."[20] The parties differed only in the extent to which they were willing to use state power to create unity in the rising generation. After Thorbecke passed from the scene (1872), his successors, the more radical "Young Liberals," would be implacable in their hostility to confessional schooling. Their liberalism, in contrast with his, had an ideological quality, compounded of anticlericalism and a desire to increase state intervention in many aspects of social (though not of economic) life.[21]

Despite the guarantee of educational freedom in the new Constitution, there were continuing difficulties in the 1850s over the establishment of confessional schools in many communities. In some cases village public schools were converted to private status by demand of the local parents, but in other communities—where leadership tended to remain in the hands of a theologically liberal elite—local authorities refused approval of schools that would compete with the public school. In the village of Uithuizen in Groningen, for example, a group sought permission, in 1851, to establish a "school with the Bible"; refused by local authorities, they appealed in vain to the central government. In 1854 a hundred orthodox Protestants from the village immigrated to America, where they could educate their children as they wished.[22]

It was nine years before a new school law was enacted to replace that of 1806 with new provisions consistent with the Constitution. The drafting of this law produced a momentous split between Groen van Prinsterer and one of the leading proponents of confessional schools, the attorney J. J. L. van der Brugghen.

Van der Brugghen, though sharing Groen's orthodox Protestantism, opposed the use of the state's authority to promote Christianity; he and other members of the "ethical tendency" within the Réveil held that Christianity was a "moral life force," working like yeast in public as well as private life, not a set of doctrines or requirements that could be enforced by government. It was thus foolish to speak of the Netherlands—as did the conservative Great Protestant party—as a Christian state. The people might, in the overwhelming majority, be Christian, but the state could only be neutral. "The sphere of the state," he wrote, "is not and cannot be that of absolute truth, since it is not the sphere of the Gospel."

It was important, in Van der Brugghen's thinking, to limit the pretensions of the state while also limiting Christian claims to dominate the state. Neither political parties nor government-operated schools should seek to be explicitly Christian, though Van der Brugghen did include in his School Law of 1857 a provision that the purpose of education was to develop in children "all Christian and social virtues." It was his conviction of the limits on how much of the religious truth could legitimately be taught in government schools that made Van der Brugghen an early and strong supporter of private confessional schools; this conviction also brought him into conflict with his coreligionists like Groen who were not yet ready to abandon the belief that the state could be explicitly Christian and indeed Calvinist.[23]

After the failure of an earlier attempt to adopt a school law, Van der Brugghen was called by the king to form a cabinet with the specific charge to "assure that no one's conscience be injured, without departing from the principle of the common [*gemengde*, or "mixed"] school, by which the nation has been knit together since 1806."[24] The law that emerged was almost totally satisfactory to the Liberals and Conservatives and disappointing to supporters of confessional schooling. Van der Brugghen's one serious effort to deal fairly with the concerns of the latter, a provision that a state subsidy could be provided to private schools, was eliminated during legislative debate from the School Law of 1857.

Groen and most supporters of confessional schooling had pressed for a provision that would allow a "voluntary division" of public schools along confessional lines in communities where numbers and demand made that practical. Failing in this, they turned to the creation of a network of orthodox Protestant schools without public subsidy.

Parallel developments occurred among Catholics, just emerging from the subordinate position to which the defeat of Catholic Spain two centuries earlier in the wars of independence had condemned them. The alliance with Thorbecke and his "Old Liberals" to gain educational freedom was replaced by an alliance with Groen and his Antirevolutionary party in 1879 on the common ground of support for confessional schools.

The period after the passage of Van der Brugghen's School Law of 1857 was one of struggle to organize and support confessional schools. The Catholic bishops issued a pastoral letter in 1868, inspired by the papal Syllabus of Errors (1864), that identified schooling as a primary battleground with the false spirit of the age and gave a death blow to the alliance with the Liberals. The Association for Christian National Education was formed in 1860, bringing together in uneasy cooperation supporters of Protestant schooling with theological perspectives ranging from the Center to the Right, while liberal Protestants continued to be strong supporters of the public "mixed" school. Political conflicts among Antirevolutionaries, Catholics, and Liberals sharpened and grew more ideologically defined. In Parliament Groen van Prinsterer and one Catholic colleague could be counted upon to protest government aggression against confessional schooling, but without effect.

The Constitution—in response to pressures from the Maatschappij tot Nut van 't Algemeen and from public schoolteachers—required that government provide for schooling in every community, and this was interpreted to call for the establishment of public schools even in cases where every parent had chosen a confessional school. In order to assure an enrollment for such schools, more and more local authorities decided to waive the traditional tuition fees and support public schools entirely out of taxes. The supporters of confessional schooling noted that this generally happened only when a private school had been established or was planned. It was thus a matter of real sacrifice for Catholic or orthodox Protestant parents, most of them in humble circumstances, to send their children to confessional schools for which tuition was necessary.

In other cases, public schoolmasters responded to the threat of competition by finding ways to stress the Bible and even the catechism in their instruction. Groen himself was not at first willing to abandon the explicitly Christian character of public education; when defeated on that issue, he turned to a demand that *all* reference to a generalized and (to him) profoundly misleading Christianity be removed from public schools. He was resisted in this demand by Thorbecke and by the Conservatives, who insisted that public schools were profoundly religious precisely in their refusal to recognize sectarian doctrines.[25]

Conflict between supporters of confessional and public schools sharpened during the late 1860s. In 1868 the Nut launched a nationwide campaign, calling upon its 300 branches to work to increase support for public education; this mobilization led to an increase in membership made up of many who saw confessionalism as a threat to national unity and enlightenment. The orthodox were quick to respond: Abraham Kuyper published a book arguing that the Nut's claim of religious neutrality—and that of the public schools—was in fact an assault on religious conviction of every kind.

> For the sake of tolerance the "Nut" seeks to remove every conviction that raises itself above the superficial. It wants unity, but the false kind that is created through killing life. . . . A specific, a settled conviction is in its eyes a "prejudice," an "outdated," an "immoderate notion." . . . Tolerance, yes, but tolerance out of indifference, out of superficiality, out of lack of principles. . . . It is the undermining of any solid conviction, under the slogan of the struggle against witch-hunts and sectarian conflict and religious hatred. . . . I have no hesitation about setting against the "Nut"'s dogma—"tolerance through removal of doctrinal differences"—this other: "respect for the convictions of others based on the solidity of one's own convictions."[26]

The conflict was further heightened by the organization of a more militant anticonfessional organization, Volksonderwijs ("Popular Education," now the Association for Public Education), in the period 1866–70 and the increasing political ascendancy of the Young Liberals. Liberal leader J. Kappeyne van de Coppello declared war on the confessional school in a celebrated speech in 1874, insisting that the orthodox minority deserved to be oppressed, because it was the fly that spoiled the whole ointment "and has no right to exist in our society." Kuyper responded in the same debate that, if Kappeyne's program of compulsory attendance were implemented, the lion—symbol of freedom—might as well be removed from the shield of the Netherlands, to be replaced by an eagle with a lamb in its claws.[27]

The eagle had its opportunity four years later, when Kappeyne's ministry obtained passage of legislation increasing substantially the physical and staffing requirements for all elementary schools, requirements that would make it far more difficult to maintain confessional schools. The national government would contribute 30 percent of the cost of public schools, lightening considerably the burden on municipalities of meeting these new requirements, but would not help confessional schools. The latter would remain free, Kuyper noted, "yes, free to hurry on crutches after the neutral train that storms along the rails of the law, drawn by the golden locomotive of the State."[28]

The Liberals had overreached themselves. This threat against the schools that many of them had labored to establish aroused the orthodox common people and created a movement that, in a decade, reversed the political fortunes of the Liberals and brought state support for confessional schools. The first stage was a massive petition drive that collected, in five days, 305,102 signatures from Protestants and 164,000 from Catholics asking the king to refuse to sign the Kappeyne school law. That having failed, a national organization, "The Union 'A School with the Bible,'" created a permanent mechanism for mobilization of orthodox Protestants. Catholics were equally active: in 1883 the first Catholic political program was drawn up, and the Roman Catholic State party and Groen and Kuyper's Antirevolutionary party together gained a majority of the Parliament by 1888. As a historian of Dutch liberalism observes, "no one has done so much harm to liberalism as Kappeyne." Thinking that he was smothering the last flickering flame of traditional religion, he fanned it into vigorous life.[29]

The School Law of 1889, introduced by the ministry of Antirevolutionary Baron Mackay, provided the same 30 percent state subsidy to confessional as for public schools and began a process that would lead, in 1920, to the full financial equality of all schools that met general requirements set by the central government. Throughout this period the Maatschappij tot Nut

248

van 't Algemeen, the association of public schoolteachers, and Volksonderwijs continued to fight a rear-guard action, but they were undermined by the decision of the Socialist party, in 1902, to support state subsidies for confessional schools. As Socialist leader Troelstra put it, they were willing to let the religious struggle rest in order to win the class struggle by gaining the support of Catholic and Protestant workers.[30]

In the Netherlands the effort to implement the common school in the interest of creating national unity, especially as promoted vigorously by the anticlerical Young Liberals, was for decades the primary cause of national disunity. By contrast, the "Pacification" of 1920 freed political and social energies to address the challenges of the postwar world. By giving parents the right to choose freely among educational options, the Dutch educational system avoided a tyranny of the political majority *or* of the education profession. The cracks that have appeared in this system in recent years have been the result of secularization—and thus confusion about the "identity" of confessional schools—and the growing claims of the welfare state, not of any breakdown in the system itself.

The United States: "The One Best System"

It is possible to give something like a connected narrative of developments in French and Dutch popular education in the later nineteenth century. Policies adopted at the national level in response to nationwide political and social changes have a coherence that lends itself to comparing the two experiences. In France the Catholic church overreached itself in forming an alliance with Napoleon III to dominate education; the subsequent republican (that is, in French terms, politically though not socially "radical") triumph made the substitution of a "secular faith" (Buisson's *foi laïque*) the cornerstone of government policy in education. In the Netherlands, by contrast, it was the radical Young Liberals who overreached, provoking a reaction by Catholics and orthodox Protestants that swept them out of office and led, eventually, to the virtual "disestablishment" of the public school.

The history of education in the United States is less visible, less coherent, because of the lack of a strong national role or even, in many instances, of strong state leadership. Horace Mann and his successors over the next century did not possess a fraction of the authority employed by Jules Ferry and the other education ministers of the Third Republic to impose their program through an "army of schoolmasters."

Despite the lack of central guidance and of uniformity of implementation, the implementation of American popular education evolved in directions roughly parallel to those taken by French education, and in marked contrast with the Dutch experience. This evolution has been described in many of its local manifestations, and recent accounts by Tyack and Hansot, Ravitch, Peterson, and others have told a story of parallel developments by which the common school agenda was confirmed and extended.[31]

We will not go over this story again here but simply describe three of its primary themes, each of which represents a working-out of the logic of the program articulated by Horace Mann and his allies.

POLITICAL CONTROL OF SCHOOLS. The first of these themes is the assault, by progressive reformers, on the control of city schools by politicians primarily responsive to the concerns of working-class and immigrant parents. Though a part of the concern of the reformers was with efficiency and the elimination of patronage and corruption, a larger part—so recent historians argue—had to do with homogenizing the urban population through suppressing the cultural patterns and idiosyncrasies brought from a score of foreign countries.

There can be no question that this was a major and unavoidable challenge; in 1908 investigators found that 72 percent of the students in New York, 67 percent in Chicago, and 64 percent in Boston had fathers who were born abroad.[32] The public schools were the favored instrument of assimilation, but to do their work most effectively, reformers believed, they must be insulated from the demands and concerns of parents. Local control of schools was seen as the major impediment to the true professionalization of education, and thus its capacity to transmit values that differed from those represented by parents.

"Reforms" in school governance, Tyack and Hansot observe, "often blocked the political channels by which the cities' working-class and ethnic communities had traditionally expressed their political interests in education. In the process they also enhanced the power of cosmopolitan elites."[33]

Historian Diane Ravitch has described the struggle between reformers and the decentralized New York City schools in the 1890s. The state legislature enacted "reform" legislation in 1896 that sought to eliminate political—and thus, for good or ill, popular—influence on the schools altogether, despite a petition with 100,000 signatures opposing the abolition of local boards. As the governor was advised, "it was not a good thing in a city 'largely impregnated with foreign influences, languages and ideas that the school should be controlled locally; for in many locations the influences that would control would be unquestionably un-American.' "[34]

The assault on the interest of parents in transmitting their distinctive values and loyalties to their children was exactly parallel to that of the Young Liberals in the Netherlands. The American reformers were more politically successful because of the prevalent xenophobia of the majority of American voters including, in Massachusetts, emigrants from British Canada who were especially hostile toward their Catholic fellow immigrants. State legislatures were easily persuaded to undercut the power of city-based politicians.

The Boston School Committee was reduced, in 1875, from 116 members elected by districts to twenty-four elected at large, and four years later women were given the vote in school elections, in well-founded confidence that Protestant women were much more likely than Catholic women to register and to vote.[35]

One of the most dramatic episodes in this process of undercutting the influence of immigrant parents on the public schooling of their children occurred in Boston in 1888, when British-Americans and other militant Protestants mobilized to overturn what threatened to be an Irish domination of the School Committee and to defeat Irish-born Mayor Hugh O'Brien. The Committee of One Hundred issued a series of exposés of an alleged Catholic plot to

> take the control of the public schools out of the hands of those who would conduct them in accordance with American ideas and on a nonsectarian basis, that they might conduct them thereafter in the interests of the Church of Rome.

In their efforts the committee was "wonderfully aided by some local and patriotic organizations of [Protestant] women," while Catholics sought to register their own women to vote; in a few weeks 25,000 women had paid the poll tax. The 1888 election was a triumph for the Protestants, and for a decade "election after election increased the numbers of Protestants on the Boston School Board, and no Catholic was elected mayor of Boston."[36]

SUPPORT FOR CONFESSIONAL SCHOOLS. Closely related to the question of controlling public schools to Americanize the children of immigrants was that of public funding for parochial schools. One of the anti-Irish initiatives in Massachusetts in 1888, for example, was a bill to provide state inspection and regulation of parochial schools. The following year more than 3,000 Massachusetts citizens signed a petition to Congress supporting a constitutional amendment to "prevent the interference of any religious sect with the 'common school system,' or the appropriating of any of the public funds for sectarian uses," to protect "our time-honored and truly endeared methods of teaching and training our youth for the duties and responsibilities of American citizenship." One of the sponsors of this petition told a Senate committee that the public schools faced "a hostile

251

system—a system that, in its methods and spirit, from beginning to end, is positively antagonistic to the institutions of our American nation." [37]

The proposed amendment had been submitted by Senator Henry Blair of New Hampshire; it forbade the granting of public funds to sectarian schools but also required that public schools provide instruction in "virtue, morality, and the principles of the Christian religion." Blair was a strong supporter of federal funding for public schools, convinced that they represented the best hope for shaping future citizens. Hearings on the amendment provided repeated opportunities for the restatement of the common school agenda. As a representative of the anti-Catholic Evangelical Alliance told the committee,

> the task of absorbing and Americanizing these foreign masses . . . can only be successfully overcome by a uniform system of American schools, teaching the same political creed. . . . State schools of differing character, of different languages, of different creeds, of antagonistic political doctrines, of opposing sentiments, ideas, and methods, some representing the highest elements of American civilization and others the lowest type of foreign advance in the opposite direction, would prepare the way for domestic quarrels between such antagonistic and irreconcilable elements.

The amendment would "continue us in the future, as in the past, a united, homogeneous people" by assuring "a common system of training for American citizens, and that that training should be marked by the Christian ethics to which we owe our high civilization and which are the only guarantee of civil and religious liberty." After all, few of the immigrants "understand or appreciate our institutions or the Christian and philanthropic spirit that inspired them . . . all unfitted as they are by their hereditary instincts and foreign education to understand the blessings of free institutions." [38]

To proponents of such an amendment, nothing less was at stake than the future of the nation. They were fond of quoting General Grant's warning to a veterans' organization, in 1876, that

> If we are to have another contest in the near future of our national existence, I predict that the dividing line will not be Mason and Dixon's, but it will be between patriotism and intelligence on one side, and superstition, ambition, and ignorance on the other. . . . Encourage free schools, and resolve that not one dollar appropriated to them shall be applied to the support of any sectarian school; resolve that any child in the land can get a common school education, unmixed with atheistic, pagan, or sectarian teachings.

Grant had supported an earlier amendment to the Constitution, proposed by James G. Blaine in 1875, requiring the states to "establish and maintain free public schools adequate to the education of all the children, in the rudimentary branches . . . irrespective of sex, color, birthplace, or religion; forbidding the teaching in said schools of religious, atheistic, or pagan tenets," and forbidding also public funding for "any religious sect or denomination." [39]

Although the national amendment failed, so-called Blaine amendments were adopted in a number of states. In Massachusetts a constitutional provision forbidding state support to "sectarian schools" had been adopted in the anti-immigrant fervor of 1853, but an even more explicit ban was proposed at the end of the century, excluding nonsectarian private schools as well.

Development and passage of this amendment represented a compromise; Catholics, led by Boston "boss" Martin Lomasney, were determined that, if their schools were ineligible for tax support, the institutions created and patronized by Protestants would be excluded as well. They refused to accept that the private "academies" that served in lieu of town high schools in some communities were any less "sectarian" than their own schools. One speaker at the constitutional convention held in 1917–18 described a parochial school in Quincy:

> that school is doing just the kind of work the gentleman from Deerfield claims his school is doing. It is going out into the streets of Quincy; it is taking inside its rooms the children of the poor and the rich; it is educating them. It is saving the city thousands of dollars a year. Why, if the Deerfield Academy is to receive money, should not that institution also receive money?

Logic—and growing Catholic political power—required non-Catholic legislators to accept the cutting off of support to the rural academies and even to the Massachusetts Institute of Technology so as to be able to continue to resist demands for support of parochial schools. They were determined to avoid the polarization on education issues that had occurred in France (though Catholic and Protestant speakers at the convention appraised the French experience differently). Accommodating Catholic power did not mean, as in the Netherlands, satisfying the demands of Catholics and Protestants alike for their own schools, but rather meant denying those demands more evenhandedly.

Catholics, a Protestant spokesman for the committee that developed the amendment pointed out to the convention, "felt that [the 1853 antisectarian amendment] did exclude all Catholic schools and institutions from public aid, but that [it] did not so exclude all Protestant institutions and schools

253

... [and this] was unfair to them and in a manner discriminated against them." It might be asked, "Do you not then sacrifice the non-sectarian private institutions for the sake of settling the religious controversy?" The answer, though hedging, made it clear that this was exactly what the committee had in mind.[40]

Despite an obvious desire to deny that any policy differences on confessional lines were possible in Massachusetts, the convention delegates reflected the continuing authority of the common school agenda. One supporter of public schools described immigrants as coming "over here more or less dirty, immoral and thriftless, and in the third generation they were changed to native Americans" through the "principal cause of the progress of this Nation," the public school system. Catholic delegates argued eloquently that their own schools were "educating their children to become good citizens" and that "the prejudice of this day against parish schools" was unjust and socially divisive. "We are legislating," one accurately observed, "in mutual fear and distrust."[41]

The committee that drafted the amendment confessed itself unable to define "sectarian" or "religious beliefs," noting that the same act could have religious meaning within one tradition and not another. In answer to a challenge from a fellow delegate, however, they insisted that atheism or agnosticism would be considered a "denominational doctrine" that could not be taught in a publicly supported school. "We did not want to leave it," a spokesman for the committee told the convention, "that our schools ever should become atheistic or agnostic."[42]

The overall effect of this measure was to strengthen the public school monopoly; "the trend of the times," one delegate announced without contradiction, "is toward public education." The underlying agenda continued to be the creation of uniformity of belief. No support should be provided to any institution, another delegate said, that "is teaching, inculcating, or promoting a doctrine that is not common to all the people of the Commonwealth and in which all the people do not believe." This was not an issue of religious doctrines alone, since there were "many other principles, inculcated in these institutions, that are not public and are not common to the whole citizenship of the State, and that are equally objectionable with that of the teaching of sectarian principles." Public schools should "teach and inculcate only those doctrines, only those principles, which are laid down by public officers and public agents."[43]

There could not be a clearer statement of the contention of this study, that the common school was concerned with the development of a common, public orthodoxy sharply distinguished from all sectarian doctrines as well as from atheism but resembling them in intention. It was seen as a legitimate exercise of state power (through funding and through regulation of what local government could fund) to insist upon the teaching of a "common faith" in all public schools.

Few voices were raised in protest, within the convention at least. A Mr. Pelletier of Boston, a Catholic, did put the case for acknowledging that confessional schools provided a public service:

> with all the professions of liberality, no man has risen here to say . . . "I move . . . that the Commonwealth and every city and town shall have the right to appropriate money for any worthy charitable, educational or religious cause." Why not go the limit? . . . It makes no difference whether there is a cross or a weather-vane on the top of the school; if it is teaching pupils what the State says at a certain age they ought to know, what difference if they get a little something moral?

He had no illusions about the chances of such a proposition, however, since "underneath us all there is uneasiness. . . . We do not seem to understand one another. We do not seem to be able to trust one another."[44]

The only solution, a Protestant leader insisted, was "a proper division of the time of all our children between the education the State must provide for its own protection and that which the church must provide for the full development of those intrusted to its care." After all, "education that leaves without culture the religious faculties is education that cripples by partial development."[45]

This would, indeed, be the characteristic American solution to the problem of religious teaching: a state-controlled educational system that (at least in theory) would be neither religiously sectarian nor hostile to religion, and a massive voluntary effort to provide religious instruction through Sunday schools, released time, and "vacation Bible schools." It rested upon the assumption—itself a key element of the modernization of consciousness—that experience and meaning could be compartmentalized. Religion may be honored—indeed, it may provide decisive meaning—in some aspects of life and yet be utterly excluded from other aspects. In this "pluralization of social life-worlds" a cleavage is made between public and private life, and the state comes to assert more and more global claims on all that does not belong to a shrinking private domain.[46]

This was an arrangement that Protestant and Catholic leadership, in general, were willing to accept in the period in question; the differences had to do with where the line of separation between the public and the private sphere should be drawn. Protestants tended to seek to broaden the scope of public intervention in private behavior, as in the prohibition of alcoholic beverages, whereas Catholics were in a process of broadening the "private" sphere dominated by religious themes to cover more and more aspects of life.

In contrast with France, American Catholics did not seek to impose their agenda upon the state; in contrast with the Netherlands, American Protestants did not seek to elaborate a religiously dominated comprehensive sphere of "private" institutions. The characteristic American pattern became an essentially neutral though Protestant-flavored public sector with a large Catholic subsociety with its own institutional expressions.

THE ISSUE OF LANGUAGE. Although German-speaking immigrants sustained classes in their language in Boston in the 1860s, Oscar Handlin observes that "attempts to preserve German were futile. . . . French and German easily became second languages which could be acquired by the immigrants' children in the public schools." The great majority of newcomers to Massachusetts through the nineteenth century were English-speaking Irish and Canadians from the Maritime Provinces.[47] The relation of language to assimilation did not, as a result, become an issue in the development of the common school agenda until late in the century.

This was not the case elsewhere in the country. As we have seen in Chapter 8, the desire to preserve a language and the culture expressed in that language was an important factor in the organization of confessional schools in the Midwest. In addition, public schools often responded to the demands of parents that their native languages find a place in the curriculum, though ordinarily this was supplemental rather than, as in many confessional schools, the primary language of instruction. By 1900, David Tyack reports, 231,700 children were studying German in public elementary schools, and smaller numbers were taught in Polish, Italian, Czech, Norwegian, French, Spanish, Dutch, and other languages.[48]

Offering foreign-language instruction was "a necessary concession" to bring the children of immigrants within range of the assimilating and value-shaping influence of the common school. The superintendent of schools in San Francisco argued, in 1877, that until public schools began offering French and German "hundreds of children of foreign parents were attending private schools in order that they might receive instruction in the language of the 'Fatherland.' Now they are found under the care of American teachers, and are being molded in the true form of American citizenship." Public schools in Chicago began offering German in confidence that "the number of private schools now to be found in every nook and corner of the city will decrease, and the children of all nationalities will be assembled in the public schools, and thereby be radically Americanized."[49]

By the late 1880s eight states had statutes permitting bilingual instruction in public schools; in 1872 Oregon legalized monolingual German schools.[50] This was a reasonable compromise, one that enabled the public school to be more truly "common" through making accommodations to parental concerns. Such accommodations were exceptional, however, and were abandoned as the common school agenda with its stress upon the loyalty-shaping role of public schools grew more compelling.

Americans had always been of two minds about the appropriateness of offering instruction in a language other than English. Benjamin Franklin urged, in 1753, that the German immigrants to Pennsylvania be thoroughly mixed with the English: "establish English schools, where they are now too thickly settled." Benjamin Rush, on the other hand, called in 1786 for free public schools in every community: "let children be taught to read and write the English and German languages and the use of figures."[51]

By the last decades of the century the changing character of immigration and the continuing development of the "myth" of a nation-forming common school led to a reaction against the use of languages other than English below the secondary level.

Wisconsin, in which more than one-third of the population was German-born, adopted the Bennett Law in 1889, making it "the duty of county and State superintendents to inspect all [that is, not just public] schools, for the purpose and with the authority only to require that reading and writing in English be taught daily therein." This law, establishing compulsory attendance in schools in which "reading, writing, arithmetic, and United States history" were taught in English, had been drafted originally by the Committee of One Hundred in Boston as part of its attack on parochial schools.[52]

Reaction to the Bennett Law, by German Protestants as well as Catholics, led to defeat of its Republican sponsors and repeal of the law in 1891. A subsequent Wisconsin bill, in 1912, requiring that private schoolteachers be able to speak English fluently, was defeated as well, but North Dakota the same year restricted the use of German or Scandinavian languages in private schools to religious instruction.

Though many confessional schools continued to use home languages for at least part of their instruction, there was increasing sentiment to end the accommodation of languages in the common school. By 1913 seventeen states required that English be the sole language of instruction at the elementary level in public schools, and the anti-German sentiment of the war years led twenty-one states to add such a requirement for private schools as well. In Nebraska, for example, it became law in 1919 that "No person, individually or as a teacher, shall in any private, denominational, parochial, or public school teach any subject to any person in any language other than the English language." Exception was to be made only after a student had completed the eighth grade, as certified by public authorities.[53]

The immediate occasion for much of this legislation was the emotion aroused by America's involvement in the war, and it was often associated with political conservatives, but the ground had been prepared by liberal reformers decades earlier. Thus, in 1891, a committee reported to the National Council of Education, the policy-formulating arm of the National Education Association, that "foreign influence has begun a system of colonization with a purpose of preserving foreign languages and traditions and . . . of destroying distinctive Americanism. It has made alliance with religion."[54]

This "foreign influence"—read, the Catholic church—stood in the way of achievement of the common school agenda, a continuing priority for reformers. Jacob Riis observed, in *The Children of the Poor* (1892), that "the immediate duty which the community has to perform for its own protection is to school the children first of all into good Americans, and next into useful citizens."[55] The sequence is significant: Like Horace Mann a half-century before, Riis placed his primary stress upon the shaping of loyalties, with only secondary concern for the utilitarian aspects of schooling.

Stanford professor Ellwood Cubberley who, more than anyone else in this period, emulated Horace Mann in elaborating the myth of the common school, insisted in 1909 that

> to assimilate and amalgamate these people as a part of our American race, and to implant in their children, so far as can be done, the Anglo-Saxon conception of righteousness, law and order, and popular government, and to awaken in them a reverence for our democractic institutions and for those things in our national life which we as a people hold to be of abiding worth

was the highest mission of public education.[56]

Similarly, an official of the Federal Office of Education, in a report commissioned by middle-class reformers in 1917, "attacked the teaching of foreign languages in the schools, which San Francisco had been doing, and insisted on a comprehensive 'Americanization' to break down ethnic settlements."[57]

In Massachusetts the language issue developed most acutely with respect to French Canadian parochial schools. By 1920 there were sixty-one parishes supporting schools in which French was used as a language of instruction, enrolling nearly 32,000 students, far more than the thirteen Polish schools, three Italian, two German, and one Portuguese school.

The Board of Education expressed its "grave apprehension," in 1893,

> that so large a portion of our children of school age (in parochial schools
> 10.6 per cent . . .) should be drawn away from our public schools. . . .
> Great as these mischiefs inevitably are, they will be indefinitely enhanced
> should we remain a polyglot nation . . . Without a common language we
> cannot become a nation. Without the execution of our school laws we
> cannot attain to a common language.

The board was informed by one of its "agents" that parochial schools "absorb a large fraction of the natural increase of children of school age."[58]

A decade later the board's report included an extensive report on the nativity of public and private school students. Statewide "the majority of all the school children (51.16 per cent) are either foreign born or of foreign descent" in the sense that at least one of their parents was foreign-born. Students of foreign descent were especially concentrated in parochial schools, and the enrollment of the latter had increased more than eightfold since 1873.[59]

The board returned to the theme again the following year, noting the establishment of seven new parochial schools, of which two were in Italian and one in a French parish. This "had led to the withdrawal of a large number of children from the public schools."[60]

The initiative to address the issue of language of instruction came not from the board but from a legislative commission that reported, in 1914, on "the problem of immigration in Massachusetts." The commission reported on visits to thirty-nine parochial schools in nineteen communities in which instruction was provided in a language other than English—Polish, Italian, Portuguese, French, or Greek—for at least half the day. These were only a sample of more than ninety such "bilingual schools." While expressing appreciation for the spiritual and cultural contributions of these schools, the commission noted that

> It is . . . of importance to the Commonwealth that in the secular instruc-
> tion in these schools, the study of English should be given first place, and
> that all studies, except religion and the native language of the children,
> should be conducted in the English language. The study of the foreign
> language should be made clearly subordinate to that of English.

Draft legislation to mandate this result was included in the report.[61]

As it developed, the legislature was concerned not only with language but also with "training in the duties of citizenship," making it a required subject in public schools. As the commissioner of education Payson Smith told the board in 1918, "With two-thirds of her population foreign-born, or born of foreign-parentage, it is manifest that *training in the duties of citizenship* has an important bearing in Massachusetts upon the problem of Americanization." The following year Smith noted that "nearly 350,000, or about ten percent of the entire population of Massachusetts, cannot read or write English," and reported on extensive Americanization efforts in the schools and in industry. After all, "the most conspicuous present need is a far more complete recognition of the responsibility of the State for the education of its citizens."[62]

The challenge of "Americanization" was not new; as we have seen, it has always been of the essence of the common school agenda. The urgency with which this challenge was felt during and after the First World War led, in Massachusetts, to increased pressures to assure that instruction "in all the subjects required by law is in the English language" in parochial schools and to create explicit programs of civic education for the great majority of students who attended public schools.[63]

As we have seen, this was part of a nationwide pattern and was not simply the result of the sentiments aroused by the war. After all, the French combatants were "noble allies," unlike the Germans whose American cousins experienced so much suspicion. It was not the French language in the abstract about which Massachusetts educators and civic leaders were concerned but immigrant French-Canadians who threatened to be unassimilable.

The language issue was closely tied to religion, in the broadest sense, to the *religio* of cultural minorities as well as to that of the common school as a dominant cultural institution.

The incorporation of languages other than English, in some states and for a time, into the public school curriculum was an accommodation of the growing pluralism of American life. The fact that the common school found it easier to accept languages that "competed" with English than competing religious views confirms the validity of the argument advanced in this study, that the educational reformers were more concerned to develop a religious (in Durkheim's sense) basis for morality and citizenship than to assure that particular skills were mastered.

This tolerance of linguistic diversity waned as immigration changed its character and as the common school became ever more controlled by "educationists" and rational bureaucracies rather than by local—and accommodating—elites. But the temporary willingness to accommodate language differences throws into perspective the consistent refusal to accommodate differences of religious conviction. The common school could accept a competing language more easily than it could a competing belief system; English was not of the essence of the common school, but beliefs and loyalties were. Minority languages were increasingly exiled as they came to be identified with competing loyalties. Somehow they shifted from the sphe.. of utility to that of symbol. Once this change in the meaning of language had occurred, the possibility of diversity, choice, and accommodation of parental concern had passed—for a time.

Summary

In the United States, as in France and the Netherlands, the mission of the common school was defined largely in terms of the creation of convictions and loyalties, of shaping a common mind or soul for the nation. So defined, the control and specification of the content of instruction were obviously of critical importance, as was the participation of *all* children, or at least those of the common people, in state-directed schooling.

In vain, in the United States, did ethnic parochial schools claim "that they Americanized children even more effectively than the public schools, in part because they built on rather than destroyed family, religious, and ethnic traditions."[64] They were struggling against what Ravitch describes as "the popular myth that the public schools had single-handedly transformed immigrant children into achieving citizens."[65]

This was the dominant myth of American education in the nineteenth century, and it has persisted with undiminished force in the twentieth, despite all evidence that public schools are in no sense "common" and that the assimilating forces of modern life itself create more uniformity than may be good for us.

10

The Common School
Called into
Question

Recapitulation

THE LAST DECADES of the nineteenth century and the first of the twentieth saw the full development of systems of universal education in the three nations whose history we have been following. Elementary education became obligatory, and this legal mandate was seconded by new employment opportunities that required reading and writing. Virtually every girl and boy experienced at least five years of schooling, and the brightest had an opportunity to go on to secondary education that, as yet, was far from universal.

Although the system could not have been put in place absent the developing economies of this period, the purpose of education continued to be defined, in terms articulated by Pestalozzi and Hebart in the Napoleonic era, as consisting primarily of the development of character. Not just *any* character was to be produced but that most suited to the requirements of society and state, as understood by a national elite that set the agenda for schooling.

We have seen that this goal was articulated by the generation stimulated by the revolutionary events of the 1790s into a concern for nation building and that it was implemented effectively in the early years of the next century in the Netherlands and in the 1830s in France and Massachusetts. Horace Mann and his contemporaries were conscious of being part of an international movement of educational reform. As nationalism gathered force in elite circles late in the century, the common school came to seem the key institution by which their vision could penetrate what seemed the inert and inchoate mass of the people. Those who demanded the right to provide or obtain schooling marked by traditional religion were seen as divisive of national and social unity.

This phenomenon—"sectarian liberalism" seeking to use state-controlled education to counter what it perceived as a threat posed by ecclesiastical authority and religious loyalties—was not limited to France, the Netherlands, and Massachusetts. As historian Carlton Hayes has noted,

> Elaborate systems of state-supported and state-directed elementary schools, whose teachers would be lay employees of the government and in which normally no religious instruction should be given, were inaugurated in Hungary in 1868, in Austria in 1869, in England in 1870, in Switzerland in 1874, in the Netherlands in 1876, in Italy in 1877, in Belgium in 1879, in France between 1881 and 1886; and in Germany, where state schools had long been the rule, they were largely secularized in the '70's. . . . Nor did the Liberals evince any squeamishness about invoking in behalf of popular education that very principle of compulsion which they were credited with abhorring. . . . To the legacy of religious toleration, Liberals of the '70's added an emphasis upon secularization, upon the transference of many social functions and agencies from church to state. The most important of these were educational. . . . the Liberalism of the '70's was essentially sectarian and . . . a distinguishing feature of its sectarianism was firm belief in the supreme menace of ecclesiastical authority, particularly that of the Catholic Church, to the material and intellectual and national progress of a new age, a conviction so compelling as to justify the taking of extreme and exceptional measures.[1]

The relative development of state-controlled schooling in these decades reflected quite directly the degree to which the nation-building task was taken seriously. It was taken very seriously indeed in Germany in the 1860s, consolidating scores of independent states into the triumphant Reich, and—in direct reaction—in France in the 1880s, restoring national unity after Sedan and the Commune. In America after the Civil War educating black and white southerners was a primary goal of northern elites, and the flood of immigration that peaked just before the First World War was a further impetus to the unifying mission of the public school. The fact that the Netherlands and Britain were more concerned in this period with social conflict based in a growing working class than with more direct challenges to national unity helps to explain why liberals in both countries were unsuccessful in asserting a state predominance in education. Confessional schools were recognized, in these societies, as having an appropriate role in the face of the "social crisis."

The resolutions reached in popular education in the decades before the First World War produced what the Dutch describe as a "pacification" of issues that had been deeply troubling in the nineteenth century. Although challenged from time to time, it is only in the past few years that this pacification has shown signs of coming apart. In this final chapter we shall see how the "common school," the major conceptual and institutional creation of the nineteenth-century school reformers, is being called into question today.

The primary focus of these contemporary debates varies somewhat from nation to nation, illustrating different aspects of the theme that we have traced in the historical development of systems of popular education. In France, concerns have focused above all upon the role of the common school in creating national and social unity. In the Netherlands, it is the nature of educational diversity that is called into question in a system in which parent choice is strongly supported. Although in both nations subsidies are provided to confessional schooling in the name of liberty of conscience, the debate has called into question whether religious conviction is truly the motive for most parents who choose nonpublic schools.

In the United States, by contrast, the rights of parents whose beliefs clearly differ from those of the majority have become a major legal and policy issue. American education is in a sense confronting a dilemma that France and the Netherlands have already resolved—the accommodation of religious conviction within a state-controlled educational system—only to find new issues arising on the other side of this resolution. Comparative study of the three systems can thus both suggest how our present conflicts might be dealt with and allow us to anticipate the new conflicts that might lie ahead.

France

The high tide of hostility to the Catholic church had ebbed in France before the outbreak of World War I, and the teaching orders were able to resume providing an alternative to *l'école laïque*. In 1914 about 20 percent of all primary students attended private schools—without state subsidy—and roughly this proportion was maintained between the wars.

The "school struggle" did not die away completely: In 1925 and 1936, for example, the bishops condemned secular public schools (with their "revolutionary virus") as undermining moral and social order, and in 1927 the teachers' union demanded the nationalization of nonpublic schools, but these gestures had no impact on the actual arrangements. It was the French defeat in 1940, bringing the Third Republic to an inglorious conclusion, that threatened its proudest creation. General Weygand told the Vichy government that "all the disasters of the Fatherland come from the fact that the Republic chased God out of the schools. Our first duty must be to bring Him back." Chaplains were restored to secondary schools, the teacher training institutes (the "seminaries of laicism") were abolished, and subsidies were provided to Catholic schools. Protestants, always strong supporters of public education, refused such subsidies for their few schools.

These new arrangements were immediately canceled by the Liberation in 1944, but the Fourth Republic was soon forced to deal with a massive campaign by the Catholic hierarchy and parents of private school students, complaining of the injustice of a system that required them, in order to satisfy the demands of conscience, to provide an education parallel to that supported by their taxes. The *loi Barangé* of 1951 and the *loi Debré* of 1959 provided financial support to confessional education, and the Fifth Republic's *loi Guérmeur* of 1977 extended this further; they were "so many defeats for the secular camp."[2]

These victories for confessional schooling were not easily won. The teacher unions and other powerful groups formed, in 1953, the National Committee for Secular Action (CNAL), an umbrella organization that has continued to be closely associated with the parties of the Left; their petition against the *loi Debré* collected 10 million signatures. The goal of the CNAL has continued to be "to bring together in a common school, in the name of science and of brotherhood, all the children of the one Fatherland, thus cementing French unity and preparing that of humanity."[3]

Nonpublic schools in France may select among several forms of subsidization, depending upon the extent to which they are determined to remain independent of state requirements. The "simple contract" provides for state payment of teacher salaries, with limited oversight of the operation of the school, whereas the "contract of association" provides for the operating expenses of the school as well, with more strings attached.

The political compromises enacted in these statutes were threatened in 1981 with the election of François Mitterand as president. In his campaign, Mitterand had called for "un grand service public, unifié et laïque de l'Education nationale," including "all establishments and all staff." Though the meaning he attached to these words was left deliberately obscure, and though they had formed part of the Socialist and Communist party platforms for years, the close association of his Socialist party with the CNAL suggested that he intended to make a move against the independence of—or the subsidies for—nonpublic schools.

There were good reasons why Mitterand included in his program an assault upon the existing arrangements. Half of the delegates making up his Socialist majority in the National Assembly were teachers, and the largest teachers' union, the left-wing FEN, was strongly opposed to subsidies for private schools. The union was particularly angered by the fact that the proportion of total enrollment in private schools had risen to 16 percent, from 12 percent in 1968. This opposition had been nursed through long years of conservative dominance of national government—when it could be said that "the Right governs and the Left teaches"—and was based upon principles as well as material interests.

The principles involved were expressed with particular clarity by an influential figure in educational policy, Louis Legrand, in an argument for the common school (*l'école unique*) published in 1981. Legrand acknowledged that this issue was deeply divisive:

> "the common school is opposed or supported, not on the basis of technical concerns . . . but [on the basis] of its goal. The common school is necessary, or detestable, to the extent that the awareness of cultural differences seems to require either the imposition of uniformity and the disappearance of these differences or the institutional affirmation of diversity.

As a result, "our era is returning little by little to the quarrels or ideological wars which accompanied the foundation of the public school of the Republic."[4]

The secular school was never, Legrand insisted, intended to be truly neutral; it was to be the instrument of a profound ideological transformation of the nation, to establish bourgeois republicanism—finding spiritual expression in Comtean positivism—at the expense of clerical and royalist influence among the people. This goal, deplorable as it may have been from a Socialist perspective, at least produced coherent education. The Fifth Republic, unlike the Third, has no clear ideological foundation, and as a result its schooling has become "emptied of all content."

> It has become neutrality, accepting as the content of instruction only that which is based in no value, pure knowledge, and technique. . . . But this neutrality is impossible, as the many incidents of recent years demonstrate, especially the growing and disquieting indifference of youth toward academic studies. . . . This pseudo-neutrality is basically a school of social conformity—or of anarchical revolt against such conformity. The ideological vacuum leads in fact to the sterility of the institution.

For Legrand the answer was not to abandon the goal of the common school but to rediscover a sense of positive secularity, a set of values rooted in a humanistic perspective that could with confidence be taught to all students.

> Neither faith in God nor faith in Progress remains as a secure principle. A vague religiosity and a mistrust of scientific and technical progress have penetrated spirits with a nostalgic desire to go backward. Does that not arise from a sense that something else is possible, that another concept of man is being born and could again give meaning to human life and to education? . . . One can ask whether . . . the concept of man in the world

266

that emerges from anthropology would not make it possible to establish a new unifying ethic, acceptable to all.[5]

National unity has been a theme of particular resonance in the development of popular education in France at all times. An alternative Catholic perspective on how such unity could best be realized was spelled out in an important book by Jacques Bur in 1959. Respect for freedom of conscience, Bur wrote, demands that believers be allowed to choose how their children will be educated; the common school cannot, by its very nature, satisfy all citizens in a religiously diverse society.

> The unity of citizens is not achieved by imposing on all a silence about the beliefs of some in order not to offend the unbelief of others. . . . It is not by leveling spiritual diversity that national unity is to be sought, but by bringing it into greater relief in a higher harmony that binds together the various individuals and groups in a common desire to enrich the national ideal.

Thus "an educational system that is corporative and pluralistic, far from dividing youth, will permit a harmonious unity that will not in the slightest resemble administrative uniformity or totalitarian mechanization, but is made up of a fertile and organic association among diversities."[6]

Although they urged opposite policies, Legrand and Bur clearly shared a common view of education as consisting above all in the shaping of students by a clearly articulated ideal. Both rejected a purely instrumental view of schooling.

Bur wrote at a moment when the Catholic position on confessional schooling still stood firm, but it would be profoundly shaken over the next decade. It was in 1959, indeed, that an increasing number of priests began to abandon their vows, several years before the same phenomenon affected other branches of the church. Those remaining were, to an increasing extent, more pro-Socialist than the laity; many of the most influential at the diocesan and national levels had ministered as chaplains to various Catholic movements on the Left rather than as parish priests. They were more interested in collaboration in the interest of social progress than in the maintenance of confessional institutions.

It may be that the Socialists were emboldened to risk reopening the educational battles of the Third Republic, in the interest of a unifying common school, by the wavering of the Catholic hierarchy and intelligentsia in their support for Catholic schools. Whereas in 1959 the bishops had taken a leading role in obtaining the *loi Debré*, they grew more reticent in the 1960s and 1970s. In a statement issued at Lourdes, in 1969, they went so far as to note that many good Catholics "render testimony to Christ" by working in public education and that the choice, for parents, between Catholic and secular schools was "legitimate and respectable."

Thus Legrand could conclude optimistically that it should be possible for the common school to accommodate what he saw as the remaining demands of Catholics—optional religious instruction—without losing its character as "neutral" in a positive sense. "A separate Catholic school has no more reason to exist, since it can rightfully function within the common public school," Legrand wrote.[7]

French public opinion, on the other hand, was favorable to the continued independence of private schools, and less than one voter in four wanted to see state financial aid discontinued. The organization of parents of students in nonpublic schools (UNAPEL) had nearly a million members, easily mobilized in defense of continued subsidies and against any intrusions upon the prized independence of their schools.

Socialist education minister Alain Savary acknowledged that opinion supported a flexible pluralism in education and did not support an ideologically motivated attempt to mandate educational unity. He hoped, nevertheless, to take steps that would increase the "public" nature of subsidized schools by limiting their scope to define the distinctive character of their program—and to select staff based upon their adherence to this *caractère propre*. He spoke in terms of "the desire to unite, permanently and progressively, the too-divided elements of our national education system."[8]

The supporters of Catholic education were alarmed by these proposals, despite Savary's assurances that "a pluralism of ideas, of beliefs, of identities, and the indispensable right to be different will find free scope and development within a public and secular educational service." Once their schools were absorbed into a vast system of state education, how could they preserve their identity and thus their purpose? Selection of school directors and staff by the public education authorities and the training of all teachers in public institutions would surely destroy the Christian character of Catholic schools.[9]

In what has been described as a decisive turning point for the French Catholic church, the bishops reaffirmed in 1981 their full support for Catholic schooling. That there are places at the very heart of the educational process, they reminded the nation, where values inspired by the Gospel are affirmed is an important contribution to young people who are searching for meaning for their lives.[10] This reassertion of the traditional Catholic position on education—perhaps in response to the pope's challenge in 1980, "France, eldest daughter of the Church, are you still faithful to your baptismal promises?"—was widely taken as a sign that the progressive elements that had come to dominate the church in the 1960s were losing influence.

For the next three years one of the most bitter political conflicts in post-war France took place over the issue of Catholic schooling. Gigantic demonstrations—the last of them bringing a million or more supporters to Paris—showed how strongly parents felt about retaining an alternative to the state system of schooling. The CNAL organized its own rather smaller demonstrations to show the continuing strength of anticlerical sentiment. The upshot, in mid-1984, was the resignation of Savary and the abandonment of any efforts by the Socialists to change the ground rules for education. The subsequent defeat of the party in the 1986 elections was attributed, by many observers, to this debacle.

In addition to the struggle over the status of nonpublic schooling, the French common school experienced attacks from conservative critics who questioned whether education was well served by a government near monopoly. Thus Jacques Chirac warned, in a radio speech, that "those who are determined to defend liberty" would not accept the attempted "seizure, by Socialists and Communists in power, of the minds of our children."

A sweeping indictment of education under Socialist control was published by Didier Maupas on behalf of the conservative study group Le Club de l'Horloge. Maupas argued in *L'école en accusation* (1984) that an egalitarian ideology had had the effect of emptying education of most of its content and all sense of the need for effort and discipline. The only answer, according to Maupas, was to destroy the bureaucratic control of education and encourage diversity, choice, and a renewal of high expectations; this would require "breaking with the illusion of the common school" and "adapting education to human diversity."[11]

Sociologist Robert Ballion noted, in *Les consommateurs d'école* [The education consumers] (1982) that "the state school seeks to express a universalism that no longer exists." Schools should be allowed to respond in a differentiated manner to particular groups of parents, who would thereby be encouraged to act as wise "consumers" of services for their children. Quite apart from ideological considerations, he urged,

> private education, in its present forms, is moving in the direction of an improved functioning of our educational system. . . . by legitimizing a new attitude toward education, that of the preeminence of the consumer, private education places public education more and more on the defensive, entering into competition with it and thus creating a new situation of which no one can predict the consequences.[12]

One who was willing to try to make such a prediction was Alain Madelin, a rising star among conservatives in the legislature. In *Pour libérer l'école: L'enseignement à la carte* (1984), Madelin reiterated many of the themes covered at more length by Ballion and Maupas, insisting that "effectiveness, freedom, justice, democracy" could all be enhanced by a system of diversity and choice in education.

> A new idea, a crossroads, this can unite the French people, give a contemporary expression to their determination not to submit, either for themselves or for their children, to decisions in which they have had no part; it can solidify the popular attachment to freedom of choice. In the school, as in so many other areas, freedom must be expanded.[13]

With the conservative victory in the March 1986 elections, there was speculation that Madelin and others might press for the "privatization" of schooling as of other aspects of the French welfare state. It may be that the entrenched power of the education bureaucracy was such that this seemed an unpromising task; Madelin accepted the portfolio of minister of industry, and the Chirac government has already experienced several painful defeats in attempting to implement its program for education.

At present, then, there is a standoff in French education. The Socialists were not able to dismantle the compromises under which Catholic and other private schooling enjoy public subsidies or to bring all schools into a single educational system. The conservative parties, on the other hand, have made no moves against a public education system heavily dominated by their opponents.

The Netherlands

The settlement of the "school struggle" was the basis for tremendous growth of the portion of Dutch life divided along denominational lines (*verzuild*) during the 1920s and 1930s, in every case on the model of proportional representation and support first developed for schooling. Emancipation of the "little people" for whom their Roman Catholic or Calvinist beliefs were central, their emergence into public life bringing their convictions with them, required organization. The passions and the habits of organization developed during the struggle for confessional schooling found expression across the whole range of social life. One Dutch political scientist notes that "*verzuiling* ['pillarization of society'] is inexplicable apart from the 'school struggle.'"[14]

As the issue of confessional education had led the way to the development of power blocs in the political arena, so the implementation of such education after the compromise "Pacification" of 1920 played a leading role in the institutionalization of confessional differences. Whereas in 1920 55.3 percent of elementary students attended public schools, the proportion had dropped to 37.7 percent by 1930 and to 26.8 percent by 1960, rising again to 31.7 percent in 1980. Of more than 1 million students attending nonpublic elementary schools in 1960, 37 percent attended Protestant and 60.4 percent Catholic schools; by 1980 these proportions had shifted to 43 percent Protestant, 57 percent Catholic.

Despite the imposing scope and elaboration of this system of differentiated schooling, based upon a willingness to take "educational freedom" to its logical conclusion in the age-old Dutch tradition of respect for group and individual differences, the Pacification has recently been called into question. A new "school struggle" is troubling Dutch public life and has thrown open for discussion the assumptions and the principles upon which the present system rests. The resulting debate is extraordinarily relevant to our own hesitating attempts, in the United States, to come to grips with how education should function in a pluralistic democracy.

The nineteenth and early twentieth centuries saw public education and the ideal of the common school on the defensive, but in recent years it has been the turn of confessional schooling to struggle to maintain a challenged status quo.

Though the immediate occasion for the present conflict is the need to consolidate the Dutch education system in the face of declining enrollments and budgetary constraints, it draws its sharpness from three developments in Dutch society. The first is a growing secularization, in which the weakening of traditional religious loyalties has reduced not only church attendance but also commitment to *verzuilde* institutions. The second, related in a complex fashion to the first, is a "loss of nerve" among those upon whom confessional schooling depends to confirm its purpose, from church hierarchies to teachers. The third is a new and aggressive advocacy of the common school, seen as the means of bridging not only confessional and class differences but the growing ethnic differences within Dutch society as well.

One of the lasting heritages of the Pacification has been a determination by Dutch political and communal leaders not to allow it to be called into question, lest the divisive "school struggle" be revived. "Freedom of education," seen as consisting of the freedom to establish schools (*oprichting*), to give them a specific character or flavor (*richting*), and to manage them (*inrichting*), has been included in the positions of all major political parties. Their actual preference for public or confessional schooling has been expressed in those nuances of policy that the Dutch are so skilled at reading.

This consensus has been disturbed by the increasing militancy of the Association for Public Education (VOO). The VOO has called for a new "school struggle" to sweep away what it considers the outmoded and counterproductive relics of *verzuiling*. In alliance with the union representing

271

public educators (ABOP), the VOO has argued that confessional education is neither demanded by parents nor provided by most Catholic and Protestant schools and presents an obstacle to the "constructive educational policy" that national and local government should be free to pursue in the interest of social justice and equality.[15]

These acts of aggression have not gone unmarked by supporters of confessional schooling. Protestant education leader K. de Jonz Ozn. asked whether the Pacification was in danger, and denied that public schools were truly neutral in a sense that would make them acceptable for Christian parents. The VOO itself, he charged, was trying to give public schools a distinctive *richting*, whereas the ABOP made no secret of its desire to promote a distinctive (leftist) ideological flavor. Many public schools, he suggested, were strongly marked by the flavor sought by the Humanist League. Similar charges were made by the policy specialist of the Central Bureau for Catholic Education.[16]

The responses have not been altogether defensive, however; leaders of confessional schooling are themselves conscious of the reality of the social developments that have brought their enterprise into question and are laboring to find an appropriate response.

As the Catholic *zuil* in the Netherlands has faced the corrosive effects of secularization, the situation has been complicated by what David Martin describes as "a civil war within the middle class," in which

> the intellectual elite of theologians were supported by other intellectuals and new middle class groups like journalists . . . whereas the administrative elite turned for support to the traditional leaders of profane organizations in agriculture and commerce and members of the older middle class, like shopkeepers.

This is consistent with Thurlings's observation that the apparent revolution in views within the church was "not so much that people changed their attitudes, but much more that the conservative members remained conservatives, but fell in the prestige hierarchy within the church, while the progressive members, remaining progressive, were rising." There was, in other words, a change in the elites setting the tone for Catholics and for Catholic institutions.[17]

Parents who continue to want confessional schooling for their children may not have their way. It is striking to an observer of Dutch education that many—perhaps a majority of—Catholic and Protestant schools are experiencing a great deal of difficulty in maintaining their distinctive identities. This has little to do with pressures related to government funding and oversight.

One of the main problems seems to be a loss of conviction among teachers that there is a distinctive religious heritage worth passing along to their students. Statements developed by faculties tend to stress "the ideals of Jesus Christ" or "respect for human diversity" rather than the distinctions of Catholicism or Protestantism. In Van Kemenade's 1966 study of parents and teachers associated with Catholic schools at various levels, 57 percent of the parents declared that the maintenance of Catholic schooling was necessary, but only 30 percent of the teachers agreed. Though teachers generally asserted that it was part of their professional responsibility to contribute to the religious formation of their students, only one in five reported that they deliberately sought in their teaching to stress the religious and ethical implications of the material.[18]

The decision of the Catholic bishops to replace the catechism with more open-ended religious instruction has been deplored by some as leading to confusion at the school level. "Belief is a question not of learning something," they told the faithful in a 1965 Lenten letter, "but primarily of living something." Incontestably true as this statement is, it seemed an open invitation to the Catholic school to stress social concerns to the exclusion of specific doctrines.[19]

Further confusion was caused by a proposal, advanced in 1972 by a leading Catholic educator, that public and confessional schools work together in a *tertium*, or "third way," based upon "a well-considered choice for spiritual pluriformity." The main reason for developing this option, State Secretary for Education C. E. Schelfhout told Parliament, was that citizens demanded it for principled reasons. It was thus not to be seen merely as a way to increase efficiency or to lower costs but as a step forward in Dutch education, away from the *verzuilde* system that he had earlier served as director of the Central Bureau for Catholic Education.[20]

This incident, which produced more sensation than concrete results, is characteristic of the "loss of nerve" on the part of the leaders of confessional education—the same pattern as in France. The issue was not only unclarity about the essentials of the faith that could and indeed must be taught to a rising generation but also a growing sense that a new pedagogy was called for, one that would in some ways be the antithesis of what had gone before. One could imagine Catholic and Protestant schools simply teaching less and less doctrinal material and confining themselves to the development of secular knowledge and skills. This is not at all what happened. The new pedagogical ideal was as heavily normative and indeed "religious" as that which it replaced.

Equally uncertain signals came from the Council for Affairs of Church and School of the largest Protestant church. In 1975 the council expressed a preference for schools in which various points of view are represented and respected, and one of its leaders, B. Buddingh', warned that "the Christian school" may serve primarily as an instrument of "propaganda and the maintenance of a particular life style." The next year he expressed his reservations about "the school as a single-family dwelling"; his strong preference was for the "dialogue school," in which stress is laid upon the two "core themes of the Gospel: Liberation and Solidarity." Several years later the council expressed its concern that "exclusive maintenance of the traditional *verzuilde* education fails to do justice to new developments that take account of pedagogical heterogeneity." The council's latest report expresses concern about the negative effects of the *verzuiling* of education and calls for schools in which "rules a climate of tolerance, in which teachers and children and the children among themselves can accept and respect one another, precisely with respect to their differences."[21]

In his recent inaugural lecture as professor of education history at Utrecht, N. L. Dodde predicted that confessional education would essentially destroy itself from within. Confessional schools had become nothing more than Protestant- or Catholic-flavored versions of public education: "there is no pedagogical justification for the school struggle." The irresistible tendency, Dodde stated, was toward "general" schooling, not as a matter of educational policy but because of the development of society. This schooling would be based essentially upon humanistic educational goals.[22]

Public school advocate Fons van Schoten has asserted, even more emphatically, that the secularization of confessional education is proceeding apace, despite the successful public resistance of its interest groups, "from the inside out."[23]

Two staff of the VOO, Van Schoten and Wansink, argued in a controversial book in 1984 that a loss of distinctive identity on the part of confessional schools calls into question their claim upon public support as an alternative to public and nonsectarian private schools. In contrast with the pattern of recent decades, in which nonpublic schooling has been the rule and the government has "filled in" where that failed to meet the needs of particular groups or areas, these advocates of public schooling argue that the common school should again become the norm for Dutch education.

A "new school struggle" is necessary—indeed, has already begun—according to Van Schoten and Wansink. In the first place, they argue, the evolution of society requires that schooling be seen as a primary instrument of government policy. They do not hesitate to refer to this as a "state pedagogy," while conceding that to call it a "constructive education policy" will be less controversial.

Education, as a collective provision, serves to provide for the constantly changing needs of the community. That is what the society pays for. The authorities commission education to make a contribution to the removal of social inequalities and cultural *apartheid* as the precondition for the full participation of everyone in the life of the society. The quality of this contribution forms the main issue of the new school struggle.

Because private (and especially confessional) schooling was established to perpetuate rather than to remove group loyalties, it cannot contribute to cultural integration. "Whenever a private school seeks to contribute to cultural integration, it is faced with a dilemma: give preference to its testimony or to dialogue with those who think otherwise." This would require treating their views as of equal value and expressing this concretely by the appointment of teachers, parent council, and governing board members who hold these views. It would require, indeed, placing the identity, the *richting*, of the school up for discussion. A private school that refused to make such fundamental changes in its nature and direction could not, by Van Schoten and Wansink's definition, be of equal quality with a public school in terms of the new expectations placed upon education. Thus the authorities would be justified, even compelled, to withdraw financial support. A private school that did accept such conditions might as well be a public school in any case; having lost its distinctive *richting*, it would have lost its claim upon support as an educational alternative. Therefore all schools (at least all schools receiving public support) should be operated directly by government. Q.E.D.[24]

This is as clear a statement of the rationale for the common school as was ever offered by Horace Mann.

The second line of argument employed by Van Schoten and Wansink starts from the other end, from the demands and interests of parents. Since the slogan under which the school struggle was waged was "the school belongs to parents," they seek to show that the present *verzuilde* system does not respond to what parents want. Their argument here has two parts. On the one hand, they cite the findings of parent surveys to argue that confessional education is a matter of secondary concern for most parents with children in Protestant or Catholic schools. On the other, they point to the resistance of the leadership of confessional education to a legislative proposal requiring that all schools elect decision-making councils representing all of the parents. This they take as evidence that confessional education is rooted in the distinctions of a no longer relevant past and is afraid to be subject to the priorities of today's parents.

The point that Van Schoten and Wansink seek to demonstrate with parent surveys is that there is far more confessional education available—and

275

state-subsidized—in the Netherlands than parents actually want. Unfortunately for their case, the data that they provide seem to show a fairly close correspondence of supply and demand, at least at the elementary level, particularly if those parents who do not select one of the four major options are left out of account. Of the 83.7 percent of parents who make such a selection, virtually all appear to be able to have the kind of schooling that they prefer. Thus 31.4 percent of elementary education is public, and 35.7 percent of parents said in 1979 that they wanted public elementary schools for their children—hardly a striking difference. Protestant education was preferred by 27.3 percent, and 28.1 percent of elementary children were enrolled in Protestant schools. Comparable figures for Catholic education were 34.3 percent and 37.9 percent and, for "neutral" private education, 2.7 percent and 2.6 percent.[25]

That the argument from the preferences of parents is not truly central to the case for a "new school struggle" becomes evident when this argument is set beside the first, and more central, reason given by Van Schoten and Wansink for restoring the primacy of the public school.

If the public common school is primarily an instrument of "constructive educational policy" by the government, it can in the last analysis matter little what parents want. Though confessional organizations are accused of resisting the imposition of elected parent councils to supplement governing boards and possibly to change the *richting* of schools, the VOO concedes that such councils could in no case imprint a distinctive flavor upon a public school. "It is in fact of no significance," Van Schoten and Wansink wrote in answer to a Catholic critic, "that a specific group of parents in a specific public school may perhaps have a strongly experienced group feeling. That may be fine for the group of parents, but it can have no influence upon the public school as such."[26] Thus the VOO is an advocate for more participation by parents in decision making, as long as the parents endorse what the VOO takes to be the mission and character of the public school.

After all, the primary argument for vesting control of public schools in local government is to assure that they remain accessible for all and offensive to none, as well as an effective part of a comprehensive social policy.

In 1975 J. A. van Kemenade, then minister of education for the Labor party, issued a discussion memorandum called "Contours of a Future Education System in the Netherlands." The role of the government, as presented in this document, was no longer primarily concerned with the fair distribution of funds among various types of schools. Through "constructive educational policy," society could be reshaped. As characterized by Dodde, "in constructive educational policy the national government takes many tasks upon itself out of the attitude that the educational system is too comprehensive and too differentiated to be left to the opinions and activities of well-meaning individuals and groups in Dutch society, whether expert or not."[27]

In Wansink's formulation, "the essential thing is no longer the right to provide education according to the inward-turning vision of a group sharing a common view of life, but 'the right to individual fulfillment.'" Thus the claims of group life upon the individual are to be minimized, and the present system of education is seen as a principal obstacle to "the removal of social inequality and cultural *apartheid*." The subtitle of the 1983 article in which Wansink expressed these views is "from *verzuiling* ["pillarization"] to encounter as the model for emancipation"; ironically, it was the creation of confessional schools and other *verzuilde* institutions that provided structure to the "emancipation" of the Catholic and Protestant common people in the nineteenth century.[28]

In the spirit of the "new school struggle," the principal of a public school in Utrecht told ABOP members that "private education is essentially a form of segregation, and segregation is in modern society an outdated and discriminatory phenomenon." Another supporter of public schools argued that confessional schooling was based upon indoctrination and managed "to form a group of slavish, locked-in believers scarcely able to take the slightest self-reliant actions." The result was "deformed personalities, certainly never free from anxiety and permanently dependent upon those who present themselves as their 'spiritual' leaders." Only public schools could prevent this unfortunate result.[29]

In short, the confessional school and the "Pacification" upon which its present status rests are being called into question to an unprecedented extent. The attack rests less upon solid evidence that parents have ceased to value religious education for their children (whatever their own convictions) than it does upon a shift in definition of the mission of schooling.

Those who are pressing for a redefinition of this mission to include a broad responsibility for reshaping society are in fact—consciously or not—returning to the nation-building goals of Van der Palm and others who first established the government-controlled system of popular education in the first decades of the nineteenth century.

This is no longer the agenda of the Dutch Liberal party. State Secretary for Education (and prominent Liberal) N. J. Ginjaar-Maas describes the early nineteenth-century policies as a "centralizing-autocratic education system" and insists upon the commitment of present-day Liberals to ever more educational freedom. Nor is it the official position of the Labor party, despite recurrent suspicion, by confessional organizations, that Labor has a hidden agenda to favor public schools. The Christian Democrats are, naturally, strongly in favor of the present system.[30]

A 1983 proposal, in the face of the need for cuts in the education budget, that the costs directly attributable to the *verzuiling* of education be determined drew conflicting legislative motions from all three major parties, based upon fine nuances of intention. Catholic educational leader L. A. Struik used the occasion to seek to link the Dutch Socialists to the unpopular proposals of the Mitterand government in France to bring Catholic schools under direct government control. Socialist spokesmen Van Kemenade and David van Ooijen responded with unusual heat. More recently, Van Ooijen and his colleague Jacques Wallage took care to stress the support of the Labor party for "educational freedom." Van Ooijen insisted that Socialists did not want to identify themselves with the public school, while Wallage called for less rather than more state oversight in education and argued that there was much in common between social democratic thinking about placing responsibility at the "base" and the Catholic and neo-Calvinist concepts of "subsidiarity" and "sphere sovereignty."[31]

In short, even the Labor party, however it may have flirted a decade ago with a preference for a single state system of education, is concerned to distance itself from such an idea today. The diversity and parent choice that characterize Dutch education are popular, and many Labor supporters send their own children to nonpublic schools. Despite the urging of VOO chairman Lex van der Jagt, in 1983, that the Labor party come out squarely for the public school as a matter of principle, there is no indication that this will happen any time soon.[32]

Does this mean that the "new school struggle" is no more than a flash in a pan? Not at all. The issues raised in the past few years, issues of the erosion of school identity, issues of the assimilation of new ethnic minorities into Dutch life, issues of social justice and common purpose, of tolerance and conviction, will not go away. They are being debated within the education community and beyond with a degree of explicitness that may be unparalleled in the world.

The United States

The 1980s have seen public education under attack in the United States, and not only on the familiar basis of ineffectiveness in teaching basic skills or preparing students for higher education. For the first time, virtually, since Horace Mann, voices are heard questioning the very premises upon which the "myth of the common school" is based.

Several cases that are making their way through the federal court system are causing alarm among supporters of public education. A spokesperson for the National Education Association commented that the ruling in a Tennessee case, *Mozert* v. *Hawkins County*, "creates chaos in the classroom." Anthony Podesta, president of People for the American Way (PFAW), predicted that the ruling would lead to "the disintegration of public school classrooms . . . chaos in the public schools . . . a recipe for disaster."[33]

In another case pending before a court in Alabama, the brief filed on behalf of twelve parents intervening (with support from PFAW) for the defense claims that victory for another group of parents who are the plaintiffs would be "disastrous for . . . the public schools' goal of preparing our young for participation in a democratic and pluralistic society." In such an event it would "be difficult, if not impossible, to stop short of dismantling the entire system of public education as we now know it." Public education would, indeed, "become impossible."[34]

Perhaps the most interesting comment came from an official of the American Library Association, a leader in the fight against "censorship." Judith Krug is reported as saying, "The question is whose values are going to be taught, the parents' or the state's. There's always a battle for children's minds."[35] That is indeed the perennial question in education, whether the state has a right (or a duty) to insist upon compulsory socialization of children in values that conflict with those of at least some parents, in the name of some higher social good. There *is* always a battle for children's minds.

The actual "relief" sought by the plaintiffs in Tennessee and in Alabama could be provided with relative ease by the school systems affected: excusal of certain students from certain reading lessons in Hawkins County, Tennessee; a review of textbooks in Alabama to eliminate those that "advance humanism."

There is a deeper level to the issue, though, that justifies concern among supporters of the present system of public education. The plaintiffs in the two cases challenge, in different ways, the common school itself, and they do so at the most basic level of constitutional principle.

The American constitutional system, based upon majoritarian rule, provides protection for racial and cognitive minorities through the courts. "The primary constituency of the federal courts in constitutional cases," write legal scholars Michael Rebell and Arthur Block, "is 'discrete and insular minorities,' whose rights may need protection from majoritarian biases." Though it has been black plaintiffs who have been most conspicuously successful in recent years in asserting constitutional rights, there is a growing trend for groups whose beliefs differ from those of the majority to turn to the courts for protection.[36]

279

The landmark Supreme Court ruling, during the Second World War, that children could not be required to pledge allegiance to the flag if their Jehovah's Witness parents objected on grounds of conscience, established that such convictions must be respected. "If there is any fixed star in our constitutional constellation," the Court held, "it is that no official, high or petty, can prescribe what shall be orthodox in politics, nationalism, religion, or other matters of opinion" (*West Virginia State Board of Education* v. *Barnette* 319 U.S. 624 [1943]).

The Court made oblique reference, in its opinion, to the traditional view of the common school as the prime guarantor of national unity:

> As governmental pressure toward uniformity becomes greater, so strife becomes more bitter as to whose unity it shall be. Probably no deeper division of our people could proceed from any provocation than from finding it necessary to choose what doctrine and whose program public educational officials shall compel youth to unite in embracing. Ultimate futility of such attempts to compel coherence is the lesson of every such effort.

It is in the tradition of this ruling that a group of "Fundamentalist" parents in Hawkins County, Tennessee, challenged the requirement that their children use textbooks that reflect world views offensive to their beliefs. They have won the first round of the battle, and their children will be excused from lessons that the parents find offensive.

Minorities with views sharply in conflict with those of the majority can be accommodated in this manner. They renounce, in effect, any claim to influence the school's overall program in exchange for exemption from its objectionable aspects. Thus the ruling in Tennessee stands in the tradition of the *Barnette* case, allowing the children of Jehovah's Witnesses to refrain from saluting the flag, and of the *Yoder* case, allowing Amish parents to withdraw their children from school after the eighth grade. This is consistent with the world-shunning posture characteristic of Protestant fundamentalists.

Evangelicals, though resembling fundamentalists in beliefs, have a very different relation to the prevailing culture. They see themselves as yeast in the society, with a culture-transforming role. The Tennessee plaintiffs are fundamentalists, but those in Alabama can better be described as evangelicals. Rather than seeking that their children be exempted from objectionable aspects of the curriculum, these plaintiffs—teachers as well as parents and students—are calling for basic changes in the curriculum itself.

In terms of First Amendment law, the fundamentalists in Tennessee are seeking the "free exercise" of their religion within the public school, whereas the evangelicals in Alabama are challenging the entire curriculum of public schools as an "establishment of religion" hostile to their beliefs.

From the point of view of a public educator, the first claim would be relatively easy to accommodate with some administrative flexibility, whereas the second has the potential for creating a genuine crisis. This is not to say that it is necessarily to be deplored, only that it forces us to ask deeper questions about the goals of schools and their relation to a pluralistic society than we are accustomed to ask.

These parents are by no means alone; it is clear that millions of Americans share their objections. We have seen the results of this growing concern not only in litigation but also in the quieter but more significant withdrawal of hundreds of thousands of children from public schools to private schools or home schooling. Between 1970 and 1985 the enrollment in private schools in kindergarten through eighth grade rose by 6 percent while equivalent public school enrollments were falling by 17 percent!

The basic objection of the fundamentalist parents in Hawkins County, their attorney Michael Farris told reporters, was not to one item or to a few but to books that "were systematically violating these peoples' beliefs." The examples cited with such open bewilderment by the national media were objectionable not so much in themselves as in context; they represented one perspective, with the other—that of importance to the parents—entirely missing.

The Alabama case originated in a similar complaint about a religiously offensive element of schooling, ironically coming from the other side, from a militantly secularist parent. The case was brought by Ishmael Jaffree on behalf of his three children, charging that the Alabama law authorizing a moment of silent prayer represented an "establishment of religion" and was teaching them to pray against his will. The Mobile County School Board noted, in a filing with the Supreme Court, that Jaffree had made ongoing efforts "to silence speech of many types if possible," including the Pledge of Allegiance and the national anthem. In the case of the "moment of silence," he was successful on appeal, after Federal District Judge Brevard Hand ruled against him in 1983.

The judge did not acquiesce in the reversal of his ruling by the Supreme Court but encouraged a group of parents who had intervened in defense of the state of Alabama and of silent prayer to become plaintiffs in a second stage of the case. In this stage, he said, he would accept testimony on whether other aspects of the school program constitute an establishment of the religion of secular humanism; indeed, he made it clear that he was already convinced of as much.

281

In brief, the first stage of this litigation asked that elements of explicit Christianity be permitted in Alabama public schools and called into question previous rulings of the Supreme Court to the contrary. That approach having failed, the continuing inclusion of another belief system, "secular humanism," was challenged. "If our beliefs can't find a place in the school alongside them," the plaintiffs are saying, in effect, "then we will insist that your beliefs be excluded as well!"

It is a peculiarity of educational policy making in the United States that such challenges are not generally resolved in the political arena, by negotiation and accommodation on the basis of compromise as in the Netherlands and France. Our unwillingness to consider matters of conviction as a fit subject for public policy requires that they be cast in the categories of First Amendment interpretation for resolution (ultimately) by the Supreme Court. One of the effects is to raise the stakes dramatically; a decision on the basis of the Constitution has the potential of overturning long-established arrangements that would merely need to bend a little to achieve an accommodation.

Though the plaintiffs employ a number of avenues of attack, it is central to their case to establish that certain elements of the curriculum—if not the whole—represent an "establishment of religion" just as surely as do Bible reading or periods of silent prayer. The boldness of this frontal attack gives the case its particular resonance; the plaintiffs are seeking not accommodation, as in Tennessee, but victory.

The freedom of belief guaranteed by the Constitution and by popular consensus rests upon another freedom, the plaintiffs argue, that of *the formation of those beliefs*. They cite in support of this position a 1980 law review article. Authors Stephen Arons and Charles Lawrence contend that

> If the government were to regulate the development of ideas and opinions ... freedom of expression would become a meaningless right. . . . the development as well as the expression of those beliefs, opinions, world views and aspects of conscience that constitute individual consciousness should be free from government manipulation.[37]

This line of argument (spelled out more fully in Arons's book, *Compelling Belief*) calls into question the mission of the common school as articulated by Horace Mann and others, for whom "the development of ideas and opinions" was the highest calling of public education. It draws support from several Supreme Court rulings restricting the power of public education to seek to foster "a homogeneous people with American ideals" (*Meyer* v. *Nebraska*, 1923), "to standardize its children" (*Pierce* v. *Society of Sisters*, 1925), or to achieve an "officially disciplined uniformity" (*West Virginia* v. *Barnette*, 1943).

But *do* public schools attempt to prescribe any orthodoxy? Wouldn't it be more accurate to describe them—as does Secretary of Education Bennett—as a wasteland in which a "pervasive and almost pathological aversion to controversy" has led to avoidance of value-laden statements altogether? [38]

The plaintiffs' case in Alabama depends upon demonstrating that public schools are not neutral, either in the positive sense intended by Horace Mann or in the negative sense deplored by Bennett. The plaintiffs claim that schools continue in fact to be religious and that the religion they express is that of secular humanism. They rely upon the Supreme Court's ruling, in *United States* v. *Seeger* (1965), that the test of whether a conviction is religious is not belief in a Supreme Being but "whether a given belief that is sincere and meaningful occupies a place in the life of its possessor parallel to that filled by the orthodox belief in God." By this standard, they argue, the secular humanism inculcated in Alabama public schools is religious.

Evangelicals and humanists in Alabama are engaged in a struggle the outcome of which may well be a further purging from public education of those qualities about which both are deeply concerned. Such litigation can only lead to an ever more obsessive avoidance of materials, ideals, examples, convictions that could contribute to the development of character and civic virtue. A continual purging from the curriculum of elements that give meaning and direction to human life, and thus are "religious," cannot be good for schools.

Let us stipulate, for the purpose of this discussion, that there are many parents for whom the home economics curriculum used in Alabama and elsewhere around the country reflects precisely their own values and those they wish communicated to their children. Daniel Yankelovich writes that one American in five lives by the humanistic psychology of "self-actualization." Should they not be able to see their values reflected in the public schooling of their children? But, by the same token, should parents with traditional religious and moral values not have the same right? After all, as a federal court held in a New Jersey case involving transcendental meditation (*Malnak* v. *Yogi*, 1977), "new religions appear in this country frequently and they cannot stand outside the first amendment merely because they did not exist when the Bill of Rights was drafted." [39]

Conclusions

In France and the Netherlands existing systems of parent choice in education—the result of political compromise after decades of conflict—have been challenged lately by proponents of the government-operated common school. These voices, primarily from the Left, argue that the distinctively confessional nature of most private schools, on the basis of which a right of conscience was successfully asserted, has largely been lost. In France, for example, religious motivations are reported as primary by about one parent in four with children in private schools; the corresponding proportion in the Netherlands is around 40 percent. Critics take this as evidence that the existing system really serves class rather than conscience and should be abolished in the name of social justice.

Lest this be taken as an encouragement for confessional schools to develop a more sharply profiled identity (as many are now endeavoring to do), the same critics argue that distinctively "sectarian" education destroys national unity. In short, confessional schools are spiritually divisive if they express a clearly defined world view and socially divisive if they do not! In either case they are to be deplored.

There is nothing new about this case for a unitary educational system; we have seen how it was made by Jacobins in France, Patriots in the Netherlands, Republicans in the United States in the 1790s.

For millions of parents in the three countries, on the other hand, the opportunity to choose among schools, whatever the motivation, is clearly a treasured right. Though religious instruction may not be the primary consideration, surveys in each country have shown that the majority of private school parents desire religious instruction for their children; there are indications, in fact, that they value this more highly than do many religious educators!

Nationwide polls in the United States have shown repeatedly that choice is highly valued by parents. Although 87 percent of American students attend public schools, 49 percent of the parents of public school children responded, in 1986, that they would prefer to send their children to a private or church-related school. As in previous years, nonwhite respondents were even more supportive of a system of educational vouchers (54 percent for, 33 percent against) than were white respondents (45 percent for, 42 percent against).[40]

Support for educational choice does not indicate that the idea or "myth" of the common school is on its last legs. California superintendent of public instruction Bill Honig stated the case for the common school recently in terms that Horace Mann (or Van der Palm or indeed Robespierre) could have endorsed:

> Here we are with an institution that is essential to this democracy, to this society. It is the way we pass down our basic values. You don't play around with that institution lightly. And what this voucher plan would do would say anybody can set up a plan, a school, and they can teach anything. No checks, no determination. And so we will have in Berkeley, California,

284

we'll have schools teaching the Marxist-Leninist view of history, we will have Farrakhan schools, we will have schools that teach the La Rouche point of view, and nobody can do anything about it. If you think that's healthy for this society and this democracy, when our Founding Fathers were very clear that the only way this democracy and freedom and liberty and individual choice that you like is going to survive is to transmit what the rules of the game are, a sense of freedom, a sense of how this government is organized and what we believe in. So I think for us to choose, for us to have freedom, we are going to have to at least assure that our student body get these ideas and that our young people get these ideas.[41]

Honig overlooks the fact that millions of Americans over the past century have been educated in schools not under government control, without noticeably divisive effect.

Unfortunately, we may have set ourselves an impossible task in seeking to provide a single model of education that is to be at once capable of nurturing character and civic virtue and yet inoffensive to the convictions of any parent. As Stephen Arons has observed, "parents can usually find some fundamental value difference between their family and the least common denominator in the public school."[42]

Public educators and their supporters may congratulate themselves—as did the attorney for the Hawkins County School Board—on the fact that parents who object can always have recourse to private schools. This has the effect, however, of making the exercise of conscience and of parental rights contingent upon the ability to afford a private education.

Can we agree, as a matter of education policy—not of legal wrangling—that parents should not be forced to betray their convictions and their sense of what they owe to their children for the sake of obtaining for them a free and adequate public education? And can we also agree that the education of no child is served by continuing to remove every ounce of juice and flavor in the curriculum, for fear of something that might offend?

The only solution is to allow parents to place their children in schools that correspond to their own convictions while meeting those common requirements of the society stressed by Bill Honig: schools with the cohesiveness to develop character and civic virtue, as well as to be educationally effective. Is our national unity really so fragile that it depends upon the indoctrination of the young? If so, we do well to be concerned, for an increasing number of parents are withdrawing their children from our public schools. As the Supreme Court pointed out with respect to the compulsory flag salute, for schools to insist upon teaching a single orthodoxy "is to make an unflattering estimate of the appeal of our institutions to free minds."

Repudiation of public education by religiously conservative parents is—as we have seen—not a new phenomenon in American life. The largely unprecedented element in the present situation is that such parents have been joined by a number of intellectuals for whom a virtual government monopoly of schooling seems unwise or unjust. Extension of parent choice, with some degree of government oversight, is becoming an increasingly discussed public policy option.[43]

Whether from the libertarian perspective of Milton Friedman and Stephen Arons or from the neo-Calvinist perspective of James Skillen, Rockne McCarthy and others associated with the Association for Public Justice, these critics take care to set their critique explicitly within a context of social justice. As Arons points out, "the primary victims of the unequal distribution of liberty in education are the poor, working people and racial minorities."[44]

"Education vouchers" enjoyed a brief vogue in the late 1960s among academics on the left, but perhaps the most influential book in starting the current debates was *Education by Choice: The Case for Family Control* by two law professors at the University of California. John Coons and Stephen Sugarman argued that

> society's general presumption that parents should speak on behalf of their children is simply abandoned with respect to education. . . . With respect to food, clothing, and shelter, all families are fit to choose; in matters respecting basic loyalties, intellect, and fundamental values—in short, where the child's humanity is implicated—the state must dominate the prime hours of the average child's day. Whether a distinction of this sort among economic classes is good public policy is the basic issue.[45]

It is an understatement to say that the case for parent choice has by no means convinced public educators. The National Education Association, in particular, has expressed serious reservations, and its affiliates have battled hard and often successfully against efforts to promote choice at the state level. There are recent signs of movement, however, and the 1986 report of the National Governors Association, *A Time for Results*, explicitly endorsed choice among public schools. President Albert Shanker of the American Federation of Teachers has given his cautious endorsement to such public school choice.

The most notable inroads of parent choice have been in school desegregation. Mandatory reassignments (code-named "forced busing") have been so unpalatable to local decision makers that they have grasped eagerly at the idea of magnet schools as an alternative. Students enroll in a thousand or more magnet schools on the basis of choice, subject to constraints that achieve racial integration goals. By and large, however, the connection between magnet schools and proposals for choice has been curiously weak; the Reagan administration, for example, has called strongly for parent choice while ignoring and seeking to defund a $75 million magnet school program forced upon it by Democrats. Only in the past several years have magnet schools been seen as a model for how public education in general could be organized to promote school-level accountability and effectiveness as well as educational freedom.[46]

What remains is to apply our experience with school choice as a remedy for racial inequities to the current challenge of dealing equitably with the religious convictions of parents and students. Rational as such an approach may be, however, we can expect it to arouse deep resistance among educators. As sociologist James Coleman pointed out in 1978,

> the polarization of opinion about such plans reflects a division on very deeply held values, involving beliefs about the proper division of authority between the state and the family, beliefs about the dangers to social cohesion of deviant doctrines, beliefs about the relative abilities of professionals and their clients to decide what is best, and beliefs in the importance of maintaining the existing institutional order.[47]

In one important respect the debates over religion in public schools today are remarkably similar to those during the formative period before the Civil War: the characteristics of the opposing parties. On the one hand, we have elites utterly convinced of their own disinterestedness and lofty tolerance and of their adversaries' determination to shackle truth and to impose fanatical views on the rising generation; on the other, an opposition confused by the co-optation and use against them of many of the cherished values of American society—education and fairness for all, the spirit of mutual respect, freedom of conscience, cooperation for the common good.

The result, in the last century, was that those for whom transmission of traditional religious convictions was central to the mission of the school were increasingly marginalized and prevailed only among immigrant groups that were themselves marginal. The advocates of a common faith of which the school itself was not only the propagator but also the highest expression were able to impose their vision. The common school, seeking to teach a common understanding of life, became *the* American school.

Although the alignment is essentially similar in the current debates, there is one significant difference that could produce a different outcome. The public school has largely abandoned the role that was of such central importance for Horace Mann and his contemporaries: developing character and conveying moral principles for which there was a societal consensus. It was this mission that gave the common school its almost sacred character in American life from the middle of the nineteenth to the middle of the twentieth century.

This is not to say that the contemporary public school is truly neutral with respect to values and world view. Without necessarily concurring with the entire argument of the plaintiffs in the current Alabama textbook case, we can agree that schools inevitably present a view of reality that has the effect of relativizing other views. The stress on "self-actualization" and the neglect of high ideals and altruism in the curriculum are a clear message about the meaning and purpose of human life.

The difference is that, in Horace Mann's day, the moral objectives of the school were essentially congruent with those of the public, but this is no longer the case. Mann drew upon a consensus about right and wrong that, as he often pointed out, was largely independent of the diverse religious convictions of the times. Those who rejected the public schools did so on theological grounds that, except when reinforced by a strong identification with an immigrant church, were of secondary importance. For most parents, as Tocqueville found, sectarian differences in a common Protestant Christianity were cheerfully accepted.

This consensus on the moral content of education no longer exists. The values most strongly stressed in public schools and, even more significantly, those ignored or subtly denigrated are in many cases matters over which Americans divide more clearly than over any theological issue.

It is only by stressing another contemporary—though equally controversial—theme, the expansion of parent choice, and working with the utmost care to develop a diversity of schooling that offers distinctive approaches to the common goals essential to our society that we can rebuild broad support for public education.

Introduction

1. Mary Jo Maynes, *Schooling in Western Europe: A Social History* (Albany: SUNY Press, 1985), p. 60.

2. Samuel Bowles and Herbert Gintis, *Schooling in Capitalist America* (New York: Basic Books, 1976), p. 224. For the late development of industry in the Netherlands, see E. H. Kossmann, *The Low Countries, 1780–1940* (Oxford: Clarendon Press, 1978), p. 133: Early nineteenth-century "Dutch industry continued to be on a small scale, often employing fewer than ten workmen in its factories. . . . Steam-engines were little used in Dutch factories; in 1837 there were only 72 of them with a total of 1,120 horsepower."

3. See the discussion of Max Scheler's "sociology of knowledge" in Peter L. Berger and Thomas Luckmann, *The Social Construction of Reality: A Treatise in the Sociology of Knowledge* (Garden City, N.Y.: Doubleday Anchor, 1967), p. 8.

4. Maynes, *Schooling*, p. 127. For a corroboration of this conclusion, see an important study of the impact of change on a rural community in France, *Mon village*, by Roger Thabault (Paris: Delagrave, 1943). Thabault found that, despite the school reform efforts of Guizot and others, school attendance did not become substantial until the railroad changed agriculture and commerce in ways that created new employment opportunities available to those possessing a substantial degree of literacy. Bowles and Gintis, *Schooling*, p. 160.

5. Peter Berger, Brigitte Berger, and Hansfried Kellner, *The Homeless Mind: Modernization and Consciousness* (New York: Random House [Vintage Books], 1974), passim. The authors characterize technological production and bureaucracy as "primary carriers of modern consciousness," formal schooling as among the "secondary carriers."

6. Bowles and Gintis, *Schooling*, p. 240.

7. Edward Shils, *The Intellectuals and the Powers, and Other Essays* (Chicago: University of Chicago Press, 1972), pp. 6, 9.

8. See, e.g., Michael B. Katz, *The Irony of Early School Reform: Educational Innovation in Mid-Nineteenth Century Massachusetts* (Boston: Beacon Paperback, 1970), and *Class, Bureaucracy, and Schools* (New York, 1971); Stanley K. Schultz, *The Culture Factory: Boston Public Schools, 1789–1860* (New York: Oxford University Press, 1973).

9. See Thomas Bender, *Toward an Urban Vision: Ideas and Institutions in Nineteenth Century America* (Baltimore: Johns Hopkins University Press, 1975); Paul Boyer, *Urban Masses and Moral Order in America, 1820–1920* (Cambridge, Mass.: Harvard University Press, 1978).

10. Edward Shils, *The Constitution of Society* (Chicago: University of Chicago Press, 1982), pp. 4, 58–59.

11. Berger and Luckmann, *Social Construction of Reality,* pp. 92–93.

12. Diane Ravitch, *The Great School Wars, New York City, 1805–1973: A History of the Public Schools as Battleground of Social Change* (New York: Basic Books, 1974), p. 244.

13. Jean Jacques Rousseau, *Du contrat social* (Geneva: Constant Bourquin, 1947), pp. 365, 369.

14. Berger and Luckmann, *Social Construction of Reality,* p. 92.

15. Shils, *Constitution of Society,* p. 41.

16. Peter Berger, *The Sacred Canopy: Elements of a Sociological Theory of Religion* (Garden City, N.Y.: Doubleday [Anchor Books], 1969), p. 12.

17. John Stuart Mill, "On Liberty," in *The English Philosophers from Bacon to Mill,* ed. Edwin A. Burtt (New York: Random House [Modern Library], 1939), pp. 1033–34.

18. Bowles and Gintis, *Schooling,* pp. 154–55.

19. Mary Peabody Mann, *Life of Horace Mann, by His Wife,* Centennial Facsimile Edition (Washington, D.C.: National Education Association, 1937), p. 83; *Common School Journal* (Boston) 1, no. 1 (November 1838): 14.

1. Guizot: The Government of Minds

1. See Guy de la Fontainerie, ed., *French Liberalism and Education in the Eighteenth Century* (New York: McGraw-Hill: 1932); Peter Gay, *The Enlightenment: An Interpretation* (New York: Norton, vol. 1, 1966, vol. 2, 1969). It was the custom of the revolutionary assemblies, to show their approbation of speeches and reports, to order that they be printed and distributed to all of the departments into which France had just been divided. Since, as a result of the Terror, few opinions were expressed in the Convention of which the majority did *not* approve, we have a fairly complete record of the debates on education: M. J. Guillaume, ed., *Procès-verbaux du comité d'instruction publique de la Convention Nationale* (Paris: Imprimérie Nationale, 1891). These debates were the subject of several studies in English in the 1960s: H. C. Barnard, *Education and the French Revolution* (Cambridge: Cambridge University Press, 1969); Robert J. Vignery, *The Revolution and the Schools: Educational Policies of the Mountain* (Madison: University of Wisconsin Press, 1965). For the education statutes and regulations of the Revolution, see *Recueil de lois et règlemens concernant l'instruction publique, depuis l'édit de Henri IV, en 1598, jusqu'à ce jour* (Paris: Brunot-Labbe, 1814).

As a result of this abundant documentation and analysis, we are in a good position to describe and assess the education proposals put forward by the radical leaders of the Revolution. Although they differed in details, there is essential agreement on certain elements of the Enlightenment program: hostility to revealed religion and to the power of the church, desire to assert the monopoly of the state over the education of its citizens, intention of using this power above all to shape the beliefs and values of students into those believed essential to the political order.

2. Bernard Grosperrin, *Les petites écoles sous l'Ancien Régime* (Rennes: Ouest France, 1984), p. 146, et passim. See also Maurice Gontard, *L'enseignement primaire en France de la Révolution à la loi Guizot (1789–1833)* (Paris: Les Belles Lettres, 1959), pp. 5–51.

3. Grosperrin, *Les petites écoles,* pp. 12–18; Jean Délumeau, *Le Christianisme: va-t-il mourir?* (Paris: Hachette, 1977), p. 27, et passim.

4. Gontard, *L'enseignement primaire,* p. 55.

5. Fontainerie, *French Liberalism and Education.*

6. Ibid., and Douglas Dakin, *Turgot and the Ancien Régime in France* (New York: Octagon, 1965), p. 27.

7. Morelly cited in Alexis de Tocqueville, *The Old Regime and the French Revolution* (Garden City, N.Y.: Doubleday, 1955), p. 164; see also L. Talmon, *The Origins of Totalitarian Democracy* (New York: Praeger, 1960); Du Pont de Nemours cited in Grosperrin, *Les petites écoles,* p. 24; Holbach cited in Gontard, *L'enseignement primaire,* p. 58.

8. Jean Jacques Rousseau, *Du contrat social* (Geneva: Constant Bourquin, 1947), p. 228.

9. Jean Jacques Rousseau, "Considérations sur le gouvernement de Pologne" (1772), in *Oeuvres complètes,* vol. 3, Bibliothèque de la Pléiade (Paris: Gallimard, 1969), pp. 966, 968.

10. Gontard, *L'enseignement primaire,* p. 61.

11. John Hall Stewart, ed., *A Documentary Survey of the French Revolution* (New York: Macmillan, 1951).

12. See the fascinating study by Mona Ozouf, *La fête révolutionnaire* (Paris: Gallimard, 1976).

13. Jacques-Nicolas Billaud-Varenne cited in Carol Blum, *Rousseau and the Republic of Virtue: The Language of Politics in the French Revolution* (Ithaca, N.Y.: Cornell University Press, 1986), p. 183; Robespierre cited in ibid., p. 193.

14. A. Aulard, ed., *Paris sous le Consulat: Recueil de documents* (Paris: Maison Quantin, 1903), 1:107–8. Evidence for the extent to which the radical program was actually implemented, and for the forms this implementation took, is less satisfactory than that for the goals of the program. In part this may be attributed to the nature of the question; it is only in recent years that social scientists have shown an interest in tracing the details of the implementation of programs of government-sponsored social change, and this represents another order of difficulty than studying legislative debates and reports. In addition, although the French already manifested their passion for reports to the central government, the chaos of administration during the Terror and even the Directory make such reports of very uneven value. Those making them were, in general, passionate advocates of the radical program for education, and their triumphs and frustrations seem invariably exaggerated. The information available on implementation, then, must be assessed with caution. It comes from two types of sources. On the one hand, there are detailed collections of public documents from Paris under the Commune, the Thermidorean Reaction, the Directory, and the Consulate; these make occasional reference to elementary education. It is worth noting that the editor of these collections, historian Alphonse Aulard,

took an active part in the efforts to secularize the schools during the Third Republic and was author of several of the textbooks in history and moral education that were condemned by the Catholic church for their anticlerical tone.

On the other hand, there are at least five unfriendly nineteenth-century studies of schooling under the Revolution. J.-B.-G. Fabry published his polemic *Génie de la Révolution considéré dans l'éducation; ou, Mémoires pour servir à l'histoire de l'instruction publique depuis 1789 jusqu'à nos jours* in three volumes (1817–18); it is a rich source for the very ideas he attacks. Four other studies were made late in the nineteenth century by Allain, Babeau, Duruy, and Pierre (see nn. 18, 19, 22, 31). These studies, though incorporating invaluable materials, are by no means objective. The radical and other anticlerical education reformers of the Third Republic made explicit claim on the program of the Revolution as their precedent; public elementary schools were to teach "love of the principles of the Revolution"; their teachers were "sons of the Revolution," and the "ideals of '89" were frequently set against the doctrines of the church. Opponents of this program sought to discredit it by showing how it had been an oppressive failure when first tried. This led to a search of administrative and other records for an impressive quantity of material. There is no doubt that this material was selected to place the school of the Revolution in a bad light, and certainly we must be cautious about the biases of the authors. These accounts are intended as controversial literature. There is no reason to believe that the material presented was in any way falsified, however, and more recent studies reach similar conclusions: Jean Vassort, "L'enseignement primaire en Vendômois à l'epoque révolutionnaire," *Revue d'histoire moderne et contemporaine* 25 (1978): 625–55; Robert M. Stamp, "Educational Thought and Educational Practice during the Years of the French Revolution," *History of Education Quarterly,* fall 1966, pp. 35–49; Jonathan E. Helmreich, "The Establishment of Primary Schools in France under the Directory," *French Historical Studies* 2, no. 2 (fall 1961): 189–208. Though drawing upon the anecdotal material in the nineteenth-century studies, my conclusions are confirmed by the mature scholarship of Maurice Gontard (*L'enseignement primaire*).

15. A. Aulard, ed., *Paris pendant la Réaction Thermidorienne et sous le Directoire: Recueil de documents* (Paris: Maison Quantin, 1903), 5:168–69.

16. Ibid., pp. 273–74.

17. Ibid., p. 478.

18. Albert Babeau, *L'école de village pendant la Révolution* (Paris: Didier, 1881), p. 68.

19. Victor Pierre, *L'école sous la Révolution française* (Paris: Librairie de la Société Bibliographique, 1881), pp. 86–87.

20. Ibid., pp. 91–92.

21. Ibid., pp. 70–71.

22. Albert Duruy, *L'instruction publique et la Révolution* (Paris: Hachette, 1882), pp. 160–61.

23. Gontard, *L'enseignement primaire*, p. 161. See also Michel Vovelle, *Religion et Révolution: La déchristianisation de l'an II* (Paris: Hachette, 1976). For an in-

dication that these wounds have not yet healed, see Jean Dumont, *La Révolution française ou les prodiges du sacrilège* (Limoges: Criterion, 1984).

24. Aulard, *Paris sous le Directoire*, 4:348; Gontard, *L'enseignement primaire*, p. 163.

25. Babeau, *L'école de village*, pp. 218–337.

26. Ibid., pp. 143–49.

27. Ibid., p. 154.

28. See Pierre, *L'école sous la Révolution*, p. 71. This theme of "deux jeunesses" would become one of the staples of anticlerical propaganda during the nineteenth century, receiving its classical statement by General Foy in 1822. See René Rémond, *L'anticléricalisme en France de 1815 à nos jours* (Paris: Fayard, 1976), pp. 113–14.

29. Georges Lefebvre, *The French Revolution*, trans. John Hall Stewart and James Friguglietti (New York: Columbia University Press, 1964), 2:202–4.

30. Babeau, *L'école de village*, p. 157; Gontard, *L'enseignement primaire*, pp. 170–71.

31. E. Allain, *L'oeuvre scolaire de la Révolution, 1789–1802* (1891) (New York: Franklin, 1969), p. 100; Pierre, *L'école sous la Révolution*, 184; see also Aulard, *Paris sous le Directoire*, 5:115, 478.

32. Pierre, *L'école sous la Révolution*, pp. 184–86. See also Allain, *L'oeuvre scolaire*, p. 105.

33. Duruy, *L'instruction publique*, p. 348.

34. Aulard, *Paris sous le Directoire*, 5:169.

35. Babeau, *L'école de village*, p. 105.

36. Ibid., pp. 106–13; see also Pierre, *L'école sous la Révolution*, p. 93.

37. Duruy, *L'instruction publique*, pp. 164–71.

38. Babeau, *L'école de village*, pp. 163, 230.

39. Pierre, *L'école sous la Révolution*, pp. 198–99.

40. Helmreich, "Establishment of Primary Schools," p. 200; Gontard, *L'enseignement primaire*, p. 178.

41. Allain, *L'oeuvre scolaire*, p. 101.

42. See Duruy, *L'instruction publique*, p. 178.

43. Pierre, *L'école sous la Révolution*, pp. 214–15.

44. Louis Girard, *Les libéraux français, 1814–1875* (Paris: Aubier, 1985), p. 83.

45. Gontard, *L'enseignement primaire*, p. 282.

46. Ibid., pp. 284–86, 293.

47. Ibid., pp. 327, 474.

48. Ibid., p. 282. Early members included the duc d'Orléans (future King Louis Philippe), the duc de Broglie, scientists Cuvier and Ampère, economist J.-B. Say, prominent bankers, the comte de Saint-Simon, Lafayette, Carnot, Chateaubriand, Champollion; "parmi eux figuraient les noms les plus illustres de l'époque."

49. Girard, *Les libéraux français*, p. 71.

50. Quoted from *Archives philosophiques, politiques, et littéraires* (April 1818), in Pierre Rosanvallon, *Le moment Guizot* (Paris: Gallimard, 1985), p. 50. My dis-

cussion of Guizot's political thought draws heavily upon Rosanvallon's definitive study.

51. Girard, *Les libéraux français*, p. 77.

52. Quoted from *Des moyens de gouvernement et de l'opposition dans l'état actuel de la France* (October 1821), in Rosanvallon, *Le moment Guizot*, pp. 36–37.

53. Quoted from *Archives philosophiques, politiques, et littéraires* (September and December 1817) and from *Des moyens*, in Rosanvallon, *Le moment Guizot*, p. 42.

54. François Guizot, *Memoirs to Illustrate the History of My Time* (London: Bentley, 1860), 3:64.

55. Ibid., 2:6.

56. Quoted in Rosanvallon, *Le moment Guizot*, pp. 232–33.

57. Quoted from *Essai sur l'histoire et sur l'état actuel de l'instruction publique* (1816), in ibid., p. 234n.

58. Guizot, *Memoirs*, 3:71–72.

59. Sources: Félix Ponteil, *Histoire de l'enseignement en France, 1789–1965* (Paris: Sirey, 1966); Antoine Prost, *Histoire de l'enseignement en France, 1800–1967*, 2nd ed. (Paris: Colin, 1968).

60. Guizot, *Memoirs*, 3:14.

61. Ibid., pp. 327, 330–31.

62. Rosanvallon, *Le moment Guizot*, p. 237.

63. Guizot, *Memoirs*, 3:14–16.

2. Hofstede de Groot: The Defense of the Common School

1. Charles Brooks, *Elementary Instruction: An Address Delivered before the Schools and the Citizens of the Town of Quincy, July 4, 1837* (Quincy, Mass.: John A. Green, 1837), pp. 12, 10, 13.

2. My primary sources for Hofstede de Groot's life and thought, besides his own published books and his articles in *Waarheid in Liefde*, have been a recent study of his "circle," J. Vree, *De Groninger Godgeleerden: De Oorsprongen en de Eerste Periode van hun Optreden (1820–1843)* (Kampen: Kok, 1984), and an older and uncritical biography, J. B. F. Heerspink, *Dr. P. Hofstede de Groot's Leven en Werken* (Groningen: Noordhoff, 1898).

3. For the report itself, see Georges Cuvier and François Noël, *Première Partie du Rapport sur les établissements d'instruction publique, en Hollande* (The Hague, 1816), and a translation in "Rapport wegen het Lagere Schoolwezen in Holland," in *Bijdragen ter Bevordering van het Onderwijs en de Opvoeding. . .* (Haarlem: Enschede & Zoonen, 1812). For French reactions to the report, see Maurice Gontard, *L'enseignement primaire en France de la Révolution à la loi Guizot (1789–1833)* (Paris: Société d'Edition "Les Belles Lettres," 1959), pp. 260–62.

4. Victor Cousin, *De l'instruction publique en Hollande* (Paris: Levrault, 1837).

5. Cuvier and Noël, *Première Partie*, p. 24; Cousin, *De l'instruction publique*, pp. 65, 167.

6. Cousin, *De l'instruction publique*, p. 137.

7. Professor Aart de Groot of the Theological Faculty, University of Utrecht, comments that "The governmental centralization which was realized after the founding of the Batavian Republic, and later on by the French authorities, has been a necessary part of the evolution of the loosely connected provinces toward the modern Dutch state"; private communication, September 1986. This is an important reminder, and indeed the role of the national government in defining expectations for education is much more powerful in the Netherlands today than in the United States, or than state government is in Massachusetts. What I consider an "aberration" is the attempt to impose a single religious character on Dutch schools through a single organizational model, as in France. A case could be made that it was a necessary stage that was later transcended; this would give encouragement to the advocates of "disestablishing" American public education!

8. A detailed discussion of the education available in villages in the province of Utrecht between 1580 and 1800 is provided by Engelina Petronella de Booy, *De Weldaet der Scholen* (Utrecht: Stichtse Historische Reeks, 1977). Primary schools in France during the same period are described in Bernard Grosperrin, *Les petites écoles sous l'Ancien Régime* (Rennes: Ouest-France, 1984). Two recent accounts of education in colonial and provincial New England are found in Lawrence A. Cremin, *American Education: The Colonial Experience, 1607–1783* (New York: Harper Torchbooks, 1970); and Sheldon S. Cohen, *A History of Colonial Education, 1607–1776* (New York: Wiley, 1974). For Prussia, see Anthony J. La Vopa, *Prussian Schoolteachers: Profession and Office, 1763–1848* (Chapel Hill: University of North Carolina Press, 1980). All of the authors stress the very extensive schooling available *before* the organizing efforts of the early nineteenth century.

9. For this period, see Simon Schama, *Patriots and Liberators: Revolution in the Netherlands, 1780–1813* (New York: Knopf, 1977); C. H. E. de Wit, "La République batave, 1795–1805," in *Occupants occupés, 1792–1815* (Brussels: Université Libre, 1968); and I. Leonard Leeb, *The Ideological Origins of the Batavian Revolution* (The Hague, 1973).

10. Siep Stuurman, *Verzuiling, Kapitalisme en Patriarchaat* (Nijmegen: Socialistiese Uitgeverij, 1983), p. 107.

11. Fernand Braudel, *The Perspective of the World*, trans. Sian Reynolds (New York: Harper & Row, 1984), pp. 196–97.

12. W. W. Mijnhardt, "Het Nut en de Genootschapsbeweging," in Mijnhardt and A. J. Wichers, eds., *Om het Algemeen Volksgeluk: Twee Eeuwen Particulier Initiatief, 1784–1984* (Edam: Maatschappij tot Nut van 't Algemeen, 1984), p. 191.

13. Martin Berk, "Over de Opvoeding der Kinderen: Opvoedkundige Denkbeelden in de Spectatoriale Geschriften, 1730–1780," *Pedagogische Verhandelingen* 7, no. 1 (1984): 7; see also J. Stouten, *Verlichting in de Letteren* (Leiden: Nijhoff, 1984).

14. The two-hundredth anniversary of the Nut was celebrated by the publication of *Om het Algemeen Volksgeluk*, ed. Mijnhardt and Wichers, from which these facts are drawn. The quotation is translated from p. 9 of this book.

15. For the Pietist educational tradition in Germany, see August Hermann Francke, *Paedagogische Schriften,* ed. Hermann Lorenzen (Paderborn: Schoeningh, 1957); Francke et al., *Pietistische Paedagogik,* ed. Gerhardt Petrat (Heidelberg: Quelle & Meyer, 1970); Gerhard Schmalenberg, *Pietismus—Schule—Religionsunterricht: Die christliche Unterweisung im Spiegel der vom Pietismus bestimmten Schulordnungen des 18. Jahrhunderts* (Bern and Frankfurt: Lang, 1974). For the application of this tradition in the Netherlands, see J. van den Berg and J. P. van Dooren, eds., *Pietismus und Reveil* (Leiden: Brill, 1978).

16. See J. Kuiper, *Geschiedenis van het Christelijk Lager Onderwijs in Nederland* (Groningen: Wolters, 1904), pp. 36–38, 62–63; a more recent study by E. P. de Booy on schools in the early nineteenth century is included in vol. II of the recently completed *Algemene Geschiedenis der Nederlanden,* but I did not have this available in preparing the present study. See also L. Kalsbeek, *Theologische en Wijsgerige Achtergronden van de Verhouding van Kerk, Staat, en School in Nederland* (Kampen: Kok, 1976). Schama, *Patriots and Liberators,* p. 69, notes that the Patriots did not adopt their goals directly from the French Enlightenment; the "yoking of Wolffian rationalism to the Arminian and Remonstrant traditions of heterodoxy produced in the Dutch version of 'natural religion' a more aggressive attitude toward toleration and the pluralism of Christian belief."

17. Kuiper, *Geschiedenis,* pp. 37, 56.

18. Mijnhardt, "Het Nut," p. 189.

19. For the societies, see ibid., and also Nicholas Hans, "Holland in the Eighteenth Century *Verlichting* (Enlightenment)," *Paedagogica Historica* 5, no. 1 (1965).

20. Mijnhardt, "Het Nut," p. 203; based upon an unpublished study by J. van Veen in 1982.

21. Aart de Groot, "'God wil het waar geluk van't Algemeen': Nutspublikaties van de eerste viftig jaar over godsdienst en zede," in Mijnhardt and Wichers, *Om het Algemeen Volksgeluk,* p. 237; Mijnhardt, "Het Nut," p. 193.

22. Schama *Patriots and Liberators,* pp. 72–73; de Booy, *De Weldaet der Scholen,* p. 119.

23. Leeb, *Ideological Origins,* p. 263.

24. Petrus Johannes Blok, *History of the People of the Netherlands* (1912), trans. Oscar Bierstadt (New York: AMS Press, 1970), 5: 314–15.

25. Schama, *Patriots and Liberators,* pp. 14, 216.

26. Cited in Mary Jo Maynes, *Schooling in Western Europe: A Social History* (Albany: SUNY Press, 1985), p. 41.

27. Schama, *Patriots and Liberators,* p. 534; quotation from Simon Schama, "Schools and Politics in the Netherlands, 1796–1814," *Historical Journal* 13, no. 4 (1970): 609.

28. Schama, *Patriots and Liberators,* p. 380.

29. Stuurman, *Verzuiling,* pp. 116–17.

30. Kalsbeek, *Theologische en Wijsgerige Achtergronden,* p. 138.

31. Cited in Aart de Groot, *Leven en Arbeid van J. H. van der Palm* (Wageningen: Veenman, 1960), pp. 59, 84.

32. "Christendom boven geloofsverdeeldheid." This formulation, which came to have a central place in the common school agenda in the Netherlands, seems to have made its first appearance in connection with efforts to unite the various religious communions as part of the "Batavian" or Patriot program of national unification. Thus, for example, a society of young men was formed in Delft in 1797 with this objective and employing this slogan. A. J. Rasker, *De Nederlandse Hervormde Kerk vanaf 1795* (Kampen: Kok, 1981), p. 36.

33. A. de Groot, *Leven en Arbeid,* p. 63.

34. De Booy, *De Weldaet der Scholen,* p. 125.

35. A. de Groot, *Leven en Arbeid,* p. 67.

36. Ibid., pp. 82, 84, 89. The need for educational leadership by central government had been argued as early as 1778 in the winning essay of a competition sponsored by the Zeeland Scientific Society. We can be sure that Van der Palm was familiar with this essay, since his father's essay in the same competition earned him a national reputation. One historian comments that "a nationalist bias in the thought of the authors is unmistakable; with the renewal of the mind went the growth of national consciousness." Van der Giezen, quoted in Hans, "Holland," p. 29. See Kalsbeek, *Theologische en Wijsgerige Achtergronden,* p. 137; see also De Booy (1977), *De Weldaet der Scholen,* pp. 118–19.

37. Kuiper, *Geschiedenis,* pp. 34–35.

38. De Groot, *Leven en Arbeid,* p. 86.

39. Kalsbeek, *Theologische en Wijsgerige Achtengronden,* p. 146.

40. T. M. Gilhuis, *Memorietafel van het Christelijk Onderwijs: De Geschiedenis van de Schoolstrijd,* 2nd ed. (Kampen: Kok, 1975), pp. 48–49.

41. Quoted in Kalsbeek, *Theologische en Wijsgerige Achtengronden,* pp. 151–55; see also Gilhuis, *Memorietafel,* pp. 50–52.

42. Heerspink, *Hofstede de Groot's Leven,* p. 61; Vree, *De Groninger Godgeleerden,* p. 68.

43. E. H. Kossmann, *The Low Countries, 1780–1940* (Oxford: Clarendon Press, 1978), p. 148.

44. Rasker, *De Hervormde Kerk,* p. 44.

45. See Otto de Jong, *Nederlandse Kerkgeschiedenis* (Nijkerk: Callenbach, 1978), the standard overall history; for this period, see Rasker, *De Hervormde Kerk.* On the revival, see M. Elisabeth Kluit, *Het Protestantse Reveil in Nederland en Daarbuiten, 1815–1865* (Paris-Amsterdam, 1970). See n. 47 for several recent publications on the secession of orthodox Protestants.

46. "X" [P. Hofstede de Groot], *Die Unruhen in der Niederlaendisch-Reformirten Kirche waehrend der Jahre 1833 bis 1839,* ed. J. C. L. Gieseler (Hamburg: Perthes, 1840), p. 55; Heerspink, *Hofstede de Groot's Leven,* p. 168.

47. J. Vree, "De Nederlandse Hervormde Kerk in de Jaren voor de Afscheiding," in W. Bakker et. al., eds., *De Afscheiding van 1834 en Haar Geschiedenis* (Kampen: Kok, 1984), p. 43. In the same collection of essays, J. van Gelderen analyzes the social background of the theological students at the seminary of the orthodox Protestants who "seceded" from the semiestablished church after 1834. Between 1854 and 1869, twenty-four were farmers, eight farm laborers, a

dozen teachers or student teachers, about thirty artisans, and others servants; these were the elite of the protesting group! "'Scheuring' en Vereniging, 1837–1869," p. 133. See also the essay by W. J. Wieringa, "De Afscheiding en de Nederlandse Samenleving," in the same collection. See also the study by A. Graafhuis of the social status of members of a "seceding" church in Utrecht, "De Afscheiding in de Stad Utrecht," in *Aspecten van de Afscheiding*, ed. Aart de Groot and P. L. Schram (Franeker: Wever, 1984). In recent decades the social position of members of the orthodox Protestant churches has increased dramatically, with resulting strains between assimilation and maintenance of their distinctive lifestyle; this process is studied in great detail by C. S. L. Janse, *Bewaar het Pand* (Houten, 1985; includes summary in English), and the controversies to which it has led are described in Anne van der Meiden, *Welzalig is het Volk* (Baarn, 1976).

48. F. L. Bos, *Archiefstukken betreffende de Afscheiding van 1834* (Kampen: Kok, 1940), 2: 110–20; Gilhuis, *Memorietafel*, p. 70.

49. Gilhuis, *Memorietafel*, p. 10.

50. See J. Hendriks, "De Emancipatie van de Gereformeerden," in J. C. Boogman and C. A. Tamse, eds., *Emancipatie in Nederland: De Ontvoogding van Burgerij en Confessionelen in de Negentiende Eeuw* (The Hague: Nijhoff, 1978); James W. Skillen and Stanley W. Carlson-Thies, "Religion and Political Development in Nineteenth-Century Holland," *Publius,* summer 1982.

51. G. Groen van Prinsterer, *De Maatregelen tegen de Afgescheidenen aan het Staatsregt getoest* (Leiden: Luchtmans, 1837), pp. 9–10, 26–27. For a brief biography of Groen, see G. J. Schutte, *Mr. G. Groen van Prinsterer* (Goes: Oosterbaan & Le Cointre, 1977). An older biography is P. A. Diepenhorst, *Groen van Prinsterer* (Kampen: Kok, 1932). A thorough discussion of Groen's relation to the school issue is provided by D. Langedijk, *Groen van Prinsterer en de Schoolkwestie* (Den Haag: Voorhoeve, 1947).

52. Heerspink, *Hofstede de Groot's Leven,* pp. 42–43, 47.

53. For example, de Groot wrote that "we regret deeply that a division occurred in our church in 1618 and 1619, in which the Dordt Fathers [that is, the delegates to the Synod of Dordt, by which the standard of orthodox teaching was set for the Reformed church in the Netherlands] showed a zeal in word and deed that was not the work of the holy spirit of Christ." P. Hofstede de Groot, *Een Woord aan de Hervormde Gemeente te 's Gravenhage over de Groninger Godgeleerden en hunne Bestrijding in "Den Nederlander"* (The Hague: Susan, 1851), p. 10. Later in the same polemic he referred to the "lordship of foreign Calvinism" (p. 17). In a major address marking twenty-five years as a professor, he implied that the Remonstrants, who broke away from the Reformed church in 1619, had possessed the appropriate spirit, and he referred again to the "foreign" theology of Calvin, brought by Huguenot refugee pastors. *De Groninger Godgeleerden in hunne Eigenaardigheid* (Groningen: Scholtens, 1855), p. 213.

54. Rasker, *De Hervormde Kerk,* p. 48; Vree, *De Groninger Godgeleerden,* pp. 324–25; Petrus Hofstede de Groot, "Over het al of niet bestaan eener Gron-

inger School," *Waarheid in Liefde* 1 (1844): 102–5: "God's revelation is to be found, not in a particular teaching of Jesus or the apostles by itself, but in the whole person of Jesus Christ."

55. A. Goslinga, "De Bescrijving van de Geschiedenis van den Schoolstrijd" (1925), quoted in Gilhuis, *Memorietafel*, p. 61. De Groot himself wrote that his was the "century of education," with states and churches struggling over its control and bookcases being filled with books on a topic which, since Plato, had attracted little attention. *Waarheid in Liefde* 2 (1849): 670.

56. Petrus Hofstede de Groot, "Over de Opvoeding van Kinderen in Navolging van de Opvoeding des Menschdoms door God," *Waarheid in Liefde* 4 (1849): 670, 702; Vree, *De Groninger Godgeleerden,* pp. 257, 274, 340; Johann Gottlieb Fichte, *Addresses to the German Nation,* trans. R. F. Jones and G. H. Turnbull (Chicago: Open Court, 1922), pp. 13, 15.

57. In 1837 they launched "Truth in Love, a theological journal for cultured Christians," by which their influence would be largely exerted over the next decades. The introductory essay begins, "'What is truth? What in Christianity is truth, eternally enduring truth, to which we can hold fast despite all changes in opinions and doctrines?' That is the great question of our days." *Waarheid in Liefde* (Groningen: Oomkens, 1837), p. 1.

58. Groen van Prinsterer, *De Maatregelen,* p. 8.

59. D. Langedijk, *De Schoolstrijd* (The Hague: Van Haeringen, 1935), p. 27; Langedijk, *Groen van Prinsterer,* p. 15. See the same author's extraordinary *Bibliographie van den Schoolstrijd, 1795–1920* (The Hague: Kuyper Stichting, 1931).

60. Langedijk, *Groen van Prinsterer,* p. 18.

61. P. Hofstede de Groot, "De Denkbeelden van Graser, Van Heusde, Cousin, en Van Bommel over de Betrekking van de Godsdienst en de Wetenschap tot het Onderwijs Medegedeeld en Vergeleken," *Waarheid in Liefde* 2 (1841): 408.

62. P. Hofstede de Groot, *Zijn Afzonderlijke Scholen voor de Verschillende Kerkgenootschappen noodig of Wenschelijk?* (Groningen: Scholtens, 1844), pp. 13, 17, 18, quoting from J. W. Gefken, *Over Christelijke Volksopvoeding en Vrijheid van Onderwijs in Nederland* (The Hague, 1841).

63. P. Hofstede de Groot, *Zijn Afzonderlijke Scholen,* p. 14, quoting Van den Ende from Cousin, *De l'instruction publique;* p. 20, quoting his own 1840 book, *Bedenkingen over de Zoogenoemde Vrijheid van Onderwijs.*

64. Ibid., pp. 96, 123. Note that de Groot anticipates the argument of the great opponent of the common school, Abraham Kuyper, that each of the various "spheres" of the creation order has its own distinctive rights and duties. Kuyper added the school, which he insisted should not be subject to the state.

65. Ibid., pp. 100, 102, 125.

66. Petrus Hofstede de Groot, *Wat hebben wij van het Ontwerp van Gewijzigde Grondwet te verwachten met Betrekking tot Godsdienst en Onderwijs?* (Groningen: Van Bolhuis Hoitsema, 1848), p. 5.

67. Ibid., pp. 22–25.

68. Ibid., pp. 28–31.

69. Petrus Hofstede de Groot, *Over de Belangrijkheid der Mattschappij: Tot Nut van 't Algemeen, in de Toekomst, welke wij tegengaan, Redevoering . . . den 8 November 1848 uitgesproken* (Groningen, 1848), pp. 4, 16.

70. C. P. Hofstede de Groot, *William Ellery Channing, een Apostel der Evangelisch-Catholieke Kerk* (Groningen: Oomkens, 1858), pp. 48, 53. The title is a program in itself: By presenting Channing as an "apostle" of the emerging purified Christianity, both evangelical and catholic, C. P. Hofstede de Groot was hinting at the similar reconciling role his father claimed for himself.

71. Ibid., pp. 172, 59, 67, 29. As early as 1834, in his response to De Cock's charges, Petrus Hofstede de Groot had insisted that the real issue was not what Christians should believe but whether one had a right to impose his beliefs on another. Vree, *De Groninger Godgeleerden*, p. 98. See also the first issue of *Waarheid in Liefde,* 1837, p. 6: De Groot and his colleagues express their respect for Luther and Calvin, "not for the particular doctrines that they adhered to" but for the truth that they sought.

72. [William Ellery Channing], review of William Woodbridge's *Annals of Education* in the *Christian Examiner* (Boston), November 1833.

73. Vree, *De Groninger Godgeleerden*, p. 92.

74. Bos, *Archiefstukken*, p. 110; Vree, *De Groninger Godgeleerden*, p. 96.

75. Quoted in Okko Nanning Oosterhof, *Isaac da Costa als Polemist* (Kampen: Zalsman, 1913), p. 33; compare the reaction of the American media in the 1980s to "fundamentalism."

76. Isaac da Costa, *Bezwaren tegen den Geest der Eeuw* (Leiden: Herdingh, 1823), p. 20.

77. G. H. van Senden, "De dweeperij," *Waarheid in Liefde* 2 (1845): 379.

3. Social Anxiety and the Common School

1. Quoted from Emerson's *Journals* for September 14, 1839, 5:250, in Arthur Burr Darling, *Political Changes in Massachusetts, 1824–1848: A Study of Liberal Movements in Politics* (New Haven: Yale University Press, 1925), p. 250.

2. Bernard Bailyn, *The Ideological Origins of the American Revolution* (Cambridge, Mass.: Harvard University Press, 1967), p. ix.

3. Darling, *Political Changes,* p. 2.

4. Carl F. Kaestle and Maris A. Vinovskis, *Education and Social Change in Nineteenth-Century Massachusetts* (Cambridge: Cambridge University Press, 1980), p. 111.

5. Quoted in Daniel Walker Howe, *The Unitarian Conscience: Harvard Moral Philosophy, 1805–1861* (Cambridge, Mass.: Harvard University Press, 1970), p. 245.

6. Glyndon G. Van Deusen, *The Jacksonian Era, 1828–1848* (New York: Harper Torchbooks, 1959), pp. 116–17.

7. Oscar Handlin, *Boston's Immigrants: A Study in Acculturation,* rev. and enl. ed. (New York: Atheneum, 1968), pp. 51–52.

8. *Common School Journal* (Boston) 3, no. 13 (July 1, 1841): 204.

9. *Twelfth Annual Report of the Secretary of the Board* (Boston: Dutton & Wentworth, 1849), p. 135.

10. Quoted in Stanley K. Schultz, *The Culture Factory: Boston Public Schools, 1789–1860* (New York: Oxford University Press, 1973), p. 256.

11. Quoted in ibid., pp. 269–70.

12. Ibid., p. 286.

13. Quoted in Edith Abbott, *Historical Aspects of the Immigration Problem: Selected Documents* (Chicago: University of Chicago Press, 1926), p. 338.

14. *Nineteenth Annual Report of the Secretary of the Board* (Boston: William White, 1856), pp. 42–43.

15. "Inaugural Address of His Excellency Henry J. Gardner," *Acts and Resolves of 1855* (Boston, 1855), pp. 978–79.

16. "Notes on the State of Virginia," in Thomas Jefferson, *Writings* (New York: Library of America, 1984), p. 211.

17. Quoted in John C. Miller, *The Federalist Era, 1789–1801* (New York: Harper Torchbooks, 1963), pp. 229–30.

18. Quoted in Thomas J. Curran, *Xenophobia and Immigration, 1820–1930* (Boston: Twayne, 1975), p. 18.

19. Quoted in *The Alien in Our Midst,* ed. Madison Grant and Charles Stewart Davison (New York: Galton, 1930), p. 215.

20. Ray Allen Billington, *The Protestant Crusade, 1800–1860: A Study of the Origins of American Nativism* (Chicago: Quadrangle Paperbacks, 1964), p. 44.

21. *The Biblical Repertory and Theological Review* (Philadelphia, 1830), p. 225.

22. *Christian Examiner* (Boston), September 1835, pp. 54–56.

23. [Samuel F. B. Morse], *Foreign Conspiracy against the Liberties of the United States* (New York: Leavitt, Lord, 1835), pp. 33, 10, 102–3.

24. "An American," *Imminent Dangers to the Free Institutions of the United States through Foreign Immigration and the Present State of the Naturalization Laws* (New York, Clayton, 1835; rpt., Arno Press, 1969), pp. 28, 10, 13.

25. Billington, *Protestant Crusade,* pp. 96–97.

26. Abbott, *Historical Aspects,* pp. 738–39.

27. William Allen et al., *Report on Popery, Accepted by the General [Congregational] Association of Massachusetts* (Boston, 1844).

28. G. E. E., "The Massachusetts Legislature and the College of the Holy Cross," *Christian Examiner* (Boston), July 1849, pp. 57, 60–61.

29. Abbott, *Historical Aspects,* pp. 745, 747.

30. Ibid., pp. 584, 588.

31. Ibid., p. 599.

32. Curran, *Xenophobia and Immigration,* pp. 35, 40.

33. Henry Greenleaf Pearson, in *Commonwealth History of Massachusetts,* ed. Albert Bushnell Hart (New York: States History, 1930), 4:488–91.

34. Gardner, "Inaugural Address," pp. 979–80.

35. Quoted in Handlin, *Boston's Immigrants,* p. 202.

36. Quoted in Curran, *Xenophobia and Immigration,* p. 40.

37. Ibid., p. 20; Sherman M. Smith, *The Relation of the State to Religious Education in Massachusetts* (Syracuse, N.Y., 1926), p. 108; Kaestle and Vinovskis, *Education and Social Change,* p. 171.

38. Schultz, *Culture Factory,* pp. 27–29.

39. *Eighth Annual Report of the Boston Sabbath School Union* (Boston, 1837), p. 3; see also Howe, *Unitarian Conscience,* p. 248, for Unitarian Sunday school efforts.

40. David Tyack and Elisabeth Hansot, *Managers of Virtue: Public School Leadership in America, 1820–1980* (New York: Basic Books, 1982), p. 38.

41. *Nineteenth Annual Report of the American Bible Society* (New York, 1835), p. 33.

42. *Thirtieth Annual Report of the American Bible Society* (New York, 1846), p. 100.

43. Quoted in Howe, *Unitarian Conscience,* p. 247.

44. Ibid., p. 251.

45. See Lyman Beecher, *A Plea for the West,* 2nd ed. (Cincinnati: Truman & Smith, 1835).

46. James G. Carter, *Essays upon Popular Education, Containing a Particular Examination of the Schools of Massachusetts, and an Outline of an Institution for the Instruction of Teachers* (Boston: Bowles & Dearborn, 1826), pp. 48, 24, 49, 16.

47. Edward Everett, *Orations and Speeches on Various Occasions,* 5th ed. (Boston: Little, Brown, 1859), 2:316.

48. "On the Education of Youth in America" (Boston, 1790), in Frederick Rudolph, ed., *Essays on Education in the Early Republic* (Cambridge, Mass.: Harvard University Press [Belknap Press], 1965), pp. 45, 63, 64, 66–68.

49. Quoted in Schultz, *Culture Factory,* p. 253.

50. Handlin, *Boston's Immigrants,* table 5, p. 242.

51. Quoted in Milton M. Gordon, *Assimilation in American Life: The Role of Race, Religion, and National Origins* (New York: Oxford University Press, 1964), p. 94.

52. Schultz, *Culture Factory,* p. 254.

53. Whitney R. Cross, *The Burned-Over District* (Ithaca, N.Y.: Cornell University Press, 1950), pp. 274–75.

54. Gabriel Compayré, *Horace Mann et l'école publique aux Etats-Unis* (Paris: Paul Delaplane, n.d. [1905?]), p. 29.

55. Jonathan Messerli, *Horace Mann: A Biography* (New York: Knopf, 1972), p. 114.

56. Mary Peabody Mann, *Life of Horace Mann, by His Wife,* Centennial Facsimile Edition (Washington, D.C.: National Education Association, 1937), p. 83.

57. Ibid., p. 86.

58. Ibid., p. 105.

59. *Third Annual Report of the Secretary of the Board* (Boston: Dutton & Wentworth, 1840), p. 96.

60. *Common School Journal* 1, no. 1 (November 1838): 14.

61. Ibid., 3, no. 1 (January 1, 1841): 15.

62. Ibid., 4, no. 1 (January 1, 1842): 8–9.

63. Vincent P. Lannie, ed., *Henry Barnard: American Educator* (New York: Teachers College Press, 1974), p. 87.

64. *Ninth Annual Report of the Secretary of the Board* (Boston: Dutton & Wentworth, 1846), p. 27.

65. *Tenth Annual Report of the Secretary of the Board* (Boston: Dutton & Wentworth, 1847), pp. 232–33.

66. *Twelfth Annual Report of the Secretary of the Board*, pp. 90–96.

67. Schultz, *Culture Factory*, p. 54.

68. Ibid., p. 59.

69. *Eighth Annual Report of the Secretary of the Board* (Boston: Dutton & Wentworth, 1845), pp. 16–17.

70. *Ninth Annual Report of the Secretary of the Board*, pp. 64–65.

71. Schultz, *Culture Factory*, p. 258.

72. Ibid., p. 284.

73. Ibid., p. 291.

4. Sources of the Common School Idea

1. Quoted in Dumas Malone, *Jefferson and the Ordeal of Liberty* (Boston: Little, Brown, 1962), p. 47.

2. John C. Miller, *The Federalist Era, 1789–1801* (New York: Harper Torchbooks, 1963), p. 127.

3. Jefferson to William Short, January 3, 1793, in Thomas Jefferson, *Writings* (New York: Library of America, 1984), p. 1004; see also comment by Malone, *Jefferson*, p. 185, that in subsequent years Jefferson "continued to regard the French as crusaders for human liberty."

4. Jefferson to George Wythe, August 13, 1786, in Jefferson, *Writings*, p. 859.

5. Benjamin Rush, "A Plan for the Establishment of Public Schools and the Diffusion of Knowledge in Pennsylvania...," in Frederick Rudolph, ed., *Essays on Education in the Early Republic* (Cambridge, Mass.: Harvard University Press [Belknap Press], 1965), pp. 17–18, 22.

6. *Procès-verbaux du Comité d'Instruction Publique de la Convention Nationale*, published and annotated by M. J. Guillaume (Paris: Imprimérie nationale, 1891), 1:616.

7. Rudolph, *Essays on Education*, p. 22; see also Lawrence A. Cremin, *American Education: The National Experience, 1783–1876* (New York: Harper & Row, 1980), pp. 116–21.

8. Rudolph, *Essays on Education*, pp. 17–18.

9. Jean-Jacques Rousseau, *Oeuvres complètes,* Bibliothèque de la Pléiade (Paris: Gallimard, 1969), p. 966.

10. Rudolph, *Essays on Education*, pp. 210, 190.

11. *Procès-verbaux*, pp. 196–97.

12. Rudolph, *Essays on Education*, pp. 170, 192–93, 211.

13. Ibid., p. 194.

14. Ibid., pp. 216, 219, 221.

15. Ibid., pp. 309–10.

16. Ibid., p. 311.

17. Ibid., pp. 315, 332–33.

18. Ibid., pp. 82, 127.

19. Ibid., pp. 242, 247, 239.

20. "Samuel J. May," in Henry Barnard, *American Educational Biography* (New York, 1859), p. 39.

21. Newton Edwards and Herman G. Richey, *The School in the American Social Order,* 2nd ed. (Boston: Houghton Mifflin, 1963), p. 303.

22. Henry Barnard, "The American Institute of Instruction," *American Journal of Education,* August 1856, pp. 19n., 23.

23. Ibid., pp. 25–26.

24. George B. Emerson, *History and Design of the American Institute of Instruction* (Boston: Ticknor, Reed, & Fields, 1849), p. 4.

25. See Barnard, "American Institute of Instruction," pp. 30–32, for a list of papers.

26. David Tyack and Elisabeth Hansot, *Managers of Virtue: Public School Leadership in America, 1820–1980* (New York: Basic Books, 1982), p. 49.

27. Edwards and Richey, *School in American Social Order,* p. 306.

28. Barnard, *American Educational Biography,* pp. 274, 330, 340; George B. Emerson, *Education in Massachusetts: Early Legislation and History* (Boston: Wilson, 1869), p. 31n.

29. Heman Humphrey, *Great Britain, France, and Belgium: A Short Tour of 1835* (New York: Harper & Brothers, 1838), 2:143–44.

30. John Griscom, *A Year in Europe, Comprising a Journal of Observations . . . in 1818 and 1819* (New York: Collins, 1823), 2:161.

31. Alexander Dallas Bache, *Report on Education in Europe to the Trustees of the Girard College for Orphans* (Philadelphia: Lydia Bailey, 1839), p. 207.

32. *The Princeton Review* 12 (April 1840): 248–51.

33. Vincent P. Lannie, ed., *Henry Barnard: American Educator* (New York: Teachers College Press, 1974), p. 46.

34. W. E. Hickson, *An Account of the Present State of Education in Holland, Belgium, and the German States . . .* (London: Taylor, 1840), pp. 23, 34–37; see also *Common School Journal* 3, no. 6 (March 1841): 94–95.

35. Lannie, *Barnard,* p. 54.

36. Robert Ulrich, *A Sequence of Educational Influences* (Cambridge, Mass.: Harvard University Press, 1935).

37. Charles Brooks, *Remarks on Europe Relating to Education, Peace, and Labor; and Their Reference to the United States* (New York: Francis, 1846), pp. 6–7.

38. Quoted in Edwards and Richey, *School in American Social Order,* p. 307.

39. *Christian Examiner* (Boston), November 1833.

40. Ulrich, *Sequence of Influences,* pp. 47–48; Jonathan Messerli, *Horace*

Mann: A Biography (New York: Knopf, 1972), p. 303n.; see also Ramón de la Sagra, *Cinco Meses en los Estados Unidos de la America del Norte* (Paris: Renouard, 1836).

41. Francis X. Curran, *The Churches and the Schools: American Protestantism and Popular Elementary Education* (Chicago: Loyola University Press, 1954), p. 17.

42. William Russell, *Manual of Mutual Instruction: Consisting of Mr. Fowle's Directions for Introducing in Common Schools the Improved System Adopted by the Monotorial School, Boston* (Boston: Wait & Greene, 1826), p. 50; American Bible Society, *Twenty-eighth Annual Report* (New York, 1844), p. 86.

43. Samuel C. Jackson, *A Sermon Delivered before His Excellency John Davis, Governor . . . at the Annual Election . . .* (Boston: Dutton & Wentworth, 1843), pp. 18–19.

44. *Christian Examiner* (Boston), November 1833.

45. American Institute of Instruction, *Memorial to the Honorable, the Legislature of the Commonwealth of Massachusetts,* February 1836, p. 10.

46. Victor Cousin, *Report on the State of Public Instruction in Prussia,* trans. Sarah Austin (New York: Wiley & Long, 1835), pp. 53–55.

47. Calvin E. Stowe, *The Prussian System of Public Instruction and Its Applicability to the United States* (Cincinnati: Truman & Smith, 1836), p. 73.

48. Calvin E. Stowe, *Report on Elementary Public Instruction in Europe, Made to the Thirty-Sixth General Assembly of the State of Ohio, December 19, 1837, Reprinted by Order of the House of Representatives of the Legislature of Massachusetts, March 29, 1838* (Boston: Dutton & Wentworth, 1838), p. 42.

49. Cousins to Brooks, April 1837, in Ulrich, *Sequence of Influences,* p. 49.

50. See, e.g., Henry Barnard, *National Education in Europe,* 2nd ed. (New York: Norton, 1854), p. 597.

51. Matthew Arnold, *The Popular Education of France, with Notices of That of Holland and Switzerland* (London: Longmans Green, 1861), p. 196.

52. Mary Peabody Mann, *Life of Horace Mann, by His Wife,* Centennial Facsimile Edition (Washington, D.C.: National Education Association, 1937), pp. 213–15.

53. *Common School Journal* (Boston) 6, no. 1 (January 1844): 10–11.

54. Bache, *Report to Trustees.*

55. Barnard, *National Education in Europe,* pp. 606–7; for Cuvier and Noël, see *Première Partie du Rapport sur les Etablissements d'Instruction Publique, en Hollande* (The Hague, 1816), and a Dutch translation in *Bijdragen ter Bevordering van het Onderwijs en de Opvoeding* (Haarlem: Enschede & Zoonen, 1812), 3:5.

56. Charles Brooks, *Elementary Instruction: An Address Delivered before the Schools and the Citizens of the Town of Quincy, July 4, 1837* (Quincy, Mass.: John A. Green, 1837), pp. 12–13.

57. Curran, *Churches and Schools,* p. 24.

5. The State Assumes Educational Leadership

1. Gabriel Compayré, *Horace Mann et l'école publique aux Etats-Unis* (Paris: Delaplane, n.d. [1905?]), p. 29.

2. *Common School Journal* (Boston) 3, no. 10 (May 15, 1841): 157–58; see also George Combe, *Notes on the United States of North America during a Phrenological Visit in 1838–9–40* (Philadelphia: Carey & Hart, 1841), 2:278–80.

3. *Common School Journal* (Boston), 2, no. 3 (February 1, 1840); see also Harold U. Faulkner, "Political History of Massachusetts," in *Commonwealth History of Massachusetts,* ed. Albert Bushnell Hart (New York: States History, 1930), 4:88–89.

4. *Common School Journal* (Boston), 2, no. 3 (February 1, 1840): 88.

5. Quoted in Mary Peabody Mann, *Life of Horace Mann, by His Wife,* Centennial Facsimile Edition (Washington, D.C.: National Education Association, 1937), p. 122; see also Carl F. Kaestle and Maris A. Vinovskis, *Education and Social Change in Mid-Nineteenth Century Massachusetts* (Cambridge: Cambridge University Press, 1980), p. 214.

6. Raymond B. Culver, *Horace Mann and Religion in the Massachusetts Public Schools* (New Haven: Yale University Press, 1929), p. 172.

7. Quoted in Mann, *Life of Horace Mann,* p. 167.

8. Quoted in ibid., p. 125.

9. Kaestle and Vinovskis, *Education and Social Change,* p. 229.

10. Ibid., p. 231.

11. Quoted in ibid., pp. 215–16.

12. *Common School Journal* (Boston), 2, no. 15 (August 1, 1840): 225–26.

13. Ibid., p. 230.

14. Ibid., p. 228.

15. Ibid., 2, no. 7 (April 1, 1840): 106.

16. Thomas Robbins, *Diary, 1796–1854,* ed. Increase N. Tarbox (Boston: Beacon Press, 1887), 2:458, 469–71, 492, 495, 526, 533, 598ff.

17. George Putnam, *Sermons Preached in the Church of the First Religious Society in Roxbury* (Boston: Houghton, Osgood, 1879), pp. 113–14.

18. *Christian Examiner* (Boston), January 1840, pp. 390–91.

19. Ibid., pp. 393–94.

20. *Common School Journal* (Boston), 2, no. 7 (April 1, 1840): 107–12.

21. Glyndon G. Van Deusen, *The Jacksonian Era, 1828–1848* (New York: Harper Torchbooks, 1959), p. 122; for Rantoul, see Marvin Meyers, *The Jacksonian Persuasion: Politics and Belief* (New York: Random House [Vintage Books], 1960), pp. 206–33.

22. Mann, *Life of Horace Mann,* p. 13.

23. Chap. 143, sec. 7, March 10, 1827, *Laws of the Commonwealth of Massachusetts* (Boston: Dutton & Wentworth, 1828), 10:563 (now Chap. 71, sec. 31, of the *Massachusetts General Laws*); see also *Common School Journal* (Boston) 1, no. 7 (April 1, 1839): 100.

24. *Twelfth Annual Report of the Secretary of the Board* (Boston: Dutton & Wentworth, 1849), pp. 113–14.

25. *First Annual Report of the Secretary of the Board* (Boston: Dutton & Wentworth, 1838), pp. 61–62.

26. Ibid., pp. 32–33.

27. *Second Annual Report of the Secretary of the Board* (Boston: Dutton & Wentworth, 1839), pp. 76–77.

28. *Third Annual Report of the Secretary of the Board* (Boston: Dutton & Wentworth, 1840), pp. 96–97.

29. *Common School Journal* (Boston) 2, no. 5 (March 2, 1840): 70.

30. See Chapter 7, herein.

31. *Common School Journal* (Boston) 2, no. 15 (August 1, 1840): 228.

32. Ibid., p. 229.

33. Ibid., p. 238.

34. Ibid., 3, no. 11 (June 1, 1841): 166.

35. Henry Barnard, *American Educational Biography* (New York, 1859), pp. 428–29.

36. James G. Carter, *Essays upon Popular Education, containing a Particular Examination of the Schools of Massachusetts and an Outline of an Institution for the Instruction of Teachers* (Boston: Bowles & Dearborn, 1826), pp. 43, 49–50; for Carter, see also Keith R. Hutchison, "James Gordon Carter: Educational Reformer," *New England Quarterly* 16, no. 3 (September 1943).

37. Rousas John Rushdoony, *The Messianic Character of American Education* (Nutley, N.J.: Craig Press, 1979), p. 39.

38. Quoted in Samuel L. Blumenfeld, *Is Public Education Necessary?* (Old Greenwich, Conn.: Devin-Adair, 1981), pp. 68–69.

39. [Alonzo Hall Quint], "The Normal Schools of Massachusetts," *Congregational Quarterly,* January 1861, p. 4.

40. James McLachlan, *American Boarding Schools: A Historical Study* (New York: Scribner, 1970), pp. 33–45.

41. Charles Brooks, "Moral Education: The Best Methods of Teaching Morals in the Common Schools," *American Journal of Education,* March 1856, pp. 338–39.

42. Eben S. Stearns, "Historical Sketch," in *Memorial of the Quarter Centennial Celebration of the Establishment of Normal Schools in America, Held at Framingham, July 1, 1864* (Boston: Moody, 1866), p. 42.

43. Quoted in Blumenfeld, *Is Public Education Necessary?,* pp. 178–79.

44. *Common School Journal* (Boston) 1, no. 10 (May 15, 1839): 155; for the Dwight initiative, see Mann, *Life of Horace Mann,* pp. 100–102.

45. Edward Everett, *Orations and Speeches on Various Occasions,* 5th ed. (Boston: Little, Brown, 1859), 3:342.

46. Barnard, *American Educational Biography,* p. 394.

47. *Biblical Repository and Princeton Review,* January 1835, pp. 48–49.

48. Blumenfeld, *Is Public Education Necessary?,* p. 216.

49. Quoted in Mann, *Life of Horace Mann,* pp. 112–13.

50. Carter, *Essays,* p. 44.

51. Mann, *Life of Horace Mann,* p. 174.

52. George Willis Cooke, *Unitarianism in America: A History of Its Origin and Development* (Boston: American Unitarian Association, 1902), pp. 401–3.

53. Vera M. Butler, *Education as Revealed by New England Newspapers Prior to 1850* (Philadelphia, 1935), p. 300.

54. The members of the board in 1837 were: Gov. Edward Everett, Unitarian; Lt. Gov. George Hull, Unitarian; James G. Carter, Unitarian; Rev. Emerson Davis, Congregationalist; Edmund Dwight, Unitarian; Horace Mann, Unitarian; Edward A. Newton, Episcopalian; Robert Rantoul, Jr., Unitarian; Rev. Thomas Robbins, Congregationalist; Jared Sparks, Unitarian; Rev. George Putnam, Unitarian. Putnam replaced Mann when the latter became secretary of the board.

55. *Common School Controversy; consisting of three letters of the Secretary of the Board of Education . . . in reply to charges preferred against the Board of the Editor of the Christian Witness and by Edward A. Newton, Esq. . . .* (Boston: J. N. Bradley, 1844), p. 22.

56. Ibid., p. 23.

57. Ibid., p. 27.

58. Mann to Combe, December 1, 1844, quoted in Mann, *Life of Horace Mann,* p. 231; see Culver, *Mann and Religion,* p. 194.

59. Diary, July 2, 1837, quoted in Mann, *Life of Horace Mann,* p. 82; see Neil Gerard McCluskey, *Public Schools and Moral Education: The Influence of Horace Mann, William Torrey Harris, and John Dewey* (New York: Columbia University Press, 1958), pp. 16–17.

60. McCluskey, *Schools and Moral Education,* p. 16.

61. *Common School Journal* (Boston) 5, no. 16 (August 15, 1843): 245–46.

62. See, e.g., Mann's long article to this effect in the *Common School Journal* (Boston) 8, no. 16 (August 15, 1846), entitled "Duty of Clergymen to Visit Schools"; see also Charles E. Bidwell, "The Moral Significance of the Common School: A Sociological Study of Local Patterns of School Control and Moral Education in Massachusetts and New York, 1837–1840," *History of Education Quarterly,* fall 1966.

6. The Common School as a Religious Institution

1. Heman Humphrey, "Pilgrim Fathers" (1820), in *Miscellaneous Discourses and Reviews* (Amherst, Mass.: Adams, 1834), p. 108.

2. Quoted in Samuel L. Blumenfeld, *Is Public Education Necessary?* (Old Greenwich, Conn.: Devin-Adair, 1981), p. 154.

3. *American Journal of Education* 10 (September 1857): 122.

4. Victor Cousin, *Report on the State of Public Instruction in Prussia,* trans. Sarah Austin (New York: Wiley & Long, 1835), pp. 53–54.

5. Calvin E. Stowe, *The Prussian System of Public Instruction and Its Applicability to the United States* (Cincinnati: Truman & Smith, 1836), pp. 73–75.

6. Charles Brooks, *Elementary Instruction: An Address Delivered before the Schools and Citizens of the Town of Quincy, July 4, 1837* (Quincy, Mass.: John A. Green, 1837), pp. 10–11.

7. *American Journal of Education* 5 (August 1856): 31–32.

8. Edward Everett, "The Boston Schools" (1837) in *Orations and Speeches on Various Occasions* (Boston: Little, Brown, 1859), 2:236.

9. David B. Tyack, ed., *Turning Points in American Educational History* (Waltham, Mass.: Blaisdell, 1967), p. 125.

10. Karl Mannheim, *Ideology and Utopia* (New York: Harcourt Brace & World, 1936), p. 273.

11. Daniel Walker Howe, *The Unitarian Conscience: Harvard Moral Philosophy, 1805–1861* (Cambridge, Mass.: Harvard University Press, 1970), pp. 172–73.

12. Mannheim, *Ideology and Utopia,* p. 96.

13. Chap. 143, sec. 7, March 10, 1827, *Laws of the Commonwealth of Massachusetts* (Boston: Dutton & Wentworth, 1828), 10:563 (now *Massachusetts General Laws,* Chap. 71, sec. 31).

14. Quoted in William Kailer Dunn, *What Happened to Religious Education? The Decline of Religious Teaching in the Public Elementary School, 1776–1861* (Baltimore: Johns Hopkins University Press, 1958), p. 108.

15. Quoted in ibid., pp. 111–12.

16. R. Park, quoted in ibid., pp. 113–14.

17. [Greenwood], in *Christian Examiner,* March 1831, pp. 9–10.

18. [William Ellery Channing], review of *American Annals of Education and Instruction* in *Christian Examiner* (Boston), November 1833, p. 273.

19. *Christian Examiner,* September 1839, p. 134.

20. Benjamin O. Peers, quoted in ibid., May 1839, p. 165.

21. Ibid.

22. Quoted in Arthur M. Schlesinger, Jr., *The Age of Jackson* (Boston: Little, Brown, 1945), p. 351.

23. Ibid., p. 279.

24. Nathan O. Hatch, "The Christian Movement and the Demand for a Theology of the People," *Journal of American History* 62, no. 3 (December 1980): 547–48.

25. Arthur Burr Darling, *Political Change in Massachusetts, 1824–1848: A Study of Liberal Movements in Politics* (New Haven: Yale University Press, 1925), p. 27.

26. Figures from Neil G. McCluskey, *Public Schools and Moral Education: The Influence of Horace Mann, William Torrey Harris, and John Dewey* (New York: Columbia University Press, 1958), p. 75.

27. Quoted in Glyndon G. Van Deusen, *The Jacksonian Era, 1828–1848* (New York: Harper Torchbooks, 1963), p. 43.

28. Howe, *Unitarian Conscience,* p. 210.

29. Theodore M. Hammett, "Two Mobs of Jacksonian Boston: Ideology and Interest," *Journal of American History* 62, no. 4 (March 1976).

30. Russel Blaine Nye, *The Cultural Life of the New Nation, 1776–1830* (New York: Harper Torchbooks, 1963), p. 149.

31. Quoted in Mary Peabody Mann, *Life of Horace Mann, by His Wife* (Washington, D.C.: National Education Association, 1937), pp. 13, 15.

32. Sidney E. Ahlstrom, *A Religious History of the American People* (Garden City, N.Y.: Doubleday, 1975), 1 : 491.

33. Nathanael Emmons, "Moral Inability of Sinners," in *Sermons on Various Subjects of Christian Doctrine and Duty*, ed. Jacob Ide (New York: Dodd, 1850), pp. 296, 298.

34. Quoted in Ahlstrom, *Religious History*, 1 : 492.

35. Ibid., p. 499.

36. Quoted in Mann, *Life of Horace Mann*, p. 107.

37. Quoted in Dunn, *What Happened?*, p. 124.

38. Quoted in H. Crosby Englizian, *Brimstone Corner: Park Street Church, Boston* (Chicago: Moody Press, 1968), pp. 87, 90; for contemporary accounts illustrating the vigor of earlier and later Boston revivals in the same period, see Bennet Tyler, *New England Revivals, as They Existed at the Close of the Eighteenth, and the Beginning of the Nineteenth Centuries* (Boston: Massachusetts Sabbath School Society, 1846), and Martin Moore, *A Brief History of the Evangelical Churches of Boston, together with a more particular account of the Revival of 1842* (Boston: Putnam, 1842).

39. *First Annual Report of the Secretary of the Board* (Boston: Dutton & Wentworth, 1838), pp. 33 et passim.

40. Dunn, *What Happened?*, p. 135.

41. Ibid., p. 137.

42. *Third Annual Report of the Secretary of the Board* (Boston: Dutton & Wentworth, 1840), p. 14.

43. *Fourth Annual Report of the Secretary of the Board* (Boston: Dutton & Wentworth, 1841), p. 59.

44. *Fifth Annual Report of the Secretary of the Board* (Boston: Dutton & Wentworth, 1842), pp. 65–66.

45. *Seventh Annual Report of the Secretary of the Board* (Boston: Dutton & Wentworth, 1844), pp. 125–26.

46. Ibid., p. 174; see also p. 183.

47. *Ninth Annual Report of the Secretary of the Board* (Boston: Dutton & Wentworth, 1846), pp. 66–69.

48. Ibid., p. 157.

49. *Tenth Annual Report of the Secretary of the Board* (Boston: Dutton & Wentworth, 1847), p. 233.

50. *Eleventh Annual Report of the Secretary of the Board* (Boston: Dutton & Wentworth, 1848), pp. 31, 90–91.

51. Quoted in ibid., pp. 126–29.

52. Ibid., p. 135.

53. *Twelfth Annual Report of the Secretary of the Board* (Boston: Dutton & Wentworth, 1849), pp. 94, 96.

54. Ibid., pp. 98–99.

55. Ibid., pp. 113–16.

56. Ibid., pp. 118–19.

57. Ibid., p. 139.

58. Ibid., pp. 137–38.

59. Ibid., pp. 139, 115.

60. Carl F. Kaestle and Maris A. Vinovskis, *Education and Social Change in Nineteenth-Century Massachusetts* (Cambridge: Cambridge University Press, 1980), p. 229.

61. *Common School Journal,* January 1, 1846, p. 15.

62. McCluskey, *Schools and Moral Education,* p. 19.

63. Quoted in ibid., p. 20.

64. Quoted in Raymond Culver, *Horace Mann and Religion in the Massachusetts Public Schools* (New Haven: Yale University Press, 1929), p. 76.

65. Ibid., pp. 63–64.

66. *Fifteenth Annual Report of the Secretary of the Board* (Boston: Dutton & Wentworth, 1852), pp. 26–27.

67. *Seventeenth Annual Report of the Secretary of the Board* (Boston: Dutton & Wentworth, 1854), pp. 50–51.

68. *Eighteenth Annual Report of the Secretary of the Board* (Boston: William White, 1855), pp. 46–48.

69. Stanley K. Schultz, *The Culture Factory: Boston Public Schools, 1789–1860* (New York: Oxford University Press, 1973), pp. 64, 305.

70. Kaestle and Vinovskis, *Education and Social Change,* p. 173.

71. D. Bethune Duffield, "Education, A State Duty; or, May the State Insist on the Education of Her Youth? And to What Extent Can She Go in This Direction?" *American Journal of Education,* March 1857, p. 95.

72. Ibid., pp. 96–97.

73. "Moral and Religious Instruction in Public Schools," *American Journal of Education,* July 1856, p. 153.

74. Ibid., pp. 154, 171.

75. John A. Nietz (1952), cited in Dunn, *What Happened?,* p. 77; see also p. 289.

76. Paul Vitz, *Censorship: Evidence of Bias in Our Children's Textbooks* (Ann Arbor, Mich.: Servant Books, 1986).

77. Dunn, *What Happened?,* p. 309.

78. Ibid., p. 312.

7. The Opposition to Common School Religion

1. *Spirit of the Pilgrims* (Boston), January 1828, pp. 1, 3, 7–10, 15, 19.

2. Ibid., November 1828, pp. 561, 564, 565.

3. Ibid., 1832, pp. 282, 286–88, 291.

4. Charles Hodge, "Introductory Lecture Delivered in the Theological Seminary, Princeton, New Jersey, November 7, 1828," *Biblical Repertory and Princeton Review* (Princeton), 1829, p. 86.

5. Review, in *Biblical Repertory and Theological Review* (Philadelphia), 1831;

quoted in Lewis Joseph Sherrill, *Presbyterian Parochial Schools, 1846–1870* (New Haven: Yale University Press, 1932), p. 14.

6. "The General Assembly, Parochial Schools," *Princeton Review* 18 (1846).

7. Ibid.

8. Quoted in Raymond B. Culver, *Horace Mann and Religion in the Massachusetts Public Schools* (New Haven: Yale University Press, 1929), p. 71.

9. Quoted in ibid., p. 57.

10. Quoted in ibid., pp. 58–59.

11. Quoted in William Kailer Dunn, *What Happened to Religious Education? The Decline of Religious Teaching in the Public Elementary School, 1776–1861* (Baltimore: Johns Hopkins University Press, 1958), p. 152.

12. Quoted in Culver, *Mann and Religion*, pp. 63–64.

13. Quoted in ibid., p. 76.

14. Quoted in ibid., p. 78.

15. "Religious Instruction in Common Schools," *Princeton Review*, July 1841, p. 316.

16. Ibid., p. 362.

17. Ibid., pp. 346–47.

18. Ibid., p. 367.

19. "The Ark of God on a New Cart, a Sermon, by Rev. M. Hale Smith," in *The Bible, the Rod, and Religion, in the Common Schools* (Boston: Redding, 1847), pp. 10–11.

20. "A Review of the Sermon, by Wm. B. Fowle, Publisher of the Mass. Common School Journal," in ibid., pp. 17–19.

21. "Correspondence between the Hon. Horace Mann, Sec. of the Board of Education, and Rev. Matthew Hale Smith," in ibid., pp. 39–49.

22. Ibid., pp. 52–53.

23. *Reply to the Sequel of Hon. Horace Mann, Being a Supplement to the Bible, the Rod, and Religion, in the Common Schools* (Boston: Whittemore, 1847), p. 24.

24. Quoted in Francis X. Curran, *The Churches and the Schools: American Protestantism and Popular Elementary Education* (Chicago: Loyola University Press, 1954), p. 17.

25. "The Girard Will Case: The Christian Ministry and the Religious Instruction of the Young," in *The Writings and Speeches of Daniel Webster* (Boston: Little, Brown, 1903), 11:137.

26. Ibid., pp. 147–55.

27. Ibid., pp. 161–69.

28. "Extract from the Writings of Bishop White," in ibid., p. 181.

29. *The Common School Controversy; Consisting of Three Letters of the Secretary of the Board of Education . . . in Reply to Charges Preferred against the Board by the Editor of the Christian Witness and by Edward A. Newton, Esq. . . . .* (Boston: J. N. Bradley, 1844), p. 3.

30. Ibid., p. 5.

31. Ibid., p. 6.

32. Ibid., p. 7.

33. Ibid., pp. 11, 13.

34. Ibid., p. 20.

35. Ibid., p. 21.

36. Ibid., p. 24.

37. "A Plea for the Restoration of the Scriptures to the Schools," in American Bible Society, *Twenty-third Annual Report* (New York, 1839).

38. American Bible Society, *Twenty-fifth Annual Report* (New York, 1841), p. 85.

39. American Bible Society, *Twenty-sixth Annual Report* (New York, 1842), p. 94.

40. Quoted in Dunn, *What Happened?*, p. 207.

41. "Pastoral of 1829," in Neil G. McCluskey, ed., *Catholic Education in America: A Documentary History* (New York: Teachers College Press, 1964), pp. 53–55.

42. Diane Ravitch, *The Great School Wars, New York City, 1805–1973: A History of the Public Schools as Battlefield of Social Change* (New York: Basic Books, 1974), pp. 34–35.

43. Ibid., p. 45.

44. Quoted in ibid.

45. Quoted in Jay P. Dolan, *The Immigrant Church: New York's Irish and German Catholics, 1815–1865* (Baltimore: Johns Hopkins University Press, 1975), p. 103.

46. Ravitch, *Great School Wars*, pp. 48–49.

47. "Petition of the Catholics of New York for a Portion of the Common School Fund (1840)," in McCluskey, *Catholic Education*, p. 68.

48. Ravitch, *Great School Wars*, p. 56.

49. Quoted in Dunn, *What Happened?*, p. 254.

50. "Pastoral of 1840," in McCluskey, *Catholic Education*, pp. 58–61.

51. "Pastoral of 1843," in ibid., p. 63.

52. "First Plenary Council (1852)," in ibid., pp. 80–81.

53. Quoted in Stanley K. Schultz, *The Culture Factory: Boston Public Schools, 1789–1860* (New York: Oxford University Press, 1973), p. 290.

54. Ibid., p. 291.

55. Quoted in Robert H. Lord, John E. Sexton, and Edward T. Harrington, *A History of the Archdiocese of Boston in the Various Stages of Development* (New York: Sheed & Ward, 1944), 2:582.

56. Schultz, *Culture Factory*, p. 301.

57. Lord et al., *Hisory of the Archdiocese*, p. 598.

8. Alternatives to the Common School

1. Jonathan Edwards, "Thoughts on the Revival of Religion in New England," quoted in James McLachlan, *American Boarding Schools: A Historical Survey* (New York: Scribner, 1970), p. 35.

2. Quoted in McLachlan, *American Boarding Schools*, p. 38.

3. Quoted in Theodore Sizer, ed., *The Age of the Academies* (New York: Teachers College Press, 1964), pp. 77, 86–87.

4. Stanley K. Schultz, *The Culture Factory: The Boston Public Schools, 1789–1860* (New York: Oxford University Press, 1973), p. 32.

5. Ibid., pp. 19–21, 37.

6. Carl F. Kaestle and Maris A. Vinovskis, *Education and Social Change in Nineteenth-Century Massachusetts* (Cambridge: Cambridge University Press, 1980), p. 10.

7. Ibid., pp. 18–20.

8. Ibid., p. 34.

9. Quoted in Sizer, *Age of the Academies,* pp. 98–100.

10. Quoted in Walter H. Beck, *Lutheran Elementary Schools in the United States* (St. Louis: Concordia, 1965 [originally 1939]), p. 29.

11. Benjamin Rush, "A Plan for the Establishment of Public Schools. . . ," in Frederick Rudolph, ed., *Essays on Education in the Early Republic* (Cambridge, Mass.: Harvard University Press [Belknap Press], 1965), pp. 5, 7.

12. Beck, *Lutheran Elementary Schools,* p. 48.

13. "Wer seine Sproch verlaesst, der schaemt sich doch sehner Eltern und verlaesst noch sehne Religion und werd en Methodist. Und ist denn die englisch Sproch vornemmer und schenner als die deitsch? Ich denk nett. . . . Aver sobald der Hochmuth in die junge Leit faehrt, wolle sie englische seyn und schaeme sich, deitsch zu schwaetze"; quoted in ibid., p. 80n.

14. Quoted in ibid., pp. 82–83.

15. Ibid., pp. 116–17.

16. Ibid., p. 145.

17. Arlow William Anderson, *The Immigrant Takes His Stand: The Norwegian-American Press and Public Affairs, 1847–1872* (Northfield, Minn., 1953), p. 109.

18. Lewis Joseph Sherrill, *Presbyterian Parochial Schools, 1846–1870* (New Haven: Yale University Press, 1932), pp. 2, 7–8; see also *Princeton Review,* April 1841, p. 314.

19. Sherrill, *Presbyterian Schools,* p. 9.

20. Ibid., pp. 20–29.

21. Ibid., p. 59.

22. A. Brummelkamp and A. C. van Raalte (1846), quoted in Peter de Boer and Donald Oppewal, "American Calvinist Day Schools," *Christian Scholars Review* 13, no. 2 (1984): 123; see also James D. Bratt, *Dutch Calvinism in Modern America: A History of a Conservative Subculture* (Grand Rapids, Mich.: Eerdman's, 1984).

23. Sherrill, *Presbyterian Schools,* pp. 37, 31.

24. R. J. Breckinridge, "A Plea for the Restoration of the Scriptures to the Schools," in American Bible Society, *Twenty-third Annual Report* (New York, 1839), pp. 78–87.

25. Louis S. Walsh, *Historical Sketch of the Growth of Catholic Parochial Schools in the Archdiocese of Boston* (Newton Highlands, Mass., 1901).

26. Oscar Handlin, *Boston's Immigrants: A Study in Acculturation*, rev. and enl. ed. (New York: Atheneum, 1968), p. 168; see also, e.g., the *Eighth Annual Report of the Boston Sabbath School Union* (Boston, 1837), reference to students who have "shaken off the bonds of Popery and Satan," p. 15.

27. Louis S. Walsh, *The Early Catholic Schools of Lowell, Massachusetts, 1835–1852* (Boston: Whalen, 1901), pp. 7–14. For an account of early Lowell, see the chapter "The Factory as Republican Community," in John F. Kasson, *Civilizing the Machine: Technology and Republican Values in America, 1776–1900* (New York: Penguin Books, 1977).

28. Quoted in Sherman M. Smith, *The Relation of the State to Religious Education in Massachusetts* (Syracuse, N.Y., 1926), p. 192n.

29. Ibid., pp. 193–97.

30. *Common School Journal* (Boston), William B. Fowle (publisher), June 1, 1848, p. 164n.

31. *Fourteenth Annual Report of the Secretary of the Board* (Boston: Dutton & Wentworth, 1851), p. 29.

32. Robert H. Lord, John E. Sexton, and Edward T. Harrington, *A History of the Archdiocese of Boston in the Various Stages of Development* (New York: Sheed & Ward, 1944), 2:595–96.

33. J. A. Burns, *The Growth and Development of the Catholic School System in the United States* (New York: Benziger, 1912), p. 19.

34. Horace Mann, "The Advantages of Common Schools, and the Dangers to Which They Are Exposed: Addressed to the Professional Men of Massachusetts," *Common School Journal* (Boston) 1, no. 9 (May 1, 1839): 143, 154.

35. Ibid., 1, no. 13 (July 1, 1839): 198.

36. *First Annual Report of the Secretary of the Board* (Boston: Dutton & Wentworth, 1838), p. 56.

37. Ibid.

38. *Fifth Annual Report of the Secretary of the Board* (Boston: Dutton & Wentworth, 1842), pp. 66–68.

39. Francis X. Curran, *The Churches and the Schools: American Protestantism and Popular Elementary Education* (Chicago: Loyola University Press, 1954), p. 40.

40. "The Proposed Substitution of Sectarian for Public Schools," *Common School Journal* 10, no. 11 (June 1, 1848): pp. 166–68.

41. Editorial comment in ibid., 10, no. 10 (May 15, 1848): 146.

42. Horace Bushnell, *Discourses on Christian Nurture* (Boston: Massachusetts Sabbath School Society, 1847), p. 7. This is the edition that was subsequently withdrawn by the society.

43. "Bushnell on Christian Nurture," *Christian Examiner* (Boston), November 1847, pp. 436, 438.

44. Charles Hodge, *Essays and Reviews Selected from "The Princeton Review"* (New York: Robert Carter, 1857), pp. 303–5.

45. Ibid., p. 336.

46. Quoted in Diane Ravitch, *The Great School Wars, New York City, 1805–*

1973: A History of the Public Schools as Battlefield of Social Change (New York: Basic Books, 1974), p. 37.

47. *Life and Letters of Horace Bushnell* (New York: Harper and Brothers, 1880), pp. 299–303; also in Rush Welter, ed., *American Writings on Popular Education: The Nineteenth Century* (Indianapolis: Bobbs-Merrill, 1971), pp. 175–99.

48. Quoted in Curran, *Churches and Schools,* p. 39.

49. Ibid.

50. In American Bible Society, *Twenty-eighth Annual Report* (New York, 1844), p. 104.

51. Quoted in Ray Allen Billington, *The Protestant Crusade, 1800–1860: A Study of the Origins of American Nativism* (Chicago: Quadrangle Paperbacks, 1964), p. 291.

52. Quoted in Curran, *Churches and Schools,* p. 45.

53. Quoted in ibid., p. 28.

54. Ibid., p. 63.

55. "The Catholics and the School Question," *Christian Review* (New York) 73 (July 1853): 441–58.

9. The Triumph of the Common School

1. Robert A. Nisbet, *The Quest for Community* (London: Oxford University Press, 1953; paperback rpt., 1981), p. 109.

2. Ibid., p. 99.

3. The extent and distribution of literacy in France at various periods have been the subject of many studies. See Willem Frijhoff, *L'offre d'école: Eléments pour une étude comparée des politiques éducatives au XIXe siècle* (Paris: Institut national de recherche pédagogique, 1983), and the literature cited therein. Roger Thabault traced, in one "backward" village, the general resistance to Guizot's reforms until the coming of a railroad made literacy a valuable attainment; *Mon village* (rpt., Paris: Presses de la Fondation National des Sciences Politiques, 1982).

4. Judge Thomas G. Hull, "Memorandum Opinion," *Mozert* v. *Hawkins County Public Schools,* U.S. District Court for the Eastern District of Tennessee, October 24, 1986.

5. Michael B. Katz, *The Irony of Early School Reform: Educational Innovation in Mid-Nineteenth Century Massachusetts* (Boston: Beacon Paperback, 1970), p. 210.

6. J. Stephen Hazlett, "A French Conception of Republican Education: The Carnot Ministry, 1848," *Paedagogica Historica* 13, no. 2 (1973).

7. Félix Ponteil, *Histoire de l'enseignement en France, 1789–1965* (Paris: Sirey, 1966), pp. 230–31, 235.

8. Claude Nicolet, *L'idée républicaine en France (1789–1924)* (Paris: Gallimard, 1982), pp. 93–94.

9. There is an extensive literature on the educational reforms—and struggles—of the first decades of the Third Republic. See the Bibliography.

10. Louis Legrand, *L'influence du positivisme dans l'oeuvre scolaire de Jules Ferry: Les origines de la laïcité* (Paris: Marcel Rivière, 1961), pp. 144–45; Maurice Reclus, *Jules Ferry, 1832–1893* (Paris: Flammarion, 1947), p. 154. See also Pierre Chevallier, *La séparation de l'église et de l'école: Jules Ferry et Léon XIII* (Paris: Fayard, 1981).

11. Legrand, *L'influence du positivisme*, p. 47.

12. John Stuart Mill, "On Liberty," in *The English Philosophers from Bacon to Mill*, ed. Edwin A. Burtt (New York: Random House, [Modern Library] 1939), p. 959; Jules Michelet, *Histoire de la Révolution française*, Bibliothèque de la Pléiade (Paris: Gallimard, 1952), 1:430.

13. Edgar Quinet, *The Religious Revolution of the Nineteenth Century* (London: Truebner, 1881), p. 26.

14. Guy La Perrière, *La "Séparation" à Lyon (1904–1908)* (Lyon, 1973), pp. 62–71.

15. Pierre Barral, *Les fondateurs de la Troisième République: Textes choisis* (Paris: Armand Colin, n.d.), p. 208; see also Paul Bert, *Rapport présenté à la Chambre des Députés sur la loi de l'enseignement primaire* (Paris: Librairie de l'Académie de Médecine, 1880), pp. 48, 67, 107, 196–97.

16. Emile Durkheim, *Moral Education: A Study in the Theory and Application of the Sociology of Education*, trans. Everett K. Wilson and Herman Schnurer (New York: Free Press, 1973), pp. 3, 9, 11.

17. See, e.g., works by Mrs. Alfred-Jules-Emile Fouillée, listed in the Bibliography under "Popular Education and the Third Republic"; for the *guerre des manuels,* see Christian Amalvi, "Les guerre des manuels autour de l'école primaire en France," *Revue historique,* October-December 1979.

18. L. Kalsbeek, *Theologische en wijsgerige achtergronden van de verhouding van kerk, staat, en school in Nederland* (Kampen: Kok, 1976), p. 192; for Thorbecke, see also J. A. Bornewasser, "Thorbecke and the Churches," *Acta Historiae Neerlandicae* (The Hague) 7 (1974); J. C. Boogman, "J. Thorbecke: Challenge and Response," ibid., 7 (1974).

19. Kalsbeek, *Theologische en wijsgerige achtergronden,* pp. 193–94.

20. W. J. Wieringa, "Een samenleving in verandering," in W. Bakker, O. J. de Jong, W. van 't Spijker and L. J. Wolthuis, eds., *De Doleantie van 1886 en haar geschiedenis* (Kampen: Kok, 1986).

21. H. van Riel, *Geschiedenis van het Nederlandse Liberalisme in de 19e. Eeuw,* rev. J. G. Bruggeman (Assen: Van Gorcum, 1982), pp. 108, 111.

22. D. Langedijk, *De Schoolstrijd* (The Hague: Van Haeringen, 1935), p. 61.

23. Nicolaas van Egmond, *Consequent Christendom: Leven en Werk van Mr. J. J. L. van der Brugghen* (Wageningen: Veenman, 1964), pp. 97–98, 104; see also the discussion of this interesting and tragic figure in Kalsbeek, *Theologische en wijsgerige achtergronden,* pp. 186–90, 203–16, and in T. M. Gilhuis, *Memorietafel van het Christelijk Onderwijs,* 2nd ed. (Kampen: Kok, 1975), pp. 107–23.

24. Egmond, *Consequent Christendom,* p. 116.

25. Langedijk, *De Schoolstrijd,* pp. 99, 102.

26. Ibid., p. 125; P. N. Helsloot, "De Nutsbeweging," in W. W. Mijnhardt

and A. J. Wichers, eds., *Om het Algemeen Volksgeluk: Twee eeuwen particulier initiatief, 1784–1984* (Edam: Maatschappij tot Nut van 't Algemeen, 1984), p. 63; Abraham Kuyper, *De "Nuts"-beweging* (Amsterdam: Hoeveker, 1869), pp. 44–45.

27. Langedijk, *De Schoolstrijd*, p. 140; Gilhuis, *Memorietafel*, pp. 151–52.

28. Gilhuis, *Memorietafel*, p. 152; Langedijk, *De Schoolstrijd*, pp. 148–49.

29. Van Riel, *Geschiedenis*, pp. 128–29.

30. Langedijk, *De Schoolstrijd*, pp. 170–91; see also Kalsbeek, *Theologische en wijsgerige achtergronden*, pp. 230–34; Gilhuis, *Memorietafel*, pp. 168–82.

31. See David Tyack, *The One Best System: A History of American Urban Education* (Cambridge, Mass.: Harvard University Press, 1974); David Tyack and Elisabeth Hansot, *Managers of Virtue: Public School Leadership in America, 1820–1980* (New York: Basic Books, 1982); Diane Ravitch, *The Great School Wars, New York City, 1805–1973: A History of the Public Schools as Battlefield of Social Change* (New York: Basic Books, 1974); Paul E. Peterson, *The Politics of School Reform, 1870–1940* (Chicago: University of Chicago Press, 1985); William Issel, "Americanization, Acculturation, and Social Control: School Reform Ideology in Industrial Pennsylvania, 1880–1910," *Journal of Social History* 12, no. 4 (summer 1979); Murray N. Rothbard, "The Progressive Era and the Family," in Joseph R. Peden and Fred R. Glahe, eds., *The American Family and the State* (San Francisco: Pacific Research Institute for Public Policy, 1986).

32. Tyack, *One Best System*.

33. Tyack and Hansot, *Managers of Virtue*, p. 107.

34. Ravitch, *Great School Wars*, pp. 156–58.

35. Sam Barnes, "Progressivism on the Wane: The Entrenchment of the Bureaucracy, 1900–1945," in James W. Fraser, Henry L. Allen, and Sam Barnes, eds., *From Common School to Magnet School: Selected Essays in the History of Boston's Schools* (Boston: Trustees of the Public Library, 1979), p. 93.

36. Testimony of the Reverend Dr. James B. Dunn of Boston, in U.S. Congress, *Notes of Hearings before the Committee on Education and Labor, United States Senate . . . on the Joint Resolution (S.R. 86) Proposing an Amendment to the Constitution . . . Respecting Establishments of Religion and Free Public Schools* (Washington, D.C.: Government Printing Office, 1889), pp. 60–64; Lois Bannister Merk, "Boston's Historic Public School Crisis," *New England Quarterly* 31, no. 2 (June 1958): 194. See also the three publications of the "Committee of One Hundred": *The Public Schools Must Go; The Great Victory in Boston; An Open Letter to the Friends of Free Schools and American Liberties* (Boston, 1888).

37. U.S. Congress, *Notes*, pp. 6, 42.

38. "Rev. Dr. King of New York," in ibid., pp. 20–21, 23. See also Tyack and Hansot, *Managers of Virtue*, p. 77.

39. Ibid., p. 65.

40. *Debates in the Massachusetts Constitutional Convention, 1917–1918* (Boston: Wright & Porter, 1919), pp. 192, 163, 71, 93. The text of the amendment adopted may be found in *The Constitution of the Commonwealth of Massachusetts* (Office of the Secretary of State, 1981), p. 52. It was further amended in 1972–74 to

permit state scholarships for students attending private higher education institutions (p. 94).

41. *Debates, 1917–1918,* pp. 71, 93.

42. Ibid., pp. 97, 105.

43. Ibid., pp. 148, 157–58.

44. Ibid., pp. 189, 188.

45. Ibid., p. 202.

46. See the discussion of modernization in Peter Berger, Brigitte Berger, and Hansfried Kellner, *The Homeless Mind: Modernization and Consciousness* (New York: Random House [Vintage Books], 1974).

47. Oscar Handlin, *Boston's Immigrants: A Study in Acculturation,* rev. and enl. ed. (New York: Atheneum, 1968), pp. 163–67.

48. Tyack, *One Best System,* p. 108.

49. Peterson, *Politics of School Reform,* pp. 54–55.

50. Tyack and Hansot, *Managers of Virtue,* p. 79.

51. Walter H. Beck, *Lutheran Elementary Schools in the United States* (1939) (St. Louis: Concordia, 1965), p. 29; Frederick Rudolph, ed., *Essays on Education in the Early Republic* (Cambridge, Mass.: Harvard University Press [Belknap Press], 1965), p. 5.

52. Beck, *Lutheran Elementary Schools,* pp. 225–29.

53. Ibid., pp. 318–20, 326, 330.

54. Quoted in Tyack and Hansot, *Managers of Virtue,* p. 82.

55. Quoted in Ravitch, *Great School Wars,* p. 123.

56. Quoted in Lawrence A. Cremin, *The Transformation of the School: Progressivism in American Education, 1876–1957* (New York: Random House [Vintage Books], 1961), p. 68.

57. Rothbard, "Progressive Era and the Family," p. 121.

58. *Fifty-sixth Annual Report of the Secretary of the Board* (Boston: Wright & Potter, 1893), pp. 15, 248.

59. *Sixty-fifth Annual Report of the Secretary of the Board* (Boston: Wright & Potter, 1902), pp. 199–214.

60. *Sixty-sixth Annual Report of the Secretary of the Board* (Boston: Wright & Potter, 1903), p. 202.

61. *Report of the Commission on Immigration on the Problem of Immigration in Massachusetts* (Boston: Wright & Potter, 1914), pp. 148, 150, 224.

62. *Eighty-first Annual Report of the Secretary of the Board* (Boston: Wright & Potter, 1918), p. 100; *Eighty-second Annual Report of the Secretary of the Board* (Boston: Wright & Potter, 1919), pp. 136, 18.

63. See the excellent—and broad-minded—book by Boston superintendent of schools Frank V. Thompson, *Schooling of the Immigrant* (1920), *Americanization Studies: The Acculturation of Immigrant Groups into American Society,* ed. William S. Bernard (Montclair, N.J.: Patterson Smith, 1971).

64. Tyack, *One Best System,* p. 242.

65. Ravitch, *Great School Wars,* p. 244.

10. The Common School Called into Question

1. Carlton J. H. Hayes, *A Generation of Materialism, 1871–1900* (1941) (New York: Harper Torchbooks, 1963), pp. 83–87.

2. See the discussion of these laws in Félix Ponteil, *Histoire de l'enseignement en France, 1789–1965* (Paris: Sirey, 1966); Antoine Prost, *Histoire de l'enseignement en France, 1800–1967* (Paris: Colin, 1968); Alain Savary (with Catherine Arditti), *En toute liberté* (Paris: Hachette, 1985).

3. Albert Bayet paraphrased in Gérard Leclerc, *La bataille de l'école: 15 siècles d'histoire, 3 ans de combat* (Paris: Denoël, 1985), p. 63; see also Albert Bayet, "Libre-pensée et laïcité," in *La laïcité*, Centre de sciences politiques de l'Institut d'études juridiques de Nice (Paris: Presses universitaires de France, 1960), pp. 137–44.

4. Louis Legrand, *L'école unique: A quelles conditions?* (Paris: Scarabée, 1981), p. 13.

5. Ibid., pp. 56, 60, 70–78; see also his study, *L'influence du positivisme dans l'oeuvre scolaire de Jules Ferry: Les origines de la laïcité* (Paris: Marcel Rivière, 1961).

6. Jacques Bur, *Laïcité et problème scolaire* (Paris: Editions Bonne Presse, 1959), pp. 212, 254–55, 263.

7. Legrand, *L'école unique*, pp. 204–5.

8. Savary, *En toute liberté*, especially "Texte du projet de loi," pp. 214–34.

9. Leclerc, *La bataille de l'école*, pp. 94–95.

10. Ibid., p. 118.

11. Didier Maupas, *L'école en accusation* (Paris: Albin Michel, 1984), p. 197.

12. Robert Ballion, *Les consommateurs d'école* (Paris: Stock, 1982), pp. 284–85.

13. Alain Madelin, *Pour libérer l'école: L'enseignement à la carte* (Paris: Laffont, 1984), p. 176.

14. J. P. Kruijt and Walter Goddijn, "Verzuiling en Ontzuiling als sociologisch proces," in *Drift en Koers: Een halve eeuw sociale verandering in Nederland,* ed. A. N. J. Hollander et al. (Assen: Van Gorcum, 1962), p. 232; P. W. C. Akkermans, *Onderwijs als constitutioneel probleem* (Alphen aan den Rijn: Samsom, 1980), p. 159.

15. Fons van Schoten and Hans Wansink, *De nieuwe schoolstrijd: Knelpunten en conflicten in de hedendaagse onderwijspolitiek* (Utrecht: Bohn, Scheltema, & Holkema, 1984). See, for the ABOP position, J. van den Bosch, "De onderwijsvakorganisatie en het openbaar onderwijs," in *Opstellen over openbaar onderwijs,* ed. van Schoten and Wansink (Groningen: Wolters-Noordhoff, 1985). The concept of a "new school struggle" seems to have made its first appearance in an article by van Kemenade in May 1978; see *Bulletin,* October 1983, p. 14.

16. K. de Jong Ozn., "De pacificatie in gevaar?" *Bulletin,* January 1985, pp. 8–9; also, "Openingswoord, Werkvergadering Unie 'School en Evangelie,'" *Bulletin,* October 1984, p. 12; W. van Walstijn, "Nogmaals: schoolkeuzemotieven, een onderzoeksvoorstel voor het Openbaar Onderwijs," *School en Besturen,* June 1985, p. 7.

17. David Martin, *A General Theory of Secularization* (New York: Harper Colophon, 1979), p. 192; J. M. G. Thurlings, *De wankele zuil: Nederlandse katholieken tussen assimilatie en pluralisme,* 2nd ed. (Deventer: Van Loghum Slaterus, 1978), p. 175.

18. J. A. van Kemenade, *De Katholieken en hun onderwijs: Een sociologisch onderzoek naar de betekenis van katholiek onderwijs onder ouders en docenten* (Meppel: Boom, 1968), p. 229; for a personal reaction to two confessional schools with differing commitment to their "identity," see my article, "Two Schools in Rotterdam," *Reformed Journal,* November 1985, pp. 5–6.

19. "Twente deed op A. F. van der Heijden nooit vergeefs een beroep," in *Schoolbestuur,* April 1984, p. 29. John A. Coleman, *The Evolution of Dutch Catholicism, 1958–1974* (Berkeley: University of California Press, 1978), p. 137.

20. Suus Boef-van der Meulen, "'Een oprechte behoefte van onze tijd': Nieuwe kansen voor de samenwerkings- school?" *Onderwijs en Opvoeding,* March 1984, p. 326. Titus M. Gilhuis, *De gezamenlijke school: Voor of tegen?* (Kampen: Kok, n.d.), p. 57. See also C. E. Schelfhout, "Sociologie en onderwijs," in *Vrijheid van onderwijs,* ed. L. Box et al. (Nijmegen: LINK, 1977), pp. 75–80.

21. R. Beljon and L. de Jonge, "De vrijheid van onderwijs, beleden, en bestreden," in *Onderwijsbeleid in Nederland,* ed. J. D. C. Branger et al. (Louvain/Amersfoort: ACCO, 1984), p. 90; Titus M. Gilhuis, *Pleidooi voor een school met de Bijbel* (Kampen: Kok, n.d.), p. 13; B. Buddingh', "Christelijk onderwijs: Appel en uitdaging," in *Het onderwijs gekleurd: Zes politieke en levensbeschouwelijke visies op het onderwijs,* ed. H. Beks (Leiden: Stafleu & Zoon, 1976), pp. 78–79; *Beleidsplan en verslag van werkzaamheden, 1981–1984,* Raad voor de zaken van kerk en school van de Nederlandse Hervormde Kerk (Driebergen, n.d.), pp. 13, 9.

22. "Hoogleraar voorspelt einde van onderwijs- verzuiling," *Schoolbestuur,* September 1986, p. 6.

23. A. P. M. van Schoten, "Het publiekrechtelijke karakter van het openbaar onderwijs in gevaar?" in *Het bestuur van het openbaar onderwijs,* ed. P. W. C. Akkermans and J. M. G. Leune (Den Bosch: Malmberg, 1983), p. 59.

24. Van Schoten and Wansink, *De nieuwe schoolstrijd,* pp. 93–94.

25. Calculated from figures provided in ibid., p. 10; see also the discussion in S. Boef-van der Meulen, "Ouders en het openbaar onderwijs," in *Opstellen over openbaar onderwijs,* ed. van Schoten and Wansink, pp. 83–84.

26. Van Schoten, "Het publiekrechtelijke karakter," pp. 62–63; van Schoten and Wansink, "De maatschappelijke functie van de openbare school," *School en Besturen,* October 1985, p. 7.

27. N. L. Dodde, "Nederlandse onderwijspolitiek, 1945–1983," in Branger, *Onderwijsbeleid in Nederland,* pp. 30, 35; N. L. Dodde, *Het Nederlandse onderwijs verandert* (Muiderberg: Coutinho, 1983), p. 134.

28. Hans Wansink, "Vermaatschappelijking van de vraag naar onderwijs zet bestel under druk: Van verzuiling naar ontmoeting als emancipatiemodel," *Onderwijs en Opvoeding,* September 1982, pp. 34–39.

29. G. J. Erdtsieck, quoted in K. de Jong Ozn, "Met schaar en commentaar,"

Bulletin, October 1985, p. 24; Th. G. Bolleman, quoted in Titus M. Gilhuis, *Pleidooi,* p. 9.

30. N. J. Ginjaar-Maas, "Onderwijs in de Branding: Een Liberale visie op het onderwijs," in Beks *Het onterwijs gekleurd,* p. 99. L. A. Struik, "Frankrijk en Nederland: Een schoolstrijd (?)"; J. A. van Kemenade, "Struik op oorlogspad"; David van Ooijen, "'De jacht op het confessioneel onderwijs'"; and Struik, "Spoken?," in *Bulletin,* October 1983, pp. 8–15.

31. David van Ooijen, "'PvdA wenst zich niet te identificeren met het open-baar onderwijs,'" *School en Besturen,* April 1986, pp. 26–28; Jacques Wallage, "Naar een nieuwe pacificatie, niet naar nog een schoolstrijd," *Bulletin,* April 1986, pp. 22–27.

32. Cited from *Volkskrant,* March 17, 1983, in L. A. Struik, "Spoken?," p. 13.

33. *Education Week,* November 5, 1986; *New York Times,* October 25, 1986; televised interviews, October 24, 1986.

34. Defendant-Intervenors' Pretrial Brief, *Smith* v. *Board of School Commissioners of Mobile County,* October 1986, pp. 9, 10, 66. My thanks to George H. Mernick, III, Esq., counsel for the Defendant-Intervenors, for providing me with a copy of this brief.

35. *Education Week,* November 5, 1986; *Washington Jewish Week,* November 13, 1986; *Washington Post,* October 6, 1986.

36. Michael A. Rebell and Arthur R. Block, *Educational Policy Making and the Courts* (Chicago: University of Chicago Press, 1982), p. 9. The authors found, in a study of sixty-five federal trial court decisions between 1970 and 1977, that "Minority plaintiffs succeeded in convincing judges to order changes in school policies in 71% of their cases, whereas 'other' plaintiffs won only 35% of theirs" (p. 36).

37. Stephen Arons and Charles Lawrence, "The Manipulation of Consciousness: A First Amendment Critique of Schooling," *Harvard Civil Rights/Civil Liberties Law Review* 15 (1980): 309, 312; also available in slightly different form in *The Public School Monopoly: A Critical Analysis of Education and the State in American Society,* ed. Robert B. Everhart (San Francisco: Pacific Institute for Public Policy Research, 1982), pp. 227–28.

38. Robert Rothman, "Secretary Urges Assault on Mediocre Textbooks," *Education Week,* January 28, 1987.

39. This case, *Malnak* v. *Yogi,* 440 F. Supp. 1284 (D.N.J. 1977), *aff'd per curiam* 592 F.2d 197 (3d Cir. 1979), is cited prominently in the Plaintiffs' Memorandum of Law in *Smith* v. *Board of School Commissioners of Mobile County,* pp. 26–28, 57. My thanks to Thomas F. Parker, IV, Esq., counsel for the Plaintiffs, for providing me with a copy of this brief.

40. "Gallup/Phi Delta Kappa Poll of the Public's Attitudes toward the Public Schools," *Phi Delta Kappan,* September 1986.

41. From a partial transcript of a debate aired on William F. Buckley's "Firing Line," May 2 and 9, 1986, in *Educational Choice* 2, nos. 6, 7 (June, July 1986).

42. Stephen Arons, *Compelling Belief: The Culture of American Schooling* (Amherst: University of Massachusetts Press, 1986), p. 17.

43. See, e.g., the journal *Equity and Choice,* published by the Institute for Responsive Education at Boston University since fall 1984, and the newsletter *Educational Choice,* published by the Clearinghouse on Educational Choice since October 1985. The former is clearly liberal, the latter conservative.

44. Arons, *Compelling Belief,* p. ix. See also Rockne McCarthy et al., *Society, State, and Schools: A Case for Structural and Confessional Pluralism* (Grand Rapids, Mich.: Eerdmans, 1981); Rockne McCarthy et al., *Disestablishment a Second Time: Genuine Pluralism for American Schools* (Grand Rapids, Mich.: Eerdmans, 1982).

45. John E. Coons and Stephen D. Sugarman, *Education by Choice: The Case for Family Control* (Berkeley: University of California Press, 1978), p. 27.

46. *Family Choice and Public Schools,* Massachusetts Department of Education, 1986, includes my papers on choice prepared for the National Education Association and the National Governors' Association, a paper by my colleague Michael Alves on "controlled choice" in Cambridge, and statistics on parent choice in Massachusetts. See also my article, "The Significance of Choice for Public Education," prepared for Minnesota officials, in *Equity and Choice* 1, no. 3 (spring 1985).

47. James S. Coleman, "Foreword," in Coons and Sugarman, *Education by Choice,* p. xi.

BIBLIOGRAPHY

Educational Conflict in France

General

Brickman, William W. "The Teaching of Secular Values from Ancient Times to 1800." *Paedagogica Historica*, 12, no. 1 (1972).

———. "The Teaching of Secular Moral Values in the Nineteenth Century: U.S.A., England, France." *Paedagogica Historica* 12, no. 2 (1972).

———. "The Teaching of Secular Moral Values in the Twentieth Century." *Paedagogica Historica*, 13, no. 1 (1973).

Chevallier, P., B. Grosperrin, and J. Maillet. *L'enseignement français de la Révolution à nos jours*. Vol. 1. Paris: Mouton, 1968. Vol. 2, *Documents*. Paris: Mouton, 1971.

Cholvy, Gérard, and Yves-Marie Hilaire. *Histoire religieuse de la France contemporaine, 1800–1880*. Paris: Privat, 1985.

Cobban, Alfred. *A History of Modern France*. 3rd ed. Vols. 1–3. New York: Penguin Books, 1963.

Dansette, Adrien. *Religious History of Modern France*. Vols. 1 and 2. New York: Herder & Herder, 1961.

Frijhoff, Willem. *L'offre d'école: Eléments pour une étude comparée des politiques éducatives au XIXe siècle*. Paris: Institut national de recherche pédagogique, 1983.

Giolitto, Pierre. *Histoire de l'enseignement primaire au XIXe siècle: L'organisation pédagogique*. Paris: Nathan, 1983.

Gontard, Maurice. *L'enseignement primaire en France de la Révolution à la loi Guizot (1789–1833)*. Paris: Les Belles Lettres, 1959.

Grande Encyclopédie (for biographical data).

Hobsbawn, E. J. *The Age of Revolution, 1789–1848*. London: Weidenfeld & Nicholson, 1962.

Le Bras, Gabriel. *Etudes de sociologie religieuse*. Vol. 1. Paris: Presses universitaires de France, 1955.

Mégrine, Bernard. *La question scolaire en France*. Paris: Presses universitaires de France, 1963.

Moody, Joseph N. *French Education since Napoleon*. Syracuse University Press, 1978.

Ozouf, Mona. *L'école de la France: Essais sur la Révolution, l'utopie, et l'enseignement*. Paris: Gallimard, 1984.

Ponteil, Félix. *Histoire de l'enseignement en France, 1789–1965*. Paris: Sirey, 1966.

Prost, Antoine. *Histoire de l'enseignement en France, 1800–1967*. 2nd ed. Paris: Colin, 1968.

Rémond, René. *L'anticléricalisme en France de 1815 à nos jours*. Paris: Fayard, 1976.

Before the Revolution

Ariès, Philippe. *L'enfant et la vie familiale sous l'Ancien Régime*. Paris: Editions du Seuil, 1973.

Billington, James H. *Fire in the Minds of Men: Origins of the Revolutionary Faith*. New York: Basic Books, 1980.

Broome, J. H. *Rousseau: A Study of His Thought*. London: Edward Arnold, 1963.

Cassirer, Ernst. *The Myth of the State*. New Haven: Yale University Press, 1946.

Charvet, John. *The Philosophy of Rousseau*. Cambridge: Cambridge University Press, 1974.

Chisick, Harvey. "Institutional Innovation in Popular Education in Eighteenth Century France: Two Examples." *French Historical Studies* 10, no. 1 (spring, 1977).

Cohler, Anne M. *Rousseau and Nationalism*. New York: Basic Books, 1970.

Cragg, Gerald R. *The Church and the Age of Reason, 1648–1789*. New York: Penguin Books, 1970.

Dakin, Douglas. *Turgot and the Ancien Régime in France* (1939). New York: Octagon, 1965.

d'Alembert, Jean le Rond. *Preliminary Discourse to the Encyclopedia of Diderot*. Translated by Richard Schwab. Indianapolis: Bobbs-Merrill, 1963.

Fontainerie, Guy de la, ed. *French Liberalism and Education in the Eighteenth Century: The Writings of La Chalotais, Turgot, Diderot, and Condorcet*. New York: McGraw-Hill, 1932.

Friedrich, Carl J. *The Age of the Baroque, 1610–1660*. New York: Harper & Row, 1952.

Gay, Peter. *The Enlightenment: An Interpretation*. Vol. 1, *The Rise of Modern Paganism*. New York: Norton, 1966. Vol. 2, *The Science of Freedom*. New York: Norton, 1969.

———, ed. *The Enlightenment: A Comprehensive Anthology*. New York: Simon & Schuster, 1973.

Gershoy, Leo. *From Despotism to Revolution, 1763–1789*. New York: Harper & Row, 1944.

Goubert, Pierre. *Louis XIV et vingt millions de Français*. Paris: Fayard, 1966.

———. *The Ancien Régime: French Society, 1600–1750*. Translated by Steve Cox. New York: Harper & Row, 1973.

Grimsley, Ronald, ed. *Rousseau: Religious Writings*. Oxford: Clarendon Press, 1970.

Grosperrin, Bernard. *Les petites écoles sous l'Ancien Régime*. Rennes: Ouest-France, 1984.

Hampson, Norman. *The Enlightenment*. New York: Penguin Books, 1968.

Hermand, Pierre. *Les idées morales de Diderot*. Paris: Presses universitaires de France, 1923.

Kohn, Hans. *The Idea of Nationalism* (1944). New York: Collier Books, 1967.

Manuel, Frank. *The Prophets of Paris*. New York: Harpe & Row, 1965.

Miquel, Pierre. *Les guerres de religion*. Paris: Fayard, 1980.

Montaigne, Michel, Seigneur de. "De l'institution des enfants." In *Essais*. Bibliotheque de la Pléiade. Paris: Gallimard, 1958.

Montesquieu, Baron de. *Oeuvres complètes*. New York: Macmillan, 1964.

Nisbet, Robert A. *The Quest for Community*. London: Oxford University Press, 1953.

———. *History of the Idea of Progress*. New York: Basic Books, 1980.

Nussbaum, Frederick L. *The Triumph of Science and Reason, 1660–1685*. New York: Harper & Row, 1953.

Palmer, R. R. *Catholics and Unbelievers in Eighteenth Century France*. Princeton, N.J.: Princeton University Press, 1939.

Roberts, Penfield. *The Quest for Security, 1715–1740*. New York: Harper & Row, 1947.

Rousseau, Jean Jacques. *Du contrat social* (1762). Introduction by Bertrand de Jouvenal. Geneva: Constant Bourquin, 1947.

———. "Considérations sur le gouvernement de Pologne" (1772). In *Oeuvres complètes*. Vol. 3. Bibliothèque de la Pléiade. Paris: Gallimard, 1964.

———. "Discours sur l'économie politique" (1755). In *Oeuvres complètes*. Vol. 3. Bibliothèque de la Pléiade. Paris: Gallimard, 1964.

———. "Emile" (1762). In *Oeuvres complètes*. Vol. 4. Bibliothèque de la Pléiade. Paris: Gallimard, 1969.

Tocqueville, Alexis de. *The Old Regime and the French Revolution* (1858). Garden City, N.Y.: Doubleday, 1955.

Velde, I. van der. "Pedagogische Momenten in Rousseau's 'Economie Politique': Opvoeding tot Democratie of Opvoeding voor de Totalitaire Staat?" *Paedagogica Historica* 5, no. 1 (1965).

Voltaire, François Marie Arouet de. *Philosophical Letters*. Translated by Ernest Dilworth. Indianapolis: Bobbs-Merrill, 1961.

Vovelle, Michel. "Y a-t-il eu une révolution culturelle au XVIIIe siècle? A propos de l'éducation populaire en Provence." *Revue d'histoire moderne et contemporaine* 22 (1975).

Wilson, Arthur M. "Why Did the Political Theory of the Encyclopedists Not Prevail? A Suggestion." *French Historical Studies* 1, no. 3 (spring 1960).

Wolf, John B. *The Emergence of the Great Powers, 1685–1715*. New York: Harper & Row, 1951.

The Revolutionary Program

Barnard, H. C. *Education and the French Revolution*. Cambridge: Cambridge University Press, 1969.

Blum, Carol. *Rousseau and the Republic of Virtue: The Language of Politics in the French Revolution*. Ithaca, N.Y.: Cornell University Press, 1986.

Buchez, P.-J.-B., and P.-C. Roux. *Histoire parlémentaire de la Révolution française*. Vol. 22. Paris: Paulin, 1835.

Curtis, Eugene Newton. *Saint-Just: Colleague of Robespierre*. New York: Octagon, 1973.

Ferrero, Guglielmo. *The Two French Revolutions*. Translated by Samuel J. Hurwitz. New York: Basic Books, 1968.

Guillaume, M. J., ed. *Procès-verbaux du comité d'instruction publique de la Convention Nationale*. Paris: Imprimérie Nationale, 1891.

Hayes, Carlton J. H. *Nationalism: A Religion*. New York: Macmillan, 1960.

Kohn, Hans. *Prelude to Nation States: The French and German Experience, 1789–1815*. Princeton, N.J.: Van Nostrand, 1967.

Lefebvre, Georges. *The French Revolution*. Vols. 1 and 2. Translated by John Hall Stewart and James Friguglietti. New York: Columbia University Press, 1964.

Ollivier, Albert. *Saint-Just et la force des choses*. Paris: Gallimard, 1954.

Palmer, R. R. *The World of the French Revolution*. New York: Harper Torchbooks, 1972.

Poland, Burdette C. *French Protestantism and the French Revolution: A Study in Church and State, Thought and Religion, 1685–1815*. Princeton, N.J.: Princeton University Press, 1957.

Saint-Just, Louis-Antoine de. *Théorie politique*. Edited by Alain Lienard. Paris: Editions du Seuil, 1976.

Stewart, John Hall, ed. *A Documentary Survey of the French Revolution*. New York: Macmillan, 1951.

Sydenham, M. J. *The French Revolution*. New York: Putnam, 1965.

Talmon, L. *The Origins of Totalitarian Democracy*. New York: Praeger, 1960.

Thompson, J. M. *Robespierre and the French Revolution*. London: English Universities Press, 1952.

Vignery, Robert J. *The Revolution and the Schools: Educational Policies of the Mountain*. Madison: University of Wisconsin Press, 1965.

First Attempt to Implement the Revolutionary Program

Allain, E. *L'oeuvre scolaire de la Révolution, 1789–1802* (1891). New York: Franklin, 1969.

Aulard, A., ed. *Paris pendant la Réaction Thermidorienne et sous le Directoire: Recueil de documents*. Paris: Maison Quantin, 1903.

———. *Paris sous le Consulat: Recueil de documents*. Paris: Maison Quantin, 1903.

Babeau, Albert. *L'école de village pendant la Révolution*. Paris: Didier, 1881.

Dumont, Jean. *La Révolution française ou les prodiges du sacrilège*. Limoges: Criterion, 1984.

Duruy, Albert. *L'Instruction publique et la Révolution*. Paris: Hachette, 1882.

Fabry, Jean-Baptiste-Germain. *Le génie de la Révolution considéré dans l'éducation*. Vols. 1–4. Paris, 1817–18.

Helmreich, Jonathan E. "The Establishment of Primary Schools in France under the Directory." *French Historical Studies* 2, no. 2 (fall 1961).

Ozouf, Mona. *La fête révolutionnaire*. Paris: Gallimard, 1976.

Pierre, Victor. *L'école sous la Révolution française*. Paris: Librairie de la Société Bibliographique, 1881.

Recueil de lois et règlemens concernant l'instruction publique. Vols. 1–4. Paris: Brunot-Labbe, 1814.

Stamp, Robert M. "Educational Thought and Educational Practice during the Years of the French Revolution." *History of Education Quarterly*, fall 1966.

Vassort, Jean. "L'enseignement primaire en Vendômois à l'époque révolutionnaire." *Revue d'histoire moderne et contemporaine* 25 (1978).

Vovelle, Michel. *Religion et Révolution: La déchristianisation de l'An II*. Paris: Hachette, 1976.

Woronoff, Denis. *La République bourgeoise de Thermidor à Brumaire, 1794–1799*. Paris: Editions du Seuil, 1972.

Popular Education in France from 1803 to 1870

Agulhon, Maurice. *The Republic in the Village: The People of the Var from the French Revolution to the Second Republic*. Translated by Janet Lloyd. Cambridge: Cambridge University Press, 1982.

Anderson, Robert D. *Education in France, 1848–1870*. Oxford: Clarendon Press, 1975.

———. "The Conflict in Education: Catholic Secondary Schools (1850–1870): A Reappraisal." In Theodore Zeldin, ed., *Conflicts in French Society: Anticlericalism, Education, and Morals in the Nineteenth Century*. London: Allen & Unwin, 1970.

Artz, Frederick B. *Reaction and Revolution, 1814–1832*. New York: Harper & Row, 1963.

Aulard, A. *Napoléon Ier. et le monopole universitaire*. Paris: Librairie Armand Colin, 1911.

Bousquet, Pierre. "Une tentative de municipalisme scolaire: L'enseignement primaire parisien sous la monarchie de juillet." *Revue d'histoire moderne et contemporaine* 29 (1982).

Charlton, D. G. *Secular Religions in France, 1815–1870*. London: Oxford University Press, 1963.

Falloux, Frederic Alfred Pierre, comte de. *Discours et mélanges politiques*. Vol. 1. Paris: E. Plon, 1882.

Gabbert, Mark A. "Bishop *avant tout*: Archbishop Sibour's Betrayal of the Second Republic." *Catholic Historical Review* 64, no. 3 (July 1978).

Gerbod, Paul. "Les inspecteurs généraux et l'inspection générale de l'instruction publique de 1802 à 1882." *Revue historique* 236 (July–September 1966).

Girard, Louis. *Les libéraux français, 1814–1875.* Paris: Aubier, 1985.

Gréard, Octave. *La législation de l'instruction primaire en France depuis 1789 jusqu'à nos jours: Recueil des lois, décrets, ordonnances, arrêtés, règlements, décisions, avis, projets de lois.* Vols. 1–3. Paris: Charles de Mourgues, 1874.

Guizot, François-Pierre-Guillaume. *Memoirs to Illustrate the History of My Time.* Vol. 3. Translated by J. W. Cole. London: Bentley, 1860 (reprinted 1974).

———. *Christianity Viewed in Relation to the Present State of Society and Opinion.* London: Murray, 1871.

———. *De Christelijke Kerk en Maatschappij in 1861.* Deventer: A. ter Gunne, 1861.

Hazlett, J. Stephen. "A French Conception of Republican Education: The Carnot Ministry, 1848." *Paedagogica Historica* 13, no. 2 (1973).

Jardin, A., and A. J. Tudesq. *La France des notables.* Vol. 1. *L'evolution générale, 1815–1848.* Paris: Editions du Seuil, 1973. Vol. 2: *La vie de la nation, 1815–1848.* Paris: Editions du Seuil, 1973.

Johnson, Douglas. *Guizot: Aspects of French History, 1787–1874.* London: Routledge & Kegan Paul, 1963.

Magraw, Roger. "The Conflict in the Villages." In Theodore Zeldin, ed., *Conflicts in French Society: Anticlericalism, Education, and Morals in the Nineteenth Century.* London: Allen & Unwin, 1970.

May, Anita Rasi, "The Falloux Law, the Catholic Press, and the Bishops: Crisis of Authority in the French Church." *French Historical Studies* 8, no. 1 (spring 1973).

Moody, Joseph N. "French Anticlericalism: Image and Reality." *Catholic Historical Review* 56, no. 4 (January 1971).

Raphael, Paul, and Maurice Gontard. *Hippolyte Fortoul, 1851–1856.* Paris: Presses universitaires de France, 1975.

Rosanvallon, Pierre. *Le moment Guizot.* Paris: Gallimard, 1985.

Simon, Jules. *Victor Cousin.* Translated by Melville B. Anderson and Edward Playfair Anderson. Chicago: McClurg, 1888.

Strumingher, Laura S. *What Were Little Girls and Boys Made Of? Primary Education in Rural France, 1830–1880.* Albany: SUNY Press, 1983.

Thabault, Roger. *Mon village.* Paris: Delagrave, 1943 (reprinted 1982).

Vaughan, Michalina, and Margaret Scotford Archer. *Social Conflict and Educational Change in England and France, 1789–1848.* Cambridge: Cambridge University Press, 1971.

Zeldin, Theodore, ed. *Conflicts in French Society: Anticlericalism, Education, and Morals in the Nineteenth Century.* London: Allen & Unwin, 1970.

Popular Education and the Third Republic

PRIMARY

Barthélemy Saint-Hilaire, Jules. *A la démocratie française* (includes *De la vraie démocratie* of 1848). Paris: Baur, 1874.

Bert, Paul. *Rapport présenté à la Chambre des Députés sur la loi de l'enseignement primaire (Proposition Barodet)*. Paris: Librairie de l'Académie de Médecine, 1880.

———. *Le Cléricalisme: Questions d'éducation nationale*. Preface by A. Aulard. Paris: Armand Colin, 1900.

Buisson, Ferdinand. "Edgar Quinet." *Grande Encyclopédie*.

———. *La foi laïque: Extraits de discours et d'écrits (1878–1911)*. Paris: Hachette, 1912.

———. "Sur l'enseignement intuitif." In *Les Conférences pédagogiques faites aux instituteurs délégués à l'exposition universelle de 1878*. Paris: Delagrave, 1878.

———. *Résumé des états de situation de l'enseignement primaire pour l'année scolaire, 1885–1886*. Paris: Imprimérie Nationale, 1887.

Buisson, Ferdinand, and Frederic Ernest Farrington, eds. *French Educational Ideals of Today*. Yonkers, N.Y.: World Book, 1919.

Compayré, Gabriel. *Eléments d'instruction morale et civique*. 112th ed. Paris: Delaplane, 1896.

———. *Jean-Jacques Rousseau and Education from Nature*. Translated by R. P. Jago. New York: Crowell, 1907.

Croiset, Alfred. "Les divers types d'enseignement." In Croiset et al., *Enseignement et démocratie*. Paris: Félix Alcan, 1905.

Débidour, Antonin. *L'Eglise catholique et l'état sous la Troisième République (1870–1906)*. Vols. 1 and 2. Paris: Félix Alcan, 1906.

Devinat, E. "L'école primaire française." In Alfred Croiset et al., *Enseignement et démocratie*. Paris: Félix Alcan, 1905.

Durkheim, Emile. *The Division of Labor in Society*. New York: Free Press, 1964.

———. *Moral Education: A Study in the Theory and Application of the Sociology of Education*. Translated by Everett K. Wilson and Herman Schnurer. New York: Free Press, 1973.

———. *Suicide*. New York: Free Press, 1966.

Ferry, Jules. "Discours de M. le Ministre." In *Conférences pédagogiques de Paris en 1880: Rapports et procès verbaux*. Paris: Hachette, 1880.

———. *Discours et opinions*. Vols. 3 and 4. Edited by Paul Robiquet. Paris: Armand Colin, n.d.

Fouillée, Mrs. Alfred-Jules-Emile [G. Bruno]. *L'instruction morale et leçons de choses civiques pour les petits enfants*. 41st ed. Paris: Belin Frères, 1893.

———. *Francinet, livre de lecture courante: Principes élémentaires de morale et d'instruction civique, d'économie politique, de droit usuel, d'agricultre, d'hygiène, et de sciences usuelles*. 101st ed. Paris: Belin Frères, 1897.

———. *Les enfants de Marcel: Instruction morale et civique en action; livre de lecture courante*. 138th ed. Paris: Belin Frères, 1925.

Giradet, Raoul. *Le nationalisme française: Anthologie, 1871–1914*. Paris: Editions du Seuil, 1983.

Guillemin, Amedée. *L'instruction républicaine: Obligation—gratuité—laïcité*. Paris: Chevalier, 1871.

Laveleyé, Emile de. *L'instruction du peuple*. Paris: Hachette, 1872.

———. *Essais et études*. Vols. 1 and 2. Ghent: Vuylsteke, 1894.

Lévy-Bruhl, Lucien. *La morale et la science des moeurs*. Paris: Félix Alcan, 1903.

Lichtenberger, F. "L'education morale dans les écoles primaires." In *Recueil des monographies pédagogiques publiées a l'occasion de l'exposition universelle de 1889*. Vol. 4. Paris: Imprimérie Nationale, 1889.

Lois et règlements organiques de l'enseignement primaire. Paris: Imprimérie Nationale, 1888.

Michelet, Jules. *Histoire de la Révolution française*. Vols. 1 and 2. Bibliothèque de la Pléiade. Paris: Gallimard, 1952.

Michelet, Jules, and Edgar Quinet. *Jesuits and Jesuitism*. London, n.d.

Pécaut, Félix. *Le Christ et la conscience: Lettres à un pasteur sur l'autorité de la Bible et celle de Jésus-Christ*. 2nd ed. Paris: Joël Cherbuliez, 1863.

———. *De l'avenir du théisme chrétien considéré comme religion*. Paris: Joël Cherbuliez, 1864.

———. *Deux ministres pédagogues, M. Guizot et M. Ferry: Lettres addréssés aux instituteurs par le ministre de l'instruction publique en 1833 et en 1883*. Paris: Hachette, n.d.

Péguy, Charles. *Ouevres en prose*. Vols. 1 and 2. Bibliothèque de la Pléiade. Paris: Gallimard, 1957–59.

Quinet, Edgar. *La République: Conditions de la régénération de la France*. Paris: E. Dentu, 1872.

———. *The Religious Revolution of the Nineteenth Century*. London: Truebner, 1881.

Simon, Jules. *La politique radicale*. 2nd ed. Paris: Librairie Internationale, 1868.

Steeg, Jules. *De la mission du Protestantisme dans l'état actuel des esprits*. Paris: Librairie de la Suisse Romande, 1867.

SECONDARY

Acomb, Evelyn Martha. *The French Laic Laws (1879–1889): The First Anti-clerical Campaign of the Third French Republic*. New York: Octagon, 1967.

Amalvi, Christian. "Les guerres des manuels autour de l'école primaire en France," *Revue historique*, October–December 1979.

Anderson, Robert D. *France, 1870–1914: Politics and Society*. London: Routledge & Kegan Paul, 1977.

Barral, Pierre. *Les fondateurs de la Troisième République: Textes choisis*. Paris: Armand Colin, n.d.

Bertocci, P. A. "Positivism, French Republicanism, and the Politics of Religion, 1848–1883," *Third Republic/Troisième République* 2 (fall 1976).

Chélini, Jean. *La ville et l'église: Premier bilan des enquêtes de sociologie religieuse urbaine*. Paris: Editions du Cerf, 1958.

Chevallier, Pierre. "L'évolution de l'enseignement primaire en France de 1850 à 1963." In *La scolarisation en France depuis un siècle*. Paris: Mouton, 1974.

———. *La séparation de l'église et de l'école: Jules Ferry et Léon XIII*. Paris: Fayard, 1981.

Hayes, Carlton J. H. *France: A Nation of Patriots*. New York: Columbia University Press, 1930.

———. *A Generation of Materialism, 1871–1900* (1941). New York: Harper Torchbooks, 1963.

Hoeven, Maarten Bastiaan van der. *De Schoolstrijd in Frankrijk, in het bijzonder tijdens de Derde Republiek*. Amsterdam: Meulenhoff, 1960.

Johnston, J. Richard. "Jean Macé and the Fight for Public Education in Nineteenth Century France." *Paedagogica Historica* 12, no. 2 (1972).

Keylor, William R. "Anti-clericalism and Educational Reform in the French Third Republic: A Retrospective Evaluation." *History of Education Quarterly,* spring 1981.

La Perrière, Guy. *La "Séparation" à Lyon (1904–1908): Etude d'opinion publique*. Lyon, 1973.

Larkin, Maurice. *Church and State after the Dreyfus Affair: The Separation Issue in France*. New York: Harper & Row, 1973.

Legrand, Louis. *L'influence du positivisme dans l'oeuvre scolaire de Jules Ferry: Les origines de la laïcité*. Paris: Marcel Rivière, 1961.

Mayeur, Jean-Marie. *Les débuts de la IIIe. République, 1871–1898*. Paris: Editions du Seuil, 1973.

Moody, Joseph N. "The Third Republic and the Church." *Catholic Historical Review* 66, no. 1 (January 1980).

Nicolet, Claude. *L'idée républicaine en France (1789–1924)*. Paris: Gallimard, 1982.

Ozouf, Jacques. *Nous, les maîtres d'école: Autobiographies d'instituteurs de la Belle Epoque*. Paris: René Jaillard, 1967.

Ozouf, Mona. *L'école, l'Eglise, et la République, 1871–1914*. Cana, 1982.

Reclus, Maurice. *Jules Ferry, 1832–1893*. Paris: Flammarion, 1947.

Redmond, Sr. M. Justine. *Laicism in the Schools of France*. Washington, D.C.: Catholic University Press, 1932.

Singer, Barnett. "The Teacher as Notable in Brittany, 1880–1914," *French Historical Studies,* 9, no. 4 (fall 1976).

———. "Minoritarian Religion and the Creation of a Secular School System in France," *Third Republic/Troisième République* 2 (fall 1976).

Smith, Robert J. *The Ecole Normale Supérieure and the Third Republic*. Albany: SUNY Press, 1982.

Talbott, John E. *The Politics of Educational Reform in France, 1918–1940*. Princeton, N.J.: Princeton University Press, 1969.

Weber, Eugen. *Peasants into Frenchmen: The Modernization of Rural France, 1870–1914*. Stanford, Calif.: Stanford University Press, 1976.

Zeldin, Theodore. *France, 1848–1945: Ambition and Love*. Oxford: Oxford University Press, 1979.

———. *France, 1848–1945: Politics and Anger*. Oxford: Oxford University Press, 1979.

———. *France, 1848–1945: Intellect and Pride*. Oxford: Oxford University Press, 1980.

————. *France, 1848–1945: Taste and Corruption*. Oxford: Oxford University Press, 1980.

————. *France, 1848–1945: Anxiety and Hypocrisy*. Oxford: Oxford University Press, 1981.

Resistance to the Common School in France

PRIMARY

Anglade, Jules. *Le poison civique maçonnique et obligatoire selon la formule du Dr. Paul Bert, suivi d'un programme de résistance à la loi athée*. Paris: Société Générale de Librairie, 1882.

Chateaubriand. *Essai sur les révolutions* and *Génie du christianisme*. Edited by Maurice Regard. Bibliothèque de la Pléiade. Paris: Gallimard, 1978.

————. *Mémoires d'outre-tombe*. Vols. 1 and 2. Bibliothèque de la Pléiade. Paris: Gallimard, 1951.

Dupanloup, Félix-Antoine-Philibert. *Les alarmes de l'Episcopat justifiées par les faits: Lettre à un cardinal par Mgr. L'Evêque d'Orléans*. 4th ed. Paris: Charles Douniol, 1868.

Gilson, Etienne, ed. *The Church Speaks to the Modern World: The Social Teachings of Leo XIII*. Garden City, N.Y.: Doubleday, 1954.

Goyau, Georges. *L'école d'aujourd'hui: Le péril primaire—l'école et la Patrie—l'école et Dieu*. Paris: Perrin, 1906.

Grimaud, Louis. *Histoire de la liberté d'enseignement en France depuis la chute de l'Ancien Régime jusqu'à nos jours*. Paris: Rousseau, 1898.

La Mennais, F. de. *Oeuvres complètes*. Vols. 1–7. Paris, 1836–37; rpt., Frankfurt: Minerva, 1967.

Montalembert, Charles. *Du devoir des Catholiques dans la question de la liberté d'enseignement*. Paris: Au Bureau de l'Univers, 1843.

Pujos, Maurice. *La loi et l'instruction: Gratuité, laïque, obligatoire*. Paris: Jouby & Roger/Cotillon, 1876.

Rendu, Eugène. *L'obligation légale de l'enseignement*. Paris: Hachette, 1872.

————. *L'instruction primaire devant l'Assemblée Nationale*. Paris: Hachette, 1873.

Simon, Jules. *Dieu, patrie, liberté*. Paris: Calmann Lévy, 1883.

SECONDARY

Elwell, Clarence Edward. *The Influence of the Enlightenment on the Catholic Theory of Religious Education in France, 1750–1850*. New York: Russell & Russell, 1967.

Gadille, Jacques. *La pensée et l'action politiques des évêques français au début de la IIIe. République, 1870/1883*. Vols. 1 and 2. Paris: Hachette, 1967.

McManners, John. *Church and State in France, 1870–1914*. London: SPCK, 1972.

Moody, Joseph N. "The French Catholic Press of the 1840's on American Catholicism." *Catholic Historical Review* 60, no. 2 (July 1974).

Riasanovsky, Nicholas V. "On Lamennais, Chaadaev, and the Romantic Revolt in France and Russia." *American Historical Review* 82, no. 5 (December 1977).

Spencer, Philip. *The Politics of Belief in Nineteenth Century France*. London: Faber & Faber, 1954.

Storer, Bellamy. "The Bishops and the Schools in France: An Address before the Catholic Union of Boston, February 5, 1910." Privately printed, 1910.

Vidler, Alec. *Prophecy and Papacy: A Study of Lamennais, the Church, and the Revolution*. New York: Scribner, 1954.

Contemporary Controversies in France

Ardagh, John. *France in the 1980s*. New York: Penguin Books, 1982.

Ballion, Robert. *Les consommateurs d'école*. Paris: Stock, 1982.

Bayet, Albert. "Libre-pensée et laïcité." In *La laïcité*. Centre de sciences politiques de l'Institut d'études juridiques de Nice. Paris: Presses universitaires de France, 1960.

Boursin, Jean-Louis. *L'administration de l'éducation nationale*. Paris: Presses universitaires de France, 1981.

Bur, Jacques. *Laïcité et problème scolaire*. Paris: Editions Bonne Presse, 1959.

Centre de sciences politiques de l'Institut d'études juridiques de Nice. *La laïcité*. Paris: Presses universitaires de France, 1960.

Coutrot, Aline. "Le jour se lève sur la loi Debré." *Le monde*, May 21, 1984.

Debeyre, Guy. "La laïcité et l'enseignement public." In *La laïcité*. Paris: Presses universitaires de France, 1960.

Fédération de l'Education Nationale. "Appel aux élus de la nation." *Le monde*, May 21, 1984.

Fédération Protestante de l'Enseignement. *Laïcité et paix scolaire: Enquête et conclusions*. Paris: Berger-Levrault, 1957.

Giscard d'Estaing, Olivier. *Education et civilisation: Pour une révolution libérale de l'enseignement*. Paris: Fayard, 1971.

Houtte, J. van. "La question scolaire en Belgique." In *La laïcité*. Paris: Presses universitaires de France, 1960.

Latreille, Andre. "L'Eglise catholique et la laïcité." In *La laïcité*. Paris: Presses universitaires de France, 1960.

Leclerc, Gérard. *La bataille de l'école: 15 siècles d'histoire, 3 ans de combat*. Paris: Denoël, 1985.

Le monde, May 2, May 21, July 17, 1984.

Le monde hébdomadaire, May 16, September 5, 1984.

Madelin Alain. *Pour libérer l'école: L'enseignement à la carte*. Paris: Laffont, 1984.

Maupas, Didier. *L'école en accusation*. Paris: Albin Michel, 1984.

Naurois, Louis de. "La laïcité de l'Etat et l'enseignement confessionel." In *La laïcité*. Paris: Presses universitaire de France, 1960.

Prost, Antoine, and Groupe de Travail national sur les seconds cycles. *Les lycées et leurs études au seuil du XXIe. siècle*. Paris: Ministère de l'Education nationale, 1983.

Rémond, René. "Laïcité et question scolaire dans la vie politique française sous la IVe. République." In *La laïcité*. Paris: Presses universitaire de France, 1960.

Riedmatten, Henri de. "La laïcité en Suisse." In *La laïcité*. Paris: Presses universitaire de France, 1980.

Savary, Alain, with Catherine Arditti. *En toute liberté*. Paris: Hachette, 1985.

Conflict and Compromise in the Netherlands

General

Berg, J. van den. "Die Pluralistische Gestalt des Kirchlichen Lebens in den Niederlanden, 1574–1974." In *Pietismus und Reveil*. Edited by J. van den Berg and J. P. van Dooren. Leiden: Brill, 1978.

Beversluis, N. H. *Christian Philosophy of Education*. Grand Rapids, Mich., 1971.

Blok, Petrus Johannes. *History of the People of the Netherlands*. Vol. 1. Translated by Oscar Bierstadt. New York: AMS Press, 1970.

Bowen, James. *A History of Western Education*. Vols. 1–3. New York: St. Martin's Press, 1972–81.

Box, L., J. Dronkers, M. Molenaar, and J. de Mulder, eds. *Vrijheid van onderwijs*. Nijmegen: LINK, 1977.

Christelijke Encyclopedie. Vols. 1–6. Edited by F. W. Grosheide and G. P. van Itterzon. Kampen: Kok, 1957; s.v. "Doopgezinden," "Secularisatie," "Godsdienstonderwijs," "Humanisme," "Onderwijs."

Eby, Frederick. *The Development of Modern Education*. 2nd ed. Englewood Cliffs, N.J.: Prentice-Hall, 1952.

Frost, S. E., Jr. *Historical and Philosophical Foundations of Western Education*. Columbus, Ohio: Merrill, 1966.

Helmreich, Ernest Christian. *Religious Education in German Schools*. Cambridge, Mass., 1959.

Jong, Otto de. *Nederlandse Kerkgeschiedenis*. 2nd ed. Nijkerk: Callenbach, 1978.

Kalsbeek, L. *Theologische en Wijsgerige Achtergronden van de Verhouding van Kerk, Staat, en School in Nederland*. Kampen: Kok, 1976.

Kossmann, E. H. *The Low Countries, 1780–1940*. Oxford: Clarendon Press, 1978.

Kuiper, J. *Geschiedenis van het Christelijk Lager Onderwijs in Nederland (16 n. Chr.–1904)*. Groningen: Wolters, 1904.

Latourette, Kenneth Scott. *The Nineteenth Century in Europe: The Protestant and Eastern Churches*. New York: Harper & Brothers, 1959.

Martin, David. *A General Theory of Secularization*. New York: Harper Colophon, 1979.

Maynes, Mary Jo. *Schooling in Western Europe: A Social History*. Albany: SUNY Press, 1985.

Meyer, Adolphe E. *An Educational History of the Western World*. New York: McGraw-Hill, 1965.

Rasker, A. J. *De Nederlandse Hervormde Kerk vanaf 1795*. Kampen: Kok, 1981.

Religion in Geschichte und Gegenwart. 3rd ed. Tuebingen: Mohr, s.v. "Bildungswesen," "Erziehung," "Niederlande: Kirchengeschichte," "Niederlande: Theologie," "Privatschule."

Seiler, Friedrich. *Geschichte des deutschen Unterrichtwesens.* Vols. 1 and 2. Leipzig, 1906.

Troeltsch, Ernst. *The Social Teaching of the Christian Churches* (1911). Vols. 1 and 2. Translated by Olive Wyon. New York: Harper Torchbooks, 1960.

Welch, Claude. *Protestant Thought in the Nineteenth Century.* Vol. 1 (1799–1879); vol. 2 (1870–1914). New Haven: Yale University Press, 1972, 1985.

Background, 1618–1780

Berk, Martin. "Over de Opvoeding der Kinderen: Opvoedkundige Denkbeelden in de Spectatoriale Geschriften, 1730–1780," *Pedagogische Verhandelingen* 7, no. 1 (1984).

Booy, E. P. de. *Weldaet der Scholen.* Utrecht: Stichtse Historische Reeks, 1977.

Brienen, T., K. Exalto, J. van Genderen, C. Graafland, and W. van 't Spijker. *De Nadere Reformatie: Beschrijving van haar Voornaamste Vertegenwoordigers.* The Hague: Boekencentrum B.V., 1986.

Christelijke Encyclopedie; s.v. "Coccejus," "Comenius," "Hofstede," "Nadere Reformatie," "Pietisme," "Remonstranten."

Deppermann, Klaus. *Der hallesche Pietismus und der preußische Staat unter Friedrich III.* Vol. 1. Göttingen: Vandenhoech & Ruprecht, 1961.

Deursen, A. Th. van. *Het Kopergeld van de Gouden Eeuw: Hel en Hemel.* Assen: Van Gorcum, 1980.

Doctrinal Standards of the Netherlands Reformed Congregations. Grand Rapids, Mich., 1963.

Francke, August Hermann. *Paedagogische Schriften.* Edited by Hermann Lorenzen. Paderborn: Schoeningh, 1957.

———— et al. *Pietistische Paedagogik.* Edited by Gerhardt Petrat. Heidelberg: Quelle & Meyer, 1970.

Goeters, Wilhelm. *Die Vorbereitung des Pietismus in der Reformierten Kirche der Niederlande bis zur Labadistischen Krisis, 1670.* Leipzig: Hinrichs'sche Buchhandlung, 1911.

Haller, William. *The Rise of Puritanism . . . 1570–1643* (1938). New York: Harper Torchbooks, 1957.

Hans, Nicholas. "Holland in the Eighteenth Century *Verlichting* (Enlightenment)." *Paedagogica Historica* 5, no. 1 (1965).

Huizinga, Johan. *Erasmus and the Age of Reformation.* New York: Harper Torchbooks, 1957.

Itterzon, G. P. van. *Franciscus Gomarus.* Groningen: Castricum, 1979.

Laurie, S. S. *John Amos Comenius, Bishop of the Moravians: His Life and Educational Works.* Syracuse, N.Y.: Bardeen, 1892.

Lehmann, Hartmut. *Pietismus und weltliche Ordnung in Wuerttemberg vom 17. bis zum 20. Jahrhundert.* Stuttgart: Kohlhammer, 1969.

Linde, J. M. van der. *De Wereld heeft Toekomst: Jan Amos Comenius over de Hervorming van school, kerk, en staat.* Kampen: Kok, 1979.

Linde, S. van der. "Der Reformierte 'Pietismus' in den Niederlanden." In J. van den Berg and J. P. van Dooren, eds., *Pietismus und Reveil.* Leiden: Brill, 1978.

Parker, Geoffrey. *The Dutch Revolt.* London: Penguin Books, 1977.

Peschke, Erhard. "Die Reformideen des Comenius und ihr Verhaeltnis zu A. H. Franckes Plan einer realen Verbesserung in der ganzen Welt." In *Der Pietismus in Gestalten und Wirkungen (Martin Schmidt zum 65. Geburtstag),* ed. Heinrich Bornkamm et al. Bielefeld: Luther-Verlag, 1975.

Religion in Geschichte und Gegenwart. 3rd ed. s.v. "Arminianer," "Labadie."

Ritschl, Albrecht. "'Prolegomena' to 'The History of Pietism.'" In *Three Essays,* trans. Philip Hefner. Philadelphia: Fortress Press, 1972.

Rowen, Herbert H., ed. *The Low Countries in Early Modern Times: A Documentary History.* New York: Harper Paperbacks, 1972.

Schaller, Klaus. "Pietismus und moderne Paedagogik." In *Pietismus und moderne Welt,* ed. Kurt Aland. Witten: Luther-Verlag, 1974.

Schmalenberg, Gerhard. *Pietismus—Schule—Religionsunterricht: Die christliche Unterweisung im Spiegel der vom Pietismus bestimmten Schulordnungen des 18. Jahrhunderts.* Bern and Frankfurt: Lang, 1974.

Schmidt, Martin. "A. H. Franckes Stellung in der pietistischen Bewegung." In *Wiedergeburt und neuer Mensch.* Witten: Luther-Verlag, 1969.

Sell, Alan P. F. *The Great Debate: Calvinism, Arminianism, and Salvation.* Grand Rapids, Mich.: Baker, 1983.

Stoeffler, F. Ernest. *The Rise of Evangelical Pietism.* Leiden: Brill, 1965.

————. *German Pietism during the Eighteenth Century.* Leiden: Brill, 1973.

Stouten, J. *Verlichting in de Letteren.* Leiden: Nijhoff, 1984.

Wendel, François. *Calvin: The Origins and Development of His Religious Thought.* Glasgow: Collins (Fontana), 1965.

Liberal Program of Common School and Common Religion

PRIMARY

Aanspraak van den Voorzitter J. H. van der Palm ter Opening der Vergadering van Afgevaardigden uit de Departementale School-besturen der Bataafsche Republiek. The Hague: State Printing House, 1803.

Cousin, Victor. *Etat de l'instruction primaire dans le Royaume de Prusse à la fin de l'année 1831.* Paris: Levrault, 1833.

————. *De l'instruction publique en Hollande.* Paris: Levrault, 1837. Also, same title, Brussels, 1838.

Cuvier, Georges, and François Noël, "Rapport wegens het Lagere Schoolwezen in Holland." In *Bijdragen ter Bevordering van het Onderwijs en de Opvoeding, voornamelijk met betrekking tot de lagere scholen in Holland* (Haarlem: Enschede & Zoonen) 3, no. 5 (May 1812).

————. *Rapport sur les établissements d'instruction publique, en Hollande.* The Hague, 1816.

Fichte, Johann Gottlieb. *Addresses to the German Nation.* Translated by R. F. Jones and G. H. Turnbull. Chicago: Open Court, 1922.

Hofstede de Groot, C. P. *William Ellery Channing, een Apostel der Evangelisch-Catholieke Kerk.* Reprint from *Waarheid in Liefde.* Groningen: Omkens, 1858.

Hofstede de Groot, Petrus. "Geschiedkundige Opmerkingen over de Bijzondere Eigenaardigheid der Christelijke Kerk, dat zij zich gedurig uit den eenen Toestand in den anderen ontwikkelt." In *Waarheid in Liefde*. Groningen: Oomkens, 1838.

———. "De Denkbeelden van Graser, van Heusde, Cousin, en van Bommel over de Betrekking van de Godsdienst en de Wetenschap tot het Onderwijs Medegedeeld en Vergeleken." In *Waarheid in Liefde*. Vol. 2. Groningen: Oomkens, 1841.

———. "Het Onderscheid tusschen de Doorgaande Voorsteling van *Geloof* in de Schriften des Nieuwen Verbonds en de Betekenis van dit Woord, die in de Stelsels der Godgeleerden sedert de Alexandrijnishce Kerkvaders de Heerschende is geworden." In *Waarheid in Liefde*. Vol. 1. Groningen: Oomkens, 1842.

———. "Over het al of niet bestaan eener Groninger School." In *Waarheid in Liefde*. Vol. 1. Groningen: Oomkens, 1844.

———. *Zijn Afzonderlijke Scholen voor de verschillenden Kerkgenootschappen Noodig of Wenschelijk?* Groningen: Scholtens, 1844.

———. "Het Belang der Volksopvoeding, door een Voorbeeld uit de Geschiedenis onzer Eeuw Opgehelderd." In *Waarheid in Liefde*. Vol. 4. Groningen: Oomkens, 1845.

———. *Behoort de Staat het Christelijke Beginsel in het Lagen Onderwijs te verwijderen of te behouden?* Groningen: Scholtens, 1846.

———. *Voorlezingen over de Geschiedenis der Opvoeding des Menschdoms door God tot op de Komst van Jezus Christus.* Vols. 1 and 2. Groningen: Scholtens, 1847.

———. *De Berigten Omtrent het Onderscheidend Karakter der Groningsche Godgeleerde School, van Mr. I. da Costa toegelicht.* Groningen: Van Bolhuis Hoitsema, 1848.

———. *Wat hebben wij van het Ontwerp van Gewijzigde Grondwet te verwachten met Betrekking tot Godsdienst en Onderwijs?* Groningen: Van Bolhuis Hoitsema, 1848.

———. *Over de Belangrijkheid der Maatschappij: Tot Nut van 't Algemeen in de Toekomst, welke wij tegengaan.* Groningen, 1848.

———. "Over het Belang der Moederlijke Opvoeding, en van den Bijbel in dezelve." In *Waarheid in Liefde*. Vol. 2. Groningen: Oomkens, 1849.

———. "Over de Opvoeding van Kinderen in Navolging van de Opvoeding des Menschdoms door God." In *Waarheid in Liefde*. Groningen: Oomkens, 1849.

———. *Een Woord aan de Hervormde Gemeente te 's Gravenhage, over de Groninger Godgeleerden, en hunne Bestrijding in "Den Nederlander."* The Hague: Susan, 1851.

———. "Gedachten over de Verhouding van het Dogma tot de Waarheid." In *Waarheid in Liefde*. Groningen: Oomkens, 1852.

———. *De Groninger Godgeleerden in hunne Eigenaardigheid.* Groningen: Sholtens, 1855.

———. *De moderne theologie in Nederland.* Groningen: Noordhoff, 1870.

"X" [Hofstede de Groot]. *Die Unruhen in der Niederlaendisch-Reformirten Kir-*

che waehrend der Jahre 1833 bis 1839. Edited by J. C. L. Gieseler. Hamburg: Perthes, 1840.

Maatschappij tot Nut van 't Algemeen. *De Uitwerking van het nieuwe Art. 192 der Grondwet.* Nutsuitgeverij te Zalt-Bommel, 1918.

Notificatie van den Secretaris van Staat voor de Binnenlandsche Zaken der Bataafsche Republiek behelzende eene Algemeene Schoolorde voor de lagere scholen binnen de Bataafsche Republiek. Den Haag: Staats-Drukkerij, 1806.

O'Malley, Thaddeus. *A Sketch of the State of Popular Education in Holland, Prussia, Belgium, and France.* London: Ridgway, 1840.

Oordt, J. F. van; Petrus Hofstede de Groot; L. G. Pareau; J. J. Swiers; and J. Sonius Swaagman. "Voorberigt." In *Waarheid in Liefde.* Groningen: Oomkens, 1837.

Otterloo, M. D. van. "De Lagere Scholen met Betrekking tot de Godsdienst." In *Ernst en Vrede.* Utrecht: Kemink, 1856.

———. "De Lagere School in hare Verhouding tot Huisgezin, Kerk en Staat, Historisch Overzigt." In *Ernst en Vrede.* Utrecht: Kemink, 1856.

Schleiermacher, Friedrich. *On Religion: Speeches to Its Cultured Despisers.* Translated by John Oman. New York: Harper Torchbooks, 1958.

———. *The Christian Faith.* Edited by H. R. Mackintosh and J. S. Stewart. Edinburgh: T. & T. Clark, 1928.

W. P. Wolters, *Een Pleidooi voor de Gemengde Lagere School.* Amsterdam: Rogge, 1869.

SECONDARY

Alexander, Thomas. *The Prussian Elementary Schools.* New York: Macmillan, 1918.

Bornewasser, J. A. "Thorbecke and the Churches." *Acta Historiae Neerlandicae* (The Hague) 7 (1974).

Brugghen, J. van; G. van Reinen; and A. van Wieringen. "Overheid en Onderwijs: Een Aarzelende Verbintenis rond 1800." In L. Box et al., eds. *Vrijheid van onderwijs.* Amsterdam, 1977.

Brugmans, I. J. *Stapvoets voorwaarts: Sociale geschiedenis van Nederland in de Negentiende Eeuw.* Bossum: Fibula-Van Dishoeck, 1970.

Christelijke Encyclopedie. S.v. "Groninger School," "Hofstede de Groot," "Haagsch Genootschap," "Heusde," "Maatschappij tot Nut van 't Algemeen," "Palm," "Schleiermacher."

Dawson, Jerry F. *Friedrich Schleiermacher: The Evolution of a Nationalist.* Austin: University of Texas Press, 1966.

Fischer, Rudolf. *Religionspaedagogik unter den Bedingungen der Aufklaerung: Studien zum Verhaeltnisproblem von Theologie und Paedagogik bei Schleiermacher, Palmer, und Diesterweg.* Heidelberg: Quelle & Meyer, 1973.

Groot, Aart de. *Leven en Arbeid van J. H. van der Palm.* Wageningen: Veenman, 1960.

Heerspink, J. B. F. *Dr. P. Hofstede de Groot's Leven en Werken.* Groningen: Noordhoff, 1898.

Helsloot, P. N. "De Nutsbeweging." In W. W. Mijnhardt and A. J. Wichers, eds., *Om het Algemeen Volksgeluk: Twee eevwen particulier initiatif, 1784–1984*. Edam: Maatschappij tot Nut van 't Algemeen, 1984.

Holborn, Hajo. *A History of Modern Germany, 1648–1840*. New York: Knopf, 1964.

La Vopa, Anthony J. *Prussian Schoolteachers: Profession and Office, 1763–1848*. Chapel Hill: University of North Carolina Press, 1980.

Leeb, I. Leonard. *The Ideological Origins of the Batavian Revolution*. The Hague, 1973.

Mackintosh, Hugh Ross. *Types of Modern Theology: Schleiermacher to Barth*. New York, 1937.

Mijnhardt, W. W., and A. J. Wichers, ed. *Om het Algemeen Volksgeluk: Twee Eeuwen Particulier Initiatief, 1784–1984: Gedenkboek ter Gelegenheid van het Tweehonderdjarig Bestaan van de Maatschappij tot Nut van 't Algemeen*. Edam: Maatschappij tot Nut van 't Algemeen, 1984.

Nipperday, Thomas. *Deutsche Geschichte, 1800–1848*. Munich: Beck, 1983.

Osborn, Andrew R. *Schleiermacher and Religious Education*. Oxford: Oxford University Press, 1934.

Reardon, Bernard M. G. *Liberal Protestantism*. London: Adam & Charles Black, 1968.

Religion in Geschichte und Gegenwart. S.v. "Fichte," "Groninger Schule," "Kruedener," "Liberalismus," "Pestalozzi," "Schleiermacher," "Vermittlungstheologie."

Riel, H. van. *Geschiedenis van het Nederlandse Liberalisme in de 19e. Eeuw*. Revised by J. G. Bruggeman. Assen: Van Gorcum, 1982.

Schama, Simon. "Schools and Politics in the Netherlands, 1796–1814." *Historical Journal* 13, no. 4 (1970).

———. *Patriots and Liberators: Revolution in the Netherlands, 1780–1813*. New York: Knopf, 1977.

Schmidt, Martin. "Der Liberalismus als Problem fuer die Kirche und Kirchengeschichte im 19. Jahrhundert, inbesondere seine Stellung zum evangelischen Christentum." In Martin Schmidt and Georg Schwaiger, *Kirchen und Liberalismus im 19. Jahrhundert*. Göttingen: Vandenhoek & Ruprecht, 1976.

Spiegel, Yorick. *Theologie der bürgerlichen Gesellschaft: Socialphilosophie und Glaubenslehre bei Friedrich Schleiermacher*. Munich: Chr. Kaiser Verlag, 1968.

Vermeersch, A. J. *Vereniging en Revolutie: De Niederlanden, 1814–1830*. Bossum: Fibula-Van Dishoeck, 1970.

Vree, J. *De Groninger Godgeleerden: De Oorsprongen en de Eerste Periode van hun Optreden (1820–1843)*. Kampen: Kok, 1984.

Wiegand, Hanns-Juergen. "Friedrich Julius Stahls Bild des Liberalismus." In Martin Schmidt and Georg Schwaiger, *Kirchen und Liberalismus im 19. Jahrhundert*. Göttingen: Vandenhoek & Ruprecht, 1976.

Wit, C. H. E. de. "La République batave, 1795–1805." In *Occupants occupés, 1792–1815*. Brussels: Université Libre, 1968.

Conflict and Compromise, 1830–1917

PRIMARY

Behrns, J. H. *Wet tot regeling van het lager onderwijs.* Harlingen: Behrns, 1857.

Bos, F. L. *Archiefstukken betreffende de Afscheiding van 1834.* Vols. 1–4. Kampen: Kok, 1940.

Costa, Issac da. *Bezwaren tegen den Geest der Eeuw.* Leiden: Herdingh, 1823.

Fruin, R. *De Antirevolutionaire Staatsregt van Mr. Groen van Prinsterer.* Amsterdam: Gebhard, 1853.

Gieseler, J. C. L. "Vorrede" to *Die Unruhen in der Niederlaendisch Reformirten Kirche waehrend der Jahre 1833 bis 1839,* by "X" [Hofstede de Groot]. Hamburg: Perthes, 1840.

Groen van Prinsterer, Guillaume. *De Maatregelen tegen de Afgescheidenen aan het Staatsregt getoetst.* Leiden: Luchtmans, 1837.

――――. *Ongeloof en revolutie* (1847). Edited by H. Smitskamp. Franeker: Wever, 1976.

――――. *Vrijheid, Gelijkheid, Broederschap: Toelichting van de Spreuk der Revolutie* (1848). Rpt., Groningen: "De Vuurbaak," n.d.

――――. *Handboek der Geschiedenis van het Vaderland* (1848). 6th printing. Amsterdam: Wormser, 1895.

――――. *Welke is voor Nederland de hoop van een Christen?* Amsterdam: Mueller, 1850.

――――. *Adviezen in de Tweede Kamer der Staten-Generaal.* Utrecht: Kemink, 1857.

――――. *Le parti Anti-Révolutionnaire et Confessionnel dans l'Eglise Reformée des Pays-Bas.* Amsterdam: Hoeveker, 1860.

Hubrecht, P. F. "*Het Lastige Punt.*" The Hague: Belinfante, 1901.

Kuyper, Abraham. *De "Nuts"-beweging.* Amsterdam: Hoeveker, 1869.

――――. *Eenige Kameradviezen uit de jaren 1874 en 1875.* Amsterdam: Wormser, 1890.

――――. *Lectures on Calvinism* (1898). Grand Rapids, Mich.: Eerdmans, 1931.

――――. "*Ons Program.*" Hilversum: Hoeveker & Wormser, 1907.

Laveleyé, Emile de. *Débats sur l'enseignement primaire dans les Chambres hollandaises (Session de 1857).* Ghent: Vanderhaeghen, 1858.

――――. *L'instruction du peuple.* Paris: Hachette, 1872.

"Een Limburger," *Het Mandement van het Nederlandse Episcopaat en de zoogenaamde liberale partij.* Katholiek-Nederlandsche Brochure Vereniging, Harlem, 1870.

Schaepman, H. J. A. M. *Van strijd tot vrede? Nog een woord over Art. 194 der Grondwet.* Utrecht, 1885.

Schroeter, J. J. E. F. *Gedachten over den Toestand van Neerlands Kerk, en de daaruit Voortvloeijende Beschuldigingen, tegen de Leeraars dier Kerk ingebragt.* Amsterdam: Ouden, 1834.

Vinet, Alexandre. *Morceaux choisis.* Edited by Armand Vautier. Lausanne: Georges Bridel, 1897.

Vunderink, G. W. C. *De Schoolkwestie.* Utrecht: Ruys, 1909.

SECONDARY

Algra, H. *Het Wonder van de 19e eeuw: Van Vrije Kerken en Kleine Luyden.* Franeker: Wever, 1965.

Augustijn, C. "Kerk en Godsdienst, 1870–1890." In W. Bakker et al., eds., *De Doleantie van 1886 en haar Geschiedenis.* Kampen: Kok, 1986.

Bakker, W.; O. J. de Jong; W. van 't Spijker; and L. J. Wolthuis, eds. *De Afscheiding van 1834 en Haar Geschiedenis.* Kampen: Kok, 1984.

———. *De Doleantie van 1886 en Haar Geschiedenis.* Kampen: Kok, 1986.

Berg, J. van den. "P. Hofstede de Groot en het Reveil." In *Aspecten van het Reveil.* Kampen: Kok, 1980.

Berg, J. van den, and J. P. van Dooren, eds. *Pietismus und Reveil.* Leiden: Brill, 1978.

Billiet, J. "Vrijheid van Onderwijs en Verzuiling in Belgie." In L. Box et al., eds., *Vrijheid van onderwijs.* Amsterdam, 1977.

Boer, R. de. "Groen van Prinsterer, staatspedagoog?" In *Het Gereformeerd Onderwijs: Identiteitsbezinning,* ed. A. Joh. Kisjes and P. A. te Velde. Kampen: Kok, 1983.

Boogman, J. C. "J. Thorbecke: Challenge and Response." *Acta Historiae Neerlandicae* (The Hague) 7 (1974).

Boogman, J. C., and C. A. Tamse, ed. *Emancipatie in Nederland: De Ontvoogding van Burgerij en Confessionelen in de Negentiende Eeuw.* The Hague: Nijhoff, 1978.

Bremmer, R. H. "Historische aspecten van de Afscheiding." In A. de Groot and P. L. Schram, eds., *Aspecten van de Afscheiding.* Franeker: Wever, 1984.

Christelijke Encyclopedie. S.v. "Bavinck," "Beets," "Brugghen," "Champetie de la Saussaye," "Christelijk Volksonderwijs, De Vereniging," "Cock," "Combes," "Groen van Prinsterer," "Guizot," "Gunning," "Haagse Heren, De Zeven," "Hoedemaker," "Hoekstra," "Kuyper," "Liberalisme," "Modernisme," "Oosterzee," "Pierson," "Reveil," "Reville," "Scholte," "Scholten," "Schoolstrijd," "Unie 'School met de Bijbel,'" "Unierapport," "Vrijzinnig Hervormden."

Daalder, Hans. "The Netherlands: Opposition in a Segmented Society." In *Political Oppositions in Western Democracies,* ed. Robert A. Dahl. New Haven: Yale University Press, 1966.

Diepenhorst, I. A. *De Verhouding tusschen Kerk en Staat in Nederland.* Utrecht: Kemink & Zoon, n.d.

———. *Groen van Prinsterer.* Kampen: Kok, 1932.

Egmond, Nicholaas van. *Consequent Christendom: Leven en werk van Mr. J. J. L. van der Brugghen.* Wageningen: Veenman, 1964.

Gelderen, J. van. "'Scheuring' en vereniging." In W. Bakker et al., eds., *De Afscheiding van 1834 en haar geschiedenis.* Kampen: Kok, 1984.

Gerretson, C. "Groen van Prinsterer" (1926). In J. C. Boogman and C. A. Tamse, eds., *Emancipatie in Nederland.* The Hague: Nijhoff, 1978.

Gilhuis, T. M. *Memorietafel van het Christelijk Onderwijs: De Geschiedenis van de Schoolstrijd.* 2nd ed. Kampen: Kok, 1975.

Groen en de School (no author or other publication information; apparently published soon after Groen van Prinsterer's death).

Groot, Aart de. "Het Vroegnegentiende-eeuwse Nederland." In W. Bakker et al., eds., *De Afscheiding van 1934*. Kampen: Kok, 1984.

———— and P. L. Schram, eds. *Aspecten van de Afscheiding*. Franeker: Wever, 1984.

Hendriks, J. "De Emancipatie van de Gereformeerden" in J. C. Boogman and C. A. Tamse, ed., *Emancipatie in Nederland*. The Hague: Nijhoff, 1978.

Holtrop, P. N. *Tussen Pietisme en Reveil: Het "Deutsche-Christentumgesellschaft" in Nederland, 1784–1833*. Amsterdam: Rodopi, 1975.

————. "De Afscheiding-Breekpunt en Kristallisatiepunt." In W. Bakker et al., eds., *De Afscheiding van 1834*. Kampen: Kok, 1984.

Jong, J. de. *Mr. Groen van Prinsterer als staatsman en als evangeliebelijder*. Goes: Oosterbaan & Le Cointre, n.d.

Jong, O. J. de. "Van de Andere Kant: Hervormde Reacties op de Afscheiding." In W. Bakker et al., eds., *De Afscheiding van 1834*. Kampen: Kok, 1984.

Keizer, Willem Pieter. *Vinet en Hollande*. Wageningen: Veenman, 1941.

————. *Alexandre Rodolphe Vinet, 1797–1847*. Amsterdam: Uitgevers Mij. Holland, 1848.

Kluit, M. Elisabeth. *Het Protestantse Reveil in Nederland en Daarbuiten, 1815–1865*. Paris-Amsterdam, 1970.

Knetsch, F. R. J. "Het Reveil en de Afscheiding." In A. de Groot and P. L. Schram, eds., *Aspecten van de Afscheiding*. Franeker: Wever, 1984.

Kroef, Justus M. van der. "Abraham Kuyper and the Rise of Neo-Calvinism in the Netherlands," *Church History* 17 (1948).

Kuiper, D. Th. "De Doleantie en de Nederlandse samenleving." In W. Bakker et al., eds., *De Doleantie van 1886*. Kampen: Kok, 1986.

Langedijk, D. *Bibliographie van den Schoolstrijd, 1795–1920*. Foreword by A. Goslinga. The Hague: Kuyper Stichting, 1931.

————. *De Schoolstrijd*. The Hague: Van Haeringen, 1935.

————. *Staatsalmacht en de Vrije School*. The Hague: Unie "Een School met den Bijbel," 1937.

————. *Groen van Prinsterer en de Schoolkwestie*. Den Haag: Voorhoeve, 1947.

Lauret, A. M. "Par Mandat Imperatif." *Acta Historiae Neerlandicae* IV (Leiden) 4 (1970); résume of *Per Imperatief Mandaat, 1967*.

Mackay, James Hutton. *Religious Thought in Holland during the Nineteenth Century*. London: Hodder & Stoughton, 1911.

Mallinson, Vernon. *Power and Politics in Belgian Education, 1815 to 1961*. London, 1963.

Matthijssen, M. A. J. M. *De Elite en de Mythe: Een Sociologische Analyse van Strijd om Onderwijsverandering*. Deventer, 1982.

Mulder, L. H. "De Afscheiding sociaal-wetenschappelijk benaderd." In A. de Groot and P. L. Schram, eds., *Aspecten van de Afscheidung*. Franeker: Wever, 1984.

Oosterhof, Okko Nanning. *Isaac da Costa als Polemist*. Kampen: Zalsman, 1913.

Oosterwijk Bruyn W. van. *Het Reveil in Nederland in Verband met de Vergaderingen der Christelijke Vrienden te Amsterdam*. Utrecht: Breijer, 1890.

Religion in Geschichte und Gegenwart. 3rd ed. S.v. "Empaytaz," "Erweckungsbewegung im 19. Jh.," "Evangelische Gesellschaft," "Hoedemaker," "Hoekstra," "Malan," "Merle d'Aubigne," "Moderne Richtung in Holland," "Monod," "Reveil."

Rijnsdorp, C. "'Met Vreugd naar School' (Herinnering en tijdbeeld)." *In het honderste jaar.* Kampen: Kok, 1979.

Savorin Lohman, W. H. de. *Groen van Prinsterer.* Baarn: Hollandia, 1914.

Schram, P. L. "Wichern und Heldring in Beziehung zum Pietismus." In J. van den Berg and J. P. van Dooren, eds., *Pietismus und Reveil.* Leiden: Brill, 1978.

———. "Kerk en Maatschappij in Nederland omstreeks 1850." In *Serta Historica IV: Kerk en Samenleving in de Negentiende Eeuw.* Amsterdam: VU Boekhandel, 1982.

Schutte, G. J. *Mr. G. Groen van Prinsterer.* Goes: Oosterbaan & Le Cointre, 1977.

———. "Kerk en Maatschappij bij Thorbecke." In *Serta Historica IV: Kerk en Samenleving in de Negentiende Eeuw.* Amsterdam: VU Boekhandel, 1982.

Sietsma, S. K. "Onderwijs en Grondwet." In *Het Gereformeerd Onderwijs: Indentiteitsbezinning,* ed. A. Joh. Kisjes and P. A. te Velde. Kampen: Kok, 1983.

Skillen, James W., and Stanley W. Carlson-Thies. "Religion and Political Development in Nineteenth-Century Holland." *Publius,* summer 1982.

Skopp, Douglas R. "The Elementary School Teachers in 'Revolt': Reform Proposals for Germany's Volksschulen in 1848 and 1849." *History of Education Quarterly,* fall 1982.

Spijker, W. van 't. "De Dogmatische Aspecten van de Afscheiding." In A. de Groot and P. L. Schram, eds., *Aspecten van de Afscheiding.* Franeker: Wever, 1984.

———. "Theologie en Spiritualiteit van de Afgescheidenen." In W. Bakker et al. eds., *De Afscheiding van 1834.* Kampen: Kok, 1984.

———. *De Kerk bij Hendrik de Cock.* Kampen: Kok, 1985.

Stuurman, Siep. *Verzuiling, Kapitalisme, en Patriarchaat.* Nijmegen: Socialistiese Uitgeverij, 1983.

Tijn, Th. van. "Actergronden van de Ontwikkeling van het Lager Onderwijs en van de Schoolstrijd in Nederland, 1862–1905." In L. Box, et al., eds., *Vrijheid van onderwijs.* Amsterdam, 1977.

Vanden Berg, Frank. *Abraham Kuyper.* Ontario: Paideaia Press, 1978.

Vereniging van Christenonderwijsers aan Overheidsscholen. "De V.C.O.O. en haar Doelstelling historisch belicht." The Hague, 1966.

Verwey-Jonker, H. "De Emancipatiebeweging." In J. C. Boogman and C. A. Tamse, eds., *Emancipatie in Nederland.* The Hague: Nijhoff, 1978.

Vos, H. de. *Geschiedenis van het Socialisme in Nederland in het Kader van Zijn Tijd.* Baarn: Wereldvenster, 1976.

Vree, J. "De Nederlandse Hervormde Kerk in de Jaren voor de Afscheiding." In W. Bakker et al., *De Afscheiding van 1834.* Kampen: Kok, 1984.

Wieringa, W. J. "De Afscheiding en de Nederlandse Samenleving." In W. Bakker et al., *De Afscheiding van 1834.* Kampen: Kok, 1984.

————. "Een Samenleving in Verandering." In W. Bakker et al., *De Doleantie van 1886*. Kampen: Kok, 1986.

Wilde, W. J. de. *Geschiedenis van Afscheiding en Doleantie van Hervormd Standpunt bezien*. Wageningen: Veenman, 1934.

Wolff, I. de. *De Strijd om de Kerk in de 19e eeuw 1815–1834*. Enschede: Boersma, 1954.

Wolthuis, Jan. *Onderwijsvakorganisatie*. Amsterdam: Uitgeverij SUA, 1981.

"Verzuiling" in Society and School, 1917–Present

Many of the references are to articles in Dutch education journals. To avoid confusion, here is an alphabetical listing of these journals and their position within the "new school struggle."

Bulletin is published by the Unie "School en Evangelie," an organization that has provided advocacy and support for Protestant education for more than a century. *Bulletin* attempts to allow the full range of "reflection" on Protestant education to find a place in its pages.

De Christenonderwijzer in de Openbare School is published by an association of Christian teachers in public and "general private" schools; it opposes the present confessional divisions in Dutch education.

De Reformatorische School (DRS) is published by two organizations that promote orthodox Calvinist education. Although *DRS* maintains a dialogue with *Bulletin,* it frequently gives expression to profound alienation from many of the opinions appearing in the latter.

Inkom is published by the Association of Protestant-Christian School Boards; it corresponds in general terms to *Schoolbestuur* for Catholic education.

Inzicht is published by the Association for Public Education and is strongly hostile to confessional schooling.

Onderwijs en Opvoeding is published by the pedagogical center that provides support to schools with a "general" (nonconfessional) orientation, including especially private schools with distinctive approaches. Though it devotes more space to strictly pedagogical concerns than the other journals, its preference is clearly for "encounter" schools in which all values and beliefs stand on an equal footing.

Schoolbestuur and *School en Besturen* are published by the Central Bureau for Catholic Education; the former is a monthly oriented toward news and political developments affecting Catholic schools, the latter a semimonthly oriented toward more extended discussion of policy.

Akkermans, P. W. C. *Onderwijs als Constitutioneel Probleem*. Alphen aan den Rijn: Samsom, 1980.

Akkermans, P. W. C., and J. M. G. Leune, eds. *Het bestuur van het openbaar onderwijs*. Den Bosch: Malmberg, 1983.

Bakvis, Herman. *Catholic Power in the Netherlands*. Kingston/Montreal: McGill/ Queens University Press, 1981.

Beks, H., ed. *Het Onderwijs Gekleurd: Zes Politieke en Levensbeschouwelijke Visies op het Onderwijs*. Leiden: Stafleu & Zoon, 1976.

Billiet, J. *Secularisering en Verzuiling in het Onderwijs: Een Sociologisch Onderzoek naar de Vrije Schoolkeuse als Legitimatieschema en als Sociaal Proces*. Louvain: University Press, 1977.

Branger, J. D. C.; N. L. Dodde; and W. Wielemans, eds. *Onderwijsbeleid in Nederland*. Louvain/Amersfoort: Acco, 1984.

Coleman, John A. *The Evolution of Dutch Catholicism, 1958–1974*. Berkeley: University of California Press, 1978.

Dodde, N. L. *Het Nederlandse Onderwijs verandert*. Muiderberg: Coutinho, 1983.

Driel, L. van, and I. A. Kole. *Godsdienstbeleving van Jongeren tussen Veertien en Achttien Jaar*. Kampen: Kok, n.d.

Faber, H., and T. T. ten Have. *Ontkerkelijking en Buitenkerkelijkheid in Nederland, tot 1960*. Assen: Van Gorcum, 1970.

Gadourek, I. *A Dutch Community*. 2nd ed. Groningen: Wolters, 1961.

Gielen, Jos. J. *Naar een Nieuwe Katholieke School*. 's Hertogenbosch, 1966.

Gilhuis, T. M. *De Gezamenlijke School: Voor of tegen?* Kampen: Kok, n.d.

———. *En toch is het Anders: Over de Herkenbaarheid van het Christelijk Onderwijs*. Kampen: Kok, n.d.

———. *Pleidooi voor een School met de Bijbel*. Kampen: Kok, n.d.

Goddijn, J. J. O. *Katholieke Minderheid en Protestantse Dominant: Sociologische Nawerking van de Historische Relatie tussen Katholieken en Protestanten in Nederland, en in het Bijzonder in de Provincie Friesland*. Assen: Van Gorcum, 1957.

Goddijn, W., and H. P. M. Goddijn. *Godsdienst Sociologie: Het Groepsleven van de Christenen*. Utrecht: Spectrum, 1960.

Goudsblom, Johan. *Dutch Society*. New York: Random House, 1967.

Hemert, M. J. van. *Kerkelijke Gezindten*. The Hague: Centraal Bureau voor de Statistiek, 1971.

Hollander, A. N. J. den. *Het Andere Volk: Een verkenning van Groepsoordeel en Groepsbeeld*. Leiden: Sijthoff, 1846.

Hoogma, Marianne. "Aanbod van Onderwijs strookt niet met Vraag." *Humanist,* April 1983.

Huggett, Frank E. *The Modern Netherlands*. New York: Praeger, 1971.

Idenburg, Ph. J. *Bekostiging der Onderwijsvrijheid*. Amsterdam: De Arbeiderspers, 1957.

———. *Theorie van het Onderwijsbeleid*. Groningen: Wolters-Noordhoff, 1971.

Instituut voor Toegepast Sociaalwetenschappelijk Onderzoek van de Vrije Universiteit. *Waarom naar de Christelijke School*. Amsterdam, 1974.

Janse, C. S. L. *Bewaar het Pand: De Spanning tussen Assimilatie en Persistentie bij de Emancipatie van de Bevindelijk Gereformeerden*. Houten: Den Hertog, 1985.

Kalsbeek, L. *Een School met of zonder Bijbel?* Kampen: Kok, n.d.

Kemenade, J. A. van. *De Katholieken en hun Onderwijs: Een sociologisch Onderzoek naar de Betekenis van Katholiek Onderwijs onder Ouders en Docenten*. Meppel: Boom, 1968.

————. "Verzuiling in Nederland" and "Verzuiling en Ontzuiling in het Katholiek Onderwijs." Two radio talks published in *Verzuiling en ontzuiling*. Hilversum: KRO Radio, 1969.

————, ed. *Onderwijs: Bestel en Beleid*. Groningen: Wolters-Noordhoff, 1981.

Kisjes, A. Joh., and P. A. te Velde, eds. *Het Gereformeerd Onderwijs: Identiteitsbezinning*. Kampen: Kok, 1983.

Kruijt, J. P. "Verzuiling in Beweging?" In *Pacificatie en de zuilen*, ed. J. J. Gielen et al. Meppel: Boom, 1965.

————. *Verzuiling*. Zaandijk: Heijnis, n.d.

Kruijt, J. P., and Walter Goddijn. "Verzuiling en Ontzuiling als Sociologisch Proces." In *Drift en Koers: Een Halve Eeuw Sociale Verandering in Nederland*, ed. A. N. J. Hollander et al. Assen: Van Gorcum, 1962.

Leune, J. M. G. *Onderwijsbeleid onder Druk: Een Historisch-sociologisch Onderzoek naar het Opereren van Lerarenverenigingen in het Nederlandse Onderwijsbestel*. Groningen: Tjeenk Willink, 1976.

Lievegoed, B. C. J., et al. *De Levende School: Ouders, Leraren, en Besturen rond het Kind in de Vrije Scholen*. Zeist: Vrij Geesteleven, 1980.

Lijphart, Arend. *The Politics of Accommodation: Pluralism and Democracy in the Netherlands*. Berkeley: University of California Press, 1968.

Lipschits, I. *De Protestants-christelijke Stroming tot 1940*. Deventer: Kluwer, 1977.

Matthijssen, M. A. J. M. *Katholiek Middelbaar Onderwijs en Intellectuelle Emancipatie*. Assen: Van Gorcum, 1958.

McLaughlin, S. M. Raymond. *Religious Education and the State: Democracy Finds a Way*. Washington, D.C.: Catholic University Press, 1967.

Meiden, Anne van der. *Welzalig is het Volk: De Zwarte-kousen Kerken*. Baarb: Ten Have, 1981.

Oberzee, P. van. *Het Humanisme als Levensbeschouwing in de Nederlanden*. Amsterdam: Hafkamp, 1948.

Reller, Theodore L. "Public Funds for Religious Education: Canada, England, and the Netherlands." *Religion and the Public Order*, 1963.

Schoten, Fons van, and Hans Wansink. *De Nieuwe Schoolstrijd: Knelpunten en Conflicten in de Hedendaagse Onderwijspolitiek*. Utrecht: Bohn, Scheltema, & Holkema, 1984.

Schouten, Jac. *De Doelstellingen van het Christelijk Onderwijs*. Kampen: Kok, n.d.

Steininger, Rudolf. *Polarisierung und Integration: Eine vergleichende Untersuchung der strukturellen Versaeulung der Gesellschaft in den Niederlanden und in Oesterreich*. Meisenheim: Anton Hain, 1975.

Thurlings, J. M. G. *De Wankele Zuil: Nederlandse Katholieken tussen Assimilatie en Pluralisme*. 2nd ed. Deventer: Van Loghum Slaterus, 1978.

Ven, Frans W. M. van den. *Openbaar en Bijzonder Onderwijs samen?* Groningen: Tjeenk Willink, n.d.

Verslag van het Colloquium "Opvoeden tot Waarden." The Hague: Centraal Bureau voor het Katholiek Onderwijs, 1984.

Waterink, J. "De Verzuiling in het Onderwijs." In *Pacificatie en de Zuilen*, ed. J. J. Gielen et al. Meppel: Boom, 1965.

Westerman, W. E. *Geestelijke Stromingen*. Kampen: Kok, n.d.

The Common School "Myth" in Massachusetts

History of Education in America

Bailyn, Bernard. *Education in the Forming of American Society*. New York: Random House (Vintage Books), 1960.

Bowles, Samuel, and Herbert Gintis. *Schooling in Capitalist America*. New York: Basic Books, 1976.

Callahan, Raymond E. *Education and the Cult of Efficiency: A Study of the Social Forces That Have Shaped the Administration of the Public Schools*. Chicago: University of Chicago Press (Phoenix Books), 1964.

Cohen, Sheldon S. *A History of Colonial Education, 1607–1776*. New York: Wiley, 1974.

Cremin, Lawrence A. *American Education: The Colonial Experience, 1607–1783*. New York: Harper Torchbooks, 1970.

———. *Public Education*. New York: Basic Books, 1976.

———. *Traditions of American Education*. New York: Basic Books, 1977.

———. *American Education: The National Experience, 1783–1876*. New York: Harper & Row, 1980.

Edwards, Newton, and Herman G. Richey. *The School in the American Social Order*. 2nd ed. Boston: Houghton Mifflin, 1963.

Eschenbacher, Herman. "Education and Social Unity in the Ante-bellum Period." *Harvard Educational Review* 30, no. 2 (spring 1960).

Gordon, Mary McDougall. "Patriots and Christians: A Reassessment of Nineteenth-Century School Reformers." *Journal of Social History* 11, no. 4 (summer 1978).

Kimball, Solon T., and James E. McClellan, Jr. *Education and the New America*. New York: Random House (Vintage Books), 1966.

Krug, Edward A. *The Shaping of the American High School, 1880–1920*. Madison: University of Wisconsin Press, 1969.

Lipset, Seymour Martin. *The First New Nation: The United States in Historical and Comparative Perspective*. New York: Basic Books, 1963.

Nye, Russel Blaine. *The Cultural Life of the New Nation, 1776–1830*. New York: Harper Torchbooks, 1963.

Perkinson, Henry J. *The Imperfect Panacea: American Faith in Education, 1865–1965*. New York: Random House, 1968.

Rudolph, Frederick, ed. *Essays on Education in the Early Republic*. Cambridge, Mass.: Harvard University Press (Belknap Press), 1965.

Tyack, David B. "The Kingdom of God and the Common School: Protestant Ministers and the Educational Awakening in the West." *Harvard Educational Review* 36 (1966).

————. *The One Best System: A History of American Urban Education.* Cambridge, Mass.: Harvard University Press, 1974.

————, ed. *Turning Points in American Educational History.* Waltham, Mass.: Blaisdell, 1967.

Tyack, David B., and Elisabeth Hansot. *Managers of Virtue: Public School Leadership in America, 1820–1980.* New York: Basic Books, 1982.

Welter, Rush, ed. *American Writings on Popular Education: The Nineteenth Century.* Indianapolis: Bobbs-Merrill, 1971.

Religion in American History

Ahlstrom, Sydney E. *A Religious History of the American People.* Vols. 1 and 2. Garden City, N.Y.: Doubleday, 1975.

Banner, Lois W. "Religious Benevolence as Social Control: A Critique of an Interpretation." *Journal of American History* 60, no. 1 (June 1973).

Beecher, Lyman. *Lectures on Political Atheism and Kindred Subjects.* Boston: John P. Jewett, 1852.

Carwardine, Richard. *Trans-Atlantic Revivalism: Popular Evangelicalism in Britain and America, 1790–1865.* Westport, Conn.: Greenwood Press, 1978.

Cassara, Ernest, ed. *Universalism in America: A Documentary History.* Boston: Beacon Press, 1971.

Cole, Charles C. *The Social Ideas of the Northern Evangelicals, 1826–1860.* New York: Columbia University Press, 1954.

Cross, Whitney R. *The Burned-Over District.* Ithaca, N.Y.: Cornell University Press, 1950.

Elsbree, Oliver Wendell. *The Rise of the Missionary Spirit in America.* Williamsport, Pa., 1928.

Fraser, James Walter. *Pedagogue for God's Kingdom: Lyman Beecher and the Second Great Awakening.* Lanham, Md.: University Press of America, 1985.

Gaustad, Edwin S., ed. *A Documentary History of Religion in America to the Civil War.* Grand Rapids, Mich.: Eerdmans, 1982.

————, ed. *A Documentary History of Religion in America since 1865.* Grand Rapids, Mich.: Eerdmans, 1983.

Hammond, John L. *The Politics of Benevolence.* Norwood, N.J.: Ablex, 1979.

Handy, Robert T. *A Christian America: Protestant Hopes and Historical Realities.* 2nd ed. New York: Oxford University Press, 1984.

Haroutunian, Joseph. *Piety versus Moralism: The Passing of the New England Theology.* New York: Holt, 1932.

Hatch, Nathan O. "The Christian Movement and the Demand for a Theology of the People." *Journal of American History* 62, no. 3 (December 1980).

Johnson, Paul E. *A Shopkeeper's Millennium: Society and Revivals in Rochester, New York, 1815–1837.* New York: Hill & Wang, 1978.

Koch, G. Adolf. *Republican Religion: The American Revolution and the Cult of Reason.* New York: Holt, 1933.

Lipset, Seymour Martin. "Religion and Politics." In *Religion and Social Conflict,* ed. Robert Lee and Martin E. Marty. New York: Oxford University Press, 1964.

Lovelace, Richard F. "Evangelical Revivals and the Presbyterian Tradition." *Westminster Theological Journal* 42, no. 1 (fall 1979).

May, Henry F. *The Enlightenment in America.* Oxford: Oxford University Press, 1976.

McLoughlin, William G. *Revivals, Awakenings, and Reform.* Chicago: University of Chicago Press, 1978.

Niebuhr, H. Richard. *The Social Sources of Denominationalism* (1929). New York: New American Library, 1975.

Noll, Mark A.; Nathan O. Hatch; and George M. Marsden. *The Search for Christian America.* Westchester, Ill.: Crossway, 1983.

Reichley, A. James. *Religion in American Public Life.* Washington, D.C.: Brookings Institution, 1985.

Reist, Benjamin A. "Church and State in America." In *Religion and Social Conflict,* ed. Robert Lee and Martin E. Marty. New York: Oxford University Press, 1964.

Sandeen, Ernest R. *The Roots of Fundamentalism.* Chicago: University of Chicago Press, 1970.

———, ed. *The Bible and Social Reform.* Philadelphia: Fortress, 1982.

Schaff, Phillip. *America.* Edited by Perry Miller. Cambridge, Mass.: Harvard University Press, 1961.

Seldes, Gilbert. *The Stammering Century* (1928). New York: Harper & Row, 1965.

Smith, Timothy L. *Revivalism and Social Reform: American Protestantism on the Eve of the Civil War.* Baltimore: Johns Hopkins University Press, 1980.

Stoeffler, F. Ernest, ed. *Continental Pietism and Early American Christianity.* Grand Rapids, Mich.: Eerdmans, 1976.

Religion and Public Education

Allyn, Robert. *An Appeal to Christians: Universal Education the Duty of Christians.* East Greenwich, R.I.: John B. Lincoln, 1853.

American Bible Society. *Annual Reports.* New York, 1831–46.

American Journal of Education. August 1856–June 1858.

Beecher, Catharine E. *Religious Training of Children in the School, the Family, and the Church.* New York: Harper & Brothers, 1864.

Beman, Lamar T. *Religious Teaching in the Public Schools.* New York, 1927.

The Biblical Repertory and Theological Review (later, . . . *and Princeton Review*). 1830–1844.

Biblitheca Sacra and American Biblical Repository. Andover, Mass. 1851–71.

Brown, Samuel Windsor. *The Secularization of American Education.* New York: Teachers College Press, 1912.

Cheever, George B. *Right of the Bible in Our Public Schools.* New York: Robert Carter, 1854.

Christian Review. New York, April 1851–July 1853.

Dewey, John. *A Common Faith.* New Haven and London: Yale University Press, 1934.

Fellman, David, ed. *The Supreme Court and Education.* 3rd ed. New York: Teachers College Press, 1976.

Ford, Paul Leicester, ed. *The New England Primer* (1897). New York: Teachers College Press, 1962.

Grimké, Thomas S. *Address on the Expediency and Duty of Adopting the Bible as a Class Book in Every Scheme of Education from the Primary School to the University.* Charleston, S.C., 1829.

———. *Essay on the Appropriate Use of the Bible, in Common-Education.* "Prepared for the American Lyceum." Charleston, S.C., 1833.

Herberg, Will. "Religion and Education in America." In *Religious Perspectives in American Culture,* ed. James Ward Smith and A. Leland Jamison. Princeton, N.J.: Princeton University Press, 1961.

Holtz, Adrian Augustus. *A Study of the Moral and Religious Elements in American Secondary Education up to 1800.* Chicago: University of Chicago Press, 1917.

Littlefield, George Emery. *Early Schools and School-books of New England.* New York: Russell & Russell, 1965.

McCluskey, Neil G. *Public Schools and Moral Education: The Influence of Horace Mann, William Torrey Harris, and John Dewey.* New York: Columbia University Press, 1958.

Michaelson, Robert. *Piety in the Public School.* National Council on Religion and Public Education, 1970.

Mosier, Richard D. *Making the American Mind: Social and Moral Ideas in the McGuffey Readers.* New York: Russell & Russell, 1965.

Perkinson, Henry J. "The Role of Religion in American Education: An Historical Interpretation." *Paedagogica Historica* 5, no. 1 (1965).

Pfeffer, Leo. *Church, State, and Freedom.* 2nd ed. Boston: Beacon Press, 1967.

———. *God, Caesar, and the Constitution.* Boston: Beacon Press, 1975.

Rushdoony, Rousas John. *The Messianic Character of American Education.* Nutley, N.J.: Craig Press, 1979.

Spear, Samuel T. *Religion and the State; or, The Bible and the Public Schools.* New York: Dodd, Mead, 1876.

Taylor, Marvin J. *Religious and Moral Education.* New York, 1965.

Webster, Daniel. *Legal Arguments and Diplomatic Papers.* Vol. II in *The Writings and Speeches.* Boston: Little, Brown, 1903.

The Context of Educational Reform, 1825–1855

Bender, Thomas. *Toward an Urban Vision: Ideas and Institutions in Nineteenth Century America.* Baltimore: Johns Hopkins University Press, 1975.

Benson, Lee. *The Concept of Jacksonian Democracy: New York as a Test Case.* Princeton, N.J.: Princeton Paperbacks, 1970.

Boorstin, Daniel J. *The Americans: The National Experience.* New York: Random House, 1965.

Boyer, Paul. *Urban Masses and Moral Order in America, 1820–1920.* Cambridge, Mass.: Harvard University Press, 1978.

Brown, Richard D. "The Emergence of Urban Society in Rural Massachusetts, 1760–1820." *Journal of American History* 61, no. 1 (June 1974).

Dalzell, Robert F., Jr. *Daniel Webster and the Trial of American Nationalism, 1843–1852.* New York: Norton, 1975.

Dangerfield, George. *The Awakening of American Nationalism, 1815–1828.* New York: Harper Torchbooks, 1965.

Darling, Arthur Burr. *Political Changes in Massachusetts, 1824–1848: A Study of Liberal Movements in Politics.* New Haven: Yale University Press, 1925.

Eaton, Clement, ed. *The Leaven of Democracy: The Growth of the Democratic Spirit in the Time of Jackson.* New York: Braziller, 1963.

Faulkner, Harold U. "Political History of Massachusetts." In *Commonwealth History of Massachusetts,* vol. 4, ed. Albert Bushnell Hart. New York: States History, 1930.

Hammett, Theodore M. "Two Mobs of Jacksonian Boston: Ideology and Interest." *Journal of American History* 62, no. 4 (March 1976).

Kasson, John F. *Civilizing the Machine: Technology and Republican Values in America, 1776–1900.* New York: Penguin Books, 1977.

Meyers, Marvin. *The Jacksonian Persuasion: Politics and Belief.* New York: Random House (Vintage Books), 1960.

Miller, Perry. *The Life of the Mind in America from the Revolution to the Civil War.* New York: Harcourt Brace & World, 1965.

Nagel, Paul C. *One Nation Indivisible: The Union in American Thought, 1776–1861.* New York: Oxford University Press, 1964.

Pessen, Edward. *Jacksonian America: Society, Personality, and Politics.* Rev. ed. Urbana: University of Illinois Press, 1985.

Poulson, Barry W. "Education and the Family during the Industrial Revolution." In Joseph R. Peden and Fred R. Glahe, eds., *The American Family and the State.* San Francisco: Pacific Research Institute for Public Policy, 1986.

Robinson, William A. *Jeffersonian Democracy in New England* (1916). New York: Greenwood Press, 1968.

Schlesinger, Arthur M., Jr. *The Age of Jackson.* Boston: Little, Brown, 1945.

Tocqueville, Alexis de. *Democracy in America.* Vols. 1 and 2. Edited by Henry Reeve, Francis Bowen, and Phillips Bradley. New York: Random House (Vintage Books), 1945.

Tyler, Alice Felt. *Freedom's Ferment: Phases of American Social History from the Colonial Period to the Outbreak of the Civil War* (1944). New York: Harper Torchbooks, 1962.

Van Deusen, Glyndon G. *The Jacksonian Era, 1828–1848.* New York: Harper Torchbooks, 1959.

European Models

Arnold, Matthew. *The Popular Education of France, with Notices of That of Hollnd and Switzerland.* London: Longmans, Green, 1861.

Bache, Alexander Dallas. *Report on Education in Europe to the Trustees of the Girard College for Orphans.* Philadelphia: Lydia Bailey, 1839.

Barnard, Henry. *National Education in Europe.* 2nd ed. New York: Norton, 1854.

———. *Systems, Institutions, and Statistics of Public Instruction in Different Countries.* New York: Steiger, 1872.

Brooks, Charles. *Remarks on Europe Relating to Education, Peace, and Labor; and Their Reference to the United States.* New York: Francis, 1846.

Carstens, Henry W. *School Education in Germany.* Boston: James Monroe, 1858.

Combe, George. *The Constitution of Man Considered in Relation to External Objects.* Boston: Carter & Hendee, 1829. 6th American ed. from 2nd English ed., with an additional chapter on the harmony between phrenology and revelation by Joseph A. Warne. Boston: Ticknor, 1838.

———. *Notes on the United States of North America during a Phrenological Visit in 1838–9–40.* Vols. 1 and 2. Philadelphia: Carey & Hart, 1841.

———. *Education: Its Principles and Practice.* Edited by William Jolly. London: Macmillan, 1870.

Cousin, Victor. *Etat de l'instruction primaire dans le Royaume de Prusse à la fin de l'année 1831.* Paris: Lévrault, 1833.

———. *Report on the State of Public Instruction in Prussia.* Translated by Sarah Austin. New York: Wiley & Long, 1835 (also, London: E. Wilson, 1834).

———. *De l'instruction publique en Hollande.* Paris: Lévrault, 1837.

———. *On the State of Education in Holland as Regards Schools for the Working Classes and for the Poor.* Translated by Leonard Horner. London: John Murray, 1838.

Dyson, A. E., and Julian Lovelock, eds. *Education and Democracy.* London: Routledge & Kegan Paul, 1975.

Edgeworth, Maria, and Richard Lovell Edgeworth. *Practical Education.* New York: Harper & Brothers, 1835.

Griscom, John. *A Year in Europe, Comprising a Journal of Observations . . . in 1818 and 1819.* Vols. 1 and 2. New York: Collins, 1823.

Hickson, W. E. *An Account of the Present State of Education in Holland, Belgium, and the German States . . .* London: Taylor, 1840.

Hill, Frederic. *National Education: Its Present State and Prospects.* Vol. 1. London: Charles Knight, 1836.

Humphrey, Heman. *Great Britain, France, and Belgium: A Short Tour of 1835.* Vols. 1 and 2. New York: Harper & Brothers, 1838.

Kaestle, Carl F., ed. *Joseph Lancaster and the Monitorial School Movement: A Documentary History.* New York: Teachers College Press, 1973.

Russell, William. *Manual of Mutual Instruction: Consisting of Mr. Fowle's Directions for Introducing in Common Schools the Improved System Adopted by the Monitorial School, Boston.* Boston: Wait & Greene, 1826.

354

Sagra, Ramón de la. *Cinco Meses en los Estados Unidos de la America del Norte.* Paris: Renouard, 1836.

Sketch of the Improved Method of Education Employed by Dr. Bell, in the Asylum at Madrass; by J. Lancaster, in London; and lately introduced into several schools for poor children in New York and Philadelphia. Philadelphia: Kimber & Conrad, 1809.

Stowe, Calvin E. *The Prussian System of Public Instruction and Its Applicability to the United States.* Cincinnati: Truman & Smith, 1836.

————. *Report on Elementary Public Instruction in Europe, Made to the Thirty-Sixth General Assembly of the State of Ohio, December 19, 1837, Reprinted by Order of the House of Representatives of the Legislature of Massachusetts, March 29, 1838.* Boston: Dutton & Wentworth, 1838. Similar edition printed in Harrisburg, 1838, "by Order of the House of Representatives of Pennsylvania," etc.

————. *Common Schools and Teachers' Seminaries.* Boston: Marsh, Capen, Lyon, Webb, 1839.

Ulich, Robert. *A Sequence of Educational Influences.* Cambridge, Mass.: Harvard University Press, 1935.

Van Bokkelen, L. "Compulsory Education." *Circular of Information of the Bureau of Education for December 1871.* Washington, D.C.: Government Printing Office, 1872.

Education and Religion in Massachusetts, 1825–1855

PRIMARY

American Institute of Instruction. *Memorial to the Honorable, the Legislature of the Commonwealth of Massachusetts.* February 1836.

Barnard, Henry. *American Educational Biography.* New York, 1859.

Beecher, Lyman, ed. *The Spirit of the Pilgrims.* Vols. 1–5. Boston, 1828–32.

Blagden, G. W. *The Effects of Education upon a Country Village: An Address Delivered before the Brighton School Fund Corporation, March 30, 1828.* Boston, 1828.

Braman, Milton P. *A Discourse Delivered before His Excellency George N. Briggs, Governor . . . on the Annual Election, January 1, 1845.* Boston: Dutton & Wentworth, 1845.

Briggs, George N. "Inaugural Address". (January 4, 1845). In *Acts and Resolves passed by the General Court of Massachusetts in the Years 1843, 1844, 1845; Together with the Rolls and Messages.* Boston: Dutton & Wentworth, 1845.

Brooks, Charles. *Elementary Instruction: An Address Delivered before the Schools and Citizens of the Town of Quincy, July 4, 1837.* Quincy, Mass.: John A. Green, 1837.

————. "Moral Education: The Best Methods of Teaching Morals in the Common Schools." *American Journal of Education,* March 1856.

————. *An Appeal to the Legislatures of the United States in Relation to Public Schools.* Cambridge, Mass.: John Wilson, 1867.

355

Carter, James G. *Letters . . . on the Free Schools of New England, with Remarks upon the Principles of Instruction*. Boston: Cummings, Hilliard, 1824.

———. *Essays upon Popular Education, Containing a Particular Examination of the Schools of Massachusetts and an Outline of an Institution for the Instruction of Teachers*. Boston: Bowles & Dearborn, 1826.

Channing, William Ellery. *Works*. Vol. 1. Boston: American Unitarian Association, 1903.

Chapin, E. H. *The Relation of the Individual to the Republic: A Sermon Delivered before His Excellency Marcus Morton, Governor at the Annual Election, on Wednesday, January 3, 1844*. Boston: Dutton & Wentworth, 1844.

Common School Controversy; consisting of three letters of the Secretary of the Board of Education . . . in reply to charges preferred against the Board by the Editor of the Christian Witness and by Edward A. Newton, Esq. . . . Boston: Bradley, 1844.

Emmons, Nathanael. *Sermons on Various Subjects of Christian Doctrine and Duty*. Edited by Jacob Ide. New York: Dodd, 1850.

Emerson, George B. "Lecture on Moral Education." Pamphlet in Boston Public Library, no publication information.

———. *Observations on a Pamphlet entitled "Remarks on the Seventh Annual Report of the Hon Horace Mann, Secretary of the Massachusetts Board of Education."* N.d. (1844?).

———. *History and Design of the American Institute of Instruction*. Boston: Ticknor, Reed, & Fields, 1849.

———. *Education in Massachusetts: Early Legislation and History*. Boston: Wilson, 1869.

Everett, Edward. "Address" (January 12, 1837). In *Resolves of the General Court of the Commonwealth of Massachusetts, passed at the several sessions commencing January 1835 and ending April 1838*. Boston: Dutton & Wentworth, 1838.

———. *Orations and Speeches on Various Occasions*. 5th ed. Vol. 2. Boston: Little, Brown, 1859.

Foster, B. F. *Education Reform: A Review of Wyse on the Necessity of a National System of Education*. New York: Wiley & Putnam, 1837.

Hodge, Charles. "The Latest Form of Infidelity." In *Essays and Reviews Selected from "The Princeton Review."* New York: Robert Carter, 1857.

Hudson, C. F. *Debt and Grace, as Related to the Doctrine of a Future Life*. 5th ed. Boston: Jewett, 1859.

———. *Human Destiny: A Critique on Universalism*. New York: Carleton, 1862.

Humphrey, Heman. *Miscellaneous Discourses and Reviews*. Amherst, Mass.: Adams, 1834.

Jackson, Samuel C. *Religious Principle—a Source of Public Prosperity: A Sermon Delivered before His Excellency John Davis, Governor . . . at the Annual Election, on Saturday, January 7, 1843*. Boston: Dutton & Wentworth, 1843.

Laws of the Commonwealth of Massachusetts. Vol. 10. Boston, 1828.

Mann, Horace. *First Annual Report of the Secretary of the Board*. Boston: Dutton & Wentworth, 1838.

————. *Second Annual Report of the Secretary of the Board.* Boston: Dutton & Wentworth, 1839.

————. *Third Annual Report of the Secretary of the Board.* Boston: Dutton & Wentworth, 1840.

————. *Fourth Annual Report of the Secretary of the Board.* Boston: Dutton & Wentworth, 1841.

————. *Fifth Annual Report of the Secretary of the Board.* Boston: Dutton & Wentworth, 1842.

————. *Sixth Annual Report of the Secretary of the Board.* Boston: Dutton & Wentworth, 1843.

————. *Seventh Annual Report of the Secretary of the Board.* Boston: Dutton & Wentworth, 1844.

————. *Eighth Annual Report of the Secretary of the Board.* Boston: Dutton & Wentworth, 1845.

————. *Ninth Annual Report of the Secretary of the Board.* Boston: Dutton & Wentworth, 1846.

————. *Tenth Annual Report of the Secretary of the Board.* Boston: Dutton & Wentworth, 1847.

————. *Eleventh Annual Report of the Secretary of the Board.* Boston: Dutton & Wentworth, 1848.

————. *Twelfth Annual Report of the Secretary of the Board.* Boston: Dutton & Wentworth, 1849.

————. *Reply to the "Remarks" of Thirty-one Boston Schoolmasters on the Seventh Annual Report* . . . Boston, 1844.

————. *Lectures on Education* (1855). New York, 1969.

————, ed. *Common School Journal* 1–10 (November 1838–December 1848).

Mann, Mary Peabody. *Life of Horace Mann, by His Wife.* Centennial Facsimile Edition. Washington, D.C.: National Education Association, 1937.

May, Samuel J. "Address." In *Memorial of the Quarter-Centennial Celebration of the Establishment of Normal Schools in America, Held at Framingham, July 1, 1864.* Boston: Moody, 1866.

Moore, Martin. *A Brief History of the Evangelical Churches of Boston, together with a more particular account of the Revival of 1842.* Boston: Putnam, 1842.

Morton, Marcus. "Governor's Address" (January 22, 1840). In *Acts and Resolves passed by the General Court of Massachusetts in the Years 1839, 1840, 1841, 1842; together with the Rolls and Messages.* Boston: Dutton & Wentworth, 1842.

————. "Inaugural Address" (January 20, 1843). In *Acts and Resolves passed by the General Court of Massachusetts in the Years 1843, 1844, 1845; together with the Rolls and Messages.* Boston: Dutton & Wentworth, 1845.

Neale, Rollin H. *A Sermon Delivered before His Excellency George S. Boutwell, Governor* . . . *at the Annual Election, January 8, 1852.* Boston: Dutton & Wentworth, 1852.

Pierce, John. *A Discourse before His Excellency George N. Briggs, Governor* . . . *at the Annual Election, Wednesday, 3 Jan. 1849.* Boston: Dutton & Wentworth, 1849.

Putnam, George. *A Sermon Delivered before His Excellency George N. Briggs, Governor . . . at the Annual Election, Wednesday, Jan. 7, 1846*. Boston: Dutton & Wentworth, 1846.

———. *Sermons Preached in the Church of the First Religious Society in Roxbury*. Boston: Houghton, Osgood, 1879.

[Quint, Alonzo Hall]. *The Normal Schools of Massachusetts*. "Reprinted, with some omissions, from the *Congregational Quarterly* for January, 1861." N.p., n.d.

Raymond, Miner. *A Sermon Delivered before His Excellency John H. Clifford, Governor . . . at the Annual Election, Wednesday, January 4, 1854*. Boston: William White, 1854.

Reply to Three Letters of the Rev. Lyman Beecher, D. D. against the Calvinisitic Doctrine of Infant Damnation (expanded from The Christian Examiner). Boston, 1829.

Robbins, Thomas. *Diary, 1796–1854*. Edited by Increase N. Tarbox. Boston: Beacon Press, 1887.

Sears, Barnas. *Fifteenth Annual Report of the Secretary of the Board*. Boston: Dutton & Wentworth, 1852.

———. *Seventeenth Annual Report of the Secretary of the Board*. Boston: William White, 1854.

———. *Eighteenth Annual Report of the Secretary of the Board*. Boston: William White, 1855.

———. *Nineteenth Annual Report of the Secretary of the Board*. Boston: William White, 1856.

Smith, Matthew Hale. *Universalism Examined, Renounced, Exposed*. Boston: Tappan and Dennet, 1842.

———. *The Bible, the Rod, and Religion, in the Common Schools*. Boston: Redding, 1847.

———. *Reply to the Sequel of Hon. Horace Mann*. Boston: Whittemore, 1847.

Stearns, Eben S. "Historical Sketch." In *Memorial of the Quarter Centennial Celebration of the Establishment of Normal Schools in America, Held at Framingham, July 1, 1864*. Boston: Moody, 1866.

Storrs, Richard S. *A Sermon Delivered before His Excellency Edward Everett, Governor . . . on the Anniversary Election, January 3, 1838*. Boston: Dutton & Wentworth, 1838.

Stowe, Calvin E. *The Religious Element in Education: An Address delivered before the American Institute of Instruction*. Boston: Ticknor, 1844.

Twistleton, Edward. *Evidence as to the Religious Working of the Common Schools of the State of Massachusetts*. London: Ridgway, 1854.

Tyler, Bennet. *New England Revivals, as They Existed at the Close of the Eighteenth, and the Beginning of the Nineteenth Centuries*. Boston: Massachusetts Sabbath School Society, 1846.

Ware, Henry. *A Sermon Delivered at Dorchester, before the Evangelical Missionary Society in Massachusetts at Their Semi-annual Meeting, June 7, 1820*. Boston: Burditt, 1820.

[Withington, Leonard]. *Penitential Tears; or, A Cry from the Dust by the "Thirty-one" Prostrated and Pulverized by the Hand of Horace Mann* ... Boston, 1845.

SECONDARY

Bidwell, Charles E. "The Moral Significance of the Common School: A Sociological Study of Local Patterns of School Control and Moral Education in Massachusetts and New York, 1837–1840." *History of Education Quarterly*, fall 1966.

Blumenfeld, Samuel L. *Is Public Education Necessary?* Old Greenwich, Conn.: Devin-Adair, 1981.

Butler, Vera M. *Education as Revealed by New England Newspapers Prior to 1850.* Philadelphia, 1935.

Compayré, Gabriel. *Horace Mann et l'école publique aux Etats-Unis.* Paris: Delaplane, n.d. (1905?).

Cooke, George Willis. *Unitarianism in America: A History of Its Origin and Development.* Boston: American Unitarian Association, 1902.

Culver, Raymond B. *Horace Mann and Religion in the Massachusetts Public Schools.* New Haven: Yale University Press, 1929.

Dunn, William Kailer. *What Happened to Religious Education? The Decline of Religious Teaching in the Public Elementary School, 1776–1861.* Baltimore: Johns Hopkins University Press, 1958.

Englizian, H. Crosby. *Brimstone Corner: Park Street Church, Boston.* Chicago: Moody Press, 1968.

Filler, Louis, ed. *Wendall Phillips on Civil Rights and Freedom.* New York: Hill & Wang, 1965.

Fraser, James W.; Henry L. Allen; and Sam Barnes, eds. *From Common School to Magnet School: Selected Essays in the History of Boston's Schools.* Boston: Trustees of the Public Library, 1979.

Hovey, Alvah. *Barnas Sears: A Christian Educator, His Making and Work.* New York: Silver, Burdett, 1902.

Howe, Daniel Walker. *The Unitarian Conscience: Harvard Moral Philosophy, 1805–1861.* Cambridge, Mass.: Harvard University Press, 1970.

Hutchison, Keith R. "'James Gordon Carter: Educational Reformer.'" *New England Quarterly* 16, no. 3 (September 1943).

Jackson, George Leroy. *The Development of School Support in Colonial Massachusetts.* New York: Teachers College Press, 1909.

Kaestle, Carl F., and Maris A. Vinovskis. *Education and Social Change in Nineteenth-century Massachusetts.* Cambridge: Cambridge University Press, 1980.

Katz, Michael B. *The Irony of Early School Reform: Educational Innovation in Mid-Nineteenth Century Massachusetts.* Boston: Beacon Paperback, 1970.

———. *Class, Bureaucracy, and Schools.* New York, 1971.

Littlefield, George Emery. *Early Schools and School-books of New England.* New York: Russell & Russell, 1965.

Martin, George Henry. *The Evolution of the Massachusetts Public School System.* New York and London: Appleton, 1915.

Mattingly, Paul H. *The Classless Profession: American Schoolmen in the Nineteenth Century.* New York: New York University Press, 1975.

Messerli, Jonathan. *Horace Mann: A Biography.* New York: Knopf, 1972.

Meyer, James Conrad. *Church and State in Massachusetts from 1740 to 1833: A Chapter in the History of the Development of Individual Freedom.* Cleveland: Western Reserve University Press, 1930.

Phillips, Joseph W. *Jedidiah Morse and New England Congregationalism.* New Brunswick, N.J.: Rutgers University Press, 1983.

Richards, William C. *Great in Goodness: A Memoir of George N. Briggs.* Boston: Gould & Lincoln, 1866.

Schultz, Stanley K. *The Culture Factory: Boston Public Schools, 1789–1860.* New York: Oxford University Press, 1973.

Smith, Sherman M. *Religious Education in Massachusetts.* Syracuse, N.Y., 1926.

Wilbur, Earl Morse. *History of Unitarianism in Transylvania, England, and America.* Cambridge, Mass.: Harvard University Press, 1952.

Wilkie, Jane Riblett. "Social Status, Acculturation and School Attendance in 1850 Boston." *Journal of Social History* 11, no. 2 (winter 1977).

Winship, Albert E. "Education." In *Commonwealth History of Massachusetts,* vol. 4, ed. Albert Bushnell Hart. New York: States History, 1930.

Wright, Conrad. *The Beginnings of Unitarianism in America.* Boston: Starr King Press, 1955.

Education in Connecticut

Bushnell, Horace. *Discourses on Christian Nurture.* Boston: Massachusetts Sabbath School Society, 1847.

———. "Common Schools: A Discourse on the Modifications Demanded by the Roman Catholics" (1853). In Rush Welter, ed., *American Writings on Popular Education: The Nineteenth Century.* Indianapolis: Bobbs-Merrill, 1971.

———. *Life and Letters.* New York: Harper & Brothers, 1880.

"Bushnell on Christian Nurture." *Christian Examiner* (Boston), November 1847.

Hodge, Charles. "Bushnell on Christian Nurture." In *Essays and Reviews Selected from the Princeton Review.* New York: Robert Carter, 1857.

Keller, Charles Roy. *The Second Great Awakening in Connecticut.* Archon Books, 1968.

Lannie, Vincent P., ed. *Henry Barnard: American Educator.* New York: Teachers College Press, 1974.

Smith, H. Shelton, ed. *Horace Bushnell.* New York: Oxford University Press, 1965.

Stewart, George, Jr. *A History of Religious Education in Connecticut to the Middle of the Nineteenth Century.* New Haven: Yale University Press, 1924.

Thompson, Ernest Trice. *Changing Emphases in American Preaching* (including Bushnell). Philadelphia: Westminster, 1943.

National Unity through the Common School

IMMIGRATION AND NATIVIST REACTION

Abbott, Edith. *Historical Aspects of the Immigration Problem: Selected Documents.* Chicago: University of Chicago Press, 1926.

———, ed. *Immigration: Selected Documents and Case Records.* Chicago: University of Chicago Press, 1924.

"An American." *Imminent Dangers to the Free Institutions of the United States through Foreign Immigration . . . originally published in the New-York Journal of Commerce.* New York: Clayton, 1835.

Anderson, Arlow William. *The Immigrant Takes His Stand: The Norwegian-American Press and Public Affairs, 1847–1872.* Northfield, Minn., 1953.

Baum, Dale. "Know-Nothingism and the Republican Majority in Massachusetts: The Political Realignment of the 1850s," *Journal of American History* 64, no. 4 (March 1978).

Billington, Ray Allen. *The Protestant Crusade, 1800–1860: A Study of the Origins of American Nativism.* Chicago: Quadrangle Paperbacks (original edition Macmillan, 1938), 1964.

Curran, Thomas J. *Xenophobia and Immigration, 1820–1930.* Boston: Twayne Publishers, 1975.

David, Lawrence B. *Immigrants, Baptists, and the Protestant Mind in America.* Urbana: University of Illinois Press, 1973.

Dolan, Jay P. *The Immigrant Church: New York's Irish and German Catholics, 1815–1865.* Baltimore: Johns Hopkins University Press, 1975.

Gardner, Henry J. "Inaugural Address." In *Acts and Resolves of 1855.* Boston, 1855.

Gordon, Milton M. *Assimilation in American Life: The Role of Race, Religion, and National Origins.* New York: Oxford University Press, 1964.

Grant, Madison, and Charles Stewart Davison, eds. *The Alien in Our Midst; or, "Selling Our Birthright for a Mess of Pottage."* New York: Galton, 1930.

Handlin, Oscar. *The Uprooted.* New York: Grosset & Dunlap, 1951.

———. *Boston's Immigrants: A Study in Acculturation.* 2nd ed. New York: Atheneum, 1968.

———, ed. *Immigration as a Factor in American History.* Englewood Cliffs, N.J.: Prentice-Hall, 1959.

Hansen, Marcus Lee. *The Atlantic Migration, 1607–1860.* New York: Harper Torchbooks, 1961.

Higham, John. *Strangers in the Land: Patterns of American Nativism, 1860–1925.* New York: Atheneum, 1972.

Hofstadter, Richard. *Social Darwinism in American Thought.* Boston: Beacon Press, 1955.

Jenks, Jeremiah W., and W. Jett Lauck. *The Immigration Problem: A Study of*

American Immigration Conditions and Needs. 6th ed. Edited by Rufus D. Smith. New York: Funk & Wagnalls, 1926.

Jones, Maldwyn Allen. *American Immigration.* Chicago: University of Chicago Press, 1960.

[Morse, Samuel F. B.]. *Foreign Conspiracy against the Liberties of the United States: The Numbers of Brutus originally published in the New-York Observer.* New York: Leavitt, Lord, 1835.

Osofsky, Gilbert. "Abolitionists, Irish Immigrants, and the Dilemmas of Romantic Nationalism." *American Historical Review* 80, no. 4 (October 1975).

Report of the Committee on Immigration on the Problem of Immigration in Massachusetts. Boston, 1914.

Solomon, Barbara Miller. "The Intellectual Background of the Immigration Restriction Movement in New England." *New England Quarterly* 25, no. 1 (March 1952).

Thayer, Mrs. Nathaniel. "The Immigrants." In *Commonwealth History of Massachusetts,* vol. 4, ed. Albert Bushnell Hart. New York: States History, 1930.

SCHOOLING THE IMMIGRANT

Brumberg, Stephan F. "Tales out of School: Reports of East European Jewish Immigrants in New York City Schools, 1893–1917." *Issues in Education* 2, no. 2 (fall 1984).

Davis, Philip, ed. *Immigration and Americanization: Selected Readings.* Boston: Ginn, 1920.

Farrell, John Joseph. "The Immigrant and the School in New York City: A Program for Citizenship." Ed.D. dissertation, Stanford University, n.d.

Hartmann, Edward George. *The Movement to Americanize the Immigrant.* New York: Columbia University Press, 1948.

Hill, Frank A. *Sixty-fifth Annual Report of the Secretary of the Board of Education.* Boston: Wright & Potter, 1902.

———. *Sixty-sixth Annual Report of the Secretary of the Board of Education.* Boston: Wright & Potter, 1903.

Issel, William. "Americanization, Acculturation, and Social Control: School Reform Ideology in Industrial Pennsylvania, 1880–1910." *Journal of Social History* 12, no. 4 (summer 1979).

Martin, George H. *Sixty-ninth Annual Report of the Secretary of the Board of Education.* Boston, 1906.

———. *Seventieth Annual Report of the Secretary of the Board of Education.* Boston, 1907.

Peterson, Paul E. *The Politics of School Reform, 1870–1940.* Chicago: University of Chicago Press, 1985.

Rothbard, Murray N. "The Progressive Era and the Family." In Joseph R. Peden and Fred R. Glahe, eds. *The American Family and the State.* San Francisco: Pacific Research Institute for Public Policy, 1986.

Thompson, Frank V. *Schooling of the Immigrant* (1920). In *Americanization Studies: The Acculturation of Immigrant Groups into American Society,* ed. William S. Bernard. Montclair, N.J.: Patterson Smith, 1971.

THE THREAT OF DENOMINATIONAL SCHOOLING

Beck, Walter H. *Lutheran Elementary Schools in the United States*. St. Louis: Concordia, 1965.

Bratt, James D. *Dutch Calvinism in Modern America: A History of a Conservative Subculture*. Grand Rapids, Mich.: Eerdmans, 1984.

Bulletins for the Constitutional Convention, 1917–1918. Vol. 2. Boston: Wright & Potter, 1919.

Burns, J. A. *The Growth and Development of the Catholic School System in the United States*. New York: Benziger, 1912.

Carper, James C., and Thomas C. Hunt. *Religious Schooling in America*. Birmingham, Ala.: Religious Education Press, 1984.

"Committee of One Hundred." *The Public Schools Must Go! The Fiat Has Gone Forth from the Vatican*. Boston, 1888.

————. *The Great Victory in Boston*. Boston, 1888.

————. *An Open Letter to the Friends of Free Schools and American Liberties*. Boston, 1888.

Curran, Francis X. *The Churches and the Schools: American Protestantism and Popular Elementary Education*. Chicago: Loyola University Press, 1954.

Debates in the Massachusetts Constitutional Convention, 1917–1918. Boston: Wright & Potter, 1919.

de Boer, Peter, and Donald Oppewal. "American Calvinist Day Schools." *Christian Scholars Review* 13, no. 2 (1984).

Gregg, David. *Public Schools versus Parochial Schools*. Marlboro, Mass.: "The American" Publications, 1888.

La Noue, George R. "Religious Schools and 'Secular' Subjects: An Analysis of the Premises of Title III, Section 305 of the National Defense Education Act." *Harvard Educational Review* 32, no. 3 (summer 1962).

Lord, Robert H.; John E. Sexton; and Edward T. Harrington. *A History of the Archdiocese of Boston in the Various Stages of Development*. New York: Sheed & Ward, 1944.

McCluskey, Neil G., ed. *Catholic Education in America: A Documentary History*. New York: Teachers College Press, 1964.

McLachlan, James. *American Boarding Schools: A Historical Study*. New York: Scribner, 1970.

Merk, Lois Bannister. "Boston's Historic Public School Crisis." *New England Quarterly* 31, no. 2 (June 1958).

Notes of Hearings before the Committee on Education and Labor, United States Senate . . . on the Joint Resolution (S.R. 86) Proposing an Amendment to the Constitution . . . Respecting Establishments of Religion and Free Public Schools. Washington, D.C.: Government Printing Office, 1889.

Ravitch, Diane. *The Great School Wars, New York City, 1805–1973: A History of the Public Schools as Battlefield of Social Change*. New York: Basic Books, 1974.

Sherrill, Lewis Joseph. *Presbyterian Parochial Schools, 1846–1870*. New Haven: Yale University Press, 1932.

Walsh, Louis S. *The Early Catholic Schools of Lowell, Massachusetts, 1835–1852*. Boston: Whalen, 1901.

Since 1970: The Common School under Attack

In addition to the following, material and information are drawn from the journal *Equity and Choice,* published by the Institute for Responsive Education at Boston University, and the newsletter *Educational Choice,* published by the Clearinghouse on Educational Choice.

Arons, Stephen. *Compelling Belief: The Culture of American Schooling.* Amherst: University of Massachusetts Press, 1986.

Arons, Stephen, and Charles Lawrence. "The Manipulation of Consciousness: A First Amendment Critique of Schooling." *Harvard Civil Rights/Civil Liberties Law Review* 15 (1980). A version of this article apperas also in Robert B. Everhart, ed., *The Public School Monopoly: A Critical Analysis of Education and the State in American Society.* San Francisco: Pacific Institute, 1982.

Blumenfeld, Samuel L. *N.E.A.: Trojan Horse in American Education.* Boise: Paradigm, 1984.

Campbell, Roald F.; Luvern L. Cunningham; and Roderick F. McPhee. *The Organization and Control of American Schools.* Columbus, Ohio: Merrill, 1965.

Carper, James C., and Thomas C. Hunt. *Religious Schooling in America.* Birmingham, Ala.: Religious Education Press, 1984.

Cibulka, James G.; Timothy J. O'Brien; and Donald Zewe, S.J. *Inner-City Private Elementary Schools: A Study.* Milwaukee: Marquette University Press, 1982.

Coons, John E., and Stephen D. Sugarman. *Education by Choice: The Case for Family Control.* Berkeley: University of California Press, 1978.

Cord, Robert L. *Separation of Church and State: Historical Fact and Current Fiction.* New York: Lambeth Press, 1982.

Doyle, Denis. "Family Choice in Education: The Case of Denmark, Holland, and Australia." National Institute of Education Contract no. EPA 30032, 1984.

———. "From Theory to Practice: Considerations for Implementing a Statewide Voucher System." Sequoia Institute, 1984.

Doyle, Denis, and Chester E. Finn. "Educational Quality and Family Choice: Toward a Statewide Public School Voucher Plan." Manuscript, 1983.

Elam, Stanley M., ed. *A Decade of Gallup Polls of Attitudes toward Education, 1969–1978.* Bloomington, Ind.: Phi Delta Kappa, 1978.

Everhart, Robert B., ed. *The Public School Monopoly: A Critical Analysis of Education and the State in American Society.* San Francisco: Pacific Institute for Public Policy Research, 1982.

Glenn, Charles L. "The Significance of Choice for Public Education," *Equity and Choice* 1, no. 3 (spring 1985).

———. "Why Public Schools Don't Listen." *Christianity Today,* September 20, 1985.

———. "Putting Choice to Work for Public Education." *Equity and Choice,* 2, special issue (May 1986).

———. "What Public Schools Can Do to Accommodate Religious Diversity." *Religion and Public Education* 13, no. 4 (fall 1986).

————. *Family Choice and Public Schools*. Massachusetts Department of Education, 1986.

————. "Letting Poor Parents Act Responsibly." *Journal of Family and Culture* 2, no. 3 (1987).

————. "'Molding Citizens.'" In R. J. Neuhaus, ed., *Democracy and the Renewal of Public Education*. Grand Rapids, Mich.: Eerdmans, 1987.

————. "Religion, Textbooks, and the Common School." *Public Interest,* summer 1987.

Gross, Beatrice, and Ronald Gross, eds. *The Great School Debate: Which Way for American Education?* New York: Simon & Schuster, 1985.

Hampel, Robert. *The Last Little Citadel: American High Schools since 1940.* Boston: Houghton Mifflin, 1986.

Hill, Brian. *Faith at the Blackboard: Issues Facing the Christian Teacher.* Grand Rapids, Mich.: Eerdmans, 1982.

Hitchcock, James. *What Is Secular Humanism?* Ann Arbor, Mich.: Servant Books, 1982.

Jensen, Larry C., and Richard S. Knight. *Moral Education: Historical Perspectives.* Lanham, Md.: University Press of America, 1981.

Lines, Patricia M. *Religious and Moral Values in Public Schools: A Constitutional Analysis.* Denver: Education Commission of the States, 1981.

Manley-Casimir, Michael E., ed. *Family Choice in Schooling.* Lexington, Mass.: Heath, 1982.

McCarthy, Rockne M.; Donald Oppewal; Walfred Peterson; and Gordon Spykman. *Society, State, and Schools: A Case for Structural and Confessional Pluralism.* Grand Rapids, Mich.: Eerdmans, 1981.

McCarthy, Rockne M., James W. Skillen, and William A. Harper. *Disestablishment a Second Time: Genuine Pluralism for American Schools.* Grand Rapids, Mich.: Eerdmans, 1982.

Miller, Robert T., and Ronald B. Flowers. *Toward Benevolent Neutrality: Church, State, and the Supreme Court.* Rev. ed. Waco, Tex.: Baylor University Press, 1982.

Morgan, Richard E. *The Supreme Court and Religion.* New York: Free Press, 1972.

Munsey, Brenda, ed. *Moral Development, Moral Education, and Kohlberg: Basic Issues in Philosophy, Psychology, Religion, and Education.* Birmingham, Ala.: Religious Education Press, 1980.

Nathan, Joe. *Free to Teach: Achieving Equity and Excellence in Schools.* Minneapolis: Winston Press, 1984.

Neuhaus, Richard John, ed. *Democracy and the Renewal of Public Education.* Grand Rapids, Mich.: Eerdmans, 1987.

Oaks, Dallin H., ed. *The Wall between Church and State.* Chicago: University of Chicago Press, 1963.

Peshkin, Alan. *God's Choice: The Total World of a Fundamentalist Christian School.* Chicago: University of Chicago Press, 1986.

Phi Delta Kappa. *A Decade of Gallup Polls of Attitudes toward Education, 1969–1978.* Bloomington, Ind., 1978.

BIBLIOGRAPHY

Purpel, David E., and H. Svi Shapiro, eds., *Schools and Meaning: Essays on the Moral Nature of Schooling*. Lanham, Md.: University Press of America, 1985.
Ravitch, Diane. *The Troubled Crusade: American Education, 1945–1980*. New York: Basic Books, 1983.
Rebell, Michael A., and Arthur R. Block. *Educational Policy Making and the Courts*. Chicago: University of Chicago Press, 1982.
Sichel, Betty A. *Value Education for an Age of Crisis*. Lanham, Md.: University Press of America, 1982.
Simon, Sidney B.; Leland W. Howe; and Howard Kirschenbaum. *Values Clarification: A Handbook of Practical Strategies for Teachers and Students*. New York: Hart, 1972.
Sizer, Theodore R., ed. *Religion and Public Education*. Boston: Houghton Mifflin, 1967.
Thomas, Cal. *Book Burning*. Westchester, Ill.: Crossway, 1983.
Vitz, Paul. *Censorship: Evidence of Bias in Our Children's Textbooks*. Ann Arbor, Mich.: Servant Books, 1986.
Westerhoff, John, ed. *Who Are We? The Quest for a Religious Education*. Birmingham, Ala.: Religious Education Press, 1978.
Wynne, Edward A., ed. *Character Policy: An Emerging Issue,* Lanham, Md.: University Press of America, 1982.

366

INDEX

American Association for the Advance-
  ment of Education, 176
American Bible Society, 74, 195–96, 215,
  231
Anslijn, N., 50
Arons, Stephen, 282, 285–86

Bache, Alexander Dallas, 101–2, 109–10
Ballion, Robert, 269
Barnard, Henry, 80, 101–5, 120, 138, 148
Barzun, Jacques, ix
Beecher, Lyman, 72, 156, 162, 180–82
Bennett Law, 257
Berger, Peter, ix–x, 9, 11
Bert, Paul, 240, 243
Blaine Amendment, 253
Blair, Henry, 252
Boston School Committee, 202–3, 208–
  9, 251
Bowles, Samuel, 6, 12
Breckinridge, Robert, 196, 215
British education, influence of, 112–13
Broglie, comte de, 35
Brooks, Charles, 38, 102–3, 111, 137, 140,
  147, 149, 174–75
Brugghen, J. J. L. van der, 245–46
Buisson, Ferdinand, 243, 249
Bur, Jacques, 267
Burnside, Samuel, 152
Bushnell, Horace, 153, 160, 225–30, 235

Carnot, Hippolyte, 239–40
Carter, James, 75–76, 135–36, 141
Channing, William Ellery, 59, 103, 107,
  140, 151, 153–54
Chirac, Jacques, 269
Cock, Hendrik de, 51–52
Coleman, James, 287
Combe, George, 117, 139
Committee of One Hundred, 251, 257

Compulsion, 25–27, 75, 78, 92–93, 107,
  238, 241, 263
Comte, Auguste, 241–42, 266
Coons, John, 286
Coram, Robert, 96
Cousin, Victor, 37, 40, 103–4, 107–9,
  138, 149
Critique of state schooling in France,
  269
Cubberly, Ellwood, 258
Cuvier, Georges, 31, 40, 109, 111

DaCosta, Isaac, 61
Danton, 22
Davis, Thomas, 73
Directory, 24
Doctrinaires, The, 32–33
Dodde, N. L., 274
Dubois, John, 198
Duffield, D. Bethune, 175
Dupont de Nemours, 18
Durkheim, Emile, 243
Duruy, Albert, 22–23
Dutch Calvinist schools in the U.S.,
  214–15, 232
Dutch influence, 101–3, 109–14
Dutton, W. S., 222–25
Dwight, Edward, 137–38, 141–42

Eliot School controversy, 203
Elite reformers, 6–10, 31–34, 41–45, 82,
  87, 100, 161–62, 209–10, 262, 287
Emerson, George B., 66, 99, 101, 150,
  174
Emmons, Nathanael, 128, 159–60
Ende, Adriaan van den, 38, 49, 57
Everett, Edward, 118, 138, 140, 142, 150

Farris, Michael, 281
Fenwick, James, 197

367

Ferry, Jules, 241, 249
Fichte, J. G., 54
First Plenary Council (1852), 201
Fowle, William B., 187
Franklin, Benjamin, 211, 257
French influence, 88–96, 105–6, 121–22
Friedman, Milton, 286

Gardner, Henry J., 66, 72–73
Ginjaar-Maas, N. J., 277
Gintis, Herbert, 6, 12
Girard College case, 101–2, 190–93
Griscom, John, 101
Groen van Prinsterer, Guillaume, 53–57, 112, 245–47
Guizot, François, 33–37, 239

Hall, Samuel B., 136
Hamelsveld, Y. van, 44
Hansot, Elisabeth, 250
Hayes, Carlton, 263
Hitchcock, Edward, 210
Hixson, W. E., 102
Hodge, Charles, 132, 150, 182–83, 197, 214, 225–26
Hofstede de Groot, C. P., 59
Hofstede de Groot, Petrus, 39, 50, 53–62, 148, 172, 188–89, 244
Honig, Bill, 284–85
Howe, Mark DeWolfe, 190–94
Howe, Samuel Gridley, 135
Hughes, John, 200, 231
Humphrey, Heman, 101, 144, 147, 150

Immigrants, education of, 72–75, 84, 170, 174, 202–3, 211–19, 223–24, 234, 250–54
Immigration, 64–65, 74, 78

Jacobins, 5, 15, 19–20, 90–93
Jefferson, Thomas, 5, 66–67, 89
Jong Ozn., Klaas de, 272

Kappeyne van de Coppello, J., 248
Kemenade, J. A. van, 276–77
Ketchum, Hiram, 231
Knox, Samuel, 94–95, 127
Krug, Judith, 279
Kuyper, Abraham, 247–48

La Chalotais, L.-R., 17
Language in schools, 211–13, 256–60
Lawrence, Charles, 282
Lawrence, Mass., 217
Legrand, Louis, 266–67
Letourneux, 27
Lowell, Mass., 216–17
Luckmann, Thomas, 9, 11
Lutheran schools, 211–13
Lynn, Mass., 175

Maatschappij tot Nut van 't Algemeen, 31, 42–48, 58, 247–49
Madelin, Alain, 269
Malnak v. Yogi, 283
Mann, influence of Europe upon, 60, 101, 109, 116, 121–22, 165
Mann and private schools, 219, 222
Mann and religion, 82–83, 115, 128–32, 139–44, 158–73, 184, 217
Mann and role of the common school, 63, 163, 166–67
Mann and role of the State, 79–81, 115–39, 220
Massachusetts Board of Education, 64, 79, 116–23
Massachusetts School Aid debate, 253–55
Maupas, Didier, 269
McCarthy, Rockne, x, 286
Meyer v. Nebraska, 282
Michelet, Jules, 240, 242
Mijnhardt, W. W., 43–44
Mill, John Stuart, 12
Miller, Samuel, 213
Mitterand, François, 265
Montalembert, Charles, 240
Moral education, 152–53, 163–66, 288
Morelly, 18
Morse, Samuel F. B., 68–69
Morton, Marcus, 118–20
Mozert v. Hawkins County, 279–81
Mutual schools, 32

National Education Association, 279, 286
National Governors Association, 286
Nativism, 66–73, 157, 203
Newton, Edward, 126, 141–44, 190–92, 195

New York Public School Society, 198, 231

Nieuwenhuizen, Jan, 42

Ooijen, David van, 278

Packard, Frederick, 131, 183–86
Palm, J. H. van der, 46–48, 277
Parents, 3, 22, 29, 52–53, 82–83, 122, 238
Pastoral Letter of 1829, 198
Pastoral Letter of 1843, 201
Peirce, Cyrus, 135, 139–40
People for the American Way, 279
Pestalozzi, J. H., 50, 148, 262
Phillips Academy, Andover, 136, 207–8
Pierce v. *Society of Sisters,* 282
Podesta, Anthony, 279
Potter, Alonzo, 176
Presbyterian schools, 213–14
Private schools, 207–11
Prussian influence, 103–4, 107–10, 113, 121–22, 137–38, 148–49, 154, 165
Putnam, George, 126

Quinet, Edgar, 240, 242

Rantoul, Robert, Jr., 127, 140, 143
Ravitch, Diane, 9, 198–200, 250
Religion, traditional, 11–12, 17, 51–53, 132, 141, 156–57, 162–63, 179, 206, 280–81
Religion, traditional, hostility to, 19, 47, 61, 67–69, 83, 92, 142–43, 152–53, 159–61, 172, 229, 240–41, 263
Religion and common school, 10, 18, 37–38, 43, 47–50, 54–59, 95, 111, 140–55, 163–67
Rémusat, Charles de, 37
Riis, Jacob, 258
Robbins, Thomas, 125–26, 131, 142–44
Robespierre, Maxmilien, 20, 284
Roman Catholic schools in U.S., 215–19
Rousseau, Jean-Jacques, 5, 18, 90–91
Royer-Collard, Pierre-Paul, 34
Rush, Benjamin, 89–90

Salem, Mass., 98, 209–10
Savary, Alain, 268
Schelfhout, C. E., 273
Schoolstrijd, 52, 245–49, 271–73
Schoten, Fons van, 274–76
Schotsman, Nicholas, 61
Sears, Barnas, 66, 173–74, 217
Shanker, Albert, 286
Shils, Edward, 7–8, 11
Skillen, James, 286
Smith, Matthew Hale, 131, 187–90
Smith, Payson, 259
Smith, Samuel Harrison, 91–94
State role, 3, 22, 30–34, 48, 57, 75–77, 83, 91, 95–96, 107–9, 117–39, 145–46, 228, 236–37, 263
Stowe, Calvin, 104, 108, 149–50, 165, 190
Struik, L. A., 278
Sugarman, Stephen, 286

Teachers, 24–29, 35–37, 54, 99, 134–37
Teacher training, 37, 107, 132–40, 143–45, 243
Textbooks, 21, 28–29, 46, 49–50, 93, 95, 124–32, 163, 184–85, 244
Thiers, Adolphe, 239–40
Thorbecke, J. R., 244, 247
Ticknor, George, 136
Turgot, A. R. J., 18
Tyack, David, 250

United States v. *Seeger,* 283
Unity, 3, 44–49, 56–60, 67, 73, 84–89, 94, 155–58, 186–90, 223, 267

Vichy government, 264

Wallage, Jacques, 278
Wansink, Hans, 274–75
Ware, Henry, Jr., 181
Wayland, Francis, 98
Webster, Daniel, 102, 157, 190–92
Webster, Noah, 76–77
West Virginia State Board of Education v. *Barnette,* 280